The Emergence of Daoism

At the core of Daoism are ancient ideas concerning the Way, the fundamental process of existence (the Dao). Humans, as individuals and as a society, should be aligned with the Dao in order to attain the fullness of life and its potential. This book presents the history of early Daoism, tracing the development of the tradition between the first and the fifth centuries CE.

This book discusses the emergence of several Daoist movements during this period, including the relatively well-known Way of the Celestial Master that appeared in the second century, and the Upper Clarity and the Numinous Treasure lineages that appeared in the fourth century. These labels are very difficult to determine socially, and they obscure the social reality of early medieval China, that included many more lineages. This book argues that these lineages should be understood as narrowly defined associations of masters and disciples, and it goes on to describe these diverse social groupings as 'communities of practice'. Shedding new light on a complex and multifaceted phenomenon, the formation of Daoism as a new religion in early medieval China, this book presents a major step forward in Daoist Studies.

Gil Raz is Associate Professor at Dartmouth College, USA. He specializes in Chinese Religion, with a particular interest in Daoism, and the interaction between Daoism, popular religious practices, and Buddhism.

Routledge Studies in Taoism

Series Editors: T.H. Barrett, School of Oriental and African Studies, University of London; Russell Kirkland, University of Georgia; Benjamin Penny, Australian National University; and Monica Esposito, Kyoto University.

The *Routledge Studies in Taoism* series publishes books of high scholarly standards. The series includes monographic studies, surveys, and annotated translations of primary sources and technical reference works with a wide scope. Occasionally, translations of books first published in other languages might also be considered for inclusion in the series.

Daoism in History
Essays in honour of Liu Ts'un-yan
Edited by Benjamin Penny

Daoist Rituals, State Religion, and Popular Practices
Zhenwu worship from Song to Ming (960–1644)
Shin-Yi Chao

The Emergence of Daoism
Creation of tradition
Gil Raz

The Emergence of Daoism

Creation of tradition

Gil Raz

Routledge
Taylor & Francis Group

LONDON AND NEW YORK

First published 2012
by Routledge
2 Park Square, Milton Park, Abingdon, Oxon OX14 4RN

Simultaneously published in the USA and Canada by Routledge
711 Third Avenue, New York, NY 10017

Routledge is an imprint of the Taylor & Francis Group, an informa business

© 2012 Gil Raz

British Library Cataloguing in Publication Data
A catalogue record for this book is available from the British Library

Library of Congress Cataloging in Publication Data
Raz, Gil.
  The emergence of Daoism : creation of tradition/Gil Raz.
    p. cm. – (Routledge studies in Taoism ; 3)
    1. Taoism–History. I. Title.

BL1910.R39 2011
299.5'140901–dc22   2011016946

ISBN: 978-0-415-77849-7 (hbk)
ISBN: 978-0-203-58374-6 (ebk)

Typeset in Times New Roman by Sunrise Setting Ltd, Torquay, UK

Printed and bound in the United States of America
by Edwards Brothers Malloy

Contents

Illustrations

Figures

Table

Acknowledgments

Many people have aided and supported my work, and I cannot name all those who deserve thanks. My deepest gratitude is extended to everyone whom I have encountered along the way. Without their intellectual and material support, and most of all, friendship, my research could not have proceeded.

First, I thank my mentor, R.J. Zvi Werblowsky, who told me of the Way. Stephen Bokenkamp has been more than a teacher to me. His guidance, encouragement, support, and friendship extend far beyond the academic realm. My teachers at Indiana University, Robert Eno, Robert Campany, John McRae, and Jan Nattier, deserve special thanks for putting up with me for many years and showing me various paths and byways. John Lagerwey has been a constant source of inspiration and help. His insights and comments on my work were invaluable. Terry Kleeman and Poul Andersen have provided much help and inspiration on many occasions.

Lee Fengmao, a scholar and master, was an inspiration in all aspects of my work. I am grateful to Master Li Youkun for accepting me as a student. Professor Lee and Master Li are truly men of the Way. I am also grateful to their many students and disciples, who became my guides and friends.

I also wish to thank my colleagues in the Religion Department at Dartmouth College for their kindness, support, encouragement, and patience. Special thanks are due to the Dickey Center for International Understanding for their wonderful Manuscript Review Program. I wish to thank Chris Wohlforth at the Dickey Center for organizing the review for my manuscript and to the participants: Michael Puett, Don Harper, Christopher MacEvitt, Reiko Ohnuma, Sarah Allan, Steven Ericson, and Edward Miller. I want to thank Marianne Bujard, Paul Katz, Mark Meulenbeld, and Julius Tsai who read and commented on various early versions of the text.

I wish to thank Jonathan W. Chipman, Director, Applied Spatial Analysis Laboratory, Departments of Geography and Earth Sciences, Dartmouth College for producing the map with the locations of the four stele inscriptions. I am grateful to Bai Bin for granting me permission to use images from his co-authored volume, with Zhang Xunliao, *Zhongguo daojiao kaogu*.

Most of all, I thank Judith, who tolerated my retreat into the mountains and streams of medieval China for too many years. Without her nothing would be done. And, thank you Dina and Miki for showing me what free roaming truly means.

Abbreviations and conventions

DZ   Refers to texts *Zhengtong Daozang* 正統道藏, the canon completed in 1446 during the *Zhengtong* 正統 era. A supplement, entitled *Xu daozang* 續道藏, was completed in 1607. The two collections are published sequentially in 1120 fascicles by Hanfenlou 函芳樓 in Shanghai (1924–26) based on the *Daozang* preserved at the White Cloud Monastery 白雲觀 in Beijing. I refer to these texts following the sequential numbering in Kristofer Schipper and Franciscus Verellen, eds. *The Taoist Canon*: *a Historical Companion to the Daozang* (Chicago: University of Chicago Press, 2004).

ICS   Chinese University of Hong Kong Institute of Chinese Studies the ICS ancient Chinese texts concordance series.

T   refers to texts in *Taishō Shinshū Daizōkyō* 大正新脩大藏經 [Taishō Revised Tripiṭaka]. Chief-editor Takakusu Junjiro.

ZHDZ   Refers to *Zhonghua daozang* 中華道藏, chief-editor Zhang Jiyu 張繼禹. Beijing, Huaxia chubanshe, 2004.

References to official histories are to Beijing, Zhonghua Shuju editions; also accessible on the Scripta Sinica database in Academia Sinica, Taipei: URL: http://hanji.sinica.edu.tw/.

Introduction

Part I: the Dao that can be spoken of

The opening verse of the *Daode jing* famously cautions against forcing definitions on reality: "The *dao* that can be spoken of is not the constant *dao*; the name that can be named is not the constant name." We should bear this caveat in mind when naming complex phenomena such as religious traditions. This is particularly true in the case of Daoism, a term used in English, and other European languages, to denote several philosophical trends in early China; a multifaceted religious tradition that emerged in medieval China; and, more broadly, certain ideas or worldviews found in Chinese painting, literature, medicine, and science. Several Chinese terms may be translated as Daoism, but their connotations, too, are often broad and vague. Nevertheless, as the *Daode jing* instructs, we have to use linguistic categories to define and delimit the phenomena in the world, and thus are "forced to give it a name." This book is about the emergence of Daoism as a religion in early medieval China, and its development during this formative period to become "China's unofficial high religion."[1]

At the core of Daoism are ancient ideas concerning the *Dao* 道, the Way, the fundamental process of existence. Humans, as individuals and as a society, should be aligned with the *Dao* in order to live in harmony with the patterns of the cosmos and attain the fullness of life. The quest for attaining the *Dao* was not merely an abstract notion, but a basic premise which underlay various social, cultural, and political practices as well as an array of technical and esoteric traditions, such as medicine, alchemy, divination, and psycho-physiological practices of hygiene, gymnastics, and meditation by which the hidden potencies of the cosmos could be approached, manipulated, managed, and embodied.

While ideas about the *Dao* and various practices related to it were prevalent in early China, beginning in the second century CE (Common Era), and continuing through the following centuries, these ideas and practices were integrated in complex ways to form a new religious synthesis, which eventually came to be

---

1   Borrowing Anna Seidel's felicitous phrase from her essay "Taoism: the Unofficial High Religion of China," *Taoist Resources* 7.2 (1997): 39–72.

called Daoism, or *daojiao* 道教 in modern Chinese. With its roots extending back to ancient China, and still a living tradition today, Daoism is the only indigenous tradition in China that developed into an instititional religion.

The emergence of Daoism as a new religion in early medieval China was complex and multifaceted, and closely linked to the historical, social, and cultural upheavals over four centuries. On the one hand, this era, which began in the middle of the second century CE with the decline of the Han dynasty, was a period of political instability and social turmoil that continued through four centuries of political disunion.[2] On the other hand, this was an era of cultural efflorescence, which saw the appearance of new forms of literature and the integration of Buddhism in Chinese society and culture.

In terms of the history of Daoism, the middle of the second century witnessed the appearance of the Way of the Celestial Master (*Tianshi Dao* 天師道) in the Sichuan region, and the Great Peace (*Taiping* 太平) movement in the eastern provinces. The rise of these movements is closely associated with the collapse of the Han imperium. While the Great Peace rebellion was among the direct causes for the collapse of the Han dynasty, the movement itself did not outlast the Han. The Way of the Celestial Master was an organized community established, according to its own sources, by Zhang Ling 張陵, also known as Zhang Daoling 張道陵, following a revelation by Lord Lao, the deified Laozi, in 142. The community survived the political and social cataclysm following the Taiping rebellion, and the subsequent period of disunion. The socio-political crisis continued with the conquest of northern China by non-Han peoples, and the establishment of a diminished Chinese imperium in the south in 317. The appearance of new scriptural and ritual lineages, Upper Purity (*Shangqing* 上清) and Numinous Treasure (*Lingbao* 靈寶), in the southern coastal region in the late fourth century, is closely related to these events.

The fifth and sixth centuries were characterized by a growing sense of identity and self-consciousness among Daoists as a distinct religious movement, evident in the repeated attempts at canonization, codification, and systemization of the various scriptures and ritual programs which had appeared in the preceding

---

2   The four centuries following the collapse of the Han are known by different traditional names: the period immediately following the Han is called the Three Kingdoms (三國), referring to the contemporaneous polities of Wei, Wu, and Shu. This period ended with brief unification of the realm by the Western Jin in 280. Soon, however, north China was overrun by non-Han peoples. The Jin dynasty re-established itself in the southern coastal region. Known as Eastern Jin (318–420), this polity was the first of the Southern Dynasties, a succession of short-lived dynasties. Meanwhile, a series of non-Han dynasties ruled over the north China plain. This period is variously known as the Six Dynasties or as the Northern and Southern Dynasties. Recent studies of the historical background and historiographical issues related to the period, following the collapse of the Later Han and through the Six Dynasties period, include Albert E. Dien, *Six Dynasties Civilization* (New Haven: Yale University Press, 2007); Scott Pearce, Audrey Spiro, and Patricia Ebrey, eds. *Culture and Power in the Reconstitution of the Chinese Realm, 200–600* (Cambridge, Mass and London: Harvard University Press, 2001); Charles Holcombe, *In the Shadow of the Han: Literati Thought and Society at the Beginning of the Southern Dynasties* (Honolulu: Hawaii University Press, 1994).

centuries. These efforts at canonization and establishment of a unified orthodoxy may reflect the repeated attempts by the various dynastic regimes to reunify the realm and re-establish a unified empire, efforts that culminated in the establishment of the Sui in 589, soon followed by the Tang in 618. The four centuries between the second and the sixth centuries CE constitute the formative period of Daoism, for it was at this time that concepts and practices that are still at the core of Daoism today first emerged in new scriptures and rituals.

The neat historical scheme presented in the previous paragraph, however, belies the actual, far more complex, historical process of the development of the Daoist religion in early medieval China. First, while the Way of the Celestial Master refers to an actual community, the continuity of this community and its teachings are quite problematic. The terms *Shangqing* and *Lingbao* refer to textual corpora and not to social units. The *Shangqing* texts are described as revelations transmitted by transcendent beings to Yang Xi 楊羲 (330–86), a medium in the service of his patron Xu Mi 許謐 (303–73) and his son Xu Hui 翽 (341–c. 370).[3] Yang Xi promoted these texts, and they became valued among the southern elite families. The *Lingbao* texts also claim to be revelations of ancient teachings. But, while they appeared a generation later than the *Shangqing* revelations, the *Lingbao* texts claim to have been revealed a century earlier to a legendary sage, Ge Xuan 葛玄, said to have been active in the early third century,[4] and to have been secretly transmitted since then.[5] The texts themselves do not hint at their actual author. It is only in a disparaging note in the *Declarations of the Perfected* (*Zhen'gao* 真誥), a key document of *Shangqing* lore compiled by Tao Hongjing 陶弘景 (456–536),[6] who collated the *Shangqing* texts, that we learn that the *Lingbao* texts were composed by Ge Chaofu 葛巢甫,[7] a grand nephew of Ge Hong

---

3 Michel Strickmann, *Le Taoïsme du Mao Chan, Chronique d'une Révélation* (Paris: Mémoires de l'institut des Hautes Études Chinoises, 1981): 135–40; idem "The Mao Shan Revelations – Taoism and the Aristocracy" *T'oung-pao* 63 (1977): 1–64; Isabelle Robinet, *La Révélation du Shangqing dans l'histoire du Taôisme* (Paris: Publications de l'École Française d'Extrême-Orient, 1984).

4 His hagiography is translated by Robert Ford Campany, *To Live as Long as Heaven and Earth, A Translation and Study of Ge Hong's Traditions of Divine Transcendents* (Berkeley: University of California Press, 2002): 152–59.

5 Stephen Bokenkamp, "Sources of the Ling-pao Scriptures," in Michel Strickmann, ed. *Tantric and Taoist Studies II*, 1983: 434–86; Kobayashi Masayoshi, 小林正美, *Rikuchō Dōkyōshi kenkyū* 六朝道教史研究 (Tokyo: Sōbunsha 1990).

6 *Zhen'gao* DZ 1016, compiled by Tao Hongjing following his retirement to Mt. Mao in 492, preserves much of the original record of the Shangqing revelations along with Tao's notes, and thus forms an invaluable source for the formation of early Daoism. Robinet, *Révélation*, vol. 1: 35–50 *et passim*; vol. 2: 313–45; Yoshikawa Tadao 吉川忠夫 and Mugitani Kunio 麥谷邦夫, eds. *Shinkō kenkyū* 真誥研究 (Kyoto: Kyoto daigaku jimbun kagaku kenkyūjo, 2000).

7 This identification, based on *Zhen'gao* DZ 1016: 19.11b5, was first noted by Chen Guofu 陳國符, *Daozang yuanliu kao* 道藏源流考 (Beijing, Zhonghua shuju, rpt.1989): 67, and it has been generally accepted by scholars of Daoism; see Bokenkamp, "Sources," idem, *Early* 377. Kobayashi suggests that Ge Chaofu had composed only one text, the *Five Tablets of Perfect Writs in Red Script* (*Lingbao chishu wupian zhenwen* 靈寶赤書五篇真文, which is the source for the current *Yuanshi wulao chishu wupian zhenwen tianshu jing* 元始五老赤書玉篇真文天書經 DZ 22 while

葛洪 (283–343), himself a grand nephew of Ge Xuan. Ge Hong was a staunch defender of the quest for transcendence, who in his works, *Inner Chapters of the Master Embracing the Unhewn* (*Baopuzi neipian* 抱朴子內篇),[8] *Traditions of Divine Transcendents* (*Shenxian zhuan* 神仙傳), and others, collected dozens of methods for seeking transcendence.[9] Many of the practices elaborated in the *Shangqing* and *Lingbao* scriptures were to a large degree based on texts and practices mentioned in Ge Hong's works. But Ge Hong's works were hardly the sole inspiration for these revelations. Moreover, these textual corpora include texts from different sources, which are often at odds with other texts within the same corpus. Simplistic use of labels such as Celestial Master, *Shangqing*, and *Lingbao* I argue throughout this book, obscures the social reality of Daoism in medieval China.

Communities of practice

For reasons inherent in its very process of development, Daoism was not a clearly definable religion during its formative period and remains so to this day. We should consider the Daoist religion not as a unitary phenomenon, but as an assemblage of intersecting textual and ritual lineages with a set of shared core beliefs or attitudes which formed a commonality as opposed to other traditions such as Buddhism, on the one hand, and the practices of common religion, on the other.[10] Daoists defined themselves in particular against the sacrificial cults that dominated local religious practices.[11] In Michel Strickmann's words:

> The chief rival of early Daoism was not Buddhism, and not the so-called Confucian state. Rather it was the despised and neglected "nameless religion"

the remaining texts in this corpus were composed by later disciples, Lu Xiujing in particular; Kobayashi, *Rikuchō*, 127–80.

8 Citations of Baopuzi will refer to *Baopuzi neipian* 抱朴子內篇 DZ 1185, and to Wang Ming 王明, ed. *Baopuzi neipian jiaoshi* 抱朴子內篇校釋 (rev. edn, Beijing: Zhonghua shuju, 1985). Although all translations from the *Baopuzi* are my own, I will, for convenience, include page numbers to James Ware, 1966, (translation) *Alchemy, Medicine and Religion in the China of AD 230 The Nei P'ien of Ko Hung* (1981 rpt., New York: Dover Publications).

9 On the difficulty of determining Ge Hong's relationship to Daoism, see Nathan Sivin, "On the word 'Taoist' as a source of perplexity. With special reference to the relations of Science and Religion in Traditional China," *HR* 17 (1978): 303–30.

10 My use of "common religion" follows Donald Harper, "Warring States, Ch'in, and Han Periods" in "Chinese Religions – The State of the Field" special issue of *Journal of Asian Studies* 54 (1995): 152–60; idem, "Contracts with the Spirit World in Han Common Religion: The Xuning Prayer and Sacrifice Documents of A.D. 79" *Cahiers d'Extrême-Asie* 14 (2004): 227–67; Marc Kalinowski, "Technical Traditions in Ancient China and Shushu Culture in Chinese Religion," in John Lagerwey, ed. *Religion and Chinese Society* (Hong Kong: Chinese University Press, 2004): 223–48.

11 Rolf Stein, "Religious Taoism and Popular Religion from the Second to Seventh Centuries," in Holmes Welch and Anna Seidel, eds. *Facets of Taoism: Essays in Chinese Religion* (New Haven: Yale University Press, 1979): 53–81.

of the people... in opposition to the violent cults of the deified spirits of the dead, Daoists set the pure, primordial, uncreated Dao...[12]

Daoists constructed their new syntheses while relying on various older and contemporary practices in a complex process. This process involved interactions among diverse traditions, including local cults; shamanism (*wu* 巫); immortality cults; various technical traditions and practices associated with the Masters of Esoterica (*fangshi* 方士), such as divination, breath meditation, medicine, and alchemy; and elements of Han imperial ideology and ritual.

From the outset, the Daoist lineages distinguished themselves from other traditions, and from each other, by laying claim to the proper and most efficacious practices by which to attain the Dao. Daoist authors and redactors therefore took great pains to delineate the proper practices by which the Dao may be attained and harmony restored. Daoists thus claimed to possess the correct understanding of the patterns of the universe, which in turn proved the efficacy of particular practices. Different Daoist groups, however, claimed that their particular lineages embodied this correct understanding. The texts produced during this formative period thus need to be read as documenting complex arguments about practice, even when they may be presenting mythological narratives or cosmological schemata. Different Daoist lineages, and Daoism itself, can only be truly understood within the context of debates about efficacious ways to attain the Dao.

Daoists thus created their tradition through a complex process of debating, selecting, and distinguishing from a wide repertoire of early and contemporary practices. Daoists constructed their preferred set of practices, which were transmitted from masters to disciples in graded initiation rites. Daoist lineages can thus be defined by their practices. These lineages were not exclusive. Disciples sought teachings from more than one master, and masters transmitted different teachings to disciples. Thus, disciples of one master would share certain practices and not others; while disciples of a second master, too, might share some of the same practices. At any one time there were several distinct lineages, all claiming to represent *the* true Way. These lineages, about whom we have little, if any, information, were identified by filiations with particular masters or teachings. Rather than schools, these lineages should be understood as narrowly defined associations of masters and disciples. Also active during this time were several little known communal movements, which often defined themselves in relation to better known groups. As the distinctions between these various groups and lineages are best seen at the level of practice, we may best describe these diverse social groupings as "communities of practice."

By tracing practices rather than tracing the historical development of Daoism as a linear progression beginning with Celestial Master Daoism and proceeding through the Upper Purity and Numinous Treasure scriptures, I hope to better show

---

12 Michel Strickmann, *Chinese Magical Medicine* (Stanford: Stanford University Press, 2002): 4.

the complex social reality of early medieval China that is obscured when we use oversimplified labels.

The Daoist tradition is thus composed of various lineages and communities. Within this diversity, however, was a continual effort at integration, which was not merely rhetoric, but intrinsic to the vision of the Dao as One. The quest for individual transcendence and social harmony was perceived as a return to the primordial unity of the Dao. Nevertheless, the actual process by which the Daoist tradition was constructed was far more prosaic. I suggest that traditions are con- structed retroactively as adherents seek sources for the practices advocated by their communities in order to distinguish them from other practices. These creative genealogies of practice entail three strategies of distinction: determining the correct lineage, a mythology, and correct ritual practice. These strategies of distinction will frame many of the discussions in the following chapters as I trace the development of various Daoist practices. By tracing debates on practice, and examining the processes by which specific practices were adapted, adopted, and reformulated by particular lineages, we may come to understand the emergence of the Daoist tradition.

In each of the following chapters, I explore the emerging Daoist religion by tracing a particular practice or debate: the rise of new types of communal practice, the discourse and practice of lineage, debates on sexual practice, ritual use of tal- ismans, and, finally, efforts at creating Daoist orthodoxy. The sources for this analysis are a variety of late Han and Six Dynasties documents, including Daoist scriptures preserved in the Daoist Canon (*Daozang* 道藏), epigraphic materials, and archaeological data.

Following the historical developments of these practices will not only reveal the processes by which Daoists reformulated older practices, but also elucidate different positions Daoist lineages adopted regarding these practices. This methodology allows us to trace historical developments and, more importantly, elucidate the ways in which Daoists distinguished themselves from other lineages.

What's in a name?

As mentioned above, the danger inherent in labeling and delimiting complex social phenomena is particularly pertinent in the case of Daoism, a term that is doubly problematic. First, we must remember that Daoism is a Western term which does not correspond precisely with any Chinese term. We should be aware that the word Daoism by its construction with the suffix "ism," which resonates with other similar designations, seems to imply "systemacity ... a well-integrated and clearly demarcated whole ... a unitary, perduring thing whose permutations we simply trace through time."[13] Such implication soon leads to reification,

---

13 Robert Ford Campany, "On the Very Idea of Religions (in the Modern West and in Early Medieval China)" *History of Religions*, 42 (2003): 291–92.

and thus to misconception of the complexities of the tradition. Rather than relinquishing the label Daoism, we should follow Robert Campany's suggestion to view such labels as "imagined communities... that are repeatedly claimed, constructed, portrayed, or posited in texts, rituals, and other artifacts and activities."[14]

With these caveats in mind, let us resume our discussion of Daoism. As mentioned above, the word "Daoism" can be used to translate several Chinese terms, but the most important are *daojiao* 道教 and *daojia* 道家. These two terms are often respectively translated as "religious Daoism" and "philosophical Daoism." These translations, which may be based on the uses of these terms in modern Chinese discourse, are misleading and have in fact hampered the study of Daoism as a religion. First, we may ask whether the terms "religion" and "philosophy" are relevant and applicable in the context of early Chinese discourses and practices. This is a critical question, but it far too broad to discuss here.[15] In the case of Daoism, the use of these terms creates a false dichotomy between two types of texts, "philosophical" and "religious," and allows for denigrating definitions of the latter as a degeneration or vulgarization of the former. In the past, this dichotomy also allowed scholars of China to ignore religious Daoism as a vulgar derivative of the pristine philosophical texts. Most scholars of Daoism now reject this dichotomy.[16] Moreover, these two terms were used interchangeably by medieval Daoist authors to refer to their tradition.[17]

That the term *daojia* should not be misunderstood as referring to "philosophical Daoism" is evident by examining its earliest uses. The term was introduced by Sima Tan司馬談 (d. 110 BCE) in his discussion of six categories of learning, which he considered to encompass all the traditions of the past: yin-yang 陰陽, Ru 儒, Mo 墨, Terminologists 名, Legalism 法, and Daode 道德. These categories were constructed by Sima Tan, and, as the many recently discovered documents prove, hardly represent the actual traditions of thought and practice of early China.[18] Nevertheless, as Sima Tan's categorization was, and remains, extremely

---

14 Ibid, 316–17. The notion of "imagined communities" is based on Benedict Anderson, *Imagined Communities: Reflections on the Origin and Spread of Nationalism* (London: Verso, 1983).

15 For a cogent discussion of medieval Chinese terminology and its metaphoric implications, see Campany, "On the Very Idea."

16 Stephen Bokenkamp, *Early Daoist Scriptures* (Berkeley and Los Angeles: University of California Press, 1997; hereafter EDS): 10–15; Livia Kohn, "Introduction" in Livia Kohn, ed. *Daoism Handbook* (Leiden, Boston, Köln: Brill, 2000): xxix–xxxiii; Isabelle Robinet, *Taoism Growth of a Religion*, translated by Phyllis Brooks (Stanford: Stanford University Press, 1997): 3–6.

17 See the references in Chapter 5.

18 Sima Tan's classification is in *Shiji* 130; for Ban Gu see *Hanshu* 30: 1729–31. Ban Gu adopted the term from the no longer extant "Seven Summaries" *Qilue* 七略 by Liu Xin 劉歆 (d.23). For a concise summary of the issues related to classification and "schools," see A. C. Graham, *Disputers of the Tao* (La Salle, Il: Open Court, 1989): 370–82. The issue of Sima Tan's "invention" of schools was re-examined by Mark Csikszentmihàlyi and Michael Nylan, "Constructing lineages and inventing traditions through exemplary figures in early China" *TP* 89 (2003): 59–99, and by Kidder Smith, "Sima Tan and the Invention of Daoism, 'Legalism,' *et cetera*," *Journal of Asian Studies* 62.1 (2003): 129–56.

influential we should pay attention to what he actually says, particularly about *daojia*, his favorite tradition. I translate *daojia* in this context as "Daoist tradition":

> The Daoist tradition enables man's numinous essence to be concentrated and unified, so as to move in unison with the formless, and to provide adequately for the myriad things. As for its methods, it follows the great compliance of the Yin-yang specialists, picks out the best of the Confucians and Mohists, and adopts the essentials of the Terminologists and Legalists. It shifts with the times and changes in response to things. In establishing customs and carrying out affairs, there is nothing it is not suitable for. It is simple to grasp and easy to hold onto; there is much achievement for little effort.[19]

> 道家使人精神專一, 動合無形, 澹足萬物. 其為術也, 因陰陽之大順, 采儒墨之善, 撮名法之要. 與時遷徙, 應物變化. 立俗施事, 無所不宜, 指約而易操, 事少而功多.

Clearly, Sima Tan's definition of *daojia* refers to practices, such as meditation, that allow the adept to "move in unison with the formless," that is, to attain the *dao*. *Daojia* is superior because its adepts select and integrate the best characteristics of all the other traditions.

The term *daojia* was adopted as a bibliographic category in Ban Gu's 班固 (32–92 CE) bibliographic treatise as a collective term for 37 different texts. While the referents of *daojia* as used by Sima Tan and Ban Gu are similar, they are not identical. In both cases, though, the term is best understood as a plural expression referring to "traditions/lineages that focus on the Dao" rather than to a singular Daoist school. It is also evident that the understanding of *daojia* as referring to "philosophical Daoism" is misleading.

The Chinese term which most closely coheres with the Western designation "Daoism" is *daojiao* 道教, which is used in modern Chinese to designate the religion under study here, but this term too is not without difficulty. While the modern use of this term is as a noun, the early uses of the term were as noun-verb constructions, literally meaning "teaching of the *dao*." Similarly, the Chinese term for Buddhism, *fojiao* 佛教, literally means "teaching of the Buddha."[20]

It was only in the fifth century that *daojiao* came to designate the Daoist tradition. In its earliest usages, in *Mozi*, *daojiao* referred to the teachings of the Ru 儒, that is the followers of Confucius.[21] This meaning was still frequent in early medieval

---

19 *Shiji* 130.3388–92; *Hanshu* 62. 2710.
20 For cogent remarks on Chinese terminology, see Campany, "On the Very Idea," 300–10.
21 This usage appears twice in Mozi 墨子: "The Ru consider it [fate 命] to be the teaching of the way; but they are the robbers of the people of the world" 而儒者以為道教, 是賊天下之人者也. *Mozi zhuzi suoyin* 墨子諸子索引: 9.7/64/19; *Mozi xiangu* 墨子閒詁, 290–91; Ian Johnston, *The Mozi: A Complete Translation* (New York : Columbia University Press, 2010), 353; "that by which the world lives is the teaching of the way of the ancient rulers" 天下之所以生者, 以先王之道教也 (*Mozi zhuzi suoyin* 11.3/101/10; *Mozi xiangu*, 429; Johnston, *The Mozi*, 647.

China, as for example in Gao Rou's 高柔 memorial to emperor Ming of the Wei (Cao Rui 曹叡, r. 227–40):

> 'I argue that the erudites should find their source in the way and their ancestor in the six arts. In their practice they should distinguish right and wrong in accord with their learning and array their ranks regardless of position. They should uphold and esteem the teaching of the way in order to exhort those learning, so that the transformation [of the people] will be widespread.' The emperor accepted this.[22]

The *Xiang'er Commentary to the Laozi*, the earliest extant Celestial Master text, composed in the late second century, uses *daojiao* in precisely this sense:[23]

> The true Dao is hidden, deviant words emerge. Those in the world regularly say that the artificial and contrived are the teachings of the Dao (*daojiao*), but these are all false, and must not be used. What are deviant words? Deviance has entered half of the five classics. Beyond the five classics, all books, commentaries, and records are the products of living corpses. They are all deviant.[24]

In this passage *daojiao* is not used as a proper noun designating a "religion" but still maintains the sense of "teaching of the way" in a more general sense.[25] The point here is that adherents of various teachings, including the erudites of the Confucian classics, claim to possess the teaching of the Dao, but these teachings are in fact false. The true teachings of the Dao are the words of this very text. I discuss the rhetoric of "true" and "artificial" later in this chapter; here suffice it to say that the term *daojiao* in the *Xiang'er Commentary* cannot be translated or understood as Daoism. Indeed, during this period, some Buddhists also used this term to designate the teachings of the Buddha.[26]

---

22 *Sanguozhi* 24.685–86. For more examples, see Kobayashi Masayoshi, *Chūgoku no dōkyō* 中國の 道教 (Tokyo: Sōbunsha, 1998): 7.

23 Dunhuang MS S 6825, the only extant witness to this text, is preserved only partially, containing only the section paralleling Chapters 3–38 of the traditionally received version of the *Daode jing*. The text is not dated, but there is general agreement that it was composed within the early Celestial Master community in the late second century. The manuscript is published in Ōfuchi Ninji 大淵忍爾, *Tonkō dōkyō zurokuhen* 敦煌道經: 圖錄篇 (Tokyo: Fukubu shoten, 1978): 421–34. Major studies include Ōfuchi Ninji, *Shoki no dōkyō* 初期の道教 (Tokyo: Sōbunsha, 1991): 247–366; Rao Zongyi (Jao Tsung-i) 饒宗頤, *Laozi xiang'er zhu jiaozheng* 老子想爾注校證 (Shanghai: Shanghai guji, 1991; a revised edition of *Laozi xiang'er zhu jiaojian* 老子想爾注校踐, Hong Kong: Tongnam, 1956); Bokenkamp, *Early*, 29–148, is a full translation and study. Line numbers in Bokenkamp follow the numbering in Ōfuchi. For the date of the text, see Bokenkamp, *Early*, 58–60.

24 Bokenkamp, *Early*, 104, line 246.

25 Bokenkamp, *Early*, 39, 68 n.29.

26 Xie Ao 謝敷 *Anpan shouyi jing xu* 安般守意經序 (*Chu sanzang jiji* 出三藏記集, 6) T 55.602 cited in Kobayashi, *Chūgoku*, 7.

It is only in the fifth century that the term *daojiao* begins to be used as a designation contrasting Daoism with Buddhism and Confucianism. Among the earliest examples is Gu Huan's 顧歡 (420–83) *Yixia lun* 夷夏論 [Discourse on Barbarians and Chinese] (composed in 467) which states: "The Buddha's teachings are spread by their embellished writings, the essence of the Dao teachings are unadorned and marvelous."[27]

The term, however, appears earlier in the fifth century in the context of Daoist polemics. The most intriguing use of the term is in Kou Qianzhi's寇謙之 (365–448) *Lord Lao's Scripture for Chanting the Precepts*.[28] Kou Qianzhi claimed to have received this scripture in a revelation from Most High Lord Lao in 415 along with the title of Celestial Master, while he was in reclusion on Mt. Songgao.[29] *Daojiao* is also used in the section on Daoism in the "Treatise of Buddhism and Daoism" in the *Weishu*, which is essentially a hagiography of Kou Qianzhi.[30]

As a reformulation of the Celestial Master tradition, the *Lord Lao's Scripture for Chanting the Precepts* advocated a rejection of the practices promulgated by Zhang Ling, the first Celestial Master, and his descendants. The practices most severely criticized were the sexual initiation rites known as "yellow and red," which had been the subject of intense debate among Daoists for centuries:

> [false followers] wildly transmitted the sexual methods of the yellow and the red that they personally received from Zhang Ling and presented them to husbands and wives. Licentiousness was thus rampant, and *daojiao* was disgraced.[31]

安傳陵身所授黃赤房中之術, 授人夫妻, 婬風大行, 損辱道教

27 佛教文而博, 道教質而精, *Yixian lun* is preserved in Gu Huan's biography in *Nanshi* 75.1874–1880 and *Nanqi shu* 54.931–35. This text is among the earliest polemical treatises composed by Buddhists and Daoists in an extended series of debates between the adherents of the two religions. For translations and summaries of the key texts, see Livia Kohn, *Laughing at the Tao, Debates among Buddhists and Taoists in Medieval China* (Princeton: Princeton University Press, 1995).
28 *Laojun yinsong jiejing* 老君音誦誡經 DZ 785.
29 Studies include Yang Lien-sheng 陽聯陞. "*Laojun yinsong jiejing* jiaoshi" 老君音誦誡經校釋 *BIHP* 28.1 (1956): 33–92; Richard Mather, "K'ou Ch'ien-chih and Taoist Theocracy at the Northern Wei Court, 425–45," in Holmes Welch and Anna Seidel, eds. *Facets of Taoism* (New Howen and London: Yale University Press, 1979): 103–22; John Lagerwey, "The Old Lord's Scripture for the Chanting of the Commandments," in Florian C. Reiter, ed. *Purposes, Means, and Convictions in Daoism* (Wiesbaden: Harrassowitz, 2007): 29–56.
30 *Weishu* 魏書114.3048–3055. For a Japanese translation and study, see Tsukamoto Zenryu 塚本善隆, *Gisho Shakurōshi* 魏書釋老志 (rev. edn Kyoto: Heibonsha, 1989). The Buddhist section of the text was translated by Leon Hurvitz, "Wei Shou, Treatise on Buddhism and Taoism: An English Translation of the Original Chinese Text of Wei shu CXIV and the Japanese Annotation of Tsukamoto, Zenryū," in *Yün-kang: The Buddhist Cave Temples of the Fifth Century A.D. in North China*, vol. 16 (Kyoto: Kyoto University, Institute of Humanities, 1956). There is an outdated translation of the Daoist section by James Ware, "The *Weishu* and the *Suishu* on Taoism," *JAOS* 53 (1933): 240–53.
31 DZ 785.2a.

The same passage continues to criticize those who transmit the office of libationer from father to son, thus "causing the teachings of the *dao* not to illuminate" 使道教不顯 (2b). In both lines, and throughout this passage, Kou Qianzhi attacks the improper conduct of Celestial Master Daoists. Kou Qianzhi thus uses the term *daojiao* as a designation for Celestial Master Daoism only, and not as an overarching term that integrates the various Daoist traditions. This is even clearer in the following example from the same text:

> Lord Lao said: I initially established the Celestial Master, and bestowed upon him the Daoist (daojiao) parish registers, talismans and tallies.[32]
>
> 老君曰: 吾初立天師, 授署道教治籙符契

The term is used with precisely the same meaning in the "Treatise on Buddhism and Daoism," which states the charge by the Most High Lord Lao to Kou Qianzhi in the following words:

> You are to promulgate my new code, purify and correct the teachings of the Dao. Expunge the false methods of the three Zhangs, the collection of rice levies, and the method of merging pneumas of male and female. The great Dao is pure and void, how can it have such practices?[33]
>
> 汝宣吾新科, 清整道教, 除去三張偽法, 租米錢稅, 及男女合氣之術; 大道清虛, 豈有斯事?

It appears, therefore, that whether we translate *daojiao* as "teachings of the *dao*" or as Daoism, we must note at the same time that Kou Qianzhi uses *daojiao* exclusively as a designation for Celestial Master Daoism.

We find that *daojiao* came into use among adherents of Celestial Master Daoism during the fifth century as part of their efforts to recreate their own tradition in response to perceived challenges. Scholars tend to point to the growing popularity of Buddhism as the main challenge facing Daoists, but I argue that the reformist efforts of various adherents of Celestial Master Daoism in the fifth century are in fact indicative of a different challenge: the success of the *Shangqing* and *Lingbao* scriptures and rites in capturing the imagination and allegiance of both upper and lower echelons of society.[34] As I discuss in detail in Chapter 5, the *Lingbao* scriptures in particular were a conscious effort to encompass earlier

---

32 DZ 785.6a.
33 *Weishu* 114.3051.
34 The spread of Lingbao Daoism among the public is evidenced by the Daoist steles of the Northern Wei. A large selection was published by Zhang Yan 張燕, *Beichao fodao zaoxiang bei jingxuan* 北朝佛道造像碑精選 (Tianjin: Tianjin guji, 1996). Preliminary studies of these stele include Stephen Bokenkamp, "The Yao Boduo Stele as Evidence for "Dao-Buddhism" of the Early Lingbao Scriptures," *Cahiers d'Extrême-Asie* 9 (1996–97): 55–67; Stanley Abe, "Heterological Visions: Northern Wei Daoist Sculpture from Shaanxi Province" *Cahiers d'Extrême-Asie* 9 (1996–97):

Daoist traditions within the cosmology of the Three Caverns (*sandong* 三洞) in the face of Buddhism.[35] While incorporating Zhang Daoling, the first Celestial Master, into its mythology, the Lingbao scriptures did not include the texts of Celestial Master Daoism as one of the Caverns.

I should note here that my use of Celestial Master Daoism is also rather problematic. This term is a loose translation of *Tianshi dao* 天師道, better translated as the Way of the Celestial Master. We should note that the texts associated with the Celestial Master tradition do not refer to their own tradition as *Tianshi dao*, but as *Covenantal Authority of Orthodox Unity* 正一盟威, or simply as *zhengyi*. Official histories of the late Han and the period of disunion refer to this group as the Way of the Five Pecks of Rice (*Wudoumi dao* 五斗米道), or sometimes as "rice-bandits," due to the rice levy imposed on the adherents of the Celestial Master.

Intriguingly, the title *Tianshi* appears in an inscription dating to 173 CE, which may be the earliest extant reference to the Celestial Master.[36] The title appears in a four character phrase followed by the words *dao* and *fa*, meaning methods or teachings. This phrase could thus be understood as "the methods of the Way of the Celestial Master" or as "the ways and methods of the Celestial Master." I discuss this inscription further in Chapter 2. Suffice it here to say that this brief and enigmatic text alludes to the transmission of scriptures to six libationers (*jijiu* 祭酒). Whether this transmission marks their ordination as libationers, or indicates a further advance on a path of initiation is unclear. Most importantly, the text exhorts the libationers to promulgate the teachings or methods of the Way of the Celestial Master 天師道法. The text also refers to the Orthodox and Unitary (*zhengyi* 正一), used here as an adjective of the primordial *qi* of the Dao.

The earliest references to the term *Tianshi dao* in official histories are in the *Jinshu* completed in 644 at imperial behest under the editorship of Fang Xuanling (房玄齡) (579–648). The term appears in the biographies of Yin Zhongkan 殷仲堪 (d. 399) and Chi Yin 郗愔 (313–84), who are described as upholding *Tianshi dao*.[37] Despite the clear labeling in their official biographies, these individuals reveal the difficulty of ascertaining religious affiliation of medieval Chinese figures, and the complex networks of practice associated with medieval Daoists.

Yin Zhongkan was a high official under the Jin. He is mentioned in the sixth century Daoist hagiographic collection *Biographies of Students of the Dao* (*Daoxue zhuan* 道學傳) by Ma Shu馬樞 (522–81).[38] The *Daoxue zhuan* describes Yin as

---

69–83; Hsieh Shuwei, "Image and Devotion: A Study of the Yao Boduo Stele" (M.A. Thesis, Indiana University 2002).

35 Bokenkamp, "Sources," 434–86.

36 Sometimes referred to as "Libationer Zhang Pu" inscription 祭酒張普; preserved in *Li Xu* 隸續 vol. 3, 309 (3/8a-b), compiled by Hong Gua 洪适 (1117–1184). See Chapter 2 for details.

37 For Yin Zhongkan see *Jinshu* 54.2199; for Chi Yin (the graph of his name is alternatively given as 郗) see *Jinshu* 67.1802; JS 77.2031.

38 This text is not extant except in fragments. An early collation of the fragments was done by Chen Guofu in *Daozang yuanliu kao*, vol. 2, 454–504. Stephan Peter Bumbacher, *Fragments of the Daoxue Zhuan: Critical Edition, Translation and Analysis of a Medieval Collection of Daoist Biographies* (Frankfurt am Main: Peter Lang, 2000) is a full annotated translation and study.

from a young age upholding the Way of the Celestial Master. He received [a post] in a parish of Correct Unity; he practiced the teachings with utmost sincerity, and did not seek material wealth. Whenever anyone was ill at his house, he personally made petitions and talismans.[39]

This biographical fragment presents Yin Zhongkan as following standard practices of Celestial Master Daoism.

References to Chi Yin in Daoist texts, however, do not portray him as a follower of Celestial Master Daoism. Chi Yin is mentioned several times in the *Declarations of the Perfected*, a key document of Shangqing lore. As one of the recipients of Yang Xi's revelations from the netherworld, Chi Yin learns of his father Chi Jian's 郗鑒 (266–339) murderous crimes while alive.[40] Other references in the text indicate that he may have received the esoteric *Biography of Perfected Pei* and teachings by the Lady of Purple Tenuity.[41] Significantly, in the latter case he is referred to as Xu Mi's "fellow student" 同學. Nowhere does the *Declarations* indicate that Chi Yin was an adherent of the Celestial Master, and this oblique reference suggests an initiation into Shangqing Daoism.

It seems that the editors of the *Jinshu* adopted the *Daoxue zhuan* passage in its description of Yin Zhongkan, albeit with some changes,[42] and then borrowed this terminology to name the religious tradition followed by Chi Yin. While one of these medieval figures was indeed a follower of the Way of the Celestial Master, the second figure is quite difficult to label. The terminology adopted by the Tang editors occludes the complex religious history of the medieval period. Despite the complexity of the naming practices of Daoists and historians in medieval China, I will use the term Way of the Celestial Master or Celestial Master Daoism to label the tradition started by Zhang Daoling, although, as I discuss below, the continuity of this tradition is quite problematic.

In summary, the basic terms we use, whether in English or Chinese, are all fraught with complex implications, which would have been understood by contemporaries, but are often lost to us. Labels such as *Tianshi dao* and *daojiao* are not neutral and objective, and we should recognize the particular historical context in which they appeared, how they were used, and how these uses changed over time. The term *daojiao* appeared among adherents of the Celestial Master in response to the challenge of the Lingbao scriptures and its notion of the Three Caverns, which excluded the texts and practices of Celestial Master Daoism.

---

39 *Daoxue zhuan* citation in *Sandong zhunang* 三洞珠囊 DZ 1139: 1.5a; Bumbacher, *Fragments*, 274 ff. *et passim.*

40 DZ 1016: 8.5b–8b, 15.7. For a detailed study of these events and revelations, see Stephen Bokenkamp, *Ancestors and Anxiety: Daoism and the Birth of Rebirth in China* (Berkeley: University of California Press, 2007): 113 ff. *et passim.*

41 DZ 1016: 2.18b; 3.6b7.

42 The relevant *Jinshu* line omits the reference to petitions and talismans, and, perhaps more tellingly changes the phrase "he practiced the teachings with utmost sincerity" 精心事法 to "he worshipped the spirits with utmost sincerity" 精心事神.

Rather than a marker of integration of the Daoist tradition, the earliest use of the term *daojiao* indicates distinction, competition, and contestation among Daoist lineages. While the early use of *daojiao* reveals contention within the emerging Daoist tradition, by the late Six Dynasties the term did come to label the tradition as a whole. Nevertheless, the contents of the term remain fluid and problematic to define. The complexities of *daojiao* need not discourage us from using the term Daoism. We should, however, be aware of the implications of our choice of terminology and of the definitions we use.

Towards a polythetic definition of Daoism

Many diverse lineages and traditions may be seen as Daoist depending on the definition one adopts. In most cases, however, such definitions are either overly restrictive, leaving out too much, or too loose, being so inclusive as to be almost meaningless. And yet, notwithstanding the difficulties of formulating a definition, it is clear from the writings of contemporaries that Daoism was a recognized category of social practice, although rarely do we find explicit statements regarding definitions.

Among the first to formulate a definition that recognized Daoism as a social category and which tried to encompass the Daoist tradition in its full complexity was Michel Strickmann. In order to provide a clear and limiting working definition of Daoism which would help determine which lineages could be deemed Daoist, Strickmann proposed the following set of criteria: "those who recognize the historical position of Zhang Daoling, who worship the pure emanations of the Dao rather than the vulgar gods of the people at large, and who safeguard and perpetuate their own lore and practices through esoteric rites of transmission."[43]

With this formulation, Strickmann managed to move beyond the earlier debates, which tended to focus on the obscure relationship between the ancient Daoist classics and the later religious communities. Strickmann pointed to the social basis of the religion, its self-cognizant differentiation from the common religion, and its theological basis. This was indeed a breakthrough in the study of Daoism. Little wonder then that this definition of Daoism has been influential and generally accepted by recent Western scholarship.

Implicit to this definition, however, is the identification of Daoism with the Way of the Celestial Master Daoism. This definition of Daoism closely follows the historical vision introduced by Lu Xiujing 陸修靜 (406–77) in his *Abridged Codes of Master Lu for the Daoist Community*.[44] As I discuss further in Chapter 5,

---

43 Strickmann, "Mao Chan" 1981: 132–3, idem., "On the Alchemy of T'ao Hung-ching," in Holmes Welch and Anna Seidel, eds. (New Howen: Yale University Press, 1979): *Facets of Taoism* 165–6 (Transcription altered).

44 *Lu xiansheng daomen kelue* 陸先生道門科略 DZ 1127. For a detailed study of *Lu xiansheng daomen kelue* see Peter Nickerson, *Taoism, Death and Bureaucracy in Early Medieval China* (University of California at Berkeley: Ph.D. Thesis, 1996); for a translation, see Peter Nickerson, "Abridged codes of Master Lu," in *Chinese Religions*, Donald Lopez, ed. (Princeton: Princeton University Press, 1996): 347–59.

this perception of Daoism was advocated by some Daoist lineages in the latter years of the Six Dynasties, but not all accepted it. The construction of this historical vision was in fact a crucial stage in the history of Daoism, but it cannot serve as a definition for Daoism itself. While this Daoist *imaginaire* should be a useful starting point to explore the tradition, it cannot serve as an account of the history of the tradition. Moreover, Lu Xiujing's own vision of Daoism seems to have shifted considerably between his *Codes for the Daoist Community*, which was an attempt to reform the Celestial Master community, and his later attempts at constructing orthodoxy, which were based on the *Lingbao* scriptures and expressed in his systematization of the Lingbao ritual scheme,[45] and his compilation of the first Daoist canon, the *Catalogue of the Scriptures of the Three Caverns* 三洞經書目 錄, presented to the throne in 471.[46]

Scholarship on Daoism has thus tended to follow the historical vision presented by Lu Xiujing, and to focus on the Daoist lineages that appeared during early medieval China and the canonic collections that preserved their scriptures. This scholarship tends to present a linear history of Daoism, with one lineage following the other, to culminate in the production of the canons of the fifth century. This presentation of the history of Daoism relies to a large degree on the mythohistorical vision of the Daoists themselves, and does not take into account the various debates and agendas which led to the construction of this vision. Moreover, while this vision became the dominant view among Daoists after the sixth century, it was not the only historical vision which appeared among the Daoists of the preceding centuries. I examine several of these visions in Chapter 5.

A crucial point to note is that the names of these better known lineages refer to either textual or ritual categories and are very difficult to determine socially. Viewing Daoist history through the lens of the textual compilations leads to several problems. First, the canonic compilations of *Shangqing* and *Lingbao* were produced several decades after the appearance of the texts, and while these compilations are presented as coherent in ideology and ritual, the texts included in these canons are actually multivocal and often at odds with each other. The canons, and individual texts within them, are clearly composed of writings originating from disparate sources. By focusing on a set of characteristics that seem to define the texts within a specific canonic grouping, we are prone to ignore the polyvocality of the texts and to ignore differences, inconsistencies, and debates

---

45 Catherine Bell, "Ritualization of Texts and Textualization of Ritual in the codification of Daoist Liturgy," *History of Religions* 27.4 (1988): 366–92.

46 This catalogue is not extant. An earlier *Catalogue of the Lingbao Scriptures*, compiled in 437, is extant as copied into Song Wenming's 宋文明 (fl. 549–51) *Tongmen lun* 通門論, also known as *Lingbao jing yishu* 靈寶經義疏, preserved as Dunhuang manuscripts P 2861B and P 2556. Published in Ōfuchi, *Tonkō dōkyō zurokuhen*, 725–26, 726–34; ZHDZ, vol. 5, 509–18. The preface of the earlier catalogue, *Lingbao jingmu xu* 靈寶經目序, is preserved in *Yunji qiqian* DZ 1032: 4.4a–6a. For Lu's catalogues, see Stephen Bokenkamp, "Buddhism, Lu Xiujing and the first Daoist Canon," in *Culture and Power in the Reconstitution of the Chinese Realm, 200–600*, ed. Pearce *et al.*, (Cambridge, MA and London: Harvard University Press, 2001), 181–99.

within and among the texts. Moreover, by focusing on the canonic compilations, we may simply ignore the many texts which were not included in these compilations, and which include some of the most important texts in the Daoist tradition: *Huangting jing* 黃庭經 [Scripture of the Yellow Court],[47] *Laozi zhongjing* 老子中經 [The Central Scripture of Laozi],[48] and the *Taishang lingbao wufuxu* 太上靈寶五符序 [Array of the Five Talismans of Lingbao DZ 388].[49] The latter text is particularly interesting as this third century compilation was a model and inspiration for several of the later Daoist texts, in particular the Lingbao scriptures that appeared in the late fourth and early fifth centuries. Yet, despite its early provenance, it was listed as one of the Lingbao revelation texts in Lu Xiujing's *Catalogue of Lingbao Scriptures* (compiled in 437). I examine various canons developed by Daoists during the Six Dynasties period, in Chapter 5, where I argue that integration of the various teachings became an intrinsic aspect of Daoism.

Another type of definition of Daoism depends on religious rather than social criteria. One such definition is employed by Liu Yi 劉屹, who describes the process by which the reverence for heaven gradually developed into a reverence for a personified Dao.[50] It is the latter stage that he defines as Daoism, while

47 The *Huangting jing* is preserved in the *Daozang* in two versions, a *Jade Scripture of Outer Landscape of the Yellow Court* 太上黃庭外景玉經 DZ 332. Schipper argues that this is the original version, which dates back to the late Han or early Three Kingdoms era (Schipper and Verellen, *Daozang*, p. 96). This version was renamed "Outer" by the Shangqing lineage in order to distinguish it from their own version, the *Jade Scripture of Inner Landscape of the Yellow Court* 太上黃庭內景玉經 DZ 331. The importance of the *Huangting jing* in Shangqing Daoism is well known (Robinet, *Taoist Meditation*, Chapter 2). Moreover, there are hints that it was used in the early Celestial Master community as well (Bokenkamp, *Early,* 172).

48 The *Laozi zhongjing* consists of 55 sections that name the spirits of the human body, correlating them with gods in the macrocosm, and provides methods for contacting these spirits. The text is preserved in two almost identical versions in the *Daozang*: as an independent scripture, entitled *Taishang Laozi zhongjing* 太上老子中經 DZ 1168, and as *Laozi zhongjing* 老子中經, alternately titled *Zhugong yuli* 珠宮玉曆 in *YJQQ* DZ 1032, *juan* 1819. Studies of this text include: Kristofer Schipper, "Le Calendrier de Jade – Note sur le Laozi zhongjing," *Nachrichten der Gesellschaft für Natur und Völkerkunde Ostasiens*/Hamburg 125 (1979): 75–80; Shi Zhouren 施舟人 (Schipper), "'*Laozi zhongjing*' chutan" '老子中經' 初探 in *DJWH* 16 (1994): 204–16; Maeda Shigeki 前田繁樹, "'*Roshi chukyō' oboegaki*" '老子中經' 覺書, in Sakade Yoshinobu 阪出祥伸, ed. *Chūgoku kodai yōsei shisō sōgōteki kenkyū* 中國古代養生思想 綜合的研究 (Tokyo: Hirakawa, 1988); Kato Chie 加藤千惠, "Roshi chukyō to naitan shisō no kigen" '老子中經' と内丹思想の起源, *TS* 87 (May 1996): 22–38, Chinese translation '老子中經' 與内丹思想的起源 in *Zongjiaoxue yanjiu* 1997.4: 40–47; John Lagerwey, "Deux écrits taoïstes anciens," *Cahiers d'Extrême-Asie* 14 (2004): 139–71. The provenance of this text remains unclear. Kristofer Schipper dates the *LZJJ* to the late Han text, but the text is not cited or mentioned in any other text before the late Six Dynasties. Clearly preserving Han-era material, it is difficult to affiliate this text with any of the medieval lineages.

49 Max Kaltenmark, "Quelques remarques sur le 'T'ai-chang ling-pao wou-fou siu'," *Zimbun: Memoires of the Research Institute for Humanities, Kyoto University* 18 (1981): 1–10; Gil Raz, "Creation of Tradition: The Five Numinous Treasure Talismans and the Formation of Early Daoism." Ph.D. Thesis (Bloomington: Indiana University, 2004).

50 Liu Yi, *Jingtian yu chongdao – zhonggu daojiao xingcheng di sixiangshi beijing zhi yi* 敬天與崇道: 中古道教形成的思想史背景之一 (Beijing: Zhonghua shuju, 2005).

the former is viewed as part of the general traditional belief system in early China. According to Liu's analysis, this process, which extends from the Han dynasty through the Six Dynasties period, reaches the point which adheres to Liu's definition only in the fifth century. Prior to that stage, which Liu dubs "Scriptural Daoism" (*jingjiao daojiao* 經教道教) the various movements, including the late Han groups and the fourth-century Shangqing and Lingbao lineages, are dubbed "Technical Daoism" (*daoshu daojiao* 道術道教). This analysis, of course, consigns the entire period of early Daoism to a stage best described as pre-Daoism. Nevertheless, contemporaneous movements of the Six Dynasties identified themselves as distinct from common religion, without necessarily adopting a particular overarching term, like Daoism, to define themselves, or specifying the content of such identity. There seems to be a discrepancy between the emic definitions, which may vary among different groups, and the criteria adopted by scholarly studies of Daoism.

Stephen Bokenkamp has proposed another definition, which is based on the texts studied and translated in his *Early Daoist Scriptures*. As these texts are representative of the three major lineages of the period, their view should be authoritative. Bokenkamp has distilled the various teachings into the following statement:

> Daoism is by its own account the higher religion of China, characterized by the doctrine that the primordial and eternal Dao acts in human history both directly, through the agency of its hypostases, particularly Laozi, and indirectly, through a pantheon of deities that includes those resident in the human body.[51]

The problem with such definitions is that they construct a model of Daoism based on certain characteristics which exclude major scriptures and practices. The texts mentioned above, for instance, are certainly problematic, as they do not conform to definitions based on lineages recognizing Zhang Daoling, as suggested by Strickmann, or to the theologically based criteria suggested by Liu Yi. Bokenkamp's definition, though less restrictive than those proposed by Strickmann and Liu Yi, does not include a social dimension and criteria that would allow us to differentiate between lineages.

However, as early texts, practices, and lineages were evidently of great importance for Daoists during the creative period of the Six Dynasties, we should be able to construct a definition which would allow their inclusion in Daoism, albeit with nuances and degrees of inclusion. Daoism, therefore, does not refer to a unitary phenomenon, but should be used as an inclusive label applied to a plurality of lineages that share certain ideas and practices, but not others. It may be useful here to recall that there are two kinds of models by which criteria determine membership of specific entities in a group. The first model is monothetic in which "the possession of a unique set of attributes is both sufficient and necessary for membership." This type of definition assumes a rigid and fixed set of criteria, and restricts membership to those who possess all criteria.

---

51 Bokenkamp, *Early*, 12.

The second model is polythetic, in which the group is defined by a set of attributes such that each entity possesses most of the attributes and each attribute is shared by most members.[52] This definition is dynamic, providing room for changes and developments, as members share some, but not necessarily all, of a set of criteria. A polythetic definition would allow us to differentiate between lineages that share several criteria, while allowing others to remain as marginal or borderline cases.

I suggest at this point the following set of criteria, which allows a wide variation within the Daoist religious groups, while conforming to what Daoists themselves seem to have accepted as Daoism:

1   The primary criterion is a view of the Dao as an overarching and effective force, but not necessarily personified, simultaneously prior to the emanation of the cosmos and yet active in the manifested world.
2   This force can be effectively approached by humans through ritual means, and those who are successful with this quest achieve transcendence.
3   These means are secret and guarded within strict lineages of transmission.
4   These lineages reject all practices that do not revere the direct manifestations of the Dao. Daoists thus replace sacrificial and other blood rites with other, usually bureaucratic, means of communication with the extra-human realm.
5   An eschatological vision underlies the quest for transcendence, differentiating Daoism from the earlier tradition of seekers of longevity.

These criteria are based on several texts of medieval Daoism, and would allow the canonic texts of the Three Caverns and Celestial Master Daoism to remain at the center of the emerging Daoist tradition, while also accommodating various other lineages of the Six Dynasties, which may share some characteristics, but not others. These more nuanced views allow us to understand which lineages and practices were eventually enveloped in the growing Daoist orthodoxy, either explicitly or implicitly, as well as which were excluded. This will finally help explain why certain lineages and practices were explicitly rejected, while others went through diverse processes of manipulation and adaptation.

Defining religions

While the history of Daoism needs to be understood within the context of traditional Chinese religious culture and Chinese history, the problem of defining the field is not restricted to the study of Daoism. A similar problem of definition has vexed scholars of Hinduism, and more recently has become a problem for scholars of early Christianity. In a recent compilation of essays concerning Hinduism,

---

52 Peter Burke, *History and Social Theory* (Ithaca: Cornell University Press, 1992), 32; Rodney Needham, "Polythetic Classification, Convergence and Consequence," *Man* 10 (1975): 349–69. The notion of 'family-resemblance' is derived from Wittgenstein's linguistic studies.

Julius Lipner has argued that Hinduism should be seen as "macrocosmically one though microcosmically many, a polycentric phenomenon imbued with the same life-sap, the boundaries and (micro)centers seeming to merge and overlap in a *complexus* of oscillating tensions."[53] He goes on to argue that such plurality is in fact intrinsic to all religions:

> the various designations for the world religions may be regarded as cluster terms for different families comprising what may be described as "belonger" traditions… in the different families of religions individual traditions may be identified as belonging to a particular family on the basis of shared characteristics. These characteristics may include a distinctive form of discourse, a particular set of symbols and/or myths, a specific pattern for behavior, and so on.[54]

Daoism is indeed such a "cluster term," referring to several lineages of practice that appeared in early medieval China, and which continued to develop and interact among themselves and with other traditions of practice in China until the present. Evidently, then, the polythetic definition I suggested above will need refinement and elaboration were we to trace the history of Daoism beyond the era I am focusing on in this book.

Perhaps more intriguing are the unexpected parallels that we find between the development of Christianity and Daoism. Not only does the formative period of Daoism coincide with the formative period of Christianity, but there are several parallels in the developmental trajectory of the traditions. In both cases we find an inherent relationship between the emerging tradition and imperial collapse, and in both cases visions of reunification of the realm are crucial for understanding the continuing relationship between the clerical and secular realms. Another parallel is the ambiguous relationship between Christianity and Daoism on the one hand and the local traditions in their respective spheres. The interaction between the emerging Daoist tradition and local cults is the focus of Chapter 1. I briefly discuss the complex relationship between the empire and Daoism in Chapter 5, but this should be seen as no more than a preliminary foray into a topic that deserves a complete study.[55]

More pertinently, while earlier histories of Christianity have tended to stress the triumphal march of a "remarkably universal religion, endowed with common

53 Julius J. Lipner, "Ancient Banyan: An Inquiry into the Meaning of 'Hinduness'," in J.E. Llewellyn, ed. *Defining Hinduism* (Routledge: New York, 2005): 31.
54 Lipner, "Ancient Banyan," 32.
55 Anna Seidel, "Imperial Treasures and Taoist Sacraments – Taoist Roots in The Apocrypha," in Michel Strickmann, ed. *Tantric and Taoist Studies* (Bruxelles: Institut Belges des Hautes Etudes Chinois, 1983): vol. II, 291–371; John Lagerwey, "Rituel taoïste et légimité politique," BEFEO 84 (1997): 99–109; Gil Raz, "Imperial Efficacy: Debates on Imperial Ritual in Early Medieval China and the Emergence of Daoist Ritual Schemata" in Florian Reiter, ed. *Purposes, Means and Convictions in Daoism, a Berlin Symposium* (Wiesbaden: Harrasowitz, 2007): 83–109.

codes which could spring up in many different environments," Peter Brown in his recent *The Rise of Western Christendom* stresses that in medieval Europe, Christianity "was not necessarily a unitary, still less a uniform religion… As long as we think of the 'localization' of Christianity as a failure to achieve some ideal of unity, we seriously misunderstand this phenomenon."[56] The "principal feature" of Christianity, Brown argues, "resided in its very diversity." Brown thus adopts the term "micro-Christendoms" to describe local varieties of Christianity. Moreover, in discussing the social reality of Christianity in its many variants, Brown stresses that the voices of the theological elite were a minority within the wide range of popular practices, such as the cult of saints or the taboos and restrictions. Rather than "a later 'contamination' of Christianity by 'archaic' mentality," these practices "grew directly out of its late antique Mediterranean background."[57] The rejection by scholars of such practices as "a decline from some more 'pure' state of belief" is predicated on a false notion of a "highly 'spiritualized'" early Christianity.[58] Brown shows that in terms of orthopraxy this process extended well into the second millennium.

Complementing Brown's analysis of the social realities of variant local Christianities, Bart Ehrman's *Lost Christianities* presents a rich variety of Christian ideologies and budding theologies from the first to the third centuries. These variant Christianities were all eventually suppressed by the emerging orthodoxy of the Catholic Church.[59] Ehrman's careful reading of the various texts which were excluded from the Christian canon reveals the debates and tensions between these divergent Christianities. Among the most important strategies in which rival Christian groups framed their theological debates were claims and counterclaims regarding authenticity and forgery. Thus, each group would assert the truth of its own teachings by claiming its texts to be authentically derived from the earliest Christian community, or Jesus himself, while claiming that rival teachings were forgeries.[60] Ehrman traces the creation of a Christian orthodoxy that was institutionally debated in the council of Nicaea in 325, which determined a set of theological statements that created the orthodox understanding of Christianity, and was codified in the Nicene Creed. Debates on the correct texts continued through the fourth century. The list of books that was to become the canonic New Testament was first promulgated in a letter by Athanasius in 367, but was accepted only 30 years later at the synod of Hippo in 393, and with the support of Augustine.[61] The textual codification of orthodoxy, along with the determination of the orthodox creed, created the dominant vision of Christianity

---

56 Peter Brown, *The Rise of Western Christendom: Triumph and Diversity, A.D. 200–1000* (Oxford: Blackwell, 2003): 14–15.
57 Ibid, 19.
58 Ibid, 18.
59 Bart Ehrman, *Lost Christianities: The Battles for Scripture and the Faiths We Never Knew* (New York: Oxford University Press, 2003).
60 Ehrman, *Lost*, 9–10, 31–2.
61 Ehrman, *Lost*, 245.

to the present. But, as Ehrman reminds us, the creation of orthodoxy was a historical process. We must not allow this process, which was associated with a determined effort at erasing all dissenting voices, to blind us to the diversity of early
Christianities.

These studies of early Christianity reveal that even a religion which begins with
a small, identifiable community, soon develops into complex and multifarious
variety. Unlike Christianity, however, Daoism did not originate from a single
community, but rather had multiple sources. Unlike Christianity, Daoist leaders
never managed to determine a binding orthodoxy and orthopraxy, although, as we
will see below, this was not for lack of trying. Little wonder, then, that Daoism,
like Hinduism, is much more difficult to conceptualize and define.

Part II: an episodic history of Daoism

The usual presentation of the historical development of Daoism follows a neat
scheme, not unlike the brief summary presented at the beginning of this book. My
intention in this section is to show how such narratives occlude the complex history of Daoism. I will not provide a full history, but simply point to particularly
problematic issues that illustrate the need for a history that traces debates among
"communities of practice."

Histories of Daoism usually begin with a lengthy exposition of the pre-Qin
philosophers Laozi and Zhuangzi, often stressing the mystical facets of their
thought.[62] These studies usually eschew grounding these texts in their social contexts. Moreover, while these Warring States "philosophers" are clearly important,
the links between them and the religious communities that developed some six
centuries later are tenuous. The narrative then turns to Han-period traditions
of practice. These traditions are, of course, the immediate precursors of many
medieval Daoist practices. They were, however, diverse in their practices and
social context, and they were not univocal in their cosmological assumptions.
Their impact on the emerging Daoist tradition was very complex, as different
lineages adopted and adapted distinct practices at different times and places.
These links, therefore, need to be examined very carefully. I trace some of these
in the following chapters.

The tale then focuses on the two famous religious groups that appeared at the
end of the Han. The rebellious "Great Peace" (*Taiping* 太平) movement in the
eastern coastal regions developed in the second half of the second century, and
erupted in a violent rebellion in 184. Though short lived, this rebellion hastened
the fall of the Han. The second group, known in historical sources as the Way of

---

62 Recent examples include Russell Kirkland, *Taoism: the Enduring Tradition* (New York:
   Routledge, 2004); Livia Kohn, *Daoism and Chinese Culture* (Cambridge: Three Pines Press,
   2001); Isabelle Robinet, *Taoism: Growth of a Religion*, trans. Phyllis Brooks (Stanford: Stanford
   University Press, 1997).

Five Bushels of Rice (*Wudoumi dao* 五斗米道), emerged in the Sichuan region. This is the community that was to become the Way of the Celestial Master.[63]

The history of this community, however, is very problematic. According to Celestial Master sources, this community was established by Zhang Ling in 142, later known as Zhang Daoling, following the revelation of Lord Lao, the deified Laozi, who bestowed upon him the title Celestial Master. There are, however, very few internal texts documenting the early Celestial Master community.[64] We therefore need to rely on the earliest references to this group in official historical sources, which are less interested in doctrinal matters, and tend to be biased against the religious practices they deemed to destabilize and threaten the polity. The information in these sources is somewhat contradictory. In short, it is difficult to ascertain the precise social and historical reality of the early Celestial Master community.

References in the official histories raise several intriguing questions regarding the origins of the early Celestial Master movement, and its relationship to other groups, which followed similar practices. The *Dianlüe* 典略, a third century text,[65] provides one of the most extensive descriptions of the movement, here labeled the Way of Five Bushels of Rice. This text does not refer to Zhang Ling. According to this text, the Way of Five Bushels of Rice was established by Zhang Xiu 張修, who is said to have been one of three contemporaneous rebel leaders ("demonic bandits" *yaozei* 妖賊), along with Zhang Jue, the leader of the Great Peace movement, and the otherwise unknown Luo Yao 駱曜 who arose in the capital region (*sanfu* 三輔). The latter is said to have instructed his followers in a Method for Contemplating Faults (*mianni fa* 緬匿法).[66] While the details of this

---

63 For an excellent survey of these events see Grégoire Espesset, "Later Han Religious Mass Movements and the Early Daoist Church," in John Lagerwey and Marc Kalinowski, eds. *Early Chinese Religion, Part One: Shang through Han (1250 BC–AD 220)* (Leiden: Brill, 2010): vol. 2, 1061–102.

64 For recent attempts at reconstructing the social reality of the community, see Terry Kleeman, "Community and Daily Life in the Early Daoist Church" in John Lagerwey and Lü Pengzhi, eds. *Early Chinese Religion: the Period of Division (220–589 AD)* (Leiden: Brill, 2010): vol. 1, 395–436; idem, "Daoism in the Third Century," in Florian C. Reiter, ed. *Purposes, Means and Convictions in Daoism* (Wiesbaden: Harrasowitz, 2007): 11–28.

65 Composed by Yu Huan 魚豢; cited in *Sanguo zhi* 三國志 8.264. The *Sanguo zhi* was compiled by Chen Shou 陳壽 (233–c.300), presented to the Jin throne in 274; the current text includes a commentary by Pei Songzhi 裴松之 (372–451), compiled in 429 under imperial order. For details, see Rafe de Crespigny, *Generals of the South, The Foundation and Early History of the Three Kingdoms State of Wu* (Internet edition, 2004; originally published in 1990 as No. 16 of the Asian Studies Monographs: New Series of the Faculty of Asian Studies at The Australian National University), Chapter 9; Howard Goodman, *Ts'ao P'i Transcendent: the Political Culture of Dynasty-Founding in China at the end of the Han* (Seattle: Scripta Serica, 1998): 228–31. For the date of *Dianlüe*, see de Crespigny, *Generals*, Chapter 9, 7.

66 Yamada Toshiaki argues that *ni* 匿 "hidden" should be read as *te* 慝 "evil act"; Yamada Toshiaki 山田利明, *Rikuchō dōkyō girei no kenkyū* 六朝道教儀禮の研究 (Tokyo: Tōhō-shoten, 1999): 175. See also Morohashi, 4.4560, #11100. This is accepted by Lü Pengzhi, *"Daoist Rituals,"* in Lagerwey and Lü, *Early Chinese Religion*, 1252, and idem. *Tangqian*, 18.

method are unknown, its title and proximity to the practice of "meditating upon offenses" (*siguo* 思過), employed in both other movements, suggests that these various methods were similar. With such little evidence we cannot proceed further in analysis, beyond pointing to the fact that this indicates that new understandings of "offense," which were developed in great detail by later Daoist lineages, had appeared in three distinct communities of practice.

Perhaps more importantly, the text suggests that the distinctive practices of the Way of the Celestial Master were in fact initiated by Zhang Xiu. It was he who set up Chambers of Tranquility (*jingshe* 靜室) where the ill were sent to meditate upon their offenses. He also appointed a priesthood consisting of Officers of Depravity (*jianling* 姦令) and libationers (*jijiu* 祭酒), who were in charge of having communal recitation 都習 of *Laozi's Five-thousand Graphs* 老子五千文. Other officials, entitled Demon Officers (*guili* 鬼吏), were in charge of petitioning the cosmic bureaucracy of the Three Bureaus of heaven, earth, and water on behalf of the sick.

After Zhang Xiu was killed, his community was taken over by Zhang Lu, who recognized that the locals "had faith in and practiced Xiu's techniques." Zhang Lu is said to have embellished Zhang Xiu's methods by establishing a system of "charity inns" (yishe 義舍), which were to provide rice and meat for travelers.

According to the *Dianlüe*, the Way of the Five Bushels of Rice was initiated by Zhang Xiu and was taken over by Zhang Lu. Other early accounts also suggest that the community in Hanzhong coalesced around the healer Zhang Xiu.[67] It seems, therefore, that the practices attributed to Zhang Lu in his biography originated with Zhang Xiu. Several of the practices attributed to Zhang Xiu remained at the basis of Celestial Master Daoism through the Six Dynasties. These include the Chambers of Tranquility that were the central ritual sites at the homes of Celestial Master adherents through the Six Dynasties era. Libationer remained the title for the priests of the Celestial Masters. The bureaucratic mode of communication with the Three Bureaus remained at the core of Celestial Master practice.[68] Interestingly, the charity inns, which the final lines of the passage suggest were an innovation by Zhang Lu, are not mentioned in any of the medieval Daoist texts. While the secular sources cannot be taken at face value, they do suggest that the origins of the Way of the Celestial Master are less clear than later Daoist texts claim.[69]

67 The "Annals of Emperor Ling" in the *Houhan shu* reports that "in the seventh month of the first year of *Zhongping* era (184) the demon-shaman Zhang Xiu of Ba commandery rebelled" 巴郡妖巫張修反 (*HHS* 8.343). A note to this passage cites the *Record of Liu Ai* 劉艾紀, an alternative title to Liu Ai's "Biography of Emperor Ling," which dates to the 180s–190s: "At that time the medium Zhang Xiu of Ba commandery healed the sick. Those cured were to pay with five bushels of rice, hence he was called 'Master of five bushels of rice'" (*HHS* 8.349). This text is examined in detail by Howard Goodman, "Celestial Master Taoism and the Founding of the Ts'ao-Wei Dynasty, The Li Fu Document," *Asia Major*, 3rd Ser., 7 (1994): 5–33.
68 Among the best examples for the bureaucratic mode of communication are the hundreds of petitions preserved in *Master Redpine's Almanac of Petitions Chisongzi zhangli* 赤松子章歷 DZ 615.
69 A concise summary of these issues may be found in Bokenkamp, *Early*, 32–5.

Following the fall of the Han, Zhang Lu allied himself with the burgeoning power of the Cao family, which was soon to establish the Wei. After Zhang Lu capitulated to Cao Cao 曹操 in 215, thousands of Zhang's adherents were moved to the north.[70] Zhang Lu's daughter was married to Cao Cao's son, and his five sons were all enfeoffed.[71] It is not quite clear when Zhang Lu died,[72] but there is intriguing evidence for a collapse of the community soon after. The *Commands and Admonitions for the Families of the Great Dao*, a revelation in the voice of the Celestial Master dating to 255, complains that:

> Of all male and female officers of the various ranks granted previously, not very many are still with us. Ever since the fifth year of the Grand Harmony reign-period [231], each of the holders of parish positions has been self-appointed. Their selection and promotion no longer emanates from my pneumas… Sometimes one parish has redundant officers, while in other parishes offices remain empty.[73]

Yangping Parish 陽平治, an early text devoted to the establishment of the Celestial Master administrative system of the 24 parishes, and which follows *Commands and Admonitions* in the same codex, has an even earlier date for the collapse of the communal order:

> Ever since the first year of the *huangchu* era (220) the various headmen and libationers declared their own teaching and each established his own parish. They no longer attained their post in accord with the ancient ways and methods. They did not follow the previous teachings of my parish [administration] of Yangping, Lutang, and Heming.[74]

There is no further discussion of either of these dates and the event, or events, that may have triggered the break-up of the communal order, but there are repeated exhortations in later texts regarding the sorry state of the community. We can surmise that following the move north, and after Zhang Lu's death, the cohesion of the institutional community was lost. Nevertheless, adherents of the Celestial Master were apparently quite successful in spreading their religion and gaining new adherents. This success may be gauged by the number of northern

---

70   *Sanguozhi* 15.472 reports that tens of thousands were moved to Chang'an; according to *Sanguozhi* 23.666 over 80,000 were moved to Loyang and Ye. It is unclear whether these two reports should be considered separately or together.

71   A tomb inscription discovered in Luoyang is from the tomb of Zhang Sheng, Zhang Lu's third son; for details Liu Zhaorui 劉昭瑞, *Kaogu faxian yu zaoqi daojiao yanjiu* 考古發現與早起道教研究 (Wenwu: Beijing, 2007): 46–51.

72   There is evidence that he died in Ye in 216; Bokenkamp, *Early*, 150–2, 162 n.6.

73   DZ 789.17a; the translation is from Bokenkamp, *Early*, 178.

74   DZ 789.21a.

aristocrats mentioned in the official histories as followers of the Celestial Masters.[75]

Following the conquest of the north by non-Han invaders and the establishment of the Eastern Jin, in 317, in the southern coastal region, developments in the Celestial Master tradition seem to have bifurcated into two distinct lines of development, due to their different circumstances. These are sometimes referred to as Northern and Southern Celestial Masters.[76] The southern Celestial Master tradition is supposedly characterized by its interaction with the local technical and esoteric traditions, such as alchemy, of the southern coastal region.

In the fifth century, the two branches of the Celestial Masters allied themselves with different imperial projects. In the south, one branch supported the rise of Liu Yu 劉裕 (Emperor Wu, r. 420–3) and the establishment of the Song dynasty (420–77) (also known as Liu-Song). In the north, Kou Qianzhi allied itself with the Northern Tuoba Wei dynasty (386–534).[77] Thus, through careful political maneuvering, remnants of the community, established by Zhang Lu at Hanzhong, survived the political upheavals of the period of disunion to emerge finally as the Way of the Celestial Master. The political success of Daoism culminated during the Tang dynasty, when the imperial Li clan identified Laozi as their ancestor, and adopted Daoist ritual as their ancestral rite. By the end of the Tang dynasty, following complex developments, the Celestial Masters became the recognized leaders of the orthodox Daoist religion.[78]

Paralleling the historical development of the Celestial Masters, new movements appeared in the southern coastal area following the conquest of the north by nomadic non-Han tribal groups, the cataclysmic sack of the capital Luoyang in 311, and the consequent retreat of the Jin dynasty to the south. The social and political upheaval led to a massive population shift from north to south, which was to have resounding effects in all political, economic, and cultural aspects.

Unsurprisingly, the northern émigrés arriving in the south were accompanied by libationers of the Celestial Masters, thus causing religious friction that exacerbated the socio-political tensions between the northern and southern elites. The southern elites had their own traditions of practice, many of which were collected by Ge Hong into his works. From Ge Hong, references in the *Shangqing*

---

75 Among the best known examples are the family of the famous calligrapher Wang Xizhi 王羲之 (303–361), which is said to have "for generations revered the Way of the Five Pecks of Rice of the Zhang clan" (*Jinshu* 80.2103), and the Sun clan of the rebel Sun En which is said to have upheld the Way of the Five Pecks of Rice for generations (*Jinshu* 80.2631).

76 See, for instance, Peter Nickerson, "The Southern Celestial Masters" and Livia Kohn, "The Northern Celestial Masters" in Livia Kohn, ed. *Daoism Handbook* (Leiden: Brill, 2000): 256–82, 283–06.

77 For the short-lived Daoist "theocracy" during the Tuoba-Wei, see Mather, "K'ou Ch'ien-chih."

78 Timothy H. Barrett, *Taoism Under the T'ang: Religion and Empire During the Golden Age of Chinese History* (London: Wellsweep, 1996; rpt. Warren: Floating World, 2006); Livia Kohn and Russell Kirkland, "Daoism in the Tang (618–907)" in Livia Kohn, ed. *Daoism Handbook* (Leiden: Brill, 2000): 339–83.

scriptures, and other contemporary sources, we learn of several distinct lineages of practice. These references are too brief to allow for complete understanding of these lineages and their practices. Nevertheless, these were the traditions from which Yang Xi and Ge Chaofu borrowed as they created the *Shangqing* and *Lingbao* scriptures and practices.[79] The various texts and practices transmitted within the Ge, Xu, and other inter-related clans were crucial in the development of Daoism. Texts inspired by both scriptural revelations continued to appear through the fifth century. By the middle of the fifth century a process of ortho-doxy building and canonization eventually led to an apparent amalgamation of the various scriptural lineages with a unified ordination and initiation sequence.

It was precisely in this context of creating orthodoxy that Lu Xiujing composed the *Abridged Codes of Master Lu for the Daoist Community*, in which he intro-duced his view of Daoist history. In this text Lu ascribes the emergence of Daoism to the revelation of Lord Lao to Zhang Daoling, and makes no reference to any other Daoist group, including the *Shangqing* and *Lingbao* scriptural lineages. Yet, in his project of textual canonization and codification of ritual, the *Shangqing* scriptures are presented as the highest revelation, while the *Lingbao* scriptures are at the base of his ritual systemization.

We should note that the historical views adopted in systemizing scriptures such as the *Abridged Codes* are based on the preferred interpretation of events by their respective authors and redactors. These authors tended to purposefully obscure the complex reality of their own history and the presence of rival lineages. These rival lineages, while following similar practices with similar cosmological per-ceptions, were aligned with different traditions, and defined by distinct lineages of transmission. As Daoism became more institutionalized, and as its orthodoxy was determined, these lineages were further obscured.

Obscure origins and lost lineages

An early example of a Daoist community which disappeared from the later scrip-tural record is a Daoist lineage which was active in the Sichuan basin in the latter half of the second century. This sect is known through a single Dunhuang manu-script, *Laozi bianhua jing* 老子變化經 [*Scripture on Transformations of Laozi*], analyzed in Anna Seidel's seminal study.[80] This community was contemporary with Celestial Master Daoism, yet there is no hint of its existence in any of the writings by the Celestial Masters, and it was not included in the canon of the Three Caverns established by Lu Xiujing.[81] Nevertheless, the *Scripture on Transformations of*

---

79 Robinet, *Révélation*, is particularly attentive to the complex sources of the Shangqing material; for the Lingbao material, see Bokenkamp, "Sources."

80 *Laozi bianhua jing* S 2295; published in Ōfuchi Ninji 大淵忍爾, *Tōnko dōkyō* 敦煌道經 (Tokyo: Fukubu shoten, 1978), *mokurokuhen* 目錄篇, 324, *zurokuhen* 圖錄篇, 686; *ZHDZ*, v.8, 181; Anna Seidel, *La Divinisation de Lao Tseu dans le Taoisme des Han* (Paris: EFEO, 1969). I follow the line numbers in Ōfuchi and Seidel.

81 On the development of these canons, see Chapter 5.

Laozi was preserved and transmitted through the centuries, until it was copied during the Sui at the Xuandu guan 玄都觀 [Observatory of the Mystic Capital] in the capital Chang'an.[82] This institution, originally named Tongdao guan 通道觀 [Observatory of the Pervasive Dao], was established by Emperor Wu of the Northern Zhou in 574, for the purpose of collating and editing a Daoist canon. This project was part of the imperial effort of political reunification, which included an attempt to establish a state religion based on the "three religions" (*sanjiao*) 三教, incorporating Confucianism and Buddhism within a Daoist framework. Wang Yan 王延 (d. 604) was placed in charge of this Daoist institution, which continued its work of collating Daoist texts, even after the establishment of the Sui, when it was renamed Xuandu guan.[83]

Kristofer Schipper considers the inclusion of the *Scripture on Transformations of Laozi* as evidence that "the work of Wang Yan and his colleagues was no longer limited by the scriptures of the Three Caverns and the Zhengyi canon, but had been extended to encompass works such as this popular text from the Later Han period." It is not quite clear, though, why Wang Yan did not feel constrained by the canons, nor why the "editors treated the primitive messianic text with much respect, as all ancient and corrupt characters were copied verbatim."[84] Was the text to be included in another canon being determined at the Xuandu guan? Why was it held in such high regard? It is impossible to answer these questions, but we can safely speculate that Daoists at the Xuandu guan recognized the *Laozi bianhua jing* as closely related to the texts included in the canon.

The community that produced the *Laozi bianhua jing* did not recognize Zhang Ling as a sage or recipient of a new revelation. Thus, according to Strickmann's definition, this community would not be classified as Daoist. Yet, this community shared intriguing aspects of discourse and practices with Celestial Master Daoism and later Daoist lineages. These differences are best highlighted by a close comparison with the *Xiang'er Commentary to the Laozi* of the late Han, the earliest extant Celestial Master text.

By applying the criteria of the polythetic definition I proposed, we may see precisely which aspects of discourse and practices expressed in this text are shared with later Daoist lineages, and where they differ. Thus, rather than asking whether this is a Daoist group or not, the polythetic definition allows us to actually trace similarities and differences between the community that produced the *Scripture on Transformations of Lao zi* and the early Celestial Master community which composed the *Xiang'er Commentary*. These distinctions, I suggest, reveal critical debates among closely related communities.

82　A colophon to the text states it was copied by the scribe Wang Shou 王儔 on the fourteenth day of the eight month, in the eighth year of the *Daye* 大業 era (September 14, 612); Seidel, *Divinisation*, 60.

83　For a brief introduction, see Schipper and Verellen, *The Taoist Canon*, 17–18; for a detailed analysis, see John Lagerwey, *Wu-shang pi-yao Somme Taoiste de VIe siècle* (Paris: EFEO, 1981): 620.

84　Schipper and Verellen, *The Taoist Canon*, 18.

The *Scripture on Transformations of Laozi* offers a vision of Laozi as identical with the Dao: "sometime existent and sometime absent, he is prior; and when formed is human" 存亡則為先, 成則為人. Laozi as the Dao participates in the cosmogonic process. Laozi, in fact, is not a mundane human, but a manifestation of the Dao, who "borrowed physical form in mother Li, and within her womb transformed his body" 託形李母, 胎中易身 (l.6). The text first provides nine alternative names to Laozi, all surnamed Li, but with different names (*ming* 名) and styles (*zi* 字) (l.30–38) that represent nine transformations.[85] Following these avatars of Laozi, the text lists several ancient manifestations of Laozi in which he appeared as a counselor to rulers 帝王師, beginning with the ancient Three Sovereigns and Five Thearchs 三皇五帝,[86] and extending to the Han. Most importantly, the text then claims a recent set of manifestations, beginning in 132 on Mt. Pianjueming 鶣爵鳴 near Chengdu. Laozi next appears in 144 on Mt. Bailu 白祿 where he is said to have "entrusted himself to burial in the valley" 託葬澗 (l.64).[87] Two years later, he reappeared at a shrine on this mountain, with the name Zhong Yi 仲伊. At this time he dwelt, or administered, the heights.[88] Laozi appeared again in Chengdu in 148, where he is said to have "destroyed his physical form and became a perfected person" 壞身形為真人 (l.66).[89] Laozi reappeared in 155 on Mt. Bailu, with the title Great Sage of the Slaves 僕人大賢. The text claims a final transformation will occur in 30 years, when a temple will be erected on Mt. Bailu 白鹿, and Laozi will become a Celestial Preceptor 天傅.[90]

The text then provides teachings in the voice of Laozi. Perhaps the most crucial is the repeated assertion that "after death I live again," which may also be read as "consigning myself to death, I live again" 託死更生 (l.72), or "dying, I am again alive" 死復更生 (l.74). These statements, on the one hand, are authenticated by the first part of the text, which lists the various manifestations of Laozi in the

---

85 On the significance of these "nine transformations" see Seidel, *Divinisation*, 92–105.
86 The Three Sovereigns are here listed as Baoxi 苞羲, Shennong 神農, Zhurong 祝融, the Five Thearchs are Zhuan Xu 顓頊, Diku 帝嚳, Yellow Thearch 黃帝, Yao 堯, and Shun 舜. Ancient sources provide various listings of both groups of ancient sages rulers. There were at least two distinct lists of the Five Thearchs: (1) the list in "Yueling" 月令 chapter in *Liji* 禮記 and *Lüshi chunqiu* 呂氏春秋: Taihao 太皓, Flame Thearch 炎帝, Yellow Thearch, Shaohao 少皓, Zhuanxu; (2) *Dadai liji* chapter "Wudi de" provides the following: Yellow Thearch, Zhuanxu, Diku, Yao, Shun. The latter list is the basis for *Shiji* 1 "Wudi Benji." For a preliminary discussion, see the notes to *Shiji* 1 "Wudi benji" 五帝本紀 in William H. Nienhauser, Jr., ed. *The Grand Scribe's Records* (Bloomington: Indiana University Press, 1994): 119. The sequence in *Lao zi bianhua jing* follows the order in "Wudi benji," but places Zhuanxu first. For archaeological evidence concerning the formation of these variant lists, see Wang Hui 王暉, "Chutu wenzi ziliao yu wudi xinzheng," 出土文字資料與五帝新證 *Kaogu xuebao* 2007.1, 1–28.
87 This line is not translated by Seidel. There is a Jian river 澗水 not far from Luoyang, but this cannot be the referent here.
88 *Zhicui* 治崔. There was a Cui town in Qi (in modern Zhangqiu county in Shandong) during the Spring and Autumn era. It cannot be the referent here. Does the verb *zhi* relate to the administrative parishes (*zhi*) of the Celestial Master?
89 Seidel translates this line correctly, but suggests the graph *huai* 壞 is wrong (68 n.6).
90 I follow Seidel's suggestion, and disagree with Wang Ka's emendation to *zhuan* 傳.

ancient past. On the other hand, these ancient manifestations and claims authenticate the recent manifestations, which seem to have been distinct individuals claiming to be Laozi, and who died soon after their appearance. We should note the use of the verb *tuo* 託 that appears three times in this text. This word has the semantic range of "consign," "commit," "entrust with someone," "rely on," "borrow the use of an object," and is here used in the phrases "borrow physical form" 託形 (1.6), "entrusted himself to burial" 託葬 (1.64), and "consigning myself to death, I live again" 託死更生 (1.72). In all three instances the use of *tuo* implies that the visible event is only a pretense, a simulacrum of a mundane event in order to fool the common. The cognoscenti recognize the true intention of these events. Thus, Laozi may have been born from a womb, but in actuality he is a pervasive presence and he only "borrows" physical form in order to manifest in the human realm. Similarly, death is interpreted as giving up one's physical corpse, but not as extinguishing life. Rather, the text implies, that soon after the apparent deaths of the manifested Laozi, he soon reappeared in other forms.

The third phrase, translated by Bokenkamp as "feigning death," appears in the *Xiang'er Commentary* in two passages that assert that the worthy adherents of the community do not die as do all mortals, but rather pass through the palace of Grand Darkness 太陰 where they refine their forms 練形: "When there is no place for them to stay in the world, the worthy withdraw and feigning death, pass through Grand Darkness, and have their images reborn on the other side. This is to be 'obliterated without perishing'."[91]

The notion of "feigning" or "borrowing death" in these two texts exemplifies how Daoist lineages reformulated ancient notions and practices. Among the ancient practices for attaining longevity were methods for evading death by means of a "simulated corpse" (*shijie* 尸解),[92] sometimes translated as "release by means of a corpse," whereby an adept escaped death by providing the netherworld authorities with a simulated corpse, produced through ritual means, and accompanying documentation. Presented with such proof of death, the bureaucracy of the netherworld of the dead would then remove one's name from the registers of the living and inscribe it among the dead.[93] By this combination of ritual and bureaucratic wizardry the adept would escape his fated death and continue to live hidden from the world.

91 Bokenkamp, *Early*, 102, line 227–29; *ZHDZ* 9.174c. The second passage states: "When the practice of a person of the Dao is complete, the spirits of the Dao summon him to return. He departs from the world through feigned death and passes through Grand Darkness, and is born again. They die but do not perish, hence they have longevity" 道人行備, 道神歸之, 避世託死過大陰中, 復生, 去為不亡, 故壽也 (Bokenkamp, *Early*, 135, line 515; *ZHDZ* 9.182c).

92 I borrow this translation term from Campany's detailed discussion, with extensive examples, of *shijie* in Campany, *To Live*, 52–60, *et passim*.

93 For some of the earliest evidence of the netherworld bureaucracy, see Donald Harper, "Resurrection in Warring States Popular Religion," *Taoist Resources* 5.2 (1994): 13–28; Yuri Pines, "History as Guide to the Netherworld: Rethinking the *Chunqiu shiyu*," *Journal of Chinese Religions* 31 (2003): 101–26.

The two texts under discussion here demonstrate how this notion of individual evasion of death was recast with new cosmological and eschatological understanding. In the *Xiang'er Commentary* we find the notion of "feigned death" expanded to include all members of the community. While the "profane are unable to accumulate good deeds, so that when they undergo death, this is a real death, and they belong to the earth offices,"[94] the deaths of the adherents of the Celestial Master are only apparent. In fact, their death in the mundane world is no more than relinquishing their gross physical body, as they would undergo refinement in the palace of Grand Darkness and they would continue to live as "transcendent nobles" 仙士.[95] In the *Scripture of Transformations*, on the other hand, the notion of "feigned death" is applied only to the human manifestations of Laozi who appear to die but then reappear in another human form. This text does not advocate a particular practice that leads to this attainment, nor does it imply that this attainment is accessible to the members of the community.

The claim of the distinct quality of the body of the community leaders, who claim to be manifestations of Laozi, is enhanced by asserting that the external form of the individual leader is unimportant, for "externally I am a lost slave, but within I am perfected" 外為亡僕, 內自為真 (l.74–5). This vision of Laozi as the embodiment of the Dao is vastly different from the vision expressed in the imperial "Inscription to Laozi" (*Laozi ming* 老子銘), which I discuss in Chapter 1. There, Laozi is depicted as an adept who attained the Dao through practice, and who thus functions as a model practitioner to be emulated. In this text, Laozi, and the leader who claims to be his manifestation, is a physical manifestation of the Dao, and cannot be directly emulated by the adherents of the sect. The claim by the leaders of this community to be physical manifestations of Laozi also contrasts sharply with Celestial Master Daoism. While Celestial Master Daoism also claimed to have received their teachings from the Most High Lord Lao (*Taishang laojun* 太上老君), the divine form of Laozi, they did not claim themselves to be manifestations of Laozi or the Dao.

The practices advocated by this text include recitation of the *Five-thousand Graphs*, the same title as is used in Celestial Master texts to refer to the *Daode jing*, confession, meditation, and abstention from alcohol. The *Daode jing*, in fact, seems to have inspired much of this community's teaching: Laozi's speech begins with the lines "I frolic in purity, I manage by clarity," (l.71) 吾敖以清, 吾事以明 and states its goal by declaring "without artifice, without desire, you will not be distressed by calamities; the way of the valley will adhere to your body, and you will be able to cross over" 無為無欲不憂患, 谷道來附身可度矣 (l.85). Purity, clarity, without artifice (*wuwei*), without desire, (*wuyu*), and valley are all key terms in the *Daode jing*.[96]

---

94 Bokenkamp, *Early*, 102, line 229 俗人不能積善, 行死便真死, 為地官去也.
95 Bokenkamp, *Early*, 41, 97, line 185.
96 While these words appear frequently in *Daode jing*, the actual phrases used here do not appear in any of the known recensions of the text. For a complete comparative analysis of the variant *Laozi*

Recitation of the *Daode jing* and confession were both basic practices in Celestial Master Daoism.[97] The meditation technique alluded to in the text is not quite clear, but seems to include a visualization and circulation of the five colored pneumas within the body:

> Green and white at the surface, yellow and black inside, red produces me.[98] Follow the One and commence, within there is yellow pneuma … life pneuma on left, primal pneuma on the right, yellow pneuma at the center. Cause your primordial yang to rise and penetrate the nine palaces of the limitless.
>
> (lines 82–3, 86–7)

While this technical terminology is suggestive of a clearly defined practice, it is insufficient to determine and analyze the actual practice.[99]

The cosmological changes and transformations of Laozi are at the core of the eschatological vision of this text. Laozi, having personally "initiated the offices of the Han, by changing form" 吾發動官漢令自易身 (l.76) will now personally "turn the cycle and smash the Han regime 吾轉運衝托漢事. He will choose the "good people" 良民 who will be saved from the coming calamities. It is precisely this type of eschatology, claiming the imminent end of the cosmic cycle embodied by Han, and salvific expectations of a savior who will deliver his selected people from the coming catastrophe, that link this text with the Daoist texts of the following centuries.[100]

We thus see that the *Scripture of Transformations of Laozi* shares several ideas and practices with medieval Daoist texts. First, the text expresses a vision of the Dao as a cosmogonic process that is interested and intervenes in human history by taking on human form. As Anna Seidel has shown, the identification of Laozi with Dao became a crucial aspect of Daoism, but the claim that the successive

texts, including Heshang gong 河上公 (late Han), Wang Bi 王弼 (226–49), Fu Yi 傅奕 (555–639), the Mawangdui 馬王堆 silk documents, and the Laozi parallels discovered at Guodian 郭店, see Liu Xiaogan 劉笑敢, *Laozi gujin – wuzhong duikan yu xiping yinlun* 老子古今－五種對勘與析評引論 (Beijing: Zhongguo kexue chubanshe, 2006).

97 Bokenkamp, *Early*, 35.
98 The reproduction of S 2395 in Ōfuchi clearly has "red" 赤, and is followed by Seidel. The *ZHDZ* edition has *shi* 示 (vol. 8, 182b).
99 Anna Seidel suggests a possible link to the "method of transforming the colors of the five viscera" 化色五倉之術 (*Hanshu* 25B.1260), as well as listing several parallels in later Daoist texts (72 n. 1).
100 Anna Seidel, "The Image of the Perfect Ruler in Early Taoist Messianism," *History of Religions* 9, 2/3 (November 1969/February 1970): 216–47; idem, "Taoist Messianism," *Numen* 31 (1984): 161–74. For a general survey of Daoist eschatological writings, see Lee Fengmao 李豐楙, "Chuancheng yu duiying: liuchao daojing zhong 'moshi' shuo de tichu yu yanbian" 傳承與對應：六朝道經中'末世'說的提出與衍變, *Bulletin of the Institute of Literature and Philosophy* 9 (1996): 91–130. For a partial translation and study of one of the most important eschatological scriptures, *Taishang dongyuan shenzhou jing* 太上洞淵神咒經 DZ 335, see Christine Mollier, *Une Apocalypse taoïste du Ve siécle: le Livre des Incantations Divines des Grottes Abyssales*, (Paris: Collège du France, Institut des Hautes Études Chinoises, 1990).

leaders of the community were embodiments of Laozi is quite distinct to this group. The eschatology of this text also resonates with medieval Daoist texts. Most intriguing, however, are the links between the community which produced the *Scripture on the Transformations of Laozi* and Celestial Master Daoism. We already saw that the practices advocated in this text, recitation of the *Daode jing* and confession, were also basic to Celestial Master Daoism. More significantly, the first recent appearance of Laozi mentioned in this text, on Mt. Pianjueming, which is not mentioned elsewhere,[101] resonates intriguingly with narratives associated with Zhang Daoling, who is said to have studied the Dao on Mt. Heming, which, according to Celestial Master texts, was the site of Lord Lao's revelation to Zhang Daoling. Seidel cogently suggests that the community that produced this text was a distinct group within the same milieu from which emerged the community that followed the Celestial Master. Indeed, the dating of the appearance of Laozi a decade earlier than the revelation to Zhang Daoling may not be coincidental, but a direct challenge to the developing mythology of the Celestial Master.[102]

Our exploration of the *Scripture of Transformations of Laozi* shows the variety of practices and communities at the very outset of communal Daoist religion. This variety requires that we allow these diverse aspects to be represented in the history and within the category that we label Daoism, and indeed in the earliest records of the communal Daoist movements. This diversity is a vivid reminder of the obscure origins of Celestial Master Daoism, which were smoothed over in later scriptures. The early community, which at this stage may be better termed the Way of the Five Pecks of Rice, is mentioned in official historical records. These sources, however, written by historians with little interest in religious practice and affiliation – as long as the doctrines espoused did not lead to political turmoil – are hazy about the early period of the Celestial Masters. As noted above, some sources imply that Zhang Lu, Zhang Daoling's grandson, rather than succeeding his father and grandfather as leader of the Celestial Masters, had usurped a religious movement which had been established by Zhang Xiu 張修 in the Hanzhong region of Sichuan. Daoist sources are naturally silent about this and present a clear succession from Zhang Daoling to Zhang Lu.[103]

A later example of "lost lineages" concerns the history of the *Shangqing* lineage. In her seminal study of the *Shangqing* revelations, Isabelle Robinet made a major step towards elucidating the traditions predating the *Shangqing* scriptural lineage – which came to be defined by Tao Hongjing as emanating from Yang Xi's revelations in the service of the Xu family. The *Declarations of the Perfected*

---

101 A town named Pianque cheng 扁鵲城 was located in Nanzheng county 南鄭縣, near Hanzhong (*Shuijing zhu* 27, 489).

102 The same argument is made by Ad Dudink, "The Poem *Laojun bianhua jing* Introduction, Summary and Translation," in Jan A.M. De Meyer and Peter M. Engelfriet, eds. *Linked Faiths: Essays on Chinese Religions and Traditional Culture in Honor of Kristofer Schipper* (Leiden: Brill, 2000): 74.

103 For instance, the early fifth century *Inner Explanations of the Three Heavens* (*Santian neijie jing* 三天內解經) DZ 1205: 1.5b7–6b10; Bokenkamp, *Early*, 215–17.

as well as other *Shangqing* scriptures, however, incorporate other, earlier, traditions, which may have rivaled the Yang Xi's revelations at the time, but which were subsequently suppressed.[104] For example, the *Esoteric Biography of the Perfected of Purple Solarity* may have been authored by Hua Qiao 華僑, who served as a medium in the service of the Xu family.[105] He was dismissed for revealing secrets and replaced by Yang Xi. While he is consistently portrayed negatively in *Declarations*, the inclusion of the *Esoteric Biography of the Perfected of Purple Solarity* in the *Shangqing* revelations hints at a more complex history of this textual corpus. Similarly, *Declarations* includes several biographies of practitioners who became adherents of the Dao.[106] How these figures are related to the *Shangqing* revelations is difficult to tell. However, my examination in Chapter 1 of the strategies of appropriation by which cultic figures were incorporated into the Daoist pantheon will help in elucidating the complex ways in which the *Shangqing* texts incorporated earlier and contemporary cults of transcendents.

Debating practice

However, it is not only by reading little known texts that we can find such "lost" lineages. Like early Christians, Daoist authors were also concerned with authenticity of texts and teachings, and they attempted to undermine rival teachings by labeling them forgeries. Thus, we can find traces of "lost" lineages in the texts of their surviving rivals. The two major Daoist authors and compilers of the late Six Dynasties, Lu Xiujing and Tao Hongjing, asserted that their motivation in editing the textual corpora of the *Lingbao* and *Shangqing* scriptures, respectively, was to distinguish the "artificial" 偽 from the "authentic" 真.[107] Ironically, Tao Hongjing claimed that the *Lingbao* scriptures themselves were a fabrication by Ge Chaofu. More importantly, Tao Hongjing asserted that Ge Chaofu's successful dissemination of the *Lingbao* scriptures prompted Wang Lingqi 王靈期 to fabricate false *Shangqing* texts, which he sold at exorbitant prices, including to members of the Xu family. It was to distinguish the authentic *Shangqing* revelations from the forgeries that motivated Tao to retire to Mt. Mao in 492 and embark on his work of collating and editing the *Shangqing* scriptures.[108]

Such claims regarding false teachings did not originate with these authors, but are found in the earliest examples of Daoist discourse. The *Xiang'er Commentary to the Laozi* of the late Han, the earliest extant Celestial Master text, includes

---

104 Robinet, *Révélation*, 1: 55–7, *et passim*.
105 DZ 303 *Ziyang zhenren neizhuan* 紫陽真人內傳. For an annotated translation, see Manfred Porkert, *Biographie d'un taoïste légendaire: Tcheou tseu-yang* (Paris: Collège de France, Institut des Hautes Études Chinoises, 1979).
106 These are found especially in Chapters 5 and 14.
107 On Lu Xiujing see Bokenkamp, "Lu Xiujing," 181–99.
108 *Zhen'gao* DZ 1016: 19.11b; Strickmann, *Mao Chan* 1981; idem, "The Mao Shan Revelations 1977: 1–64.

several explicit condemnations of false practices and teachings. These claims exemplify how particular lineages distinguished their practices from other contemporary lineages. Among the best examples of such debates within the emerging Daoist tradition is a condemnation of "false practitioners" who assert that the Dao is located within the body:

> ... the One is the Dao. Now, where does it reside in the body of a person? How can one maintain it? The One is not in a person's body. Those who claim it attaches itself to the body are those who are forever practicing false arts in the mortal world 常偽伎. Theirs is not the true Dao 非真道. The One exists beyond heaven and earth. Entering into the space between heaven and earth, it comes and goes within the human body. It is everywhere within your skin and not in a single spot. The One disperses its form as pneuma and gathers its form as Most High Lord Lao, whose regular domain is on Mt. Kunlun. What is sometimes named "void nothingness," sometimes the "self-actualizing" or the "nameless" – these all refer to the One. Now [I, we] have promulgated the precepts of the Dao to instruct people. To maintain the precepts without transgressing them is to "Preserve the One." Not to practice the precepts is to "lose the One." Those who forever practice false arts in the mortal world point to the five viscera and call it "the One." They meditate, closing their eyes, hoping to thereby seek good fortune. This is wrong. They depart ever farther from life.[109]

This passage refers to a crucial theological, or should we say "daological," debate within the emerging Daoist tradition. The passage thus equates a meditative practice, "preserving the one" 守一, which was to become a core Daoist practice,[110] with maintaining the precepts promulgated by High Lord Lao to the first Celestial Master. These precepts formed the ethical and institutional basis of the community. On a more abstract level, the passage refers to a divergent understanding of the *Dao* itself. Another passage in the *Xiang'er Commentary* is even more specific:

> Those who continually practice false arts in the mortal world promulgate their teachings. Pointing at shapes, they call them the Dao, claiming it has a residence, colored garments and specific height, so that one may meditate upon it.[111]

---

109 Ōfuchi, 423, *Tonkō dōkyō zurokuhen*, lines 105–113; Rao, *Laozi xiang'er*, 12; Bokenkamp, *Early*, 89.
110 This seemingly simple name may refer to numerous practices. For an introduction, see Robinet, *Taoist Meditation: The Mao-shan Tradition of Great Purity* (Albany: SUNY Press 1993).
111 Ōfuchi, 425, *Tonkō dōkyō zurokuhen*, lines 212–14; Rao, *Laozi xiang'er* 19; Bokenkamp, *Early*, 100.

The *Xiang'er Commentary* is clearly condemning those who claim the One dwells within a single locus in the body, and has a specific form and attributes. Although the term "preserving the one" may refer to any of several practices, the terminology in the *Xiang'er Commentary* is strikingly similar to a passage preserved in Ge Hong's *Inner Chapters*:

> The One has a surname and name, and clothes of specific color. It is nine *cun* in height in men, six in women.[112] It is located either in the Lower Cinnabar Field 丹田, two *cun* and four *fen* below the navel, or in the Golden Porte of the Crimson Palace 絳宮金闕 below the heart, the Middle Cinnabar Field. Sometimes it is between a person's eye-brows. As you progress within, at one *cun* is the Bright Hall 明堂, two *cun* within is the Cavern Chamber 洞房 and three *cun* within is the Upper Cinnabar Field. This then has been cherished by generations of Daoists 道家 who transmitted the names as oral instruction requiring a blood oath.[113]

This passage is found in chapter 18 "Terrestrial Perfection" 地真 of the *Inner Chapters of the Master Embracing the Unhewn* which Ge Hong presents as a teaching by his teacher, Zheng Yin 鄭隱. This text is extant in another version, entitled *Scripture of the Perfect One*,[114] which is included in the Daoist canon as the last section of the *Array of the Five Talismans*, but is clearly distinct in its mythology and practices from the main text of the *Array*.[115] Intriguingly, the passage cited above is absent from the *Scripture of the Perfect One*. Is there any significance to this absence? What do the three texts reveal about Daoist ideas regarding the One, and the proper understanding associated with the practice of "maintaining the One"?

The object of criticism of the *Xiang'er Commentary* was clearly a practice very similar to that recorded by Ge Hong. The Celestial Master author was thus distinguishing his own understanding of the One from a parallel tradition that continued unrecorded until its appearance in Ge Hong's work. Ge Hong's teacher, Zheng Yin, was thus a member of a lineage that adhered to the teaching that the "One has a name." Whether this was the very lineage of "false practitioners" condemned in the *Xiang'er Commentary* is difficult to state with certainty. Nevertheless, we can thus specify at least one lineage that presented a rival teaching to that of the Celestial Master. Whether the Dao dwells within the body with a specific form or not was a crucial question, and the two positions clearly distinguish between Celestial Master Daoism and the lineage with which Zheng Yin was affiliated.

---

112 During the Han a *cun* 寸 was approx. 2.31 cm.

113 *BPZ* 18.323, repeated on page 325 as "The perfected One has a name and surname, size, clothes and color."

114 DZ 388: 3.16a9–23b7; the full title is *Scripture of the Great One and Perfected One of the Most High* 太上太一真一之經.

115 For a detailed analysis of the *Zhenyi jing* and its place in the *Array of the Five Talismans*, see Raz, "*Creation*," 175–81.

This distinction was crucial, and the redactor of the *Scripture of the Perfect One* obviously sided with the Celestial Master position and elided the problematic passage.

It is precisely by tracing arguments about practice, such as the one illustrated in the three passages cited above, that we can gain a sense of the internal arguments among Daoists, the stakes involved in these arguments, and, most importantly, follow the developments of the tradition as it distinguished itself from other communities of practice and continued the debates within the emerging tradition.

In the following chapters, I focus on specific practices that are central to the understanding of Daoism. The sequence of the chapters follows the historical development of the tradition, with Chapter 1 focusing on developments in late Han, tracing the developments of communal practices that formed the basis for the emergence of Daoist lineages, and Chapter 5 focusing on inter-Daoist debates in the late fourth and fifth centuries, and the efforts at forming an integrated orthodoxy and orthopraxy. The intervening chapters trace the discourse and practice of lineage, talismans, and sexual rites from their Han antecedents to their integration into the emerging Daoist tradition.

Chapter 1, "Immortality cults and cults of immortals," examines the emergence of new types of communal practices that differed from the traditional local cults. The chapter focuses on several second-century inscriptions celebrating the attainment of transcendence by practitioners of esoteric arts. Paradoxically, these individual seekers of immortality became foci of communal reverence. After describing the tradition of immortality seekers, the chapter examines the rise of the new communal practices the inscriptions reveal. I argue that these inscriptions reveal a typology of cults, ranging from family-based associations to local, regional, and trans-regional cults. These new communal cultic centers provided the social basis for the rise of Daoist communities that distinguished themselves from the local traditions.

Chapter 2, "Blood rites and pure covenants," is devoted to "lineage," a fundamental category in all aspects of traditional Chinese society, culture, and religion. This chapter examines the notions and practices underlying the basic social category of Daoism, the lineages of masters and disciples, focusing on the rhetorics and practices by which lineages were constructed. The chapter examines both the narrative constructions of lineages, as well as the initiations and ritual transmissions of practices by which lineages were actually constructed. Lineages, initiations, and ritual transmissions were also the core social modalities of the Masters of Techniques. By examining the differences between the Daoist practices and those of the Masters of Techniques, we will see how the Daoists distinguished themselves from the lineages from which they adopted several of their practices.

Chapter 3, "Talismans: the power of inscription," focuses on the ritual use of talismans, a practice that has characterized Daoism since the emergence of the earliest lineages, and that remains essential in contemporary practice. Linking Daoist practices of talismans and charts with ideas regarding script, Daoists viewed their talismans and scriptures as emanations of primordial *qi*, prior to the manifested world. I introduce the notion of "inscription" to analyze the efficacy and power inherent in talismans.

In Chapter 4, "The Yellow and the Red: controversies over sexual practice," I examine debates concerning sexual practice among medieval Daoists. Sexual practices were among the most basic techniques of the immortality seekers in early China, as attested by the manuals of sexual practice included in the various caches of early documents unearthed in recent years. Revealing the importance and popularity of these practices, these documents help place and contextualize the varied attitudes to sexual practices found in Daoist sources. Daoist sexual practices range from the practice of semen retention known as "reverting essence to nourish the brain," through the sexual initiation rites of the Celestial Masters, to the sublimation and internalization of the sexual process in Shangqing Daoism. Claims regarding proper sexual practice were a critical issue for Daoist lineages to distinguish themselves from other non-Daoist "communities of practice" and from each other.

Chapter 5, "Creating orthodoxy," focuses on the creation of a Daoist orthodoxy by Lu Xiujing, whose systemization of ritual, canonization project, and historical construction of the tradition remain at the core of the Ming Daoist canon, much of contemporary ritual, and the historical understanding of Daoism. Lu Xiujing, however, was neither unique nor the first in trying to unify the emerging Daoist tradition. In fact, I argue that such a vision of orthodoxy and integration was a characteristic of several of the medieval Daoist traditions. I thus begin by exploring antecedents to Lu's project. I examine the nascent canons and orthodoxies of the Lingbao scriptures and Celestial Master as rival attempts at systemization as a context for understanding Lu's project of integrating the ritual schemes, scriptural canons, and his historical vision.

1 Immortality cults and cults of immortals

Lingyang Ziming 陵陽子明 of Zhi 銍 township enjoyed fishing at Xuan 旋 stream. Once he caught a white dragon. Terrified, Ziming released it from the hook, bowed to it, and set it free. Later, he caught a white fish. In its stomach he found a text which taught him methods for ingestion [of efficacious substances]. Ziming then ascended Mt. Huang to gather the five types of stone lard, which he boiled in water. After ingesting this [compound] for three years, the white dragon arrived and escorted him to Mt. Lingyang, where he dwelt for over a century.[1]

The emergence of Daoist religion in medieval China was predicated on new social, cultural, and religious alignments. The primary defining aspect of these developments was the appearance of new types of communal religious practices that distinguished themselves from traditional common religion. A second key aspect which came to distinguish Daoism was the identification of Laozi with the Dao. This process, as Anna Seidel has shown, had by the second century transformed the ancient philosopher into a divine being, coeval with the Dao. These two aspects are in fact related, for, as Daoist scriptures tell us, it was Most High Lord Lao, *Taishang laojun*, the newly imagined form of Laozi, who appeared to Zhang Ling in 142 CE to confer upon him the title of Celestial Master and reveal to him the teachings with which to establish a new religious institution.

The deified Laozi has become one of the core elements in defining the emergence of Daoism in the late Han. The appearance of Lord Lao to Zhang Ling, and the acceptance of the latter as the initiator of Daoism, was an essential part of the history of Daoism constructed by Lu Xiujing in his *Abridged Codes*, and it was adopted by Michel Strickmann in his definition of Daoism. Yet, how unique were

---

1 *Liexian zhuan* 列仙傳 DZ 294; 2.14b. For variants and annotations, see Max Kaltenmark, *Le Lie-sien tchouan* (Collège de France: Paris, 1953; rpt. 1987): 183–7; Wang Shumin 王叔民, annot. edn *Liexian zhuan jiaojian* 列仙傳校箋 (Taipei: Institute of Literature and Philosophy, Academia Sinica, 1995): 158. *Zhi* township and *Xuan* stream are located in ancient Chu, in the southwest of modern Xiu 宿 county of Anhui province.

these developments? How novel was the deification of Laozi? Was the Way of the Celestial Master the first voluntary religious association in China, and thus a redefinition of religion in early medieval China? I explore these questions in this chapter.

I argue that the rise of Celestial Master Daoism has to be understood in a larger context of religious change during the Eastern Han. The emergence of Daoist lineages was grounded in a new type of communal practice that developed during the Han dynasty and culminated in the late Han. These new communal practices were located at cultic centers that focused on individual practitioners who were perceived as having attained the Dao and transcended the limitations of mundane space and time. Yet, despite their escape from the mundane world, or, perhaps due to it, sites dedicated to such individuals became sites of succor and beneficence for local communities. These cults, I suggest, were the basis for new communal religious movements, and a source for many of the Daoist lineages that emerged in the following decades and centuries. The emergence of Daoism should, therefore, be seen as a product of organic growth of indigenous Chinese religion.

This chapter will begin with a brief description of the tradition of seekers of transcendence and its relationship to both Han imperial religion and Han common religion. This will be followed by a study of four contemporaneous stele inscriptions, all dating to the 160s. These inscriptions from the waning years of the Eastern Han illustrate the development of seekers of immortality from small lineages of individuals linked in master–disciple relationships into communal cultic centers. In the final part of the chapter, I examine the ways in which these individuals and their cults were incorporated into the emerging Daoist lineages.

To pre-empt the complex argument of this chapter, I begin by returning to Lingyang Ziming's hagiography cited above; one of 70 short narratives concerning adepts contained in the late Han hagiographic collection *Arrayed Traditions of Transcendents* (*Liexian zhuan* 列仙傳; hereafter *LXZ*).[2] This narrative illustrates some of the main themes I will be tracing in this and the following chapters: the quest for longevity and transcendence, transmission of esoteric knowledge, and, finally, the appropriation of these techniques and practices, narrative structure, and, perhaps most importantly, the incorporation of such adepts into the Daoist tradition. Allowing us glimpses into the religious beliefs and practices of Han China, the hagiographies of seekers of transcendence also overlap with the discourse of the "Masters of Esoterica" (*fangshi* 方士), who first rose into prominence during the Qin and whose influence continued throughout the Han.[3]

---

2 *Liexian zhuan* is attributed to Liu Xiang 劉向 (77–6 BCE). Most scholars, however, agree that while it preserves some early material, its final redaction took place in late Eastern Han; see Kaltenmark, *Lie-sien*, pp. 1–2; Wang Qing 王青, *Hanchao de bentu zongjiao yu shenhua* 漢朝的本土宗教與神話 (Taipei: Hongye, 1998): 191–8.

3 The main hagiographic and biographic collections are: (1) *Arrayed Traditions*; (2) *Shenxian zhuan* 神仙傳, translated by Campany, *To Live*; (3) *Sanguozhi* 三國志 ch. 29 "Fangji zhuan" 方技傳 by Chen Shou 陳壽 (233–97) with commentary by Pei Songzhi 裴松之 (372–451); (4) *Houhan shu* 82 "Fangshu liezhuan" 方術列傳, translated in Ngo Van Xuyet, *Divination, Magie et Politique dans*

Before proceeding further, we should discuss the two terms, *xian* and *fangshi*, which are crucial for understanding the history of Daoism. Neither of these terms is clearly defined, and neither refers to clearly delineated social groups. Nevertheless, as they are used by contemporaneous authors to refer to the individuals and the practices we are examining here, we must try to understand the social, cultural, and historical contexts in which they made sense.

The word *xian*, variously translated as "immortal" or "transcendent," signifies the ultimate attainment of psycho-physical transformation. It should be best understood as attaining the Dao, although the precise connotations of such attainment vary among practitioners and traditions. The word *xian* may be written in two forms. Its more common graphic form is of a "man by mountain" 仙, with the metaphorical implication of remote reclusion in nature. An earlier form of the word, 僊, implies "ascent;" the Han dictionary *Shuowen jiezi* glosses the graph as "long-lived, ascended and departed" 長生僊去.[4] Adapted by the various Daoist lineages, the exact connotations of the attainment of *xian* varied among different practitioners and lineages. In some contexts, the attainment of *xian* was the lowest in a hierarchy of attainment.

The second term, *fangshi*, is also problematic, and several authors have suggested different translations for this term.[5] The word *fang* 方 refers to "recipes" or "methods," and in the context of the narratives we will be exploring here, the

---

la Chine ancienne (Paris: Presses Universitaires de France, 1976), and Kenneth J. DeWoskin, *Doctors, Diviners and Magicians of Ancient China: Biographies of Fang-shih* (New York: Columbia University Press, 1983). Other important sources include chapters 6 and 28 of the *Shiji*, references to *fangshi* mentioned individually in other chapters of the *Hanshu* and *Hou Hanshu* and Six Dynasties collections of tales of anomalies such as *Bowu zhi* 博物志, *Soushenji* 搜神記, on which see Robert F. Campany, *Strange Writing: Anomaly Accounts in Early Medieval China* (Albany: State University of New York Press, 1996).

4   The *Shuowen* includes an earlier form of the graph, 仚, glossed as "Man in mountain" (*Shuowen jiezi zhu* 說文解字注, ch. 8A, p. 38b). Kristofer Schipper prefers the translation "immortal" or "human mountain," see Kristofer Schipper, *The Taoist Body* (Berkeley: University of California Press, 1993): 164. Robert Campany prefers the translation "Transcendent" with the caveat that there is not "... an absolute metaphysical difference between *xian* and lesser beings, but ... they have ascended to links in the chain higher than those occupied by even the best human beings," see Campany, *To Live*, 4–5.

5   Yü Ying-shih has suggested that this term "may generally be translated as 'religious Taoists' or 'popular Taoists' since all the arts they practiced were later subsumed in the Daoist religion. In specific contexts, they may be translated as 'magicians,' 'alchemists,' or 'immortalists,'" see, Yü Ying-shih, "Life and Immortality in the Mind of Han China" *HJAS* 25 (1964): 105, n103. I find Yü's suggested translation misleading as it obscures the crucial distinctions between *fangshi* and *daoists,* which are the very subject of this chapter. Harper has suggested the almost literal translation 'recipe gentlemen' in Donald Harper, *Early Chinese Medical Literature* (London and New York: Kegan Paul International, 1998): 44. Though his reasoning is correct, I find the term unwieldy. Joseph Needham suggests technicians, thaumaturgical craftsmen, and adepts as possible translations (*Science and Civilization in China* (Cambridge: Cambridge University Press, 1974): vol. 5, part 2, 9). These terms suggest the range of activities engaged in by *fangshi*, but lack the element of gnosis which underlay their activities. In discussing the understanding of the term *fangshi*, Robert Campany also opts for "masters of esoterica" see Campany, *To Live*, 6.

term implies secret knowledge that was transmitted from master to disciple only in ritual initiations. I therefore use the translation "master of esoterica" to emphasize the aspects of gnosis and practice associated with these figures. The *fangshi* are traditionally said to have originated in the Yan and Qi coastal areas, and to be closely associated with the followers of Zou Yan 騶衍 (305–240 BCE). The earliest evidence for them in traditionally received sources is indeed from that area.[6] These practitioners transmitted legends of three islands "where transcendents and medicinals for avoiding death could be found, the beasts and birds were all white, and palaces were made of gold and silver."[7]

Archeological evidence, however, reveals that practices which may be classified as associated with *fangshi* were not limited to the coastal area. In fact, large numbers of recently unearthed documents that may be placed within the tradition of *fangshi* practices have been found in the south, in areas associated with the Chu cultural area.[8] While this may be no more than coincidence due to research priorities and circumstance, it suffices to show that *fangshi* and their practices were found throughout the Han realm.[9]

Several scholars have tried to map regional traditions among *fangshi* based on hagiographies and notices in traditional sources.[10] Such mappings of regional

---

6 The earliest reference to the term *fangshi* is in the "Fengshan" chapter of the *Shiji*: "Since the time of kings Wei and Xuan of Qi, followers of Zou Yan discussed his theory of the cyclical revolutions of the five virtues 終始五德之運. When [the king of] Qin became emperor these men of Qi memorialized to him, hence the Inaugural Emperor employed them. On the other hand, Song Wuji 宋毋忌, Zheng Boqiao 正伯僑, Chong Shang 充尚 and Xianmen Gao 羨門高, who were all of Yan, practiced the way of methods and transcendence 方僊道, of releasing the form by refinement and transformation, upon which they relied in serving the spirits. Zou Yan showed his text *Yin and yang control the revolutions* (*Yinyang zhuyun* 陰陽主運) to the various lords, but the Masters of Esoterica from the coastal regions of Yan and Qi transmitted his arts without understanding. As a result innumerable practitioners of strange and weird arts appeared." (*SJ* 28.1368).

7 *Shiji* 12.455; *Hanshu* 25A.1204.

8 For a convenient list of *fang* literature unearthed in the twentieth century, see Li Jianmin, Sisheng zhi yu, 2000: 8–16, *et passim*. Li Ling 李零, *Zhongguo fangshu kao* 中國方術考 (Beijing: Dongfang, rev. edn 2000) and *Zhongguo fangshu xukao* 中國方術續考 (Beijing: Dongfang, 2000) contain several studies of such materials. For a study of recently unearthed documents, see Enno Giele, "Early Chinese Manuscripts: Including Addenda and Corrigenda to New Sources of Early Chinese History: An Introduction to the Reading of Inscriptions and Manuscripts," *Early China* 23–24 (1998–99): 247–337. Giele's Database of Early Chinese Manuscripts and the updated "New Reports on Early Chinese Manuscripts (2010)" are both maintained on the Early China website (http://humanities.uchicago.edu/easian/earlychina).

9 Donald Harper, "Warring States Natural Philosophy and Occult Thought," in Michael Loewe and Edward Shaughnessy, eds. *The Cambridge History of Ancient China* (Cambridge, UK; New York: Cambridge University Press, 1999): 813–84; Marc Kalinowski, "Divination et astrologie dans l'empire Han: Sources Historiographiques et découvertes archéologiques récentes," in *Cahiers du Centre Gustave Glotz* 16 (2005).

10 Meng Wentong 蒙文通 delineates three distinct traditions of transcendence seekers associated with regional distinctions: herbalists based in the Yan-Qi area, ingestion of *qi* which originated in the Shu area and part of the Wu-Yue region, and sexual practices in the Chu area; Meng Wentong, "Wanzhou xiandao fen sanpai kao" 晚周仙道分三派, in *Tushu jikan* 圖書季刊 8 (1946); rpt. in *Meng Wentong wenji* 蒙文通文集 (Chengdu: Bashu shushe, 1987): v. 1, 335–42. Hu Fuchen 胡孚琛 has proposed

distinctions were constructed by methodologies which ignore considerations of historical developments, agendas of the source materials, and changes in popularity of specific practices at certain periods. If we consider these variables while tracing how certain practices are emphasized or ignored in the historical development of hagiographies, we would realize that these records reveal less about the individual practitioner than about the changing popularity of practices, as well as about the proclivities of the authors or compilers of the narratives. Sexual practices, for instance, which were relatively absent from hagiographies in *Liexian zhuan*,[11] become more important in the traditions recorded in *Shenxian zhuan* and the "Fangshu" chapter of the *Hanshu*. This may demonstrate that sexual practice grew in popularity and importance among practitioners during the Han dynasty. On the other hand, it may indicate reluctance of the redactors of *Liexian zhuan* to include sexual practices in the hagiographies they compiled. Mapping regional traditions based on hagiographical notices may thus be at best tentative.

Another avenue to examine *fangshi* is to trace practices rather than individuals. As the archaeological evidence shows, Qin- and Han-era traditions of *fangshi* and their practices are clearly traceable to developments in the Warring States era. However, as textual evidence of this period is limited, demarcating regional traditions depends on limited references to individuals who came to be categorized as *fangshi* by their practice of specific techniques only in retrospect. The individuals associated with specific practices may sometimes be legendary, and texts may borrow names of ancient practitioners as marks of prestige and authority. By focusing on practices rather than on individual adepts we can distinguish certain types of practices and thus establish a limited typology of practices. Li Ling follows the categorization of the *Hanshu* bibliographic chapter which differentiated practices into two main types:[12] *shushu* 數術, literally meaning "arts of calculations," which included practices dealing with "heaven and earth," or methods for divination from natural elements, and *fangji* 方技 which included healing, medical, and longevity practices. Each category included a variety of practices and numerous variants.

The category of *shushu* included: (1) astronomical calendrics (*tianwen lisuan* 天文曆算), astrological divination (*zhanxing* 佔星), and descrying weather (*houqi*

a different scheme: a Yan-Qi tradition, exemplified by Anqi Sheng 安其生 and Xian Mengao 羨門高, focused on ingestion of immortality drugs, particularly cinnabar; *fangshi* from Qin and Jin focused on sexual practices and revered Pengzu and Rong Cheng; and a southern tradition, in the regions of Chu, Wu-Yue, and Ba-Shu, which focused on *qi* cultivation, gymnastics, breathing practices, and meditation, and who found their exemplars in Wangzi Qiao and Master Redpine; Hu Fuchen, *Daoxue tonglun* 道學通論, 271. For other mappings of regional traditions, see Wang Qing, *Bentu*, 172–9.

11 One of the few exceptions is Laozi who is described as "adept at nourishing essence and pneuma; he valued intercourse, and did not ejaculate" 好養精氣, 貴接而不施. Kaltenmark notes that this technical terminology resonates with the tradition of sexual practice, Kaltenmark, *Lie-sien*, 63, n.4. Particularly intriguing is the entry to Rongcheng gong 容成公, who is also described as a master of sexual techniques and said to be Laozi's instructor. I discuss Rongcheng in Chapter 4.

12 *Hanshu* 30: 1763–80; Li Ling, *Zhongguo fangshu kao*, is a detailed study of the various practices.

候氣);[13] (2) methods of the *shi* cosmograph (*shifa* 式法), hemerology (*xuanze* 選擇), wind-angles (*fengjiao* 風角), and five tones (*wuyin* 五音);[14] (3) divination by turtle plastron and milfoil (*guipu shizhan* 龜卜筮占), among the most ancient methods of divination, were also employed by officials to determine royal activity; (4) dream interpretation (*zhanmeng* 佔夢), exorcism (*yake* 壓刻), and expulsion (*cirang* 祠禳);[15] (5) physiognomy (*xiang* 相), also known as "Methods of [examining] form" (*xingfa* 形法), included practices of descrying topography, geomantic placement of tombs and houses, descrying human features as well as of animals.

The category of *fangji* included: (1) medical texts (*yijing* 醫經), theoretical and comprehensive texts; (2) recipes and healing techniques (*jingfang* 經方); (3) sexual manuals (*fangzhong* 房中); (4) techniques for immortality 神僊.

These methods included specialized dietary regimens that advocated the ingestion of particular foods and medicinal substances in order to cure illness and prolong life. These practices eventually became methods for attaining transcendence. The Han category does not seem to differentiate between herbal and mineral based practices. Practitioners of alchemy, however, distinguished the compounding and ingestion of mineral elixirs from the use of herbal practices. Alchemy, known as *dan* 丹, referring to both cinnabar (mercury sulfide), the major ingredient in the alchemical process, and to the alchemical compound itself, became a major practice among seekers of transcendence. Another set of practices that were adapted by later Daoist lineages were various methods of *qi* circulation.[16]

We should note that these categories are bibliographic, that is, they were labels used in the imperial library to arrange texts, and do not indicate any social links.

---

13 Texts and methods of this category are entitled with names of various ancient legendary astronomers who are listed in the astronomical chapters of the *Shiji* and *Hanshu*.

14 Originally associated with astronomical methods, practices using the *shi* cosmograph became divorced from actual astronomical observation and relied on manipulation of the plates and their abstract symbols. For a detailed study of this process, see Marc Kalinowski, "Les Instruments astro-calendériques des Han et la méthode *liu ren*," *BEFEO* 72 (1983): 309–420. Hemerology developed from *shi* methods. By calculating interdictions and determining auspicious and inauspicious days, practitioners compiled "almanacs" (rishu 日書) by which days could be selected according to their suitability for specific acts. Such practitioners were known as "[One who selects] days" (*rizhe* 日者). The term "wind-angles" refers to methods of determining fortune and calamity according to the direction winds blow. The term "five-tones" refers to methods of divining fortune and misfortune by observing the seasonal pitch pipes. These two types of practice were usually listed together. These various methods were incorporated into manuals of military techniques. The theoretical bases for these methods were the theories of *yinyang* and five phases, which developed during the Warring States era.

15 Oneiromancy was considered secondary among divination practices. Oneiromancy was intimately linked to conceptualizations of the body, spirits, and ghosts. Ancient etiologies of disease interpreted illness, nightmares, and psychological pressures as a result of ghostly intervention. Methods of expulsion and exorcism were therefore the preferred treatment for such ailments. Strickmann, *Chinese Magical Medicine*, is a detailed study of the demonic etiology of dreams and methods for exorcising and healing.

16 Among the earliest examples of such techniques are the Mawangdui manuscripts entitled *Yinshu* and *Daoyin tu*; for translation and analysis, see Harper, *Early*, 310–27.

Individual practitioners could study and receive instruction in a variety of practices. However, it is precisely by tracing practices that we may get a clearer picture of social filiations. Moreover, as many of these practices were adopted into the Daoist ritual systems, it is by tracing how Daoist lineages adapted and manipulated them that we may learn how Daoists created their tradition.

The protagonists of the *Arrayed Traditions* are of diverse origins. Many are known from other sources, both earlier and contemporaneous, which provide them with attributes different from those given to them in *Arrayed Traditions*. Some figures, such as Master Redpine (Chisongzi 赤松子) are of ancient and obscure origins, while others like Father Cinnamon (Guifu 桂父) were probably gods of local cults. Nevertheless, once these disparate individuals were appropriated by the compiler of the *Arrayed Traditions* and provided with biographies which located them in mundane time and place, and focused on specific practices by which they attained transcendence, they became model adepts. Thus, regardless of their varied origins, the protagonists of the *Arrayed Traditions* were placed within the tradition of immortality seekers.

Despite the wide variety of skills, practices, loci, and thematic elements attributed to the protagonists of the various narratives, there are certain themes which recur throughout the *Arrayed Traditions*. Reflecting variations in the representation of adepts, other narratives, concerning many of the same figures but produced in different contexts, do not always elaborate or stress the same themes. Certain structural elements, however, remain constant through these diverse narratives. In this chapter I examine these themes in the context of cultic practice.

The hagiographic narratives often provide the source for the adept's practice. Other hagiographies, especially those adapted into Daoist texts, emphasized the importance of proper transmission of teachings and texts from master to disciple. I discuss these initiation rites and the creation of lineages in Chapter 2. Even when the source of the teaching is beyond the human realm, as in the case of Lingyang Ziming, the teaching itself is perceived as textual and seems to gain its authority by its graphic nature. This element is reminiscent of the revelation of the *River Chart and Luo Writ* (*Hetu Luoshu* 河圖洛書), mythical texts which had been presented to ancient emperors by turtles and dragons. These talismanic texts were the prototypical texts upon which the Han weft texts 讖緯 were modeled, and which, in turn, inspired the creation of early Daoist texts. I discuss the critical importance of charts, texts, and talismans in Chapter 3.

The text obtained by the adept provided knowledge of specific practices – ingestion of mineral compounds in this case – which, through proper use, led to transcendence. The narratives stress that attainment demanded lengthy and precise preparations, followed by a gradual process of refinement, both of the physical form and its spiritual components. These preparations necessitated reclusion, often on a mountain. As in the case of Lingyang Ziming, adepts were sometimes identified with a mountain to such an extent that the toponym and the names of the adept were the same. We will find such a case in our examination of Tang Gongfang.

To summarize, transcendence, as perceived in these narratives, was not a sudden realization of ineffable truth, but rather the result of a process of bodily preparation and refinement predicated on a determined regimen of specific practices, usually in reclusion on a mountain. Attainment of transcendence was a culmination of a technical procedure which required instruction and a textual basis.

As is the case with many of the adepts described in *Arrayed Traditions*, references to Lingyang Ziming in other early sources provide us with different views of the same individual. These sources describe him as a master of *qi* circulation, that is complex breathing techniques, and refer neither to ingestion of minerals, nor to the revelation of the teaching in a fish's belly noted in the hagiography in *Arrayed Traditions*.[17] Another Han dynasty text, which I discuss in Chapter 4, alludes to him as a master of sexual practices.[18] Clearly, the passage in *Arrayed Traditions* cannot be taken as a full and objective account of the tradition concerning Lingyang Ziming. Rather, the representation of Lingyang Ziming in this account is a result of selection, possibly invention, of particular elements and themes by the compiler of the *Arrayed Traditions*. This particular representation was meant to cohere with the agenda of the collection. In fact, any claim to such an objective account is patently impossible, as at each telling the narrative is subject to the particular interests and proclivities of the teller.

Still later, Lingyang Ziming was appropriated by medieval Daoist authors. He appears in the *Central Scripture of Laozi* as part of the pantheon of corporeal gods.[19] Among the mytho-historical figures mentioned as corporeal spirits in *Central Scripture of Laozi* are the Queen Mother of the West and the King Father of the East, important deities in Han common religion, and Confucius.[20]

---

17 Lingyang Ziming is said to have practiced a method of ingesting the Six Pneumas. A lost *Lingyang ziming jing* 陵楊子明經 is cited in Wang Yi's commentary to the *Chuci* 楚辭 poem "Yuanyou" 遠遊 in Hong Xingzu 洪興祖 (1090–155) comp., *Chuci buzhu* 楚辭補注 (Taipei: Da'an), 251. The system is mentioned in the Mawangdui manuscripts *Ten Questions* (*Shiwen* 十問) and *Cutting off grains and ingesting pneuma* (*Quegu shiqi* 卻穀食氣) in Harper, *Early*, 307, 395. References to the system occur in Li Yi's 李頤 commentary to the "Xiaoyao you" chapter of the *Zhuangzi* (*SBCK* 1:5a); Sima Xiangru's 司馬相如 "Daren fu" 大人賦 and comments by Zhang Yi 張揖, Ying Shao 應劭 and Fu Qian 服虔 (*HS* 57B.2599).

18 In his *Zidu jing* 子都經, Wu Yan 巫炎, named *Zidu* 子都, a *fangshi* active during the reign of Han emperor Wu, claimed to have received instruction in sexual methods from Lingyang Ziming. The *Zidu jing* is lost except for citations in Chapter 28 of Ishinpō 醫心方 comp. in 984 by Tamba Yasuyori 丹波康賴 (911–995) (Taipei, Xinwenfeng, 1976, 6 vols.); collated in Li Ling, *Fangshu kao*, 512–4. Translated in Robert H. van Gulik, *Sexual Life in Ancient China: a Preliminary Survey of Chinese Sex and Society from ca. 1500 B.C. till 1644 A.D.* (Leiden: E. J. Brill, 1961): 137 ff.; republished with a new introduction and bibliography by Paul R. Goldin (Leiden and Boston: Brill, 2003): 137 ff.

19 Lingyang Ziming appears in section 12 as the name of the father of the Perfected Zidan who dwells in the 'great storehouse' *taicang* 太倉 in the center of the stomach (*YJQQ* 18.7b-8a).

20 The King-Father of the East and Queen-Mother of the West are important figures in the *Central Scripture*, for instance, section 4 states:

> A person has two nipples; they are the ford at which the essences, pneumata, and yin and yang of the myriad spirits cross. Below the left nipple is the sun; below the right nipple is the moon. These are the residences of the King-Father and Queen-Mother. Their upper

The names of adepts, like Lingyang Ziming, served as signifiers which could be adopted by various authors and lineages to provide ancient authority for practices as well as conferring prestige on lineages. We will need to bear this in mind as we examine other hagiographies and narratives of adepts and Daoists.[21] I discuss such appropriations in the final section of this chapter.

The obvious links between the *fangshi* of early medieval China and the Daoist lineages of the Six Dynasties have been pointed out before. However, most studies have focused on tracing names and practices mentioned in Shangqing or Lingbao texts to Han antecedents. Isabelle Robinet has attempted to reconstruct the social network of practitioners and their practices linking the *fangshi* at the court of Cao Cao and the emerging Shangqing lineage. However, as these links focus on the master–disciple networks they do not explain the appearance of organized communities of adherents.

The religious practices of the *fangshi* extended from involvement in the highest levels of imperial ritual, namely the *fengshan* 封禪 rite, to local religious rites.[22] They are best known, though, for following various esoteric psycho-physical regimens intended for personal cultivation of individual practitioners. The practices of the *fangshi* were not communal practices, but were to be practiced and transmitted in secrecy within strictly defined lineages of master and disciples.

However, as the fame of individual practitioners grew they became part of the public domain, especially as their practice proved efficacious. While most formed small coteries of practitioners, some became the focus of widespread cultic practice. Of the 70 hagiographies collected in *Arrayed Traditions*, almost half refer to shrines erected in reverence of the adept at specific sites. Some specify the adept became an object of reverence in certain locales, while others seem to indicate that the cult had spread over wide areas. Some adepts, who are not associated with shrines in *Arrayed Traditions*, are reported to have received cultic reverence in other sources, such as the *Hou Hanshu* and Li Daoyuan's 酈道元 (d. 527) *Shuijing zhu* 水經注. While these examples clearly indicate that numerous *fangshi* became subjects of cultic veneration, they do not describe the actual practices associated

domain are the eyes, they cavort in the head. At rest, they are below the nipples, sleeping in the Purple Chamber of the Scarlet Palace. They are the pneumata of yin and yang.

Confucius' role in the system is relatively minor, section 17 states: "The Cinnabar field is called Essence Treasury Palace 藏精宮, its spirit is surnamed Kong 孔, named Qiu 丘, his byname is Zhongni 仲尼."

21 Campany, *To Live*, is especially attentive to the issue of refractions of ancient material in hagiographic reformulations.

22 *Hanshu* 25B reports that beginning with emperor Wu, a policy of centralizing religious practices was initiated, which included sacrifices at hundreds of altars of local gods that were erected near the capital. *Fangshi* were among the ritual specialists who performed these sacrifices. These policies were continued by emperors Cheng and Ai. See Marianne Bujard, *Le Sacrifice au Ciel dans la Chine Ancienne: Théorie et Pratique sous les Han Occidentaux* (Paris: EFEO, 2000); idem, "State and Local Cults in Han Religion," in John Lagerwey and Mark Kalinowski, *Early Chinese Religion Part One: Shang through Han* (Leiden: Brill, 2009): 777–811.

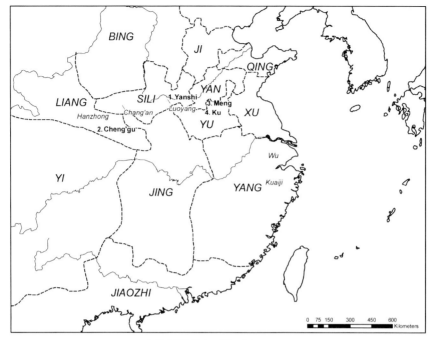

1. Fei Zhi Stele at Yanshi
2. Tang Gongfang Stele at Cheng'gu
3. Wangzi Qiao Stele at Meng
4. Laozi Stele at Ku

Figure 1.1 Sites of the four stele inscriptions.

with the particular shrine and adept, nor do they indicate the extent and form of the cult itself. We may fill in some of these gaps by examining inscriptional evidence of contemporaneous late Han cults which reveal various levels of practice and public participation.

The inscriptional evidence demonstrates that comparable instances from hagiographic collections should not be considered as "fiction" but rather as actual evidence for cultic practice and religious groupings.[23] We can also assume that similar cults were prevalent throughout the Han polity. While these inscriptions raise many intriguing questions, I will limit myself here to the following issues: first, the practices and lineage ascribed to the protagonist, and, second, the cultic practice associated with the location. I will then show how these individuals, practices, and narratives were co-opted into the emerging Daoist synthesis.

23 See Robert Campany's criticism of "fiction as a category of analysis," in Campany, *To Live*, 98–100.

Based on the scope of cultic practice associated with the inscriptions, I argue that these cults of transcendence may be usefully divided into the following typology:

1   Small cultic associations: formed around an actual individual, little known, or even unknown, beyond the immediate group; exemplified by the *Fei Zhi inscription* 肥致碑.
2   Local cultic center: a center of public worship of a local practitioner; exemplified by the *Transcendent Tang Gongfang inscription* 仙人唐公房碑.
3   General cultic center: a localized cult of a practitioner who has become part of the public domain. Already a legendary person in contemporary sources, whatever may have been the original particulars of the practitioner are no longer recoverable; exemplified by the *Wangzi qiao inscription* 王子喬碑.
4   Universal cultic center: a cultic center designated and supported by the imperial court, exemplified by the *Inscription to Laozi* 老子銘.

While a chronological progression may be postulated from type one to four, and examples of such developments may be demonstrated, the purpose of the following is not to examine the processes by which cultic associations may expand into local cults, general cultic centers, and, finally, into universal cults. Rather, the examples will show that various levels of cultic practice associated with transcendents existed contemporaneously. The language describing practices was shared across the various types. Certain phrases in this discourse are formulaic and have lost their original particular meaning or precise referent. The same terminology is found in contemporary hagiographies and, later, in Daoist practice. This continuity should alert us to the fact that despite its opaqueness this discourse referred to actual practices and that these phrases were not merely literary conventions.

I   MASTER FEI ZHI: SMALL CULTIC ASSOCIATION

A stele inscription located in the southern ante-chamber of a small tomb complex discovered near Luoyang in 1991 reveals the cultic activity centering upon Master Fei Zhi.[24] Due to obvious parallels between the language and practices of the inscription and contemporary hagiographies of *fangshi* and transcendents, on

24 The initial archaeological report: *Yanshi xian nancaizhuang xiang han Fei Zhi mu fajue jianbao* 偃師縣南蔡庄鄉漢肥致墓發掘簡報 *Wenwu* 1992.9: 37–42. For a clear reproduction of the stele and short discussion, see Stephen Little, ed. *Taoism and the Arts of China* (Chicago: The Art Institute of Chicago, 2000): 151. A translation with few notes is found in Mark Csikszentmihàlyi, *Readings in Han Chinese Thought* (Indianapolis: Hackett, 2006): 152–5. Robert Campany provides a translation in his *Making Transcendents: Ascetics and Social Memory in Early Medieval China* (Honolulu: Hawaii University Press, 2009): 225–32, which is largely based on my own early work.

the one hand, and of Daoist scriptures, on the other, this inscription has drawn considerable attention.[25]

The inscription provides a first-hand look at a small group of seekers of transcendence, centered on a single family. Unattested in other sources, Master Fei, a practitioner of esoteric arts, had attracted the attention of Xu You 許幼, a local official, also unreported elsewhere, who became his patron and disciple. Having practiced together, they may have died together (ritually?), although no specifics are given. In the final lines of the inscription, five followers state that they will ingest "stone lard 石脂" (probably, a type of silicate) and thereby "depart as transcendents." Death was obviously interpreted by this group as a passage to immortality, and it appears that the members of this group actively sought it.

The members of this group do not seem to have had links to any other group, yet the period of its activity (the stele is dated to 169 CE) is highly significant. This was the period that the community of Celestial Master Daoism was active in the Shu region while the *Taiping* movement was developing in the eastern provinces. It was also at this time that the imperially sponsored rituals to Laozi and Wangzi Qiao were performed leading to the erection of the steles discussed later in this chapter. As an example of late Han religious mentality, it sheds light on the milieu in which Daoism developed.

The terminology of the Fei Zhi inscription is similar to both Han era hagiographies and to later Daoist usage and demonstrates continuity of common understanding and practices between Han era *fangshi* and early Daoist practices. After examining the practices and lineage ascribed to Fei Zhi I will discuss the range

---

25 Fan Yousheng 樊有升, "Donghan Fei Zhi bei" 東漢肥致碑, *Shufa congkan* 書法從看 1992.2; collected in *Huaxiang zhuan shike muzhi yanjiu* 畫像磚石刻墓誌研究 (Zhongzhou guji, 1994): 168–71; Fan Yousheng, "Donghan daoshi 'Fei Zhi bei' chuxi" 東漢道士'肥致碑' 初析. *Heluo chunqiu* 河洛春秋 1997.1: 21–7; Dong Xiansi 董賢司, "Yizhu Fei Zhi bei" 譯注 '肥致碑 *Dafen daxue jiaoyu xuebu yanjiu jiyao* 大分大學教育學部研究紀要 17.1 (1995); Wang Yucheng 王育成, "Han tiandi shenshizhi lei daoren yu daojiao qiyuan" 漢天帝神使者類道人與道教起源, paper presented at the International Conference on Daoist Studies (1996), published in *Daojia wenhua yanjiu* 道家文化研究 16 (1999): 181–203; Wang Yucheng, "Donghan 'Feizhi bei' tansuo" 東漢肥致碑探索, *Zhongguo lishi bowuguan guankan* 1996.2: 34–41; Wang Yucheng, "Donghan daojiao diyi keshi 'Fei Zhi bei' yanjiu" 東漢道教第一刻石'肥致碑' 研究, *Daojiaoxue tansuo*, 道教學探索 10 (1997): 14–28; Hsing I-tien 邢義田, "Donghan de fangshi yu qiuxian fengqi – Fei Zhi bei duji" 東漢的方士與求仙風氣 — 肥致碑讀記, *Dalu Zazhi* 大陸雜誌 94.2 (1997): 49–61; Yu Wanli 虞萬里, "Donghan 'Fei Zhi bei' kaoshi" 東漢肥致碑考釋, *Zhongyuan wenwu* 中原文物 1997.4: 95–101; Li Hsun-hsiang 李訓詳 "Muzhiming haishi cisi ti ke? — du Fei Zhi bei zhaji" 墓誌銘還是祠祀提科 — 讀肥致碑札記, *Dalu Zazhi* 95.6 (1997): 286–8; Kristofer Schipper, "Une stèle Taoïste des Han orientaux récemment découverte" in Jacques Gernet and Marc Kalinowski, eds. *En Suivant la Voie Royale, Mélanges Offerts en Hommage à Léon Vandermeersch* (Paris: EFEO, 1997): 239–47; Zhang Xunliao 張勛燎, "Henan Yanshi xian nan caizhuang xiang donghan chutu daoren Fei Zhi bei ji youguan daojiao yiwu yanjiu" 河南偃師縣南蔡庄鄉東漢出土道人 '肥致碑' 及有關道教遺物研究, *Sichuan daxue kaogu zhuanye chuangjian sanshiwu zhounian jinian wenji* 四川大學考古專業創建三十五周年紀念文集 (Chengdu: Sichuan daxue, 1998): 301–11; Liu Yi, *Jingtian*, 514–34, *et passim*.

and scope of this group, and the role cults like this may have played in the formation of early Daoism.

Fei Zhi Inscription

Filial Emperor Zhang, [when] Jupiter was in *bingzi* (76 CE): recorded.

Filial Emperor Zhang

Filial Emperor He

Filial Emperor He, [when] Jupiter was in *yichou* (89 CE): recorded.[26]

[1] Stele of Master Fei of East Anle in Liang county of Henan,[27] was an Officer in Waiting of the Lateral Quarters for the Han.[28] His taboo name was Zhi, his name was Changhua. He was from Liang county.

As a youth he [2] embodied the pliability of spontaneous nature 自然, as an adult he had the conduct of one with rare customs. Always dwelling in seclusion he nourished his intentions. The Master regularly resided atop a jujube tree, and did not descend for three years. With the Dao he roamed [3] free,[29] by his harmonious conduct his name was established, his fame spread within the seas. Crowds of gentlemen respectfully came to look at him, gathering like clouds.

Once a red vapor accumulated and filled the sky. From the ministers and directors down through the hundred [4] officials there were none who could disperse it. [5] Hearing that atop a jujube tree in Liang there was a man of the

---

26 These lines are set off from the main text, arching across the semi-circular top of the stele. Schipper, Xing Yi-tian and Yu Wanli emend the transcription *beng* 崩 "Imperial death" in *Wenwu* to *ce* 冊 "record," see Yu Wanli, "Donghan," 95 for philological details. The primary reason is that Liu Da 劉炟 had just ascended the throne in the end of 75 CE. The *bingzi* year (76) was the first full year of his reign, which lasted for nine years. Similarly, *yichou* (89 CE) was the first full year of his son Liu Zhao's 劉肇 enthronement. "Record" in this context seems to refer to an official tablet bestowed by the ruler on his officials as they presented themselves at court (*Shuowen jiezi* 2b33b). Zhang Xunliao suggests the graph should be read *meng* 萌, meaning "first, initially" – referring to the emperors first years on the throne.

27 Southwest of present day Ruzhou 汝州 Henan province.

28 *Yeting* 液庭 refers to the concubine quarters. For the term "lateral quarters" and details, see David Knechtges, *Wen xuan, or, Selections of Refined Literature,* vol. 1 (Princeton University Press, 1996): 122–3. According to Hucker, 1985, # 3010 after 104 BCE the term came to refer to the Palace Disciplinary Service, which was responsible for administering and monitoring the women in the palace. "Officer in Waiting" translates *daizhao* 待詔, a term referring to persons summoned for service but still awaiting official appointment. The term is usually preceded by the name of the office in which the person will be posted (Hucker, 1985, # 6127); Charles Hucker, *A Dictionary of Official Titles in Imperial China* (Stanford: Stanford University Press, 1985).

29 The phrase yudao yaoxing 與道遙行 harks back to Zhuangzi's "free roaming" *xiaoyao* 消遙.

Dao the king dispatched an envoy to summon the Master with full etiquette. In his loyalty, the Master came to protect the king as though on wings. In accordance with the time he produced a calculation[30] [6] and dispelled the calamitous anomaly. He was honored with the post of Officer in Waiting of the Lateral Quarters, and bestowed a million cash. The Master declined and did not take the offer. In the middle ten day period of the 11th month, the Emperor desired fresh mallow.[31]

[7] The Master then entered his chamber, and in no time exited holding two sprigs of mallow. The Emperor asked the Master: where did you get them? He replied: "I received them from the governor of Shu commandery." [8] The emperor sent a dispatch rider to inquire at the commandery. The report from the commandery stated: "At dawn on the fifteenth day of the eleventh month an envoy in a red chariot came and took two sprigs of fresh mallow."

[9] This was proof of the Master's spirit-luminescence 神明.[32] He delves deeply into the mysterious and subtle, exits the abyss and enters the darkness. His transformations are difficult to know. In traveling a myriad miles, he does not shift in time. He fleetingly travels to the eight extremities and stops for a breather [10] at the transcendent court.

The Master's instructor was Zhang Wu of Wei Commandery 魏郡張吳,[33] and he was companion to Yanzi of Qi; Huang Yuan of Haishang 海上黃淵, and Master Red Pine. In life he was named Perfected Person, in his generation none [11] could rival him.[34]

The meritorious officer grand master of five,[35] transcendent teacher Xu You from East Village in Luoyang took Master Fei to be his master. With warmest reverence, he invited Fei to stay at his home. You followed the Master, [12] achieved "crossing the generations" and departed.[36]

---

30 Zhang Xunliao suggests the graph 算 should be read *ce* 策. I do not find his argument convincing.
31 *Kui* 葵 is more precisely Asian mallow, *malva verticillata L.*
32 The connotation of the term *shenming* is problematic. In some contexts, it seems to imply a perfected cognitive capacity while in other contexts it implies the presence of bodily gods. In this case, the latter meaning makes better sense. Fei Zhi was able to dispatch his bodily spirit/s to Shu and gather the plants. This concept was further elaborated in Daoism into the 24 effulgences.
33 Csikszentmihàlyi mistakenly translates as "Fei Zhi taught Zhang Wu."
34 The lineage mentioned here will be discussed below.
35 *Wudaifu* 五大夫; Hucker translates as Grandee of the Ninth Order (Hucker # 7824), the twelfth highest of 20 titles of honorary nobility 爵 conferred on deserving subjects. Below rank seven, *qidaifu* 七大夫, local officials depended on their own resources, but those above rank seven were supported by local taxation. Wang Yucheng notes officials of ranks seven and eight, *qidaifu* and *gongsheng* 公乘 were eventually absorbed into the commoners, while *wudaifu* continued to be considered eminent 高爵 (Wang 1997: 25).
36 *Dushi* here refers to the concept of living beyond one's allotted life span. The earliest references seem to be in Wang Chong's attack on the Daoist belief in immortality/transcendence, which

[I] You's son Jian, named Xiaochang,[37] whose heart is kind and whose nature is filial, constantly thinks of spirits and numina. In the second year of the Establishing Peace era [*jianning*, 169 CE] when Jupiter was in *yiyou*, [13] on *bingwu* day, the fifteenth of the fifth month, a day of Direct Establishment,[38] [I] Xiaochang arranged an altar at the side-room.[39] At dawn and evening the whole household, solemnly and without daring to relax our awe, reverently approached [14] Master Fei. Our libations and prayers accorded with the four seasons.[40] The transcendent spirit has retired in glory, resplendent as a hidden dragon.[41] Though we wished to call on him the passage way could not be followed.

I solemnly placed this stone, [15] in order to, with utmost reverence describe what is laid out above, clarify and exhort us, ignorant infants. The lyrics are:

[16] Brilliant and that is all. Anciently, the divine Master and luminous father attained great fame,[42] and ascended afar to view the guidelines. Sons and grandsons standing motionless, reverently look up to [you who are] without hindrances.[43]

serves to show that the concept was fully developed by mid Han, but does not provide positive definitions of the practices associated. This term was later adopted by Daoist lineages to designate the attainment of transcendence, while Buddhist authors adapted it as a translation of "Crossing-over into Nirvana."

37 By naming his son Xiaochang 孝萇, lit. "Filial to Chang," Xu You expressed his devotion to his teacher. Yu Wanli points out that as *zi* were given during the capping ceremony at 26 years of age, Xu You must have become Fei Zhi's disciple prior to that (Yu 1997: 98).

38 Yu Wanli suggests that the graph 十 in the text is redundant and the date should be fifth day of the fifth month. The fifteenth day of the fifth month in 169 was a *bingchen* 丙辰 day. The text, however, specifies that it was a *bingwu* 丙午 day, an auspicious day of Direct Establishment 直建 according to the hemerological system "Establishing and removal" *jianchu* 建除. This would have been ten days earlier, on the fifth. Noting a small hole by the graph 十, Yu suggests indicates a correction of a redundant graph. For explanations of the *jianchu* system, see Marc Kalinowski, "Les traités de Shuihudi et l'hémérologie chinoise à la fin des Royaumes-Combattants" *T'oung Pao* 72 (1986): 175–228, esp. 198–200; Alain Arrault and Jean-Claude Martzloff, "Calendriers," in Marc Kalinowski, ed. *Divination et Société Dans le Chine Médiévale* (Paris: Bibliothèque national de France, 2003): 103–104.

39 *Bianzuo* 便坐 seems to refer to an altar or shrine erected at a side chamber of a tomb (*zuo* refers to the emplacement of the ritual offerings in front of the deity or spirit who are said to descend and rest on the arranged seat as they partake of the offerings.) See Hsing, "Donghan," 58; Yu, "Donghan," 99; Wang, "Donghan," 15–16. For Han references, see *SJ* 103.2764, and Sima Zhen's *Suoyin* commentary (also in *HS* 46.2194) and commentary on burial practices in *Houhanshu* treatise 6.3144, n.1.

40 Wang suggests this means – "continuously present offerings". Note that the practice of offerings and "libation" 餟 is among the "aberrant practices" attacked in the *Xiang'er Commentary*.

41 Submerged Dragon is the reading of the first line of the first hexagram, *qian*. It is conventionally interpreted as the hidden potential of the Yang phase.

42 There is a debate concerning the graph 父 or 又 following the phrase: 神君皇. If it is the former, the phrase may be parsed as Divine Master and Luminous Father, referring to both Fei Zhi and Xu You, or as referring to a single person. This would however disturb the syllabic pattern of the verse. If the latter graph is meant, it would be the first graph of the following clause, simply meaning "and, moreover." (Hsing, "Donghan," 58, Yu, "Donghan," 99a).

43 *Shi* means to depend on; here I think the point is that Master Fei has nothing on which he depends, nor is anything dependent on him.

I, therefore, [17] inscribed this stone so as to reach your compassion and intelligence, wishing that you will reappear regularly and bestow your blessings and auspiciousness.

[18] The Terrestrial Transcendent 土仙者, Great Lord of Five 大伍公, had seen the void of Kunlun of the Queen Mother of the West and received the Way of Transcendence.

The followers of the Great Lord of Five were five: Tian Yu 田傴, Quan [] [19] Zhong 全 [] 中, Songzhi Ji Gong 宋直忌公, Bi Xianfeng 畢先風 and Master Xu 許先生. All will ingest stone marrow, and depart as transcendents.

According to the archaeological report, the stele was found in the southern ante-chamber of the tomb. This is probably the side-altar mentioned in the inscription. Despite the fact that the principal of the tomb is Xu You, Fei Zhi's patron, this shrine is the central feature of this familial cult. Indeed, the stele itself probably served in the ritual, as there is at the base of the stele a small ledge with three small niches, apparently for placing offerings.

It is unclear from the text when Fei Zhi and Xu You had died, and whether their deaths involved any ritual practice. However, line [12] implies that Xu You's death, interpreted as "crossing the generations," was perceived as the culmination of his practice with Fei Zhi.

The inscription serves both a commemorative as well as ritual function. While celebrating Fei Zhi's skills and prowess, the inscription also calls upon him to respond to the offerings with blessings. Intriguingly, the final lines hint at yet another form of practice – ingestion of mineral compounds in quest of transcendence. Whether this was regularly practiced at the site or was to be a ritual climax of the cult's activities is impossible to ascertain. We may conjecture, however, that this was part of the teachings imparted by Fei Zhi to his followers.

While the inscription is dated to 169 CE, it claims that Fei Zhi's main period of activity was almost a century earlier. The only two clear dates on the stele, 76 CE and 89 CE seem to refer to Fei Zhi's appearance at the imperial court. This was after he had already made a name for himself. If he was only in his twenties at the time, he would have been over a hundred years old by the 160s. The inscription clearly asserts that Fei Zhi had lived to a ripe old age. Nevertheless, the inscription implies that Fei Zhi died at an unspecified time prior to the inscription and installation of the stele. What then is the motivation for the installation of the stele in the tomb, and what is the significance of the inscription?

Political involvement [lines 3–8]

Although two reigns are mentioned in the inscription, claiming that Fei Zhi appeared at court during the reigns of emperors Zhang (r. 76–89) and He (r. 89–105) of the Eastern Han, the episodes mentioned in the text are undated. More specifically, the inscription asserts that Fei Zhi received a provisional appointment in the imperial harem as a reward for having responded to an imperial summons and resolving ominous celestial phenomena. It is unclear when this first encounter took place. At a later date, while serving in the palace, Fei Zhi satisfied the emperor's desire for mallow by instantaneously traveling to Sichuan and returning with two branches. None of these events is dated precisely, nor mentioned elsewhere. It would be easy to dismiss the whole matter as hyperbolae and pretension on behalf of Fei Zhi and his disciples. However, the significance of the two episodes goes beyond mere self-glorification on the part of a practitioner. In the first instance, Fei Zhi is perceived as resolving a threatening omen, thereby saving the emperor. In the second case, Fei Zhi claims close intimacy with the emperor. The episodes thus affiliate him with the famous *fangshi* in the Western Han courts, Zhang Liang at the court of Han Gaozu, and Li Shaojun and Dongfang Shuo at Emperor Wu's court. Moreover, as I discuss in detail below, these details may in fact allude to a narrative which presages medieval Daoist tales, such as the *Esoteric Biography of Han Emperor Wu* (*Han Wudi neizhuan* 漢武帝內傳).

Lineage [lines 10–11]

Two distinct lineages are mentioned in the inscription. The first associates Fei Zhi with a lineage not attested elsewhere, including obscure figures as well as one of the most famous adepts of all. The identification of the figures in this lineage remains problematic, partly due to the difficulty in parsing the relevant phrases. First, it is unclear whether there are two or four individuals named.[44] Second, while the first half of the phrase explicitly states "the master took as his teacher… (*shi* 師)," the second half states "…were his companions," implying that he was the equal of Huangyuan and Master Redpine, and not their disciple. It is unclear whether Yanzi should be counted among the teachers or companions. Those referred to as companions were not necessarily living "companions." Rather they were probably seen as partners in ethereal frolics. Of the four names, one is unattested elsewhere. While the identifications made of the remaining three individuals are problematic, two of them may be quite well known personages, albeit surprising.

Zhang Wu, the first person mentioned, remains unknown. Wei Commandery, some 300 km northeast of Luoyang, and its neighboring Anle, straddled the southern part of modern Hebei and Ci county (磁) in Henan, and was established during the reign of Han Gaozu. Renamed Wei City 魏城 during Wang Mang's interregnum, it reverted to its earlier name during the Eastern Han.[45] So far no further information concerning Zhang Wu has been found, but his very anonymity may indicate the authenticity of his existence.

Yanzi of Qi 齊晏子, the second individual mentioned as Fei Zhi's teacher or as one of his companions, may be Yan Ying (c. 580–500 BCE), a loyal aide to a

---

44 Schipper suggests only two persons are mentioned. Liu Yi, Robert Campany, and others agree that four distinct individuals are named.
45 HHS 12.3431.

succession of rulers of Qi.[46] Numerous speeches, remonstrations, and anecdotes by and concerning Yanzi are preserved in the *Zuozhuan* commentary and collected in the *Yanzi Chunqiu* 晏子春秋.[47] A paragon of Confucian political morality, he is not associated with esoteric practices or *fangshi* lineages in any of the received or recently unearthed texts. While this may hint at an unknown tradition concerning Yanzi, his inclusion in this lineage may be an example of co-optation of famous ancient scholars by lineages of *fangshi*. Other examples of pre Qin and early Han scholiasts co-opted into the ranks of *fangshi* and transcendents include Mozi 墨子, who is mentioned in *Baopuzi* as a master of "transformation," receives a hagiography in *Shenxian zhuan*, and was absorbed into the early Shangqing pantheon,[48] and Kong Anguo 孔安國, who is described as a practitioner of *qi* circulation and alchemy in his *Shenxian zhuan* hagiography.[49]

It is, of course, also possible that the name Yanzi does not refer to Yan Ying of the Warring States era, but to an otherwise unknown *fangshi* surnamed Yan, who would have been active in the early Han and originated from Qi.

The third individual mentioned in the lineage, Huangyuan Haishang 海上黃淵, whose name may mean Huangyuan of the Coast, is also unattested elsewhere. He may possibly be identified with Master Huang of the Eastern Sea (*Donghai*

---

46 Lord Ling 靈公 (r. 581–554), Lord Zhuang 莊公 (r.553–548), and particularly Lord Jing 景公 (r.547–490).

47 Yan Ying's biography is in *Shiji* 62.2134. On *Yanzi chunqiu* see Durrant in Michael Loewe, ed. *Early Chinese Texts: A Bibliographical Guide* (Berkeley: Society of the Study of Early China: Institute of East Asian Studies, University of California, Berkeley 1993): 483–9; for a concise summary of his thought and place in Spring and Autumn intellectual currents, see Yuri Pines, "The Search for Stability: Late-Chun ch'iu thinkers" *Asia Major*, Ser.3, 10.1–2 (1997): 18–31.

48 Ge Hong lists "Mozi's Secret Five-phases Treatise" *Mozi zhenzhong wuxingji* 墨子枕中五行記 (*BPZ* 19.333), describing it as the most important of treatises on transformation. Originally of five scrolls, it was summarized into a single scroll by Liu Jun'an 劉君安 (Liu Gen 根) prior to his departure as transcendent:

> Its methods include both medicinals and talismans, which allow one to fly up and down, hide oneself where there is no space, transform into a woman by smiling only, become an old man by twisting one's face, become a young boy by crouching on the ground, become a tree by grasping one's staff. [Using it] one can plant strange plants which will produce edible melons and fruit, draw on the floor to make rivers, and pile earth to form mountains. Sitting, one may summon the traveling canteen, raise clouds and ignite fire. There is nothing that cannot be done.

Ge Hong also provides an alchemical formula by Mozi (4.81). In *SXZ*, Mozi is said to have compounded an elixir and achieving status as a terrestrial transcendent. Mo Di was included among the transcendent sages who presented Zhou Ziyang with teachings in the fourth-century text *Ziyang zhenren neizhuan* 紫陽真人內傳. Said to dwell on Mt. Niaoshu 鳥鼠 (in Gansu) Modi presented the Central Scripture of the Inner Vision Chart of Purple Crossing and Blazing Radiance 紫度炎光內視圖中經 DZ 303: 10a3, 16a5; Manfred Porkert, *Biographie d'un taoïste légendaire: Tcheou tseu-yang* (Paris: Collège de France, Institut des hautes études chinoises, 1979): 92–93. Mozi's hagiography in *SXZ* is translated in Campany, *To Live*, 329, 508; see Stephen Durrant, "The Taoist Apotheosis of Mo Ti," *JAOS* 97 (1977): 540–6. For Liu Gen's *SXZ* hagiography, see Campany, *To Live*, 240–9, 447.

49 *TPGJ* 13.2, *TPYL* 394.2a Translated and discussed in Campany, *To Live*, 311–14. Ge Hong cites 'Kong Anguo's Secret Records' *Kong Anguo miji* 孔安國秘記 for a narrative concerning Zhang Liang and the Four Hoary Elders (Wang Ming, *Baopuzi*, 5:113, Ware, *Alchemy*, 104).

Huanggong 東海黃公), who is mentioned in Zhang Heng's "Western Metropolis Rhapsody":

> Amazing magicians, quicker than the eye: changed appearances, divided their bodies,
> Swallowed blades and spat fire; darkened the arena with clouds and mists,
> Drawing on the ground they made rivers appear, which flowed like the Wei and coursed like the Jing.
> Master Huang of Donghai, with red blade and Yue incantations,
> hoped to subdue the tiger, but could not save himself in the end.[50]

Xue Zong 薛綜 (d. 243 CE) comments on this verse: "In Donghai there was a person who could wield a red blade and [walk] Yu's pace, and used the incantation methods of the Yue people to subdue tigers. He was called Master Huang."

In his comments on these lines, Li Shan 李善 (d. 643 CE) cites an extended reference to Master Huang in *Xijing zaji* 西京雜記:

> Master Huang of Donghai, even as a child practiced [esoteric] arts 術. He could control snakes and manage tigers. He regularly wore a crimson metal blade at his belt and bound his hair with red silk. Standing he could raise clouds and mist, sitting he could make mountain and rivers appear. When he was decrepit and old, his strength was depleted, having over indulged in alcohol, he could no longer practice his arts. At the final years of the Qin dynasty a white tiger appeared at Donghai. Holding his crimson blade, Master Huang went forth to challenge it. As he could no longer practice his arts, he was killed by the tiger. The people of the capital region (Sanfu三輔) used this [story] as a basis for games, the Han emperor used it as a basis for the game of *juedi* 角抵.[51]

If Haishang Huangyuan is indeed Master Huang of Donghai, then by claiming him as an equal, Fei Zhi claimed that he too possessed skills and practices equal to this famous master of Yue practices.[52] Thus we see Fei Zhi tapping into both the *fangshi* tradition of the northern coastal region as well as to the more shamanic culture of the southern coast.

---

50 *Wenxuan* 文選 (Taipei: Huazheng shuju, 1984), *juan* 2, p.49a; translated in Knechtges, *Wen xuan*, vol. I, 233, L.731. The same narrative is also found in *Soushen ji*, 2: 39.

51 *Xijing zaji* 3.1, in Hanwei congshu 漢魏叢書, Jilin Daxue. *Xijing zaji* is attributed to Ge Hong, but was probably compiled in the 520s, William H. Nienhauser Jr, *The Indiana Companion to Traditional Chinese Literature* (Bloomington: Indiana University Press, 1986): 406. On the *juedi* games see Michael Loewe, "The chüeh-ti games: a re-enactment of the battle between Ch'ih-yu and Hsüan-yüan?" in Loewe, *Divination, Mythology and Monarchy in Han China* (Cambridge: Cambridge University Press, 1994): 236–48.

52 The region of Yue was well known for its tradition of efficacious techniques, particularly associated with breath cultivation. For a useful summary, see Harper, *Early*, 173–83.

The fourth person mentioned as Fei Zhi's companion, Chisongzi 赤松子 or Master Redpine, is arguably the most famous master of esoterica. His hagiography, which is the first one in the *Liexian zhuan*, recounts that he was Rain Master of the emperor Shennong 神農 (Divine Husbandman), whom he also taught a method for imbibing liquid jade. His main prowess was the "ability to enter fire and self-immolate" 能入火自燒. He regularly visited the Queen Mother of the West on Mt. Kunlun, a recurring topos in late Han conceptualizations of successful adepts. He also instructed the daughter of another mythical emperor, Yandi 炎帝 (Fiery Emperor).

These mythemes may be remnants of ancient shamanic rites of immolation and rain making. By the early Han, Chisongzi had become a model for *fangshi* seeking to emulate his attainments. The *Huainan zi* reports that he was a master of circulation of breath (xingqi 行氣) and other breathing techniques.[53] These techniques are mentioned in the *Shiji* biography of Zhang Liang who asks leave of Han Emperor Gaozu (r. 202–195 BCE) so he can follow the path of Chisongzi. He subsequently quits eating grains and begins practicing circulation of breath.[54] Several other Han sources mention Chisongzi (frequently together with Wangzi Qiao) as an exemplary ancient master who had attained transcendence through self-cultivation. These often formulaic references, ranging from poems collected in the Chuci 楚辭 to inscriptions on Han mirrors, attest to his popularity during this period.[55]

The final lines [18–19] of the inscription are especially problematic. It is unclear to whom the terms Terrestrial Transcendent 土仙者 and *Dawugong* 大伍公 refer, or how they are related to Fei Zhi and Xu You. *Dawu gong* had obtained his teachings from the Queen Mother of the West and had attracted five disciples, whose names are listed. The last name given, Master Xu, probably refers to Xu You as it is unlikely that Xu Jian, who authored the main text of the inscription, would refer to himself as Master.

The term *Dawu gong* itself is problematic. It is unclear whether it is a name, a title, or an epithet. Is it to be construed as Master Dawu or as "Great Lord of Five"? Moreover, the identity of the person referred to by this is unclear. Yu Wanli suggests *Dawu gong* may be an astrologer mentioned in Dongfang Shuo's 東方朔 hagiography in a Ming era compilation *Xiaoyao xu jing* 消遙墟經:

> When he was about to die, [Dongfang] Shuo told a fellow official: no one in the world was able to recognize me, except for *Dawu gong*. After he had died, emperor Wu summoned *Dawu gong* and questioned him. He claimed he had no knowledge [of the matter]. The emperor asked: "what are your abilities,"

---

53 *Huainanzi zhuzi suoyin* 淮南子逐字索引 (Hong Kong: Chinese University of Hong Kong Institute of Chinese Studies, Shangwu, 1992): 11/99/13; 20/214/15.

54 *Shiji* 55.2047 and 2049.

55 For *Chuci* references, see David Hawkes, *Ch'u Tz'u, The Songs of the South* (Boston: Beacon Press, 1962): 82, 116, 139; Wang Qing, *Bentu*, 199–216.

he replied "I am good at tracking the stars". The emperor asked: "are all the stars in their paths?" he replied: "All the stars are present. Only Jupiter has been absent for forty years, and has recently reappeared." The emperor gazed up at heaven and sighed: "Dongfang Shuo has been by my side for forty years and I didn't realize he was the [spirit of the] planet Jupiter." He then became depressed and unhappy.[56]

Yu Wanli does not pursue this further and does not try to trace the source for this late reference or explain the relationship between this astrologer, Fei Zhi, and the famous trickster-adept Dongfang Shuo. A variant of this passage is provided in the Song compilation *Lishi zhenxian tidao tongjian* 歷史真仙體道通鑒, which cites the *Xijing zaji*:

> Dongfang Shuo said: no one in the world recognizes me, except for the Grand Astrologer of the Calendar bureau 曆官太史. When Emperor Wu summoned and queried him, he replied: 'all the asterisms are present, only Jupiter is not seen.'[57]

As older hagiographies of Dongfang Shuo do not refer to the astrologer by name, Hong Zicheng's source for naming him *Dawu gong* remains unclear. These older sources do refer to Dongfang Shuo's stellar identity, beginning with *Liexian zhuan*: "Those with knowledge suspected he was the essence of Jupiter" (DZ 294: 2.7a).[58] His hagiography in *Fengsu tongyi*, however, identifies Dongfang Shuo as a manifestation of the planet Venus, as well with a number of ancient sages:

> The common people say that Dongfang Shuo was the essence of the planet Venus. During the Yellow Emperor's era he was Wind Elder 風伯, during Yao's era he was Wu Chengzi 務成子, during the Zhou he was Laodan 老聃. In Yue he was Fan Li 范蠡, and in Qi he was Chiyi zipi 鴟夷子皮.[59]

This hagiography, which Ying Shao claims originated among the "children and herd-boys," may be a late Han popular version of the legend of Dong Fangshuo. Like the deified Laozi, the historical Dongfang Shuo had been deified and transformed into a sage who repeatedly manifests himself in different epochs in different human form as a teacher to the ruler. According to this passage, Laozi himself is a manifestation of Dongfang Shuo. The final phrase identifies Dongfang Shuo with another famous *fangshi*, Fan Li, who departed for the sea after helping

---

56 DZ 1465: 1.15a9–b5. Yu however does not pursue this further, (Yu 99). *Xiaoyao xu jing* is a Ming compilation of hagiographies, collected by Hong Zicheng 洪自誠 of Xindu 新都 in Sichuan (fl. *wanli* era, 1573–1620), *Zhonghua daojiao dacidian*, 202.
57 DZ 296: 3. 21a3; composed by Zhao Daoyi 趙道一 (fl. 1294–1307).
58 DZ 294: 2.7a; Wang, *Liexian*, 103–5; Kaltenmark, *Lie-sien*, 137–8.
59 FSTY 2.7a.

king Goujian of Yue defeat the kingdom of Wu. He reappeared in Qi, having changed his name to Chiyi zipi. Still later he was known as Lord Zhu of Tao 陶朱君.[60] In his *SXZ* hagiography, Kong Anguo claims his teacher was none other than Fan Li, among whose disciples was one named Dawu 大伍.[61]

While it is impossible to cohere the chronologies of these various accounts, their coincidence is very suggestive. The historical Dongfang Shuo and Kong Anguo (d.c. 100 BCE) were both active during the second century BCE. Although Fan Li's activity is said to have spanned centuries, the only certain date mentioned is his departure from Yue some time after 479 BCE. Kong Anguo, in referring to Fan Li's disciples, including Dawu, mentions their amazing longevity, thus placing them deep in the Spring and Autumn eras. While it is possible that the astrologer referred to in Dongfang Shuo's hagiography is Fan Li's disciple, a textual tradition linking Kong Anguo's *SXZ* hagiography and *Xiaoyao xu jing* needs to be established before this hypothesis can be pursued further. This link in turn needs to be traced to Han period sources. Until such links can be demonstrated, it remains difficult to determine whether the Fei Zhi inscription partakes of this textual tradition.

The main problem with Yu Wanli's suggestion, however, is that it implies that two distinct lineages are mentioned in the inscription.[62] As the stele appears to have served as a votive and ritual site for a family-centered cult, and was dedicated to the master at the center of the cult, it seems unlikely that the final lines refer to a different lineage than that of the main part of the inscription. The Fei Zhi inscription implies that *Dawu gong* was active as a master of the group during the late Eastern Han, and makes no reference to either Fan Li or Dongfang Shuo.[63] It seems more likely that *Dawu gong* was a title adopted by Fei Zhi as the master of the cult.[64] The final lines then cohere with the main part of the inscription.

Although the most likely explanation is that *Dawu gong* refers to Fei Zhi, his choice of this title may allude to the early Han astrologer or to Fan Li's disciple, who may in fact be the one and the same. However, as the earliest attested mention

60 DZ 294: 1.6; Wang Shumin, *Liexian*, 58–9; Kaltenmark, *Lie-sien*, 102–104.
61 TPGJ 13.2, TPYL 394.2a; Campany, *To Live*, 311–14.
62 Liu Yi does not agree with Yu Wanli's identification of Dawu Gong, but he agrees that Dawu Gong and his five disciples are a distinct lineage, unrelated to Fei Zhi; Liu Yi, *Jingtian*, 523.
63 Yu Wanli considers the reference to the Queen Mother of the West to be an allusion to Dongfang Shuo. This is unwarranted considering the importance of the Queen Mother in Han period mythology. For details see Michel Loewe, *Ways to Paradise: the Chinese Quest for Immortality* (London: Allen and Unwin, 1979): 86–126; *et passim*; Suzanne E. Cahll, *Transcendence and Divine Passion: the Queen Mother of the West in Medieval China* (Stanford: Stanford University Press, 1993); Wang Qing, *Bentu*, 253–347.
64 See also the discussion in Zhang Xunliao who suggests a number of possible explanations for the identity of Dawu gong. Although he admits that this question cannot be fully resolved, he maintains that Dawu gong, be it Fei Zhi's teacher, Fei Zhi or Xu You, is within the same lineage.

of a master named *Dawu* is the Fei Zhi inscription itself, this suggestion remains tentative at best.

Despite the difficulties of determining the precise identities of the persons mentioned in the lineages mentioned in the Fei Zhi inscription, a number of lessons may be gained by our examination. First, the importance of possessing a prestigious lineage is clear. One's claim to power and knowledge must be legitimated by recognized names. In the first case, Fei Zhi's claims ultimately depend on Chisongzi. In the guise of Dawu gong, the source is the Queen Mother of the West. These two claims are, however, inherently different. The first lineage, which I term "this worldly," although obscure in details, is a construction which descends through a fully human sequence of masters and does not diverge in its claims from the ancient *fangshi* conceptions. As I stated above, the very anonymity of Zhang Wu, and the problematic identities of Huangyuan and Yanzi, should perhaps be seen as signs of authenticity.

Dawu gong's claim, on the other hand, entails a new cosmological structure, with a different form of relation between the human realm and the numinous realm. The teachings are here transmitted directly from a goddess and in the mythical realm of Kunlun, rather than in the human plane as in the case of the first lineage. The teachings are perceived as having been introduced into the human realm by a qualitatively different source. I term this type of lineage "other worldly." In earlier narratives, this type of transmission had been restricted to numinous revelations by mythical animals, such as fish, birds, and dragons, as in the cases of Lingyang Ziming and the mythical emperors. By the late Han, as this inscription shows, "other worldly" revelations were increasingly associated with deities. This trope became the typical form of revelation for Daoist teachings.

The claim by Dawu gong was not an original one. The Queen Mother of the West and her abode on Mt. Kunlun had already become a mythical destination for practitioners. The importance of this motif may be demonstrated by its inclusion in Chisongzi's hagiography in *LXZ*, the first of the collection. Having claimed himself a companion of Chisongzi, Fei Zhi in the guise of Dawu gong could then claim to have visited the mythical land of Kunlun. Tales of visits to Kunlun and encounters with the Queen Mother seem to have become common fare by the Later Han. While criticizing such claims as extravagant and without basis, Ge Hong provides descriptions of Mt. Kunlun's subterranean paradise.[65] While such a critical view may be representative of conservative and purist practitioners, like Ge Hong, it demonstrates the popularity of such claims with the general public. This motif finally became the basis for the narrative cycle of the *Hanwudi neizhuan*.[66]

---

65 See Ge Hong's criticism of Gu Qiang's 古強 claims of longevity (Wang BPZ 20.347, Ware 321) and of Cai Dan's 蔡誕 professed tour of Kunlun (Wang Ming *Baopuzi*, 5:113; Ware, *Alchemy*, 104).

66 Kristofer Schipper, *L'empereur Wou des Han dans la légende taoiste* (Paris: EFEO 1965); Thomas E. Smith, "Ritual and the Shaping of Narrative: The Legend of the Han Emperor Wu," University of Michigan Ph.D. Thesis, 1992; Li Fengmao 李豐楙, "Han wudi neizhuan yanjiu" 漢武帝內傳

Significantly, both types of lineage, "this worldly" and "other worldly," appear in the Fei Zhi inscription, signifying that both notions developed within the same *fangshi* lineages and continued to coexist within the same groups. Even more significantly, despite the claims for a far higher plane of revelation, there is little difference in the practices advocated by the two types of revelatory lineage.

Practices and abilities

A number of distinct practices are ascribed to Fei Zhi. I discuss these in tandem with the abilities they confer on the successful practitioner. Previous studies have already noted many parallels between these practices and those found in hagiographies, such as *LXZ* and *SXZ*. I will therefore focus upon such practices as described in Daoist texts.

1 Solitary asceticism and ingestion of dates

Fei Zhi's earliest accomplishment that made his name was his solitary sojourn atop a date tree for some three years – presumably feeding solely on jujube dates. Jujubes are numbered among the most efficacious of herbal sources. Anqi sheng was said to have lived on jujubes alone, giant as melons, the ingestion of which led to his transcendence and translation to Penglai.[67] Another *fangshi* who resorted to jujubes was Hao Mengjie 郝孟節, who by ingesting date stones could hold off from regular food for five and even ten years.[68] The importance of jujubes for Han practitioners may be demonstrated by the formulas inscribed on a number of TLV mirrors: "...on it are transcendents, oblivious of age. When thirsty they imbibe from the jade font, when hungry, they ingest jujubes...".[69] The possessor of the mirror is to emulate the transcendents and follow their practice.

The Fei Zhi inscription does not describe the method of ingesting jujubes or specify the expected effects of this practice. This lack is typical of most hagiographies which are formulaic in form and content. For actual methods we need to turn to Daoist texts, such as the *Array of the Five Talismans*, which provides clear instructions for a practice based on the ingestion of jujube dates entitled "Yue Zichang's Method of Ingesting Date Stones 樂子長含棗核方":

> A method of longevity: Regularly hold a date stone in your mouth, [sucking it] just as a baby suckles a nipple. Hold it for a long time until the juice fills

---

研究, in *Liuchao sui-tang xiandao lei xiaoshuo yanjiu* 六朝隋唐仙道類小說研究 (Taipei: Xuesheng, 1986): 21–122.

67 SJ 28.1385. Although this detail is absent from his hagiography in LXZ (DZ 294: 1.6; Wang, *Liexian*, 70, Kaltenmark, *Lie-Sien*, 115), it became a conventional attribute of Anqi sheng in other narratives.

68 HHS 82B.2750–1. Ngo, *Divination*, 145–6.

69 Loewe, *Ways to Paradise*, 198–200 provides translation and transcription of three mirrors with this formula C3201, C4102, and C5001.

your mouth, in three measures. Swallow two parts and keep one in your mouth. Ingest each mouthful together with air. This is called "returning the essence" 還精. When you complete [each turn] you should start again, as a continuous cycle.

When you first cut off grains, after five days there is a small climax. As your head becomes befuddled immediately stop. After fourteen days, again your head will become befuddled, and you should again stop. After twenty-one days your pneuma will be fixed. If you wish to eat, you may eat. If you do not wish to eat, your [craving] will naturally cease. Once you cut off grains you must refrain from sexual intercourse. You may eat a few jujubes and drink liquor, no more than a *sheng*. This method is the same for both men and women.[70]

Intriguingly, this method, which allowed one to cut off regular food, is related to sexual practice, or rather abstinence. Sex is explicitly forbidden for practitioners of this method. On the other hand, the practice itself is named "returning the essence," a term usually associated with sexual practices involving semen retention. The details of Fei Zhi's practice are unknown. But, if his practice too called for sexual abstinence, then his appointment to the imperial harem may not have been coincidental.

Fei Zhi's practice of ascetic solitude eventually brought him fame. Multitudes came to seek him, though it is unclear what these people expected of him. His fame finally reached the imperial palace which summoned him at a moment of crisis. Summoning of hermits and practitioners of esoterica was a common theme, not only in ancient China. By their remoteness, detachment and autonomy from the central power the practitioners gained enormous prestige, especially if they continued to elude calls to serve at the court. Conversely, their prestige, charismatic power and 'other-worldly' authority would be conferred on the ruler whom they would be willing to serve.[71]

2   *Descrying and resolving meteorological phenomena*

Fei Zhi's summons to the palace was to resolve a threatening omen: red vapor had covered the sky and none of the aides and ministers could disperse it. Yu Wanli has collected evidence showing that red vapor was an omen of war.[72] Fei Zhi performed a calculation (*fasuan* 發算) by which the anomaly was extinguished.

---

70 DZ 388: 2.36a5–36b3.
71 On the power gained by religious virtuosos, see Peter Brown, *The Cult of the Saints: Its Rise and Function in Latin Christianity* (Chicago: University of Chicago Press, 1981). On the paradox of power gained through remoteness and solitude as a source for popular attraction, see Stanley Tambiah, *The Buddhist Saints of the Forest and the Cult of Amulets: a Study in Charisma, Hagiography, Sectarianism, and Millennial Buddhism* (Cambridge: Cambridge University Press, 1984).
72 Yu: 96–7.

We should note that calculations functioned not only as prognosis, that is, a way to determine the cause of the anomalies, but also a means of dispelling the anomalies.

The category of "Observation of clouds and examination of vapors" (*wangyun xingqi* 望雲省氣) was among the important and politically engaged practices of the *fangshi*.[73] Dong Fu 董扶 of Guanghan (in present Sichuan) observed "an imperial pneuma at the celestial allotment of Yizhou" 益州分野有天子氣, which he reported to Liu Yan in 188. A year later, after both had obtained posts in Sichuan, the empire collapsed into chaos. The enthronement of Liu Bei as Emperor of Shu-Han in 221 was perceived as a verification of Dong Fu's observation.[74] Similar practices are noted for Wu Fan 吳範, a third-century practitioner at the Wu court, who "whenever there were omens of calamity would immediately perform a calculation and describe the situation, his calculations were very effective and he thereby made his name".[75]

3 Instantaneous travel

The ability to move great distances in a blink of an eye was a common ability among *fangshi*.[76] Along with the ability to be simultaneously in several places and shape shifting, this ability was proof of an adept's worth and quality. Rarely, however, were the methods which provided these abilities specified.

A common theme in these narratives is that the ability is proven by providing rare products from remote locales. Fei Zhi proved his ability by obtaining fresh mallow from Shu for the emperor.[77] The same narrative structure is found in two better known hagiographic accounts: Zuo Ci 左慈 is said to have obtained ginger from Shu for Cao Cao,[78] and Jie Xiang 介象 is reported as obtaining ginger from Shu for Sun Quan of Wu.[79] Another common theme in these narratives is the verification of the miracle. In the cases of Jie Xiang and Zuo Ci, this verification is provided by a messenger who had earlier been sent by the ruler for a different

---

73 HHS 82A 2703, 2734; Ngo 116, 160 *et passim*.

74 HHS 82A 2734 (Ngo 116). This observation depended upon the notion of *fenye* 分野, which determined celestial correspondences of regions within the imperial realm.

75 SGZ 63.1421 每有災祥, 輒推算言狀, 其數多效, 遂以顯名.

76 For example, the SXZ mentions Liu Zheng 劉政, Master Baishi 白石先生, Li Zhongfu 李仲甫, Li Yiqi 李意期, Elder of Taishan 泰山老父; see references in Campany, *To Live*, 228, 230, 292, 322, 337.

77 Yu Wanli notes that mallow flowers during the summer and was no longer available by the eleventh month, except in southern climes, such as Sichuan. The choice of mallow may not be incidental. The *Taiqing jing duangu fa* 太清經斷穀法 DZ 846.11b6 lists four recipes for resuming eating grains, which are all based on mallow. Was the emperor practicing some ascetic diet? In the *Sanyuan yanshou canzan shu* 三元延壽參贊書 DZ 851: 3.15a mallow is listed as the chief of the five vegetables. Planted in autumn, the early blooms will produce seeds in spring. These are called Winter Mallow 冬葵. Its core is toxic and can harm humans (DZ 851 was compiled during the Yuan by Li Pengfei 李鵬飛).

78 HHS 112.2747.

79 SGZ 63.1427 citing *Shenxian zhuan*; Campany, *To Live*, 191.

purpose and who encounters the master or his envoy. In Fei Zhi's case, the emperor dispatches a special envoy to inquire at the local prefecture.

Significantly, the three accounts differ on the actual practice by which the master obtains the rare delicacy. Jie Xiang provides a messenger with a talisman and staff by which he is instantly transported to the market at Chengdu. Zuo Ci, like Fei Zhi, travels to Shu, but the method is unspecified. Fei Zhi is said to have entered his chamber before reappearing with the mallow flowers. Possibly this was an early version of the meditation chamber (*jingshi* 靜室), which later became the central locus of Daoist practice.

Noting these similarities, Wang Yucheng suggests the Fei Zhi inscription, being the earliest attested text, is the original narrative that Ge Hong and Fan Ye imitated.[80] This suggestion is not warranted. Certainly, the accounts of Zuo Ci and Jie Xiang are more developed; in both cases their procurement of ginger follows a magical feat of obtaining fish from the ocean, and is thus a second proof of their prowess. While both accounts seem to be based on a common source, this source is in fact unlikely to have been the Fei Zhi inscription. After all, could Ge Hong and Fan Ye have seen this inscription? Rather, all three accounts should be seen as tapping into a common narrative motif, which probably circulated as oral legends attached to various masters before being recorded in writing.

4   Consumption of Shizhi 石脂 *"stone lard"*

Consumption of "stone lard" was not an uncommon practice. Numerous early practitioners are said to have ingested these minerals, among them the afore-mentioned Lingyang Ziming, Chixu zi 赤須子,[81] and Chisongzi.[82] Later Daoist practitioners continued this practice.[83] The term refers to siliceous clay. The *Shennong bencao jing* 神農本草經 lists it among the superior medicinal substances, specifying that there are five types of siliceous clay distinguished by color (green, yellow, black, white, and red):

> if ingested for long they replenish the bone marrow and increase pneuma, fortify the flesh and lead one to be without hunger. They lighten the body and extend one's years. The five colors of stone lard accord with the five colors [of the five phases] and replenish the five viscera.[84]

---

80 Wang Yucheng, "Donghan," 21.
81 LXZ, Wang, *Liexian*, 101, Kaltenmark, *Lie-sien*, 135.
82 *Yuejue shu* 越絕書, cited in TPYL 987.4500.2.
83 For example, Ren Dun 任敦 in the sixth-century *Daoxue zhuan*; Bumbacher, *Fragments*, 155.
84 *Shennong bencaojing* 1.9a (Sibu beiyao edn; Taiwan chung-hua shu-chu). Bernard Read and C. Pak, *Chinese Materia Medica, A Compendium of Minerals and Stones* (Taipei: SMC Materials, 1977): 3.36 provides modern accepted identifications the five types of colored earths and their chemical composition. For a short introduction to this text and its problematic provenance, see Paul Unschuld, *Medicine in China, A History of Pharmaceutics* (Berkeley and Los Angeles: University of California Press, 1986): 17–27. Ho Peng Yoke names the five siliceous clays: red, blue, Fuller's earth, kaolin, and graphite; see Ho, Peng Yoke "Alchemy on stones and minerals in

Some sources refer to these five minerals collectively as "Azure, red, yellow, white and black talismans,"[85] further emphasizing their association with the five phases.

The *Treatise on Curiosities* by Zhang Hua 張華 (232–300) mentions that: "[below Mount Kunlun] ... Crannies and caves intersect and harmonious pneuma is exuded; then stone lard and jade paste are produced. Ingesting them, one will be without death."[86] Dawu Gong's visit to Kunlun, therefore, aside from proving his personal efficacy, may also have served an etiological function for the practice of ingesting "stone lard" by his followers.

We should note that the ingestion of stone lard is specifically associated with the five followers of Dawu gong and not with Fei Zhi himself. We are not told what precise practices led to Fei Zhi's transcendence, nor does the inscription specify the precise method by which this mineral was ingested by the cult members. However, Fei Zhi's own practice was probably the model for the disciples' practice. While the details are unclear, this practice may well have resembled the practice described in the following example. These instructions for consuming the "five colored stones" as well as an explanation for the efficacy of this practice are found in *Medicinal Methods of the Transcendents for Ingesting Cinnabar and Minerals*, a text of uncertain date, but preserving early materials:[87]

> Red stone lard is sour, non-toxic; white stone lard is sweet, non-toxic, balanced; black stone lard is salty, non-toxic, balanced; yellow stone lard is bitter, non-toxic, balanced; azure stone lard is sour, non-toxic, balanced. All are medicinals that nourish the body and extend years.
>
> Method for refining Five-stone lard:
>
> Pound, place in water. Grind until very fine. Let the solution clarify. When it is like mud, with stones on the bottom, collect the upper portion. Repeat this fifteen times. Dry. Daily ingest three times. You may then cut off grains and

Chine pharmacopoieas" *Chung Chi Journal* 7 (1968): 2. On red siliceous clay, a.k.a. red bole, see Nathan Sivin, *Chinese Alchemy: Preliminary Studies* (Cambridge: Harvard University Press, 1968): 274.

85 青赤黃白黑符 See Wu Pu's 吳普 (220–64) comment in *Shennong bencao jing* 1.9b, also cited in TPYL 987.4501.1.

86 Zhang Hua, *Bowuzhi* 博物志 1.1a (Sibu beiyao edn). This passage begins as a citation of a weft text, *Hetu kuodixiang* 河圖括地象, which is cited in numerous other early sources. These citations refer to the size and subterranean topography of Kunlun, but do not mention 'stone lard'. It is, however, quite likely that Zhang Hua provides a fuller citation, and that the original *Hetu kuodixiang* did include this idea. Note that the sources for the citations collated in *Isho shusei* 6.31–46 do not include the *Bowuzhi*. For details about the *Bowuzhi*, see Campany, *Strange Writing*, 49–52, *et passim*.

87 *Shenxian fuer danshi xingyao fa* 神仙服餌丹石行藥法 DZ 420; attributed to Master Jing Li 京里先生, who is unattested elsewhere. The current text is listed in *Tongzhi Yiwenlue* 通志藝文略. It may be a remnant of the *Shenxian fushi jing* 神仙服食經 by Master Jing Li in 12 scrolls listed in *Jiutang shu* 47.2048 (listed under medical practices) and *Xintang shu* 59.1569. See Chen Guofu, *Daozang*, 406, 413, 424.

be without hunger. Your body will lighten, your pneumas will be replenished, and you will withstand wind and cold. When ingesting this you must focus your intentions and hold a purification ritual 精意齋戒. If you are unable to hold a purification ritual you must not lightly consume this medicine as it will not transform but harm you....The five stones are difficult to obtain, you must be very careful in this.[88]

The consumption of such mineral compounds was the basis for the early alchemical practices advocated by Ge Hong. Some practitioners continued to develop more advanced alchemical practices. Other Daoists, however, eventually sublimated alchemical practice as they adopted the alchemical terminology for contemplative practices, forming the basis for internal alchemy (*neidan* 內丹). Actual consumption of alchemical products seems to have been relegated to lower forms of transcendence.

Cultic practice

The importance of the Fei Zhi stele goes beyond the many parallels and common motifs that we find between the content of the inscription and various hagiographic accounts. The inscription states that the stele was set up to commemorate Master Fei Zhi and functioned as a site for offerings. As pointed out by Schipper, Wang Yucheng, and Zhang Xunliao there are three cup-shaped hollows on the ledge at the foot of the stele in which offerings were to be placed. Zhang has located a parallel arrangement described by Hong Gua (1117–84) in his discussion of the "Offering-bowls Inscription for the Five Lords" 五君杯盤文.[89] The inscription itself consists of just five names: Great Lord Lao 大老君, Lord of the Western Sea 西海君, Lord of the Eastern Sea 東海君, Lord of the Perfected 真人君, and Lord of the Transcendents 仙人君. In his discussion, Hong Gua states this stele was unlike anything he had seen before, in that by each name there were three round hollows. Moreover, Hong Gua stresses that the script was stylistically the same as that on datable steles from the Han dynasty. Whether the hollows on this stele do indeed refer to the same practice as the Fei Zhi stele awaits further investigation. In any case, the physical form of the Fei Zhi stele and the content of the inscription clearly indicate that this stele formed a focus of cultic practice.

As discussed above, Wang Yucheng has suggested that the Fei Zhi stele may be the source for some narratives and motifs of later hagiographies. Such a conclusion may be hasty. A safer interpretation of the Fei Zhi inscription is that it tapped into pre-existing lore concerning *fangshi*. Liu Yi points out that while the Fei Zhi inscription may currently be our earliest witness for particular motifs, it is unlikely

---

88 DZ 420.25b6–26a5. I have not included two sentences that describe a medicine to counteract the harmful effects of non-transformed five stones.
89 Preserved in Hong Gua 洪适, *Li Xu* 隸緒 2:3b. The stele may have originally been located at the *Shangqing gong* 上清宮 on Mt. Mang 邙 near Luoyang.

that these originated with this hitherto unknown *fangshi*. He aptly describes the Fei Zhi stele as a stereotypical example of Han-period immortality cults rather than a model for such cults.[90] I agree with this characterization, and further argue that the significance of this inscription lies in seeing the terms in the inscription as neither original nor special, but as derivative of contemporary discourse, and thus representative and exemplary of cultic practice. The Fei Zhi inscription thus vivifies for us what had hitherto been formulaic literary allusions.

II TANG GONGFANG: LOCAL CULT

The stele for Transcendent Tang Gongfang was inscribed when his shrine in the town of Chenggu 城固 in Hanzhong county was refurbished, probably during the late Eastern Han.[91] According to the inscription, Tang Gongfang had achieved transcendence with the aid of his master during the second year of Wang Mang's reign (7 CE). Falling foul of the local administrator after refusing to instruct him, Tang turned to his master for help. The latter provided Tang and his wife with an elixir which would allow them to depart (*qu* 去). Though not explicitly stated, this term clearly implied departing from the human realm. Tang's wife insisted on departing with the entire household. After daubing the house with elixir and letting the animals drink it, they all rose up to the heaven in broad daylight.

Unlike Fei Zhi, Tang Gongfang is mentioned in a number of sources, including Daoist scriptures of the Six Dynasties. As told in the inscription, the legend of Tang Gongfang taps into a mythical complex which had developed in the Hanzhong for at least a century and a half. It includes etiologies for a local toponym, the Xu 婿 stream and township, and for the strange behavior of a local type of rat. He is associated with a cycle of myths related to Li Babai, who in turn is related to the very important mythical complex of Li Hong. Untangling this network of myths and clarifying their relationships may not be possible in the present state of our knowledge, but by examining this set of mythical complexes we may learn more about the interaction of Daoism and local cults and the shifting boundaries between them.

---

90 Liu Yi, *Jingtian* 1989, p. 530.
91 The inscription appears in Hong Gua 洪适, *Lishi* 隸釋 3.9b-12b and in *Jinshi cuibian* 金石萃編 19.3a-7a. The stele is kept at the Stele Forest in Xi'an, see Xi'an beilin shufa yishu 西安碑林書法 藝術: 38 see Campany, *Strange Writing*, 187–92. Discussed and translated in Kristofer Schipper, "Le culte de l'immortel Tang Gongfang," in A. Forest, Y. Ishizawa, and L. Vandermeersch, eds. *Cultes populaires et sociétés asiatiques* (Paris: EFEO, 1991): 59–72; Schipper 施舟人, "Lijing baishi xianghuo bushuai de Xianren Tang Gongfang" 歷經百世香火不衰的仙人唐公房, in Lin Fushi 林富士 and Franciscus Verellen 傅飛嵐 *Yiji chongbai yu shengzhe chongbai* 遺跡崇拜與 聖者崇拜 (Taipei, Yun-chen wenhua, 1998): 85–99. For a partial English translation and discussion, see Campany, *Strange Writing*, 187–92, and further discussion in Campany, *To Live*. Among the first scholars to notice the importance of this stele was Yü Ying-shih, who paraphrased it in his "Life and Immortality," 107. Another paraphrase and discussion in Needham, *Science*, vol. 2, 124–6.

The leading donor of the shrine was Guo Zhi 郭芝, the governor of Hanzhong, accompanied by fifteen other local notables, including two ex-governors of Jiangyang 江陽 (modern Lu 瀘 county in Sichuan). The cult and shrines are mentioned by Chang Qu 常璩 (fl. 347) in his *Huayang guozhi*,[92] attesting to its continued presence and geographical spread.[93] Schipper traces the cult through mentions in local gazetteers to the late imperial period, and to contemporary practice in the town of Chenggu, where a shrine to Tang Gongfang still stands.

The following translation of the inscription to Transcendent Tang Gongfang is based on the text in *Lishi*, which I compared with recent transcriptions, such as Gao Wen, 1997, and Yuan Weichun, 1990.[94] Chen Xianyuan, 1996, provides a full transcription, but without specifying his sources for filling in the lacunae.[95] The translation includes his emendations, marked off with brackets that include the number of missing graphs according to the *Lishi* transcription:

> The lord's name was Gongfang, of Chenggu. He was Thearch Yao's {descendent. Thearch Yao was sincere, reverent, able yet humble, the lord truly succeeded (10 lacuna)} him. Hence, he could raise his household {achieve crossing – over, lift his home and as a transcendent (5 lacuna)} depart. He soared up to the luminous brilliance 皇耀, driving and riding *yin* and *yang*, soaring into the limpid [heavens] he treaded the floating [clouds]. His allotted longevity was boundless. Although revered by kings and lords, treasured within the four seas, he was {not be moved even by a single (5 lacuna)} hair. The nature of heaven and earth is what he most cherished.
>
> According to tradition transmitted by the elders in the second year of Wang Mang's regency (*jushe* 居攝, 7–8 CE) when the lord was serving as commandery officer, {once, during their leisure time, as, together with his colleagues (4 lacuna)} he was eating melons in the garden, there was a Perfected Person nearby, [but] none of his companions recognized him. Only the lord presented him with an excellent melon, and then followed and respectfully saluted him.
>
> The Perfected Person consequently arranged a meeting with the lord at the top of the mountain at the Xi valley entrance. There he presented the lord with divine medicine, and said: "After ingesting the medicine you will be transported by your intentions myriad *li* and you will know the speech of birds and animals."

---

92 *Huayang gu zhi* 華陽國志 2.
93 Other shrines to Tang Gongfang, include: (1) Baozhong 褒中 county (present Baocheng 褒城, in NE Hanzhong) – Shrine to *Tang Gongfang* 唐公房 (HYGZ 2.3b) and (2) Yangxian 洋縣 (present Xixiang 西鄉) (*Taiping huanyu ji*, j.188).
94 Gao Wen 高文, *Hanbei jishi* 漢碑集釋 (Kaifeng: Henan daxue, 1997); Yuan Weichun 袁維春 *Qinhan bei shu* 秦汉碑迹 (Beijing: Beijing gongyi meishu, 1990): 589–600.
95 Chen Xianyuan 陈显远, *Han 'Xianren Tang Gongfang bei' kao* 汉 "仙人唐公房碑" 考, *Wenbo* 文博 1996.2: 27–8, 48.

At that time the prefectural capital was at Xicheng 西成 over 700 *li* from [Tang's] home.[96] Traveling back and forth between official audiences, within a blink of an eye he would arrive. All the people of the commandery were surprised by this, and reported it to the prefect, who then appointed him a *yuli* 御吏.[97]

[Once] rats gnawed through the cloth of a chariot's canopy. The lord then drew a gaol on the ground, summoned the rats and killed them. [The prefect] examined their innards and indeed saw [remains] of the cloth. The prefect {set out} a banquet, and [said] he wished to follow Tang and study the Dao. Gongfang did not immediately submit. The prefect angrily ordered his officers and guards to arrest Gongfang's wife and children.

Gongfang quickly returned to Gukou and called on his Master to tell him of the urgent danger. The Master returned with him and gave Gongfang, his wife, and children an elixir to drink, and said: "you may depart." The wife and children loved their household and could not bear to depart. The Master said: "is it that you wish the entire household to depart together?" The wife and children replied: "That is our wish."

Therefore, they took the elixir and swabbed it on the house posts, and made the oxen and horses and domestic animals drink it. In a thrice a great wind and dark clouds appeared and covered Gongfang, his wife and children, the house and animals. In a burst of wind they all flew upwards and departed together.

In the past, Qiao, Song, Cui, Bo 喬松崔白 all attained the Dao alone,[98] but Gongfang raised and crossed over his entire household. Great indeed! A proverb says: "Where a worthy dwells, munificence flows for a hundred generations!" Hence, he has caused Xi village to be without mosquitoes 蚊 in spring and summer, free of frost during the winter. Pestilence 癘 and poisonous vermin do not linger, and flying insects 螟 are expelled,[99] and the hundred

---

96 Xicheng 西成 refers to 西城, the prefectural seat of Hanzhong (present Ankang 安康 city in Shaanxi).

97 Both *Lishi* and *Cuibian* have *li*, while *Lianghan jinshi ji* has *shi* 史. As *yuli* is not an attested title, the correct graph should probably be *shi*. However, *yushi* was an imperially bestowed title and not granted by local officials.

98 Qiao and Song refer to the afore-mentioned Wangzi Qiao and Chisongzi. Cui Wenzi 崔文子 of Taishan, was from a family traditionally affiliated with Huanglao teachings. He became a disciple of Wangzi Qiao. He compounded Yellow Powder Crimson Pills 黃散赤丸. The identity of Bai, or Bo, is more problematic. Schipper suggests he is Boyang, the legendary author of *Zhouyi cantongqi*, who became identified with Laozi (*Culte*, 64). Yuan suggests he should be identified with Master White Stone 白石先生 who is described in *LXZ* as a disciple of Daoist Master of Central Yellow 中黃道人. He boiled white stones for his sustenance; hence he dwelt on White Stone Mountain. He also ate dried meat and grains and drank wine. He could traverse some three or four hundred *li* a day and his appearance did not decline (*TPYL* 663).

99 *Ming* 螟 *te* 螣 are two types of insects that feed on distinct parts of plant. The *locus classicus* is *Shijing* "Datian" 大田 (Mao 218): "Expel the insects and pests" 去其螟螣 及其蟊賊. The commentary states "Those that feed on the sprouts are called *ming*, those that eat the leaves are called *te*,

grains can be harvested. Nowhere under heaven is there such efficacious virtue and succor. The multitudes of transcendents are on a par with the Dao, our native soil is irrigated by their virtue. Those who recognize his virtue are few, and through the generations none have recorded it.

I, Guo Zhi of Nanyang, named Gongzai 公載, Grand Administrator of Hanzhong, have cultivated my government like the north star,[100] and ridden the winds of the Zhou and Shao 周邵之風.[101] Joyous at the excellence of Lord Tang's spiritual efficacy, I realized that those eminent in the Dao, are renowned, and those whose virtue is distinguished are revered in temples. In order to express these auspicious thoughts, I personally offered the monies, as a leader of the group of donors 群義, to renovate and enlarge this temple. [In order to] {gather} harmony and seek blessings and to spread them among the people. We inscribed this stone with glowing verses to glorify the lord's numinous fame. The words are:

{To magnificent lord Tang/whose glory reaches Xuanhuang 軒黃 roaming free in the Lacquer garden *qiyuan* 漆園/[102] your Way matches that of Zhuang of Meng 蒙庄} consequently enjoying the divine medicine, you ascended floating to the clouds, fleeting about on wings.

The back of the stele is inscribed with 15 names, the principal donors to the refurbishment of the shrine and erection of the stele, which constitute the "donor group" mentioned in the inscription.[103] All 15 donors were local grandees of the

---

those that eat the stalk are called *mao* 蝥 and those that eat the nodes are called *zei* 賊." Where the current text of the *Shijing* has 螣 a citation of this line in *Erya* "shi chong" 釋蟲 15.54 preserves the graph 蟘. SWJZ 13A43b preserves the graph 𧕟. While *ming* has also been identified as *chilo simlex* a type of small moth, the other creatures have not been identified with any certainty. I therefore translate the term generically as 'noxious insects'.

100 Alluding to *Analects* 2.1.

101 Zhou refers to Duke of Zhou, Shao refers to Elder of Zhao 召伯, who in *Shijing*, "*Gantang*" 甘棠 (Mao): "Zhaobo, surnamed Ji 姬 named 奭, fed Zhao with vegetables."

102 *Qiyuan* is Zhuangzi's legendary place of service. Its location has been variously identified as: (1) in the north of Heze 菏澤 county in Shandong (*Zhengyi* commentary to *SJ* 63 "Zhuangzi biography"); (2) Northeast part of Shangqiu 商丘 county in Henan, site of the ancient Meng 蒙; (3) Eastern part of Dingyuan 定遠 county in Anhui. As Meng is mentioned in the complementary line in the couplet, the reference here is probably to the second of the above alternative locations.

103 *Jinshi xubian* 1.15a (SKQS edn).

  1 Yang Yan 楊宴 *zi* Pingzhong 平仲 of Chenggu, former Acting Chief of Jiangyang 故江陽守長.

  2 Zuo Jie 左介, *zi* Yuanshu 元術 of Chenggu, Local Inspector of the Eastern Sector 東部督郵 (Hucker, "Dictionary," 7332).

  3 Yang Yin 楊銀, *zi* Bo Shen 伯慎, of Nanzheng 南鄭, former Acting Chief of Jiangyang.

  4 Zhu Gui 祝龜, *zi* Yuanling 元靈 of Nanzheng, retired scholar 處士.

  5 Zhu Yang 祝楊, *zi* Kongda 孔達 of Nanzheng, Administrator at Education Bureau 司徒掾 (Hucker, "Dictionary," 8219).

  6 Zhu Dai 祝岱, *zi* Zihua 子華 of Nanzheng, retired scholar.

region where Tang Gongfang had been revered for over a century and a half. Two were natives of Chenggu, the other 13 hailed from the neighboring town of Nanzheng. Of the latter, nine are surnamed Zhu and are probably of a single clan. Both Chenggu and Nanzheng belonged to Hanzhong prefecture, as well as Baozhong, where another shrine to Tang Gongfang is reported in *Huayang guozhi*. Jiangyang, where the two men surnamed Yang are said to have served, was part of the neighboring Tewei 特為 prefecture. Both prefectures were part of Yi 益 province, the northern part of present Sichuan. The stele may be dated by the fact that Zhu Gui, the fourth on the list of donors, is mentioned in *Huayang guozhi* as having been appointed as town head of Jiameng 葭萌, a township in Hanzhong, by Liu Yan, governor of Yi Province.[104] Liu Yan was in close contact with Zhang Lu. Below I speculate on the possible relationship between the cult to Tang Gongfang and Celestial Master Daoism.

While the shrine is mentioned in *Shuijing zhu*, Li Daoyuan does not cite the inscription but presents a different tradition related to Tang Gongfang, focusing on the unfortunate fate of the rat that did not join the rest of the animals as the entire household rose into the air:

> [Tang Gongfang] studied the Dao and attained transcendence and entered Yuntai Mountain. He produced cinnabar [compound] and ingested it. In broad daylight, he ascended to the heavens. The cock crowed up above, and the dog barked in the clouds. He despised the rat, and only it was left behind. The rat was very perturbed and each month at the new moon would vomit its entrails [and die]; but would return to life. Therefore, contemporaries called it the Tang rat.[105]

Other sources also refer to this narrative of the rat.[106] Schipper speculates that Tang Gongfang was originally a rat-catcher, who was "deified" due to his success. He also provides evidence linking rat catching with alchemical methods,

---

7 Zhu Chen 祝忱, *zi* Ziwen 子文 of Nanzheng, former Retainer at Yizhou provincial office 故益洲從事 (Hucker, "Dictionary," 7176).
8 Zhu Heng 祝恆, *zi* Zhonghua 仲華 of Nanzheng, retired scholar.
9 Zhu Lang 祝朗, *zi* Deling 德靈 of Nanzheng, retired scholar.
10 Zhu Chong 祝崇, *zi* Jihua 季華 of Nanzheng, retired scholar.
11 Zhu Rong 祝榮, *zi* Wenhua 文華 of Nanzheng, scribe to the Governor 太守史.
12 Zhao Ying 趙英, *zi* Yancai 彥才 of Nanzheng, scribe to the Governor.
13 Liu Tong 劉通, *zi* Hai 海☐☐ of Nanzheng, retired scholar. ☐ (lacuna) refers to unknown graphs in the name.
14 Zhao Zhong 趙忠, *zi* Yuanchu 元楚 of Nanzheng, former Commandant of Baozhong 故褒中守尉.
15 Yang Feng 楊鳳, zi Kongluan 孔鸞 of Nanzheng, [unclear post].
104 HYGZ 10C.5b.
105 Li Daoyuan, *Shuijing zhu* (Sibu congkan edition) 27.20.
106 1 *Liangzhou ji* 梁州記 by Liu Deng 劉澄 (479–502) (cited in YWLJ 95.1658–9, TPYL 9.7b–8a): "On the mountain there is the Entrail-changing rat 易腸鼠, which every month thrice vomits and changes its intestines. Shu Guangwei 束廣微 named it Tang Rat." (Shu Guangwei is Shu Xi (261–300), who was among the officials charged with editing the documents unearthed in

probably relating the ingestion of lead and cinnabar compounds to poisoning.[107] Campany agrees that Tang was a regional god in Hanzhong and northern Sichuan, suggesting the interest of local notables in exalting the local deity and "to elevate his identity above that of a mere rodent queller".[108] I question whether Tang's function as rat-catcher was central to his apotheosis. We should remember that the narrative concerning the "entrail-changing rat" was as intriguing and attractive to Six Dynasties compilers of collectanea as it is to us.[109] The lore concerning the etiology of an odd local type of rat intersected with the narrative of Tang Gongfang, but does not necessarily reflect the most salient feature of the cult.

A similar example of the intersection of local lore with the Tang Gongfang cycle, also recorded by in the *Shuijing zhu*, provides an etiology for the toponym of the stream and township where the shrine was located:

> The Xu 婿 stream is a river valley emerging north of the Han river.[110] To the north it abuts Mt. Ting 聽山... Located by the river is Xu township 壻鄉, the stream is called Xu stream... On the day Gongfang ascended to the heavens, his son-in-law (*xu* 婿) was away and did not return and could [therefore] not pace the clouds together [with the household]. He remained and lived by the river. It is said that since then there were no calamities of heavy frost, snakes and tigers. The local people considered him a spirit; hence they called the place and the stream "Son-in-law." [In honor] the common people erected a temple here, and inscribed a stone in order to describe the miraculous events.[111]

Although the etymology for the place names given in the passage is clearly anachronistic, it demonstrates that by the Six Dynasties the local landscape was subsumed into the Tang Gongfang lore. This narrative also reminds us that the

281 CE from the tomb of Prince Xiang of Wei; the most significant of which was the *Mu tianzi zhuan* (Shu Xi's biography is in *Jinshu* 57).)

2   *Bowuzhi*: "Tang Fang ascended to transcendence together with his roosters and dogs. As he hated the rat, he did not take it. In its regret, each month the rat vomits and changes its intestines."

3   Liu Jingshu 劉敬叔 *Yiyuan* 異苑:

> The Tang Rat is like a rat in shape, but slightly longer, bluish-black in color. In its stomach there is excess matter, like intestines in form, which it emits regularly – so it is also known as Entrail-changing rat. In the past, when Tang Fang raised his home and ascended to the heavens, the roosters and dogs all departed. Only the rat was thrown out. It did not die but its intestines were pushed out some inches. In three years it changes them. The common people call it Tang Rat. It is found in the river in Chenggu.

107 Schipper, "Culte," 1991: 66.
108 Campany, *To Live*, 107.
109 For interesting thoughts on the entertainment value of ghost and anomaly literature see Poo Mu-chou, "Ghost Literature: Exorcistic Ritual Texts or Daily Entertainment?" AM 13.1 (2000): 43–64.
110 The text mistakenly has *zhi* 智 for *xu* 婿.
111 *Shuijing zhu* 27.20, the 'rat' narrative is embedded in this passage.

shrine was associated with management of natural disasters. The inscription, too, explicitly refers to the expulsion of other vermin, besides rats. Whatever may have been Tang Gongfang's original vocation, he had come to be a protector of the local crops and population.

Practices and abilities

Like Fei Zhi and other successful adepts, Tang Gongfang, too, gained the ability of "instantaneous travel." It was his travel between the capital and his home that had alerted the local administrator to his abilities. However, more impressive are the references to his alchemical practice. All the sources mention that Tang Gongfang had entered Mt. Yuntai in order to produce elixirs in his search for transcendence. While the various texts do not indicate which elixir and which procedures were employed by Tang, the efficacy of this elixir was such that daubing it on the house and feeding the animals sufficed to transport the entire household to heaven.

Schipper has pointed out that alchemical practice and rat capturing were related – probably due to the use of lead and mercury as rat poisons. Wang Changyu's 王昌遇 hagiography in *Lishi zhenxian tidao tongjian* tells of his encounter with an aged seller of rat poison. Pitying the old man, Wang would buy some each time he passed by. After Wang admitted that he bought the poison from pity rather than to poison rats, the old man confided to him that the drug would not necessarily kill the rats. Indeed, administering the drug resulted in the transformation of the rats into doves, which then flew away.[112]

An even more intriguing practice referred to in these narratives, is Tang's power of inscription by which he captured the rat. Having drawn a gaol on the earth, he summoned the rat into it. I focus on the power of inscription in Chapter 3, here suffice it to say that this practice recalls the ancient myth of Yu's tripods, whose power subdued the demonic anomalies of the realm, and is reminiscent of references in hagiographies to adepts who could "draw mountains and rivers." Importantly, these practices are closely related to the talismanic practices that were to become a hallmark of Daoist practice.

Yü Ying-shih, among the first to draw attention to the Tang Gongfang inscription, had interpreted its significance as exemplifying the "worldly" transformation of the idea of *xian*, which changed the concept of the *xian* from ascetic reclusion to a notion which allowed the successful practitioner to retain his worldly possessions, transplanting his earthly pleasures to the celestial realm. The earliest example for such a transformation was the image of the Yellow Thearch as portrayed by Gongsun Qing 公孫卿 while persuading Han emperor Wu to perform the *fengshan* rites. The Yellow Thearch was said to have ascended to heaven with his entire retinue and harem, totaling over 70 people.[113] Liu An, King

112 Schipper, "Culte," 66; DZ 296: 45.10a.
113 SJ 28.1394 , 12.468.

of Huainan, was also said to have ascended to the heavens along with his entire household, including his dogs and roosters.[114] Tang's ascent with family and household seems to follow these earlier models. In addition, Yü also points out that this inscription demonstrates that "by this time the cult of *xian* immortality had already acquired a wider social basis and was no longer an exclusive affair between *fangshi* and the ruling class". Secondly, he points out that the inscription reflects "the popular belief in drugs as the best, or rather the easiest, way to achieve immortality".[115]

Yü's points need to be tempered by the fact that the motif of ascent with one's household is very uncommon, and is so far unattested in any other context beyond the three instances mentioned above. Even if other examples were to be found, they would be heavily outweighed by the number of narratives that emphasize that transcendence is individual and necessitates total abandonment of all social links, including familial ties. As Campany has pointed out, narratives concerning *shijie* especially emphasize that the adept is to depart from his native land, change his name and never return. One such example is the Huang Chuping narrative in the *Array of Five Talismans*, which drives this point home by stressing that Huang Chuqi needs to abandon his wife and children and remain with Huang Chuping in order to emulate his brother's attainment.[116]

Appropriation by Daoist lineages

While the stele inscription mentions Tang Gongfang's association with a master, the text does not mention the master's name or any other details about the lineage and traditions associated with him. This apparent gap in the hagiography was filled in by a number of references in Six Dynasties Daoist texts, which mention that Tang Gongfang's master was Li Eight-hundred (Li Babai 李八百). It is, however, impossible to determine how early this lineage was conceived, and whether it reflects an authentic local tradition. The *Shenxian zhuan* hagiography of Li Babai refers to Li's examination of Tang Gongfang's sincerity and resolve with a series of disgusting tests.[117] It does not, however, refer to the provision of melons mentioned in the inscription. Ge Hong mentions Li Babai in his *Baopuzi* as part of his discussion of a 'Li-family Dao' 李家道. A number of scholars consider this reference to be a distant echo of Celestial Master Daoism.[118] On the other hand, Ge Hong does not mention Tang Gongfang in *Baopuzi*.

---

114 Wang Chong 王充, *Lunheng jiaoshi* 論衡校釋, comp. by Huang Hui 黃暉 (Beijing: Zhonghua shuju, 1990) 24, FSTY 2.7b.
115 Yü, 1964: 107.
116 DZ 388: 2.14a2.
117 Campany, *To Live*, 215–18. Li feigns illness, which manifests itself as boils and sores, and requests that Fang heal it by licking the open wounds. Testing of disciples is a major theme in similar hagiographies.
118 See Campany, *To Live*, 216–18.

Tang Gongfang's fame and prestige may be indicated by the position he was given in the *Shangqing* pantheon. He is listed in the *Declarations* as one of four aides to Baoming, the celestial style of Mao Ai, the youngest Mao brother: "Tang Gongfang of Xishan 西山 [is] in charge of births and deaths".[119] The *Lingbao weiyetu*, Tao Hongjing's systematized pantheon incorporated him in the right-hand ranks of sixth level.[120] In the sacred geography produced within the *Shangqing* lineage, Xishan, the domain of Perfected Tang Gongcheng [sic], was listed as the twelfth of 36 Minor Cavern-Heavens and renamed "Celestial Pillar Treasure Culmen of Mystic Heaven" (Tianzhu baoji xuantian 天柱寶極玄天).[121] Li Babai was incorporated into this system as the resident of Changli mountain parish 昌利山治. The text specifies he was Tang Gongfang's teacher.[122]

The repeated reminders in Daoist texts that Li Babai was Tang's teacher may reflect the fact that the latter continued to occupy a more important place in popular conceptualizations. The assertion of Li Babai's superiority is therefore a means of subsuming the local cult into a Daoist system. This may be interpreted as an appropriation of local cultic figures by Yang Xi, in the early *Shangqing* revelations, and subsequently in later systemizations. Such a claim implies that Yang Xi was aware of the Hanzhong-centered cult, and deemed it important enough to incorporate its saint into the *Shangqing* pantheon. Strangely enough, Li Babai himself is not mentioned in *Declarations* or in *Lingbao weiyetu*. Did Yang Xi prefer the disciple to the master? Did he include Tang Gongfang in his system following a narrative that did not include Li Babai?

While it is entirely possible that Yang Xi had included Tang Gongfang in the *Shangqing* pantheon based on his knowledge of the cult, it seems more likely that the inclusion of Tang Gongfang in a Daoist context would have occurred earlier in a Sichuan-based lineage. The links we had noted above, between Tang Gongfang and his master Li Babai and early Celestial Master Daoism, should alert us to the possibility that Tang Gongfang could have been incorporated into texts emanating from the Celestial Master milieu. We indeed find such reference in the *Scripture of Divine Incantations from the Cavernous Abyss*.[123]

---

119 DZ 1016: 13.12b7–13a6. Xishan is in Hong province 洪州, Nanchang 南昌 county.

120 *Lingbao zhenling weiye tu* 靈寶真靈位業圖 DZ 167: 21a. This is a relatively low position. The right-hand ranks are lower ranked than left-hand ranks, while the sixth level is the second lowest of seven.

121 YJQQ 27.5b1; *Dongtian fudiyuedu mingshan ji* DZ 599 does not refer to Tang Gongfang, but to Hong Ya 洪崖.

122 *Dongtian fudiyuedu mingshan ji* DZ 599.12b; YJQQ 28.8b; SDZN 7.9b8 Changli parish is in Guanghan 廣漢, 70 km north of Chengdu. Li Babai is here named Li Babo 李八伯.

123 *Taishang dongyuan shenzhou jing* 太上洞淵神咒經 DZ 335. Principal studies of the *Shenzhou jing* include: Yoshioka Yoshitoyo 吉岡義豐, "Rikuchō no zushin dōkyō" 六朝の圖讖道經 in *Dōkyō kyōten shiron* 道教經典史論 (Tokyo: Dōkyō kankōkai, 1955): 183–263; Ōfuchi Ninji, *Dōkyō shi no kenkyū*: 435–547; Miyakawa Hisayuki 宮川尚志, "Shindai doky no ikkosatsu – 'Taishō tōen shinju kyō' omegurite" 晉代道經の一考察 '太上洞淵神咒經' をめぐりて, in *Chū goku shūkyōshi kenkyū* 中國宗教史研究 (Kyoto: Dōhōsha, 1983): 149–74; Yamada Toshiaki, "'Taishō tōen shinju kyō' no zushin teki seikaku" '太上洞淵神咒經' 的圖讖性質 – 關於其成立情況, *Taisho daigaku kenkyū kiyo, bun, bukkyō gakubu* 大正大學研究紀要文佛教學部 66 (1981): 145–63; Ozaki Masaharu 尾崎正法, "Tōen shinju kyō" 洞淵神咒經, in *Kōza Tonkō*,

With a fully developed Daoist apocalyptic vision, *Divine Incantations* is one of the primary sources for studying the developments of Daoist eschatological thought, and particularly the messianic vision associated with Li Hong 李弘. The popularity of this text during the Six Dynasties may be demonstrated, on the one hand, by the number of Dunhuang manuscripts preserving various chapters of the text, and on the other hand, by the number of rebellions associated with the name Li Hong, and possibly inspired, in part, by notions advocated in the *Divine Incantations*.[124]

Most scholars agree that the earliest strata of the text consisted of the current first and second chapters, which were later expanded to four chapters and finally to ten, by the end of the Six Dynasties period. The remaining ten chapters of the current twenty were compiled by Du Guangting 杜光庭 (850–933), who also wrote a preface. There is, however, debate concerning both the time and place of compilation of the earliest textual strata. Related to these issues is the affiliation of the text, and which Daoist lineage it actually represents. Most scholars have dated the earliest strata to the late Eastern Jin and early Liu-Song period, associating the compilation with the rise of Liu Yu (363–442), known posthumously as Emperor Wu, who established the Song dynasty in 420.[125]

An intriguing hypothesis concerning the origins of the *Shenzhou jing* has been presented by Ma Chengyu, who suggests the earliest textual layers were compiled in the Hanzhong region during the early Eastern Jin.[126] The *Shenzhou jing* refers to a number of different texts and titles which presumably are the earlier strata from which it was compiled.[127] One such passage states:

> The Dao said: I have [in the past], in *Duyang gong* 杜陽宮 recited the *Scripture of Great Exorcism* (*Daqu jing* 大驅經) on behalf of the assembled

---

Tonkō to Chūgoku Dōkyō 講座敦煌, 敦煌中國道教 (Tokyo: Tohō, 1983): vol. 4, 177–82; Zuo Jianquan, "'Dongyuan Shen zhou jing' yuanliu shikao" '洞淵神咒經' 源流試考 *Wenshi* 23 (1984); Kobayashi, *Rikuchō*, pp. 367–381; Christine Mollier, *Une Apocalypse taoïste du Ve siècle: le Livre des Incantations Divines des Grottes Abyssales* (Paris: Collège de France, Institut des Hautes Études Chinoises, 1990).

124 On the eschatology of *Shenzhou jing* and Li Hong see especially Anna Seidel, "Perfect Ruler," 216–47; Tang Changru 唐長孺, "Shiji he daojing zhong suojiande Lihong" 史籍和道經中所見 的李弘, in *Weijin nanbei chao shilun shiyi* 魏晉南北朝史論拾遺 (rpt. Beijing: Zhonghua shuju, 1983): 208–17; Lee Fengmao 李豐楙, "Liuchao de Li Hong tuchen chuanshuo" 六潮的李弘圖 讖傳說, in *Liuchao Sui Tang xiandaolei xiaoshuo yanjiu* (Taipei: Taiwan xuesheng shuju, 1986): 283–304; idem, "Tangdai 'Dongyuan Shen zhou jing' xiejuan yu Li Hong" 唐代 '洞淵神咒經' 寫卷與李弘, *Di'erjie Dunhuangxue guoji yantaohui lunwenji* 第二屆敦煌學國際研討會論文 集 (Taipei: Hanxue yanjiu zhongxin, 1991): 481–500; idem, "'Dongyuan Shenzhou jing' de shenmoguan jiqi kezhishuo" '洞淵神咒經' 的神魔觀及其克制說, *Dongfang zongjiao yanjiu* 2 (1991): 133–155; idem, "'Daozang' suoshou zaoqi daoshu de wenyi guan – yi 'Nüqing guilü' ji 'Dongyuan Shenzhou jing' xi weizhu" '道藏' 所收早期道書的瘟疫觀 – 以 '女青鬼律' 及 '洞 淵神咒經' 系為主, *Zhongguo wenzhi yanjiu jikan* (1993): 417–54.

125 Mollier, *Apocalypse*, 56–7.

126 Ma Chengyu 馬承玉 "Cong Dunhuang xieben kan 'Dongyuan shen zhou jing' zai beifang de chuanbo" 從敦煌寫本看 '洞淵神咒經' 在北方的傳播, *DJWH* 13 (1998): 200–25.

127 See Mollier, *Apocalypse*, 47–8 for a table listing the various titles appearing in the text. It is unfortunately not detailed enough to allow tracing the various textual layers within the *Shenzhou jing*.

jade maidens in order to guide and transform the various beings. At that moment Perfected Tang Ping 唐平 of the Central States 中國 arrived, and said: "Recently the registers of the dead have become unclear [due to the many deaths]. From now on when will there be plagues 瘴?"[128]

While not explicitly stated here, the passage seems to imply that Tang Ping was privy to an early textual revelation.

This was certainly how Du Guangting understood the redaction process, which he described in his preface. Du attributed the revelation and compilation of the text to Wang Zuan 王纂, a Daoist of Maji Mountain 馬跡山, who witnessed the calamities, famine, and epidemics during the final years of the Western Jin. The Most High Lord of the Dao (Taishang daojun) descended to him, explained the causes of the recent calamities, and transmitted the *Divine Incantations*. In his account, the deity mentions that he had, in the past, transmitted the *Divine Incantations* to Perfected Tang Ping at Duyang gong (3a1). Elsewhere in the *Divine Incantations* we are told that Duyang gong atop Mt. Duyang is the most sacred of the myriad temples in China.[129] While most scholars have located Duyang gong at Mt. Duyang in present Fengxiang 鳳翔 county, Shaanxi.[130] Ma points out that the account in *Shuijing zhu* concerning Mt. Duyang makes no reference to Daoist activities. On the other hand, he notes that in describing the juncture of Han and Wen rivers, the section on Mianshui 沔水 states:

... [Wen] is the Men 門 river, which emanates from a cavern below a mountain north of Hucheng 胡城. The elders say that in Duyang there is a temple to a transcendent. The cavern is in front of the temple door, hence this stream is known as Men (Gateway) stream, and the river is called Men river.[131]

This Duyang was therefore located west of Chenggu in Hanzhong county. Ma concludes that Tang Ping must be a Daoist of Hanzhong, and thus associated with the local cultic center of Tang Gongfang.

Tang Ping appears elsewhere in *Divine Incantations* as a future savior, who will arrive in aid of those who had converted to Daoism during the coming cataclysmic floods:

When the great flood comes, the transcendents Tang Ping, Yu Guang, and Ma Qi, of the central states, leading 80,000 celestial beings and transcendents, will arrive riding metal boats to collect the Daoists.[132]

128 DZ 335: 5.1a3–5.
129 DZ 335: 20.16a–b. This is the locus of the Hemp Maiden 麻姑 about whom more will be said below (7.3a3).
130 Mollier, *Apocalypse*, 69 n.10.
131 Chen Qiaoy, 陳橋驛 *Shuijing zhu jiaoshi* 水經注校釋 (Hangzhou: Hangzhou daxue chubanshe) 1999; SJZ *shu*, (Jiangsu renmin).
132 DZ 335: 20.5a3. I have no information about Yu Guang and Ma Qi.

Further on in the same chapter Tang Gongfang himself is mentioned as one of the great former Daoists:

> From now until *renwu* 壬午 and *xinsi* 辛巳 years[133] there will be many female Daoists who will receive the Three Caverns [scriptures]. Among those entering mountains, women will be many, while men will be few. The Mystic Maiden will descend, transforming herself into a young maiden, and enter the human realm.[134] Following the *jiashen* 甲申 year,[135] all males and females above thirteen years of age will receive 'Ten Generals Youth 十將軍童子' [registers] and 'Celestial Yellow Book Contracts and Commands 天上黃書契令'. Why is that? Those who for generations have transmitted the faith in the Dao, Hemp Maiden (Ma Gu 麻姑), Du Lanxiang 杜蘭香, An Qisheng and Tang Gongfang when converting the people have all received them. All Daoist groups 道士門門 possess these scriptures, making offering and recitations day and night. In the south of the river 江左, Wu-Chu, Han-Qin and Shu there are many people practicing the Dao.[136]

Lord Tang is also mentioned in a passage describing the eschatological vision of the appearance of the savior Perfected Lord Li Hong in a *renchen* 壬辰 year. Lord Tang will be among a group of Perfected who will arrive to prepare the deliverance of humanity by converting the people to the correct path:

> The Perfected lord is not far-away, his name is Li Hong. Faithful Daoists will exert themselves to the utmost to convert people and transmit the teaching to them. Transcendents will arrive to greet him. Since the *renwu* 壬午 year plague demons have killed people and humanity is [almost] exhausted. The Most High will pity them and dispatch the great perfected to announce [the imminent] descent into the world of Yan Ping 嚴平, Jin Fangshi 進方社,

---

133 Years 18–19 of the sexagesimal cycle.
134 The Mystic Maiden plays an important role in *Shenzhou jing* as instructor and savior of humanity. Along with Hemp Maiden and Lady Wang 王妃, she will descend at the head of 360,000 troops who will command the demon kings in the name of the Most High to cease their cataclysmic depredations (1.2b6). When plagues were decimating humanity all the celestial jade maidens wanted to merely gather on Mt. Duyang with Hemp Maiden and travel through the five Marchmounts in order to observe whether humanity was dying. Only the Mystic Maiden intervened on humanity's behalf and appealed to the Most High, who allowed her to descend and convert the people to the Three Caverns, thus saving humanity (7.3a2–7). In another apocalyptic vision she is said to convert the three hundred wives of the king of the oceanic people, although their practice of the Dao differs from that in China (20.14a7–b3). In a passage that systematizes the officers responsible for 18 different types of death, she is listed as responsible for whoever's death is related to water (20.8a8–b8). Finally, a plurality of Mystic Maidens will descend, along with various transcendents and jade maidens, to protect the *Shenzhou jing*, upon its release in the world (20.26b4–5).
135 Year 21 of the sexagesimal cycle.
136 DZ 335: 20.13a7.

Zhou Zhengxuan 周正玄, and Lord Tang 唐君 in order to convert the people.[137]

Whether this Lord Tang is Tang Gongfang or Tang Ping is unclear. These two figures seem to have been conflated, but due to the difficulties in determining the redaction process of the text, it is impossible to determine how this may have occurred. Nevertheless, this passage demonstrates the importance of Shu-based mythology to the author(s) of the text, and to the development of the messianic figure of Li Hong.

Yan Ping, originally named Zhuang Zun 莊尊 (traditional dates 59–24 BCE), was a recluse from Chengdu during the final years of the Western Han. Making his living from divination, he would shut his stall as soon as he earned enough for the day and devoted himself to the study of Laozi and Zhuangzi. He composed a commentary on the *Daode jing* entitled *Daode zhigui lun* 道德指歸論,[138] and was the teacher of Yang Xiong 楊雄 (53 BCE–18 CE), the author of the *Taixuan jing* 太玄經.[139]

Li Hong was a contemporary Confucian scholar of Chengdu, who also gained high praise from Yang Xiong: "He did not see, hear, speak, or practice anything that was not upright."[140] His reputation rests on two incidents. When about to be appointed to office, he arranged a feast but remained drunk for a month so as not to be able to accept the post. More important was his behavior when his son had committed murder. The local magistrate was willing to absolve the son of such a worthy. Li Hong, however, chased his son away, explaining that he had chosen a middle path between Shi Jie 石碏 who had killed his son,[141] and Confucius who advocated that fathers and sons should protect each other.[142] During the late Han, the prefect of Chengdu, Wang Shang 王商, erected shrines and steles in honor of both Yan Ping and Li Hong.[143]

---

137 My translation follows P 2789; Ōfuchi, *Tonkō dōkyō zurokuhen*, 554, lines 23–27, which differs from DZ 335: 9.a 4–9 in some significant ways. DZ 335 does not mention Li Hong, and leaves out the graph *wang* 王 following Yan Ping. Mollier (*Apocalypse*, 136) seems to have misunderstood the names of the perfected, missing the reference to Yan Ping and Lord Tang.

138 *Daode zhenjing zhigui* 道德真經指歸 DZ 693 preserves the preface along with *juan* 7 to 13 of Zhuang Zun's commentary. The first six *juan* are preserved in various other anthologies in the canon. The text is collated and annotated by Wang Deyou 王德有 in *Laozi zhigui* 老子指歸 (Beijing: Zhonghua shuju, 1994).

139 HYGZ 10.1b. *Gaoshi zhuan* tells of refusal to take office even after receiving funding from a rich patron. Yan Ping summarizes his reasoning as "increasing my valuables will damage my spirits, producing a name for myself will kill my body."

140 Yang Xiong 揚雄, *Fayan zhuzi suoyin* 法言逐字索引 (Hong Kong: ICS, 1995): 11/31/12.

141 Shi Jie's son Hou 厚 participated with Zhou Yu 州呼 in murdering Wan the ruler of Wei 衛君完. Shi Jie arranged for their capture, and sent his personal assistant to kill Hou (see *Zuozhuan*, Duke Yin 4 (Legge, 17)).

142 HYGZ 10.1b–2a.

143 Pei Songzhi's commentary to Xu Jing 許靖 biography, citing the *Yizhou qijiuzhuan* 益州耆舊傳 SGZ 38.967. Much information concerning Yan Ping and Li Hong is contained in Lu Bi 盧弼, *Sanguozhi jijie* 三國志集解 (Beijing: Zhonghua shuju, 1982), *juan* 38.6a–b, 797.

In her study of eschatological messianism of Six Dynasties Daoism, Anna Seidel suggested that the selection of the name Li Hong for the future savior, and linking him to the mild-mannered Confucian scholar, was due to his surname rather than his actions.[144] Laozi's surname was of course Li.

Another intriguing possibility may be a link to a messianic Daoist state established in the Shu region during the fourth century by a local aboriginal clan surnamed Li. Adherents of Celestial Masters Daoism, they had moved north with thousands of other members of the community following Zhang Lu's surrender to Cao Cao in 215. After returning to Sichuan, they established an independent Daoist state in the Shu region. Named Great Perfection *Dacheng* 大成, this state lasted some 45 years (302–47) before its absorption by the Western Jin. Whether the *Divine Incantations* is related to this family and produced by them or their followers is a complex question, which deserves special examination and is beyond the scope of this study. It is clear, however, that the eschatological lore of the *Divine Incantations* is firmly rooted in local Shu and Ba traditions.[145]

The legend of Tang Gongfang as told in the inscription taps into a mythical complex, which had developed in the Hanzhong for at least a century and half. It includes etiologies for a toponym and for the strange behavior of a local type of rat. The narrative was later associated with a cycle of myths related to Li Babai, which, in turn, is related to the very important mythical complex of Li Hong and to early Celestial Master Daoism. These mythical complexes, which were originally distinct local traditions in the Sichuan region, were incorporated in complex ways into the lore of various Daoist lineages. While the precise filiations of the various elements of these mythical complexes remain obscure, careful examination of such networks of myths reveals the continuing interaction of various Daoist lineages and local cults, and the shifting boundaries between them.

III   STELE OF WANGZI QIAO: GENERAL CULTIC CENTER

In August of 165, Han emperor Huan (r. 147–67) dispatched an envoy, Wang Zhang, to perform a sacrifice for the transcendent Wangzi Qiao and erect a stele at the family shrine of the Wang family of Meng 蒙 (in Henan, near the Shandong border), which was established following Wangzi Qiao's appearance during the *La* (Great Exorcism) festival of 137 CE.[146] Of obscure ancient origins, Wangzi Qiao had, by the early Han, become one of the most important exemplars of successful

---

144 Seidel, "The Image."
145 The Li family were Cong 賨 aborigines of the Ba region, also known as Broadshield Man *Banshun Man* 板楯蠻. For detailed studies, see Tang Changru 唐長孺, "Fan Changsheng yu bashi ju shu de guanxi" 范長生與巴氏據蜀的關係, *Lishi yanjiu* 歷史研究 4 (1954): 115–122, and Terry Kleeman, *Great Perfection, Religion and Ethnicity in a Chinese Millennial Kingdom* (Honolulu: University of Hawaii Press, 1998).
146 The *La* was the final ritual sequence of the traditional New Year festival. For details see Derk Bodde, *Festivals in Classical China* (Princeton: Princeton University Press, 1975): 49–74.

transcendents. He is mentioned in numerous early sources, often in tandem with Chisongzi. As will become clear in the following discussion, the shrine and stele were attempts to tap into the charisma of prestigious persona. Rather than presenting the historical aspects of Wangzi Qiao, they should be regarded as attempted appropriations of a well-known figure to enhance the prestige of a local family, on the one hand, and as a means of garnering support for a weak emperor on the other. The erection of the shrine and stele thus demonstrate developments of cultic associations of the late second century in general as well as features of the specific cult.

According to his *Liexian zhuan* hagiography, Wangzi Qiao was Prince Jin, son of King Ling of the Zhou (571–45 BCE). Before any formal study, he was already skillful at playing the mouth organ 笙 and could produce the call of the crane. He roamed between the Yin and the Luo rivers. At some point he was accepted as a disciple by Master of the Dao Fu Qiu 道士浮丘 on Mt. Song'gao. Over 30 years later, he revealed himself to Huan Liang and, through him, announced to his family to gather on Mt. Goushi 緱氏山 on the seventh day of the seventh month. He indeed arrived at the appointed time on the mountain top, riding a white crane, only to bid them all farewell and depart again. The hagiography ends by mentioning shrines at both the foot of Mt. Goushi (Henan, Yanshi county) and on Mt. Song'gao. These locales are all within the vicinity of the ancient capital of Luoyang and about 600 miles away from the site of the shrine and stele.

The first line of the hagiography locates Wangzi Qiao in a known and respectable narrative context identifying him with a known historical figure. However, the references to Prince Jin in historical sources do not mention any esoteric practices. Rather, we are told he remonstrated with his father on behalf of a community that was threatened by plans for construction of a dam.[147] Some sources link him with Shi Guang 師曠, chief musician at the court of Jin, known for his divination skills using musical tones. His fame was such that his name was affixed to a book of divinations cited as one of the prime examples of esoteric texts.[148]

There is no hint of this mundane history in the hagiography that focuses on esoteric practices. His skill at playing the reed pipe and emulating the call of the crane, which may allude to his link with Shi Guang, presages his later identification with the bird itself. Although the content of his teachings is not specified, Wangzi Qiao is said to have studied with Master Fu Qiu, who is not known from other early sources. Later sources elaborate on this lineage and even provide citations of the basic text transmitted by Fu Qiu, which appears to be a teaching focusing on emulating the qualities of the crane.[149] The significance of the date of

147 Marianne Bujard, "Le culte de Wangzi Qiao ou la longue carrière d'un immortel," *Études Chinoises* 19 (2000): 115–58.
148 HHS 82A.2703, a book of divination of calamities in six chapters is attributed to him in the HHS bibliographic chapters.
149 In his commentary on Bao Mingyuan 鮑明遠 (Bao Zhao 鮑照, c. 414–466) "Rhapsody of the Dancing Cranes" *Wuhe fu* 舞鶴賦, Li Shan stated that a text entitled *Xianghe jing* 相鶴經

Wangzi Qiao's reappearance may be related to its astronomical connotations. In ancient sources, the seventh day of the seventh month signified the celestial encounter between the Weaver Maid and the Oxherd asterisms. It thus came to signify an occasion of mythic encounters and hierogamies, such as the meeting between the Queen Mother of the West and Han emperor Wu in the *Hanwu di neizhuan* cycle.[150]

A distinct, and probably older, tradition is preserved in the *Chuci* poem "Celestial Questions" (*Tianwen* 天問) and in Wang Yi's commentary, in which Wangzi Qiao is said to have manifested himself as a rainbow before transforming into a great bird.[151] By the early Han, Wangzi Qiao, often partnered with Chisongzi, became a model for emulation for the seekers of transcendence. The description given in the *Huainanzi* reveals that successful adepts were now perceived as transcending the mundane world and unifying their physical form with the Dao through their transformative practices. Through this physical self-transformation the model adepts come to embody the Dao and its endless transformations:

> The methods of the sages may be seen, but the source of their practice cannot be found. The words of discerning masters may be heard, but the cause of their words cannot be manifested. ...Now Wang Qiao and Chisong blew, puffed, exhaled and inhaled. Exhaling the old and inhaling the new they abandoned their form and rejected their consciousness, embraced the unhewn and reverted to perfection. They thereby roamed through the profound and minute and ascended to penetrate the cloudy heavens. Now, those wishing to learn their methods cannot attain their [ability at] nourishing the pneumas and fixing the spirits. They randomly exhale and inhale, sometimes constricting and sometimes dilating but they are unable to ride the clouds and ascend.[152]

Few of these themes appear in the text on the Wangzi Qiao stele. After describing the appearance of the transcendent on his grave mound and the subsequent

---

originated with Fu Qiu, who transmitted it to Wangzi Jin. Cui Wenzi who studied with Wangzi Qiao obtained this text, and secreted it in a cavern on Mt. Song'gao where it was found by the eight masters of Huainan when they were collecting herbs. Hence, it was transmitted in the world (*Wenxuan* 14.8a). Li Shan also provides a paraphrase of the text. Fu Qiu is given a hagiography in *Zhenxian tongjian* 真仙通鑒 DZ 296:4.7a–8a. The passage includes a citation of *Xianghe jing*, which is identical to Li Shan's comment in *Wenxuan*. An elaborate form of the encounter and teachings transmitted by Fu Qiu to Wangzi Qiao is given in *Huagaishan fuqiu wang guo san zhenjun shishi* 華蓋山孚丘王郭三真君事實 DZ 177: 1.1b–2b.

150 See Loewe, *Ways to Paradise*, 114–20.
151 *Chuci buzhu*, 145; David Hawkes, *The Songs of the South: an Ancient Chinese Anthology of Poems* (Harmondsworth, Middlesex, England; New York, N.Y: Penguin, 1985).
152 HNZ 11.65–6.

establishment of a shrine, the inscription claims the place became a locus of wide-ranging cultic practices:[153]

> Then, those who delighted in the Dao came from distant places to gather there. Some strummed zithers and sang of Great One (Taiyi 太一), others practiced meditation to visit their Cinnabar Fields (dantian 丹田). Those who were sick or crippled and who silently bowed and prayed for good fortune were granted it straight away, but those who were lacking in respect were struck down immediately… thus it was that it was a tomb of great virtue, the tomb of a Perfected 真人.

The importance of this inscription is in providing us with a range of public practices performed at the site. The Fei Zhi inscription with its family-centered cult and individual quest for transcendence naturally does not provide any hint as to how the public may have viewed such a shrine. The Tang Gongfang inscription, while attesting to practices of the adept, does not give any description of public performances or allude to the expectation of the general public of attending and practicing at the shrine. While it was clearly viewed as efficacious, and perceived as having some control over the weather and pests in the immediate vicinity, we have no idea what type of practice may have been performed at the site. These gaps may be filled by examining the Wangzi Qiao inscription.

The inscription does not associate any particular practice with Wangzi Qiao himself. However, the people congregating at the site performed a variety of distinct practices, which may be divided into three types. The first appears to have been communal performances of ritual music associated with Great One. The origins of this deity are unclear.[154] On the one hand, Great One is mentioned in several poems in the *Chuci*, suggesting origins in the ancient region of Chu. On the other hand, Great One is mentioned as the cosmogonic source in the recently excavated text "Great One Generated Water" (*Taiyi shengshui*),[155] which explain its place in cosmological speculations in the encyclopedic compilations of *Lüshi*

---

153 There are two extant versions of the inscription: (1) a shorter version preserved in *Shuijing zhu* 23.64, *Shuijing zhu* 15.13a–b, *Shuijing zhushu* 23.1974; (2) a longer version preserved in the Collected Works of Cai Yong *Cai zhonglang ji* 蔡中朗集 in *Hanwei liuchao yibaisan jia ji* 漢魏六朝一百三家集 2: 18b–19a; collated by Zhang Pu 張溥 (Ming) in *Congshu jicheng* (Beijing: Zhonghua shuju, 1985): Chapters 389–90. See also *Li shi* 20.16b. A full translation is provided by Donald Holzman, "The Wang Ziqiao Stele," in *Immortals, Festivals and Poetry in Medieval China*, (Aldershot and Brookfield: Ashgate Publishing, 1998); originally published in *Rocznik Orientalistyczny* 47.2 (Warsaw, 1991): 77–83. Campany, *Strange*, 193–95, discusses this stele and its relation to Wangzi Qiao hagiographies.

154 Li Ling 李零 (translated by Donald Harper), "An Archaeological Study of Taiyi (Grand One) Worship," *Early Medieval China* 2 (1995): 1–39.

155 Sarah Allan, "The Great One, Water, and the Laozi: New Light from Guodian," *T'oung Pao* 89 (2003): 237–85.

Chunqiu 呂氏春秋 and *Huainanzi* 淮南子.[156] Great One was placed at the peak of the imperial pantheon and revered by the Han emperors since the ritual innovation initiated by Han emperor Wu (141–87 BCE).[157] The inscription does provide us with a clear description of the purpose of this practice in the context of the cultic performance of the shrine. Whether it was part of a personal practice by individuals seeking transcendence, or whether it tapped into the imperial cult and had more public motivation, cannot be determined from this short reference. It is, of course, quite possible that different practitioners may have had different motivations in their performance, and that these motivations may have overlapped, as they do in modern Daoist ritual. The development of the cult of *Taiyi*, and its place in the imperial ritual system, had a crucial role in the formation of the Daoist ritual system.[158]

The second type of practice mentioned is one of the earliest references to what was to become a core practice in Daoist ritual meditations – a contemplative inner journey by the adept to the Cinnabar Field, the source of energy located below the navel. This is among the earliest references to the Cinnabar Field. The use of this term, which maps alchemical discourse onto the human body, indicates an adoption of alchemical discourse into psycho-physical meditative practice. It may also indicate that the alchemical tradition, even at this very early stage, was already tending to internalization of practice. These concepts and their developments shaped the conceptualization of the human body and the links between the human microcosm and the macrocosm, which remain at the heart of Daoist ritual. As these fascinating topics cannot be explored further here, I will simply note that the Wangzi Qiao inscription provides us with early evidence for these practices and, importantly, for their general popularity.

The third type of practice is the unspecified supplications performed by the ill and afflicted with the expectation that the numinosity of the shrine will provide them with healing and good fortune. Unlike the two types of practice mentioned above, these are not psycho-physical practices and probably did not require any special training. Rather than the practices of religious specialists and adepts, these practices were truly at the public and popular level. Whether the emperor's attention to the shrine was due to these public performances or whether it was due to the emperor's interest in personal transcendence, or, as is probably the case, a combination of both, cannot be determined with any certainty. Despite these difficulties in ascertaining the specific practices and motivations associated with the shrine, the

156 John Knoblock and Jeffrey Riegel, *The Annals of Lü Buwei* (Stanford: Stanford University Press, 2000): 136–40, *et passim*; *The Huainanzi: A Guide to the Theory and Practice of Government in Early Han China* by Liu An, King of Huainan; translated and edited by John S. Major, Sarah A. Queen, Andrew Seth Meyer, and Harold Roth (New York: Columbia University Press, 2010).

157 Bujard, *Le sacrifice.*

158 I examine these developments in my essay: "Imperial Efficacy: Debates on Imperial Ritual in Early Medieval China and the Emergence of Daoist Ritual Schemata," in Florian Reiter, ed. *Purposes, Means and Convictions in Daoism, a Berlin Symposium* (Wiesbaden: Harrasowitz, 2007): 83–109.

inscription demonstrates a merger of imperial and popular practice around a figure initially associated with the quest for transcendence. The performance of different practices, with distinct expectations, at the same site is further demonstration of the development of the cult of immortality into popular cults of immortals.

Appropriation into Daoism

As befitting one of the most famous transcendents, Wangzi Qiao was incorporated into Daoism as a recipient and transmitter of numerous teachings, methods, and texts. He received a high post in the *Shangqing* revelations, and was among Yang Xi's celestial visitors. In these revelations, he was identified as the official in charge of the Golden Court below Mt. Tong Bo 桐柏 in the Tiantai range, with the full and awesome title Perfected of Tongbo, Assistant Prince on the Right, Commander of the Five Marchmounts and Director Aide to Thearchical Dawn 桐柏真人右弼王領五嶽司侍帝晨王子喬.[159]

As recounted in *Declarations*, he first appeared to Yang Xi on the twenty-sixth night of the sixth month (third year of *xingning* 興寧, July 27, 365) in the company of seven other Perfected of the highest rank. He is described as:

> very young and formally dressed, bearing a lotus-flower cap 芙蓉冠, wearing ruby red clothes embroidered with white pearls and carrying a sword. None had seen him before. Discussing much about matters of the Golden Court within the mountain, he talked with the other Perfected. I could not understand many of his words. He was reverent to the three Perfected Ladies of Purple Tenuity, Purple Clarity, and the Southern Marchmount,[160] but spoke on equal terms with the others. This was Wangzi Qiao, the Perfected of Mt. Tongbo".[161]

Elsewhere in the *Declarations*, Yang Xi mentions Wangzi Qiao's tomb in Jingling 京陵: "When it was exposed during the Warring States period only a sword was found in the chamber. When someone tried to reach and look at it, the sword suddenly flew up into the heavens".[162]

The *Declarations* thus provides us with two distinct images of Wangzi Qiao. On the one hand, he is portrayed as a Perfected of the highest ranks. On the other hand, his tomb is described as that of a lower grade adept who attained transcendence by means of a simulated corpse – in this case a sword.[163] How should we reconcile

159 DZ 1016: 1.2b9.
160 Lady Wang of Purple Tenuity 紫微王夫人, Perfected Consort Nine Blossoms of the Upper Palace of Purple Clarity; Stephen Bokenkamp, "Declarations of the Perfected," in Donald S. Lopez, ed. *Religions of China in Practice* (Princeton, Princeton University Press, 1996): 171–9.
161 DZ 1016: 1.15a10–b4. A slightly reduced version of this passage appears in DZ 1016: 2.3a6.
162 DZ 1016: 14.18a6–9 citing from Yang Xi's *Sword Scripture* (*Jianjing* 劍經).
163 The *Array of the Five Talismans* DZ 388: 3.13b–14a includes instructions for a similar procedure, by which the adept could generate a simulated corpse by using a talisman, which the compilers consider a method of lower attainment. For more examples, see Campany, *To Live*, 70–2.

the two images of Wangzi Qiao in the *Declarations*? We need to recall that the mythology of Wangzi Qiao was continuously developing and that differing images were held at different times and at different locales. Yang Xi was clearly drawing on a number of different narratives about Wangzi Qiao. The appropriation was not a systematic process, but rather a cumulative construction of various narratives.

IV IMPERIAL INSCRIPTION TO LAOZI: UNIVERSAL CULTIC CENTER

The deification of Laozi, who came to be identified with the Dao itself and one of the three high deities of later Daoism, is a complex process. As there are several important studies regarding the changing and varied conceptions of Laozi,[164] I will only examine here one facet of it – the inscription celebrating the imperially sponsored rites to Laozi, dated to the *jiazi* day (number 1) of the eighth month in the eighth year of the *yanxi* 延熹 reign (September 24, 165 CE). The stele was erected at Ku county of Chen 陳國苦縣,[165] a site traditionally said to be Laozi's birthplace, by a local official named Bian Shao 邊詔 at the behest of Han emperor Huan 桓帝 (r. 147–67). Having ascended the throne at the age of eighteen, Emperor Huan was devoted to seeking transcendence. He established the site of the stele within two years of his ascendance. In 153, a stele bearing an inscription to Laozi's mother, the *Shengmu bei* 聖母碑, was erected at the site.[166] In February 165, Emperor Huan dispatched an official to Ku county to pay reverence 祠 to Laozi. This rite was followed by another in January 166. In September 166, the emperor personally paid reverence at the Sleek Dragon Hall.[167] The motivation for the emperor's reverence of Laozi has been the subject of many studies. I will here only examine the image of Laozi that is evident from the stele in Ku which was inscribed during this intensive ritual activity.

The inscription begins with outlining Laozi's human biography as it had come to be accepted by the Han dynasty.[168] Although his birth is associated with the changing fates of the Zhou dynasty and related to the transformations of yin and yang, he is portrayed as a man and loyal official of the Zhou, and over two hundred years in age. A short verse section provides a more numinous image:

> Those in the world who cherish the Dao, encounter his likeness and revere it.
> They believe that Laozi disperses and merges together with the pneumas of

---

164 Seidel, *Divinisation*, remains the classic study of the early stages of this process. Livia Kohn, *God of the Dao: Lord Lao in History and Myth* (Ann Arbor: Center for Chinese Studies, The University of Michigan, 1998), examines the deification of Laozi through a variety of sources ranging from the Han to the fifteenth century. See Kohn's extensive bibliography for references.

165 At Bozhou 亳州 in Chu, present Luyi 鹿邑 county in Henan.

166 The inscription is preserved in *Shuijing zhu* 23.11; partially translated in Kohn, *God*, 39; discussed in Seidel, *Divinisation*, 37, 85. Liu Yi doubts the date of the preserved inscription, and dates it to the Jin period; Liu Yi, *Jingtian*, 305–16.

167 HHS 3188.

168 For a complete translation, see Seidel, *Divinisation*, 122–28.

original chaos, and his beginning and end equals that of the three radiances. Observing the heavens, he makes prognostications; he ascends and descends to and from the dipper and stars. Following the sun he transforms nine times, he diminishes and rests in accord with the seasons. He regulates the three radiances with the four numinous beasts at his side. Contemplating his Cinnabar Field, and Taiyi in the Purple Chamber, his Dao is complete and his spirits transformed, he sloughed off his shell as a cicada and crossed the generations.

However mythical, remote, and extra-human this portrayal is, it remains a portrayal of a successful adept, and not a god distinct from humanity. In fact, despite the lyricism, the description of Laozi does not provide a more divine image than the portrayal of Wangzi Qiao in the *Huainanzi* passage cited above. Moreover, the practices by which Laozi attained his unity with the Dao are the same practices mentioned in the Wangzi Qiao inscription. The final lines of the inscription refer once more to Laozi's practices:

Unifying his radiance with sun and moon, merging with the five planets,
Entering and exiting the Cinnabar Furnace, ascending and descending from the Yellow Court,
Turning away and abandoning popular vulgar customs,
He conceals his effulgent spirits and hides his form,
Embracing the primordial, his spirits are transformed,
He inhales and exhales the ultimate pneumas.

Once again, the emphasis is on the accomplishment of perfection through practice. Some of these practices, or very similar variants, are found in several Daoist texts. We need to note that phrases referring to unifying and merging with the sun and moon and the stars are not metaphoric, nor are they references to divine qualities. Rather, these are references to meditative practices by which the adept absorbed the solar, lunar, and astral essences.

The representation of Laozi in the inscription is in sharp contrast to the image of Laozi presented in the nearly contemporaneous *Scripture on Transformations of Laozi*, discussed in the Introduction, which describes Laozi as the physical manifestation of the Dao descending in human form to the world. The Laozi Inscription, while referring to this aspect of Laozi, stresses the practices by which he attained perfection and ascended to the Dao. This is not surprising. The inscription presents the imperial view of Laozi, a vision of an adept of superior quality and attainment, who was probably a model for the personal practice of the emperor himself, whose motivation is described in the inscription:

The Imperial Highness, revering Virtue and exalting the Way, Ingesting the vast radiance, contemplating his spirits and nourishing his form, He set his intention on ascending to the clouds. He therefore fixed his mind on the

Yellow Thearch and matched tallies with the High Ancestor. Seeing Laozi in his dream he revered and offered him worship.

Emperor Huan, therefore, did not revere Laozi as a cosmic god, but rather as a successful adept who had attained extra-human status through practice. The inscription clearly implies that the emperor was determined to attain such status and had begun practicing psycho-physical meditations based on *qi* circulation even before his encounter with Laozi in a dream. The dream was interpreted as a response to having already made some progress along the path – and a request for further aid from the accomplished adept and master, Laozi, to the determined neophyte, the emperor. To sum up, Laozi, even while his divine status as an embodiment of the Dao was becoming increasingly accepted, was portrayed in the imperially sponsored stele as an accomplished practitioner. Rather than emphasizing his descent into the human realm as did the *Scripture on Transformations of Laozi* and later hagiographies, the inscription emphasized his ascent into the heavens following a specific regimen of practice. Laozi was thus depicted as the ultimate model for practitioner and especially for the ultimate practitioner, the emperor.

Conclusion

The four inscriptions analyzed in this chapter demonstrate developments within the tradition of seekers of transcendence during the Han. While these developments may be traced through the four centuries of the Han, they are particularly apparent in the final decades of the second century when the four inscriptions studied above were all erected. These inscriptions show the transformation of the individual quest for transcendence into wide-ranging cultic and communal practices. Sites associated with successful practitioners became foci of local, regional, and trans-regional cults. This transformation may be partly explained by popular perceptions of the successful adepts, who came to be revered for their efficacious aid in healing, weather and crop management, and miraculous interventions. Thus, despite the individual focus of the practice and the esoteric means by which these practices were transmitted, successful adepts became known to the public, which sought their grace outside the narrowly defined lineages and without entering into the master–disciple relationships required within the lineages. These developments eventually led to the establishment of the Daoist lineages, which based much of their ritual programs on the earlier practices of the seekers of transcendence, synthesizing them into complex integrated systems.

The best example for the early personal quest may be the Inaugural Emperor of Qin, whose administrative and ritual system was based upon the cosmological speculations of Zou Yan and who, under the influence of Masters of Esoterica from the coast, was personally devoted to the quest of transcendence. The same type of quest is evident in the Fei Zhi inscription, which suggests how the small localized family-based lineages may have been organized. By the late second century, as the three other inscriptions demonstrate, shrines to individual adepts had become foci of communal cultic practice. While the particular developments of each cult may be impossible to examine with any detail in the present state of our knowledge, the references within the Tang Gongfang and Wangzi Qiao inscriptions to earlier forms of cultic practice attest to the historical developments of these cults. The deification process of the adepts evident in the three inscriptions also demonstrates that the Laozi Inscription does not mark a unique development. While Laozi may have been perceived as the greatest of the Masters, his deification, and eventual identification with the Dao itself, must be seen within the context of the deification of other Masters of Esoterica and as part of the same spectrum.

If communal practice was an intrinsic development within the *fangshi* lineages, what, then, marks Daoism as different from these earlier lineages? I suggest that the major distinction is in the systematization of the earlier practices into large coherent systems, subsuming the practitioners into organized pantheons and reformulating the narratives of transmission into integrated mythical narratives. I examined these issues by following two lines of development.

I have shown that many of the individual adepts mentioned in early sources, including the *Liexian zhuan*, official histories and the inscriptions were subsumed into far larger narratives written by various Daoist lineages. While this co-optation is easy to demonstrate, the actual process and its implications are complicated by our lack of understanding of the actual relationships between specific lineages and texts preserved in the Daozang. We can, at best, only speculate about this process and the reasons for the selection and emplacement of particular figures in the larger narratives and pantheons.

Nevertheless, the main lineaments of the process are clear and may serve to help us distinguish Daoism from the earlier lineages. The *fangshi* lineages tended to be focused on a single adept, and his or, more rarely, her particular skills and abilities. Even when a lineage of transmission was provided, it served to focus on the individual adept rather than to pull him into a larger framework. The opposite process is at work in the Daoist narratives. The individual adepts are mentioned more as proof for the efficacy of practices and are always placed within the context of a large set of interacting lineages – a totalistic framework is evident.

Paralleling the narratological process was another process, which placed the diverse practices within a hierarchy of attainment. This process can be further elaborated by comparing the discourse of transcendence in the four inscriptions to the discourse in later Daoist texts. It is unclear whether the term "terrestrial transcendent" in the Fei Zhi inscription already has the meaning it acquired in Daoist texts, and whether this usage implies that a hierarchical conception of transcendence was at play in the discourse shared by the inscription. However, I argue that as Dawu gong, who is labeled "terrestrial transcendent" and Fei Zhi, who is labeled Perfected, are in fact the same person, then these labels do not imply hierarchy. In later Daoist texts, which explicitly placed these earlier practices within a hierarchy of attainment, we find that the terms "release by means of a corpse" and "terrestrial transcendence" signify lower levels of attainment.

It was therefore in organic developments within the lineages of the Masters of Esoterica that Daoist religion emerged. As the prestige of individual practitioners transformed them from masters of local lineages of practice into regional foci of reverence, the individual particulars were subsumed within increasingly formulaic depictions. As an individual adept was credited with greater numinous power, more complex narratives were constructed to depict his abilities. Paradoxically, this process led to a diminishing of the individual's personality. The original local lore of the transcendent was often lost within the grand narratives – sometimes to reappear in minor posts in the Daoist pantheons.

2 Blood rites and pure covenants

A pure retreat [causes the] descent of the five thearchs,
[For a] Myriad years [you] can be constant and complete.
In cinnabar and azure (*danqing* 丹青) draw up an oath of trust,
In five-eight, it will be revealed only once.
A wild goose (*honglu* 鴻鷺) with thousand-year old feathers,
Use it to summon the celestial Perfected.[1]

Daoist lineages defined themselves through proper textual transmission. Transmission functioned both ritually and rhetorically to create and maintain the self-identity of a lineage. Lineage construction was one of the primary strategies by which Daoist lineages distinguished themselves from each other, as well as from other lineages of practice. Ritual transmission of texts and practices is so significant in Daoism, that, following Strickmann, I include it among the criteria for defining Daoism.

Transmission based lineages, however, were not unique to Daoism, nor were they a Daoist innovation. Rather, lineage based traditions were a feature of classicist traditions such as the Ru and Mohists.[2] As we saw in the previous chapter, lineage was also a central feature of *fangshi* discourse. Proper transmission of a teaching, either textual or oral, was a primary determinant of the self-definition of lineages, and underlay the later retroactive constructions of schools and traditions.

---

1 *Array of the Five Talismans* DZ 388: 3.3a10–3b4.
2 Recent studies of the so-called Han schools show that these were retroactive constructions and reflect more on late Han and post Han idealized views of textual transmission than on the social realities of late Warring States and early Han. These new insights concerning Classicist schools do not invalidate my argument. Rather, they raise the intriguing question whether the textual ordination as a determinant feature of a tradition was modeled on the *fangshi* lineages. See Mark Csikszentmihàlyi, "Traditional Taxonomies and Revealed Texts in the Han," in Livia Kohn and Harold David Roth, eds. *Daoist Identity: History, Lineage, and Ritual* (Honolulu: Hawaii University Press, 2001): 81–101; Csikszentmihàlyi and Nylan, "Constructing"; Smith, "Sima Tan"; Nathan Sivin, "Drawing Insights from Chinese Medicine" *Journal of Chinese Philosophy* 34 (2007): 43–55.

Rather than schools and traditions, in my analysis I use the more delimited term "lineage of practice" to describe the community formed between a master and a disciple, and subsequent disciples, through rites of initiation in which specific teachings are transmitted. The relationship between the master as transmitter and disciple as recipient, who in turn becomes the transmitter to the next generation, was conceived as providing authority and legitimacy for a particular teaching. It was the legitimacy of properly conferred teachings that assured that the practices would be efficacious, and thus provided the lineage with its own power and authority. The authority of a teaching, therefore, lay in its pedigree and its claim to antiquity.

My use of the term "lineage" relies on the definition developed by James Watson in his studies of different kinship units. "A lineage is a *corporation* in the sense that members derive benefits from jointly-owned property and shared resources... Furthermore, members of a lineage are highly conscious of themselves as a group in relation to others whom they define as outsiders".[3] Lineages are further defined as possessing collective assets vested in the group. By wielding these assets the lineage gains power and status in society. Watson's definition refers to economic assets belonging to extended kinship units. However, I believe lineage is an apt term of description for the lineages of *fangshi* and Daoists if we consider collective assets to include intellectual capital such as the technical knowledge of the *fangshi* or the ritual prowess of the Daoists, which was transmitted within groups structured by master-disciple relationships, and if we consider the self-perception of particular groups of *fangshi* or Daoists.

Proper textual transmission does more than ensure that the esoteric practices inscribed in the text are protected from the profane. The rhetoric of the ritual asserts that the transmission of the practice has always been limited and protected. Ritual transmission simultaneously confers the status of the ancient pedigree on the initiate while ensuring the antiquity and purity of the teaching. The rite of transmission therefore functions as the essential defining strategy of a lineage within which a particular text or practice was transmitted.

The importance of transmission rites in medieval Daoism may be exemplified by the verse opening this chapter. This incantation from the *Array of the Five Lingbao Talismans* is a poetic abstract of the transmission rite of the Lingbao Talismans. The verse is followed by complete and detailed instructions for the ritual, along with a commentary. The significance of this ritual is threefold. First, this is the earliest record of a Daoist "offering" ritual (*jiao* 醮), which was a major inspiration for Daoist ritual since the medieval era. The basic structure and symbolism of this rite remain at the core of Daoist ritual today. Second, and perhaps more pertinent for our purpose, the instructions and commentary reveal the complex ways in which the ancient rite of blood sacrifice, of a wild goose in this case, was recast into a bloodless Daoist rite. Third, it is very significant that the earliest

3   Patricia B. Ebrey and James L. Watson, eds. *Kinship Organization in Late Imperial China 1000–1940* (Berkeley: University of California Press, 1986): 5.

record of a *jiao* rite is in fact a transmission ritual, that of the five *Lingbao* talismans and associated texts. In other words, the main purpose of the ritual inscribed in the text is the proper transmission of the text itself by which the lineage that produced the text ensured its own continuity. The proper transmission of the text thus functions as the essential definition of the lineage.

Appended to the verse is an anonymous commentary, which, intriguingly, presents an entirely different understanding of the ritual procedure:

> Ling had in the past received this [scripture] from the Little Lad of the Eastern Sea, who led him to tear a piece of "Southern Harmonious Cinnabar Silk," five foot long, which served as a mark of fidelity and he thereby received this [scripture]. He cut a piece of "Emerald Grove Silk," five foot long, which served as a covenant for not divulging it. "Southern harmony" means red, "emerald grove" means green. The ancients valued hair and skin hence they used pearls and jade in order to cherish (*qin* 親) them, they revered the four limbs, so they enveloped them in silk as a dwelling. Reverence for the Way and Virtue and protection of the body gods – these are the teachings of the transcendent officials.[4]

The major difference between the verse and the commentary is that in the former the major act of sealing fealty is sacrifice of a goose. While the verse also mentions colored silks, the symbolic value of these silks is unclear. In the commentary, the colored silks are defined as replacing bloody rites of fealty. These differences in ritual procedure and understanding reflect changes in transmission rites, which in turn reflect a major transition in the history of Chinese religion. The rejection of blood rites is a major mark for distinguishing Daoism from traditional Chinese religious practice.

In this chapter, I examine different notions of lineage in medieval China, with a particular focus on the process of lineage construction and its role in the emergence of Daoism. In the first part of the chapter, I explore the distinction between Daoist and non-Daoist initiation rites by tracing the transition from blood oaths to "pure" initiation rites. I argue that the critical difference between non-Daoist and Daoist lineages is the use of blood oaths in the former and its rejection by the latter. This distinction is closely related to the Daoist rejection of blood sacrifice, which was central to Chinese traditional religious practice. I begin by examining the discourse and practices of transmission in a biography of an early Han physician, and show that similar practices were reported by Ge Hong five centuries later. I then note the transition in Daoist initiation rites from blood oaths to bloodless rites of transmission, and finally to the development of schemes of textual initiations that came to define Daoism. These bloodless rites of textual transmission are one of the distinguishing marks of Daoism.

---

4   DZ 388: 3.3a10–3b2.

In the second part of the chapter, I examine the narratives of transmission given in the *Array of the Five Talismans*. First, I explore the main lineage associated with the Five Talismans by tracing the short notes appended to the various texts, practices, and instructions in the text. These notes state the origins and, often, the lineage which transmitted the specific practice. These short notices are the primary units by which the redactor or compiler of the *Array* constructed this particular tradition. By tracing the lineage constructed in the text, I show the process by which the compilers asserted their authority by claiming certain pedigrees for their preferred practices. Assuming that the compilers of the text wished their audience to imagine a particular filiation for the practices advocated in the text, references to different lineages associated with specific practices allows us to trace rivalries and debates within the emerging tradition. Authors and compilers thus retroactively constructed transmission lineages and traditions that linked their specific master-disciple lineages with larger "imagined communities" that extend to ancient sages, less remote significant masters, and status-laden names. I analyze this "imagined community" by exploring the significance of the individuals who appear in the lineage.

I then turn to examine transmission narratives of the Five Talismans in various Daoist sources. These references show that there were at least two versions of this text circulating among the same group of families. Tracing the precise filiation of the two versions of the text not only demonstrates the secrecy by which textual transmission proceeded, but also allows us to explore the actual social reality of several Daoist lineages, including some affiliated with Celestial Master Daoism, Shangqing Daoism, and others for which we have only obscure textual hints.

I   The *Fangshi* model of transmission

The Daoist discourse of lineage developed from the practices of the Masters of Esoterica of the Han dynasty. The esoteric teachings of these traditions were transmitted through strict initiation rites which formed closely defined lineages of practice. In these traditions, the master–disciple relationship was idealized as a father–son bond. Transmission rites required vows of secrecy and bloodletting. This, I argue, functioned to actualize the metaphoric familial bond and shift it from a metaphor to reality. For a glimpse into the discourse and practices of the *fangshi* our analysis of transmission rites and lineage construction begins with the *Shiji* account of Chunyu Yi's 淳于意 (216–c. 150 BCE) reception of medical knowledge.[5]

---

5   *Shiji* 105.2794–2820. Analyzed (with a partial translation) in Harper, *Early Medical Literature*, 55–67; Nathan Sivin, "Text and Experience in Classical Chinese Medicine," in Don Bates, ed. *Knowledge and the Scholarly Medical Traditions* (Cambridge: Cambridge University Press, 1995): 177–204.

Chunyu Yi first studied with Gongsun Guang 公孫光. After several years, Gongsun Guang informed Chunyu Yi that his knowledge was exhausted and suggested that Yi seek further training with Yang Qing 陽慶, whose knowledge was far more profound. Gongsun Guang himself had earlier sought Yang Qing's teachings only to be told he was "the wrong person" (*fei qiren* 非其人). Gongsun Guang concluded by saying: "He will surely recognize your delight in recipes." Chunyu Yi was indeed accepted by Yang Qing and received his teachings.

The first thing to note is the theme of recognition – the master identifies the disciple, who is qualitatively different from other potential recipients of the teachings. This theme is reinforced by the metaphor embedded in Sima Qian's laconic summary of Chunyu Yi's receipt of the teachings: "[Yang] Qing was over seventy years old and without sons. He ordered Yi to completely rid himself of the old methods. He then presented Chunyu Yi with all his restricted methods (*jinfang* 禁方)."[6] But, Yang Qing did have sons. In fact, it was through his son Yin that Chunyu Yi was introduced to him. What, then, does Sima Qian mean by stating "he was without sons"?

We should here recall Yang Qing's admonishment to Chunyu Yi: "Beware not to let my sons and grandsons know that you are studying my methods."[7] Clearly, in this passage "son" refers to the "right person," the one destined to receive the full teachings. The rhetoric of these passages implies that the expected transmission was father to son, and that the master–disciple relationship is modeled upon this hereditary filiation.

We should also note that Chunyu Yi considered the teachings he received from both of his teachers as "restricted methods." Both teachers had warned him not to divulge the teachings, and we have Chunyu Yi's reply to Gongsun Guang: "To have had the opportunity to see and serve you, and to have received your restricted methods, was fortunate indeed. Till death I would not dare to recklessly transmit them to others."[8] I agree with Donald Harper's suggestion that this sentence may well be a formulaic vow of secrecy that accompanied the rite of transmission. Although Chunyu Yi does not specify how the transmission proceeded and whether any special ritual means were required, we can get a glimpse of these procedures by examining the connotations of the term "restricted methods."[9]

The term "restricted methods" appears in Bian Que's 扁鵲 biography, which precedes Chunyu Yi's biography and is possibly a model for it. Having recognized that Bian Que is "not a common person" (*fei changren* 非常人), Lord Changsang 常桑君 tells him: "I possess restricted methods. I am old and wish to transmit them to you. You must not leak them." Bian Que responds "I respectfully accept." However fictitious this narrative may be, this exchange is probably representative

6 *Shiji* 105.2794.
7 *Shiji* 105.2815.
8 *Shiji* 105.2796.
9 Much of the following is based on Li Jianmin 李建民, "Zhongguo gudai 'jinfang' kaolun" 中國古代 "禁方" 考論 *BIHP* 68 (1997): 117–57.

of the actual formulaic exchanges between masters and disciples in the *fangshi* lineages.

Lord Changsang gives Bian Que a drug, saying "ingest this with unsullied water and after thirty days you will recognize anomalies." After presenting Bian Que with writings containing his "restricted methods," Lord Changsang disappears, evidence that he was not a regular human. After 30 days, Bian Que is indeed able to gaze into the internal organs of a patient and see the knots within and to examine the *qi* vessels.[10]

In this hagiographic narrative, we find again the themes of recognition and secrecy. Moreover, although Bian Que's teacher is not human, and the methods he transmits are presumably beyond those found in the mundane world, the teachings are textual. The textual transmission is accompanied by a practice that transforms the physician physically, providing him with new powers of perception and recognition beyond those of regular healers. Little wonder, then, that among the methods received by Chunyu Yi is *Bian Que's Writings on [qi] Vessels*. It is also clear from this passage that the term "restricted methods" did not refer to specific practices as much as to highly guarded teachings, including theoretical schemata, such as the vessel theory and the procedures for examining pulse. How then did physicians and other *fangshi* transmit their secrets?

Secrecy and proper rites of initiation are described in the *Esoteric Scripture of the Yellow Thearch* (*Huangdi neijing* 黃帝內經), a key text among medical practitioners since the Han dynasty.[11] In the words of the Yellow Thearch: "to obtain the correct person and not to instruct him, this is called 'losing the Way'; to transmit [teachings] to the wrong person is to wantonly leak celestial treasures." Qi Bo, the Yellow Thearch's instructor, responds that "without observing purification and restrictions, you cannot proceed. Beware in transmitting this".[12] The text includes several references to procedures for initiation rites, including ritual purification, selecting auspicious dates, secreting the text in special containers, and setting up sacred precincts for the rites.[13] Details of the most important procedure are given in another passage, which describes the Yellow Thearch's transmission of vessel theory and acupuncture to Thunder Sire (*Leigong* 雷公):

> The Yellow Thearch said: "This has been restricted by my former masters. To personally transmit this requires an oath of slicing the forearm and smearing the blood on the mouth (*gejian shaxue zhimeng* 割臂歃血之盟). If you wish to obtain this, would you not proceed and purify?"… After dwelling in purification for three days, Thunder Sire inquired: "I dare ask, as it is a day of

10 *Shiji* 105.2785.
11 See Nathan Sivin in Loewe, ed. *Early Chinese Texts* 196–215; Yamada Keiji, "The Formation of the Huang-ti nei-ching," *Acta Asiatica* 36 (1979): 67–89; Harper, "Warring States," 823, 875–79.
12 *Suwen* 69, 20.1b: 得其人不教, 是謂失道; 傳非其人, 慢泄天寶…非齋戒不能發, 慎傳也. Partly cited in Harper, *Early*, 63; a fuller citation in Li Jianmin, "Zhongguo," 129.
13 See references in Li Jianmin, "Zhongguo," 129–37.

Upright Yang (*zhengyang* 正陽), your little son wishes to receive the oath."
The Yellow Thearch then entered the purification chamber with him. They
cut their forearms and smeared their mouths with blood. The Yellow Thearch
personally recited an incantation: "Today is a day of Upright Yang, smearing
the blood I transmit the methods. If you dare turn your back on these words
misfortune will in turn fall upon you." Thunder Sire bowed twice and
responded: "Your little son receives them." The Yellow Thearch then grasped
him with his left hand and with his right hand presented him with the writings, saying: "Beware, beware, I will tell you about them."[14]

Blood oaths such as this were the core procedure at the initiation rites of pre
Han and Han era physicians and other *fangshi*, and they were the basis for the
Daoist rites of initiation and transmission. Daoist lineages, however, condemned
the shedding of blood and hence reformulated these rites accordingly. As we
will see below, while the ritual procedure of the *Five Talismans* was written
within the context of such blood oaths, the commentary attached to the ritual
instructions rejects the blood rite. This tension between instructions and commentary is among the earliest evidence we have for the shift away from blood rites as
an oath of fealty.

In studying the social context of physicians, Donald Harper also examined
Chunyu Yi's biography.[15] His conclusion is that there is little evidence for institutional lineages: "Three men [Chunyu Yi, Gongsun Guang, and Yang Qing] – not
one a hereditary physician, not one identified with a specific lineage of texts or
teachers extending over several generations." While I agree with Harper that there
is "little evidence… of a larger organization binding physicians into exclusive
brotherhoods,"[16] I suggest that seeking such a large institutional base is simply
anachronistic. Mark Csikszentmihàlyi and Michael Nylan show that the presence
of philosophical schools in Warring States and early Han is based on misreading
notices in the *Shiji* and the *Hanshu*. The "schools" were retroactive constructions
of lineages and traditions. Our acceptance of these schools is an anachronistic
imposition of Eastern Han and post-Han concerns onto the earlier periods.[17]
Although Csikszentmihàlyi and Nylan restrict their argument to the so-called
philosophical schools, I believe their conclusions are also apt for the *fangshi* lineages. However, I argue that the absence of large "schools" and institutionalized
traditions does not preclude the existence of numerous small lineages. The shared
discourse of these disparate lineages, who shared terminology, practices, and
maybe most importantly, mythical ascriptions of textual origins, may mislead us
into assuming wide membership in multi-generational brotherhoods – but we

---

14 *Lingshu* 48, 8.1a–b, partly cited in Harper, *Early*, 63. A fuller citation in Li Jianmin, "Zhongguo," 133.
15 Harper, *Early*, 57–67.
16 Ibid, 60.
17 Csikszentmihàlyi and Nylan "Constructing lineages."

should remember, as we saw in Chapter 1, that shared discourse does not necessarily indicate unified groupings.

Chunyu Yi had received "restricted methods" from two teachers. His acceptance of Yang Qing's as superior indicates that there was an implicit hierarchy of methods among practitioners. Chunyu Yi does not provide any systematic criteria for evaluating his respective teachers' methods, nor does he specify what the respective content of the teachings was, how they differed, and how their relative status was evaluated. However formulaic the vow of secrecy may have been, it indicates these methods were indeed restricted and that the transmission of practices between master and disciple implied an exclusive relationship modeled upon the father-son relationship. Despite this exclusivity, a disciple could receive teachings from more than one master, while a teacher could transmit his teachings to more than one disciple. We have no indication what the relationship was among the disciples of the same teacher. A lineage thus was defined vertically, that is, master to disciple, but not necessarily horizontally, among disciples.

II   Blood oaths in Ge Hong's *Baopuzi*

We may compare Chunyu Yi's learning process with Ge Hong's description of his apprenticeship with Zheng Yin, some five centuries later.[18] One of many disciples, Ge Hong claims to have been the only one to have received many of his teacher's texts. As apprentices, all worked in simple menial jobs. Ge Hong distinguished himself by his skill in writing, and was recognized as "teachable" (*kejiao* 可教). Other disciples did not receive the teachings he did. Once again, we find that the vertical link between master and disciple is of crucial importance, while there is little, if any, value to the horizontal links between disciples. Like Chunyu Yi, Ge Hong also had at least one more instructor, Bao Jing 鮑靚 (260–330?), his father-in-law, from whom he received further teachings. Stressing the importance of proper transmission of practices and the importance of the teacher, Ge Hong's view of proper initiation and receipt of longevity practices remained the same as that of the early *fangshi*:

> The greatest virtue of heaven and earth is called life, life cherishes things (*sheng haowuzhe ye* 生好物者也).[19] That is why of the things held in deepest

---

18 My summary follows BPZ 19.331–2.
19 I find Ware's translation "[life] embodies love for creation" unwarranted. This sentence is based on a passage in the *Zuozhuan*, Shao 25, which elaborates on the crucial importance of proper ritual.

> Joy is produced by pleasure, anger is produced by hatred. Therefore, [the sages] examined their conduct and were sincere in their commands, [adjudicating] misfortune and fortune, rewards and punishments and thereby managing life and death. Life is a good thing. Death is a bad thing.

喜生於好怒生於惡, 是故審行信令, 禍福賞罰, 以制生死. 生好物也, 死惡物也 (James Legge, *The Ch'un Ts'ew, with the Tso chuen in The Chinese classics*; rpt. (Taipei, Republic of China: Southern Materials Center, 1985): 704, translation on 708).

secrecy and cherished by Daoist practitioners (*daojia* 道家), none surpass the methods of longevity. Therefore, only after a blood oath (*xuemeng* 血盟) can they be transmitted. Transmission to the wrong person will be penalized by a celestial punishment.[20]

We should note here the rhetoric of secrecy, recognition of the disciple, proper ritual procedure for transmission, and punishment for improper transmission. We had seen these ideas in Chunyu Yi's biography and we will revisit them below. As in the case of Chunyu Yi and the ritual procedure for transmitting medical knowledge, the transmission of esoteric practices also required a blood oath and proffering a gift. I suggest that the blood marked a bond between master and disciple, which transformed their relationship into a filial modality.

Ge Hong reported that blood rites were also necessary for the transmission of the *Writ of the Three Sovereigns* (*Sanhuang wen* 三皇文) and *Charts of the Perfected Forms of the Five Marchmounts* (*Wuyue zhenxing tu* 五嶽真形圖), the most efficacious talismanic texts in his possession:

> Among writings about Dao none surpass in importance the *Charts of the Perfected Forms of the Five Marchmounts* and the *Inner Writ of the Three Sovereigns* (*Sanhuang wen* 三皇內文). Anciently, the most accomplished of the transcendent officials reverently hid these methods. None but those named as transcendents can receive them. They are transmitted once in forty years. Transmission requires smearing the lips with blood as a covenant and proffering a gift. These writs are within all famed mountains and the five Peaks, but they are hidden in stone chambers within the dark earth. When one who has attained the Dao enters a mountain and contemplates them with intense concentration, then in response the mountain gods open the mountain and allow the adept to see these texts. For example, when Bo Zhongli 帛仲理 would obtain such a text in a mountain, he would erect an altar and offer silk. He would regularly make one copy and then retire. If you have this writ, always place it in a pure clean place. Whenever you are about to do something you should plainly announce it to the writ, revering it as you would a lord or father. The scripture says: "A house which possesses the *Writ of the Three Sovereigns* would avoid deviant and evil ghosts, noxious miasmas, and flying harmers."[21]

While the use of blood for sealing an oath is clear enough, we should note that the term used for proffering a gift (*weizhi* 委質) in the context of the *Charts of the Perfected Forms of the Five Marchmounts*, and the *Writ of the Three Sovereigns* probably refers to sacrificing an animal as pledge. The term literally means "offering a dead body" and refers to an ancient ritual practice in which an official upon

---

20 BPZ 14.1a; Wang, *Baopuzi*, 252; Ware, *Alchemy*, 226.
21 BPZ 19. 8a6–8; Wang, *Baopuzi*, 19.336; Ware, *Alchemy*, 226; Campany, *To Live*, 136.

his first appointment would inscribe his name on a plaque and present the corpse of a sacrificial victim to the lord, swearing that if he were to waver he would be punishable by death.[22] This symbolic rite of absolute submission to the ruler was employed by the *fangshi* lineages as the rite of transmission. We should note, however, that Bo Zhongli does not receive the text from a master. Rather, the text is revealed inside a cave. Nevertheless, Bo Zhongli performs the proper ritual. This narrative suggests that the ritual is designed to signify that one is authorized to receive and possess the text. Indeed, it may be that the ritual activates the efficacy of the text.

Ge Hong reported that he received this text, along with the *Charts of the True Forms of the Five Marchmounts*, from his teacher Zheng Yin, who had received them from Ge Xuan. Ge Hong received a second variant of this text in 301 from Bao Jing 鮑靚 (260–330?), his father-in-law and teacher, who obtained this text while meditating in a "stone chamber" on Mt. Song'gao.[23] The narrative exemplifies the importance of ritual oath of transmission even in the case of revealed texts:

> In the second day, of the second month, of the second year of the *yuankang* reign (292), Bao Jing ascended Mt. Song'gao 嵩高山 and entered a stone chamber, where he sat in pure retreat 清齋. Suddenly, he saw the *Ancient Writ of the Three Sovereigns*, the graphs formed by the cracks on the rocks. As at that time he did not have a master, he presented four-hundred feet of silk as a faith offering, in accord with the regulations, and made an oath to himself 自盟. He later transmitted this text to Ge Hong.[24]

The *Writ of the Three Sovereigns* is revealed to Bao Jing after an intense period of meditation. The text literally emerges out of the natural patterns on the rock. Although it is a revealed text and not transmitted by a master, Bao Jing is still required to follow the proper ritual protocol. He therefore presents a faith offering and swears an oath, albeit to himself.

Rites of transmission involving blood oaths were required for receiving the teachings of the alchemical methods which Ge Hong valued most. The transmission rite for the *Yellow Thearch's Scripture of Divine Cinnabar of the Nine Cauldrons* (*Huangdi jiuding shendan jing* 黃帝九鼎神丹經) required that "golden figurines of human and fish be tossed into an east flowing stream as a

---

22 The *locus classicus* is *Zuozhuan*, Xi 23 (Legge 184), which is cited in the notes for *Shiji*, "Arrayed Biographies of Confucius' Disciples" (*Zhongni dizi liezhan*): "Anciently, when first taking office, one needed to first inscribe one's name on a tablet, and offer a dead animal to the lord, indicating that one pledged one's life to the lord" (*SJ* 67.2191: 古者始仕, 必先書其名於策, 委死之質於君, 然後為臣, 示必死節於其君也). Mark E. Lewis, *Writing and Authority in Early China* (Albany: SUNY Press, 1999): 19 refers to examples of the term *zhi* in the Houma 侯馬 covenant texts.

23 YJQQ DZ 1032: 4.10b–11a.

24 YJQQ DZ 1032: 4.10b–11a, 6.5b7–9, 11b9–12a2.

contract, and the lips be smeared with blood as a covenant; one without the bones of a spiritual transcendent can never get to see this method."[25] The transmission of the *Scripture of the Golden Liquor* required: "Throw a golden human figurine, weighing eight ounces, into an east flowing stream. After drinking blood as an oath you may receive the oral instructions."[26] The instructions mentioned by Ge Hong are found in the extant versions of the alchemical texts preserved in the Daozang.[27]

The references in Ge Hong to blood oaths in the transmission of alchemical texts may be compared to the transmission rite prescribed in an alchemical text *Essential Instructions of the Scripture of Transmuted Cinnabar*, probably dating to the fifth century:

> To transmit the Divine Cinnabar Scripture and Instructions requires a binding ritual and contractual oath. The disciple is to offer a golden figurine of a fish and a dragon-shaped jade ring as pledges. These offerings replace the ritual oaths requiring cutting hair and smearing the mouth with blood.[28]

> 傳受神經丹訣, 皆約齋盟誓, 用金魚八兩, 玉龍, 偃鐶, 以代剪髮歃血之誓.

This passage exemplifies the shift away from blood oaths, revealing one of the key changes made by Daoists as they adopted and adapted various practices. Significantly, this text explicitly states that the golden figurines replace the blood oath, indicating that the intended audience for this alchemical text would have expected a blood rite – but this has now been replaced.

To place this shift in context, I first consider the rejection of blood rites in the ritual system of Celestial Master Daoism. I then turn to a detailed examination of the transmission ritual of the Five Lingbao Talismans, which is not only the earliest example of *jiao* rite, but also exemplifies the transition from blood rites to pure covenants.

III   Rejection of blood rites in the way of the Celestial Master

Celestial Master Daoism condemned sacrificial ritual, claiming that only the

25 BPZ DZ 1185: 4.6a8–6b5; Wang, *Baopuzi*, 74; Ware, *Alchemy*, 75.
26 BPZ DZ 1185: 4.17a4–5; Wang, *Baopuzi*, 83; Ware, *Alchemy*, 83.
27 The first chapter of *Huangdi jiuding shendan jingjue* 黃帝九鼎神丹經訣 DZ 885 is closely related to the Nine Cauldrons seen by Ge Hong. Full translation in Fabrizio Pregadio, *Great Clarity: Daoism and Alchemy in Early Medieval China* (Stanford: Stanford University Press, 2006): 159–92.
28 *Taiji zhenren jiuzhuan huandan jing yaojue* 太極真人九轉還丹經要訣 DZ 889.5a. The text dates to the late Six Dynasties; Schipper and Verellen, *Taoist Canon*, 102; Robinet, *Révélation*, vol. 2, 389–98; Strickmann, "Tao Hung-ching," 147–50. Fabrizio Pregadio, *Great Clarity*, 192–200, provides a full translation.

deviant spirits of dead generals and warriors required such bloody offerings.[29] The pure emanations of the Dao did not eat nor drink the physical remains of animals, but rather feasted upon the insubstantial vapors released by "pure offerings," namely rice. The late second century *Xiang'er Commentary to the Laozi* is very clear on this point:

> The correct law of heaven does not reside in offering foodstuffs and praying at ancestral temples. The Dao therefore forbids these acts and provides heavy penalties for them. Sacrifices and food are means for communication with deviant forces. Hence, even if there is "excess food" or implements, Daoists must never employ or eat of them ... Those who possess the Dao will not dwell where there are offerings of sacrifice and praying at ancestral shrines.[30]

The ritual system of the early Celestial Master community was established in direct contrast to the prevailing sacrificial system of the imperial and ancestral rites. Styling itself the Covenantal Authority of Correct Unity (*zhengyi mengwei*), the texts of Celestial Master Daoism defined its *raison d'etre* as the eradication of the false practices pervading the realm. Chief among these practices were indeed the blood sacrifices offered at the various local shrines, ancestral shrines, temples to local deities, and on the imperial altars. Gods who demanded flesh and blood offerings were deemed false. Not only were they not efficacious, but their rapacious demands brought more harm on the populace.[31] Lu Xiujing's *Abridged Codes* are particularly clear on this point:

> The cosmic order lost its balance, and men and demons mingled chaotically. The stale vapors of the Six Heavens took on official titles and appellations and brought together the hundred sprites and the demons of the five kinds of wounding, dead generals of defeated armies, and dead troops of scattered armies. The men called themselves "generals"; the women called themselves "Ladies".... They arrogated to themselves authority and the power to dispense blessings. They took over people's temples and sought their sacrificial offerings thus upsetting the people, who killed the three kinds of sacrificial animals, used up all their resources, cast away all heir goods, and exhausted their produce. They were not blessed with good fortune but rather received disaster.[32]

---

29 For an excellent survey of the history of sacrifice in traditional China and the complex interaction between imperial, Daoist and Buddhist attitudes to sacrificial rites, see Terry F. Kleeman, "Licentious Cults and Bloody Victuals: Sacrifice, Reciprocity, and Violence in Traditional China," *Asia Major*, Ser. 3, 7 (1994): 185–211.
30 *Laozi xiang'er zhu* S 6825 lines 374–77; Ōfuchi, *Tonkō dōkyō zurokuhen*, 429; Bokenkamp, *Early*, 119–20.
31 Rolf Stein, "Religious Taoism," 53–81.
32 DZ 1127.1a; translation from Nickerson, "Abridged Codes," 352.

Most importantly, Celestial Master Daoism presented a completely new view of divinity and of the interaction between humans and deities. The true deities were not transformed humans, as in the imperial and local cults, and did not require the sustenance of flesh and blood. Moreover, the deities that populated the cosmos were perceived as a vast bureaucracy, and communication between human and spirits was modeled on the imperial bureaucracy.[33] The core ritual mode in Celestial Master liturgy was the submission of petitions addressed to the appropriate officials and bureaus in the cosmic bureaucracy.[34] The bureaucratic petitioning model of ritual was adopted by other Daoist lineages, and remains at the core of Daoist ritual today.

The Way of the Celestial Master was a communal religion, that is, whole families, and even communities, joined the ecclesia, which was organized into 24 parishes. Each member of the ecclesia was registered to a particular parish. The most important communal celebrations on the liturgical calendar were three annual gatherings at each parish center, where the members reported any deaths, births, and marriages to the libationer, so that the registers of the community were up to date. This aspect of the Celestial Master community was modeled on the imperial bureaucracy.

Another aspect of the community, however, was modeled on the lineages of individual practitioners. Each member of the community possessed a register (*lu* 籙) listing spirit-generals who protected the register holder against nefarious influences. These registers were transmitted in graded initiation rites. Children, boys and girls, received their first register, which listed a single spirit-general, at age seven. In later stages of initiation, initiates received registers of 10 and later of 75 generals. As was recently shown by Lü Pengzhi, these registers of spirit-generals were apparently gendered, with the generals on male registers labeled "transcendent" (*xian* 仙), and generals on female registers labeled "numinous" (*ling* 靈). The final initiation for most members of the community was a merging of the male and female registers, to attain a complete register of 150 generals. This is probably the basis for the famous, yet little understood, rite of merging *qi* (*heqi* 合氣), the sexual initiation ritual practiced by Celestial Masters initiates upon reaching adulthood.[35] I discuss this ritual in further detail in Chapter 4.

Transmission of registers (*shoulu* 授籙) became a defining mark of initiation and ordination in medieval Daoism, and was apparently not restricted to members

33 Ursula-Angelika Cedzich, "Das Ritual der Himmelmeister im Spiegel früher Quellen: Übersetzung und Untersuchung des liturgischen Materials im dritten *chüan* des *Teng-chen yin-chüeh*," Ph.D. Dissertation (Julius-Maximilians-Universität, Würzburg, 1987). Reviewed by Anna Seidel, "Early Taoist Ritual," *Cahiers d'Extrême-Asie* 4 (1988): 199–204.

34 Among the best exemplars are the dozens of petition forms preserved in *Chisong zi zhangli* 赤松子章歷 DZ 615; Franciscus Verellen, "The Heavenly Master Liturgical Agenda According to Chisong zi's Petition Almanac," *Cahiers d'Extrême-Asie* 14 (2004): 291–343.

35 Lü Pengzhi 呂鵬志, "Tianshi dao shoulu keyi – Dunhuang xieben S.203 kaolun" 天師道授籙科儀敦煌寫本考論, BIHP 77.1 (2006): 79–166; summarized in idem, Tangqian, 196–99. See also John Lagerwey, "Zhengyi Registers," *Institute of Chinese Studies Visiting Professor Lecture Series* (I), *Journal of Chinese Studies*, Special Issue (Chinese University of Hong Kong, 2005): 35–88.

of the Celestial Master community. Almost all emperors of the Northern Dynasties during the fifth and sixth centuries received registers from Daoist masters.[36]

Importantly, the transmission of Celestial Master registers, although similar to the transmission rites in the *fangshi* lineages, did not require blood oaths. The earliest record of a Celestial Master transmission ritual, which may indeed be the earliest extant record of the Celestial Master, is a fragmentary inscription dating to 173 CE:[37]

> Second year of the *xiping era* (173 CE), third month, first day. Hu Jiu [], demon soldier of the Celestial Elder, [announces]: you have followed the path to transcendence and your Dao is complete. Mystic [Heaven] has bestowed upon you an extended lifespan. The Orthodox and Unitary *qi* of the Dao have been distributed to your *hun*-soul and *qi*. It has been decided to summon the libationers Zhang Pu, Meng Sheng, Zhao Guang, Wang Sheng, Huang Chang and Yang Feng, to come and receive twelve scrolls of Subtle Scriptures. The Libationers pledge to spread the teachings of the Way of the Celestial Master without Limit!

> 熹平二年三月一日, 天 表鬼兵胡九 [ ][ ], 仙歷道成 , 玄施延 命, 道正一元 [氶], 布于伯(魂) 氣.[38] 定召祭酒張普, 萌生, 趙廣, 王盛, 黃長, 揚奉等, 詣 受微經十二卷. 祭酒約施天師道法無極才 [哉].

There is considerable debate regarding the identities of the deity Celestial Elder and of Hu Jiu, the figure making the announcement.[39] Hu Jiu's title demon soldier, however, resonates with the title "demon officers" given in the reports about the Way of the Five Bushels of Rice in the *Dianlüe* (see Introduction). More importantly, the inscription clearly refers to a transmission of twelve "subtle scriptures" to a group of libationers, who have "completed their Dao" and whose "soul and qi" are infused with the primordial *qi* of the Dao. The inscription does not hint at the actual ritual of transmission, but the final line is a ritual pledge (*yue* 約) to spread the teaching of the Way of the Celestial Master.

The main point for our purpose here is that the earliest record of the Celestial Master community concerns the ordination of libationers and transmission of texts. These texts are to be used in the further promulgation of the teachings.

36 Anna Seidel, "Imperial Treasures," Li Gang, "State Religious Policy," in John Lagerwey and Lü Pengzhi, eds. *Early Chinese Religion: the Period of Division (220–589 AD)* (Leiden: Brill, 2010), vol. 1, 193–274.

37 Preserved in *Lixu* 隸續 vol. 3, 309 (3/8a–b), which states that the inscription was originally located in Shu, but no specific location is given. Chen Yuan 陳垣, *Daojia jinshi lue* 道家金石略 (Beijing: Wenwu, 1988): 4. Long Xianzhao 龍顯昭 and Huang Haide 黃海德, eds. *Bashu daojiao beiwen jicheng* 巴蜀道教碑文集成 (Chengdu: Sichuan Daxue, 1997): 1.

38 Lü Pengzhi suggests the graph *bo* 伯 is a mistake for *po* 魄 and should be understood as hun 魂; Lü, *Tangqian*, 17 n.3.

39 Kleeman, *Great Perfection*, 69. Liu Yi argues this inscription is not related to the Celestial Master Zhang Daoist lineage, Liu Yi, *Jingtian*, 593–602.

Although fragmentary, this inscription indicates that the early community already had several ranks of initiation and ordination, and that rising in these ranks entailed textual transmission. Moreover, the transmission in this case links the libationers to the Celestial Elder, who is evidently a deity. The scriptural transmission thus binds the libationers to the celestial hierarchy, and thus presages the transmission rites of the Lingbao tradition to which I turn next.

IV   Transmission rite of the Five Talismans

We now return to our examination of the transmission rite in the *Array of Five Talismans*. Full instructions for this rite are given in the section "Ritual Instructions for a Sacrifice and Invocations" (*Jiaozhu zhi yi* 醮祝之儀) in the third *juan* of the *Array of the Five Talismans* immediately following the verse cited at the head of this chapter.[40] This ritual is a careful synthesis of several earlier unrelated practices: imperial ritual, sacrificial traditions, breath cultivation techniques, and the use of talismans. In the ritual the adept summons the Five Celestial Thearchs who dwell in the directional heavens. The Thearchs are summoned by arcane names that first appeared in the Han Weft texts, and which entailed a vision of the emperor as an embodiment of the epochal pneuma. The names of the directional heavens are based on a breathing cultivation practice entitled the Five Sprouts (*wuya* 五芽), in which the practitioner inhales the nascent pneumas of the five directions. Precise instructions for this practice, which was originally unrelated to the imperial tradition or the use of talismans, are provided in the *Zhenyi jing* section of the *Array*. Variants of the practice are mentioned in several medieval scriptures. I have elsewhere discussed the symbolic complex of this ritual and its relationship to debates on imperial ritual in medieval China.[41] My discussion here focuses on the offering of the goose and symbolism of the Cinnabar and Azure Oath, which are at the core of the rite.

The ritual was to be performed at midnight either indoors, in a meditation chamber (*jingshi* 靜室), or outside, on a temporary altar (*tingtan* 庭壇). Following a three day retreat for purification, the adept is to complete the following preparations: laying out five mats in accord with the five directions, with an incense burner placed by each; a plump white goose is sacrificed (*zai* 宰), and fine rice wine is presented. The wine is allowed to rest until it is clear of impurities. When limpid, the wine is poured into eleven cups arranged on pans. Next, the wine is poured from five of the cups onto the censer, so that the wine and smoke mingle. The remaining wine is poured into an amphora placed before the mats. After completing the wine oblations, the goose meat is placed in the pans, which are also placed before the mats. The use of wine and sacrificial meat coheres with ancient forms of *jiao* ritual.

---

40 DZ 388 3.3b9–7b3.

41 There are differences between the use of these names in the *Array* and their use in the Weft texts. I showed elsewhere that these differences reveal that the ritual in the *Array* was composed within the context of debates among imperial ritualists regarding the status of the emperor. For details, see Raz, "Imperial Efficacy." On the Five Sprouts, see Raz, *Creation*, 384–96.

Next, the five *Lingbao* talismans are placed between strips of cinnabar-red and green silk on their respective mats in accord with the five directions. Fruit is placed by each mat to enhance the efficacy of this faith offering. Incense of five fragrances is burnt.[42] Next the adept announces his presence and requests the descent of the Five Celestial Thearchs. The descent of the celestial spirits is only a preamble for the ascent of the adept's own corporeal spirits to the celestial courts. Modeled on official court audience, the incantations are formulaic and bureaucratic in style:

> I, the male disciple from A town in B county in C province,[43] who was born in D year, month and day and am so many years old, have received the Writ of the Highest Five Lingbao Talismans from Daoist master E of F commandery. In accord with the ritual instructions of the great Dao, I respectfully summon the Five Celestial Lords. I have purified myself in retreat for three days and have slaughtered a wild goose. I have cleansed and prepared the spirits of my body. Having emptied my heart, I greet the Superior Luminous Celestial Worthies.

In this first incantation the adept reiterates his preparatory actions. It is clear that the sacrifice of the wild goose is crucial for summoning the celestial deities. In the next incantation, the adept describes the externalization of his own bodily spirits who ascend to audience in the five directional heavens and requests that the celestial deities deign to descend and enjoy the offerings:

> My three cloud-souls and seven white-souls and the perfected of three bodily palaces ascend to the palaces of the nine heavens and the domains of Five Exterior regions: to the heaven of Green Sprouts (*qingya* 青芽), the Ruby-cinnabar (*zhudan* 朱丹) heaven, to the Central Yellow heaven in the mountain of the Great Emperor 太帝之山中黃之天, to the Bright Stone (*mingshi* 明石) heaven, and to the heaven of Dark Shoots (*xuanzi* 玄滋); to the heavens of the eight directions and the courts of the Five Thearchs and of the Perfected. There [my bodily spirits] will fully describe and announce the purification [and request the celestial deities] to descend temporarily to my village, in so-and-so county, in so-and-so province, to approach with their pneumas the

42   "Five fragrances" (*wuxiang* 五香) usually refers to a combination of five aromatic herbs burnt together. There are several different lists of ingredients. Several lists are presented in *Yunji qiqian*. For example, one list, which provides the efficacy of each specific ingredient, includes angelica root (*baizhi* 白芷) which expels the three worms, bark of peach wood (*taopi* 桃皮) which blocks noxious pneumas, biota leaf (*boye* 柏葉) which causes the descent of the perfected, *Lysimachia foenum-graecum* (*lingling* 零陵) which gathers the numinous sages, and root of aristolochia (*qingmu* 青木) which eradicates contamination (DZ 1032: 41.5b10). Other lists include sweet basil, cherry blossoms, melilot, costus root, and sandalwood, based on DZ 1032: 41.3b (translated in Bokenkamp, *Early*, 358 n†) and DZ 1032: 41.4a.

43   The formulaic and bureaucratic style is emphasized by the use of *mou* 某, which I render A, B, C, and so on. The practitioner is simply to add his personal details to complete the incantation.

perfection of the Five Talismans, and to enjoy this modest ceremony and meager offerings.

Upon completing these incantations the adept faces the mats and kowtows twice. He is now ready to summon the superior spirits. Visualizing the forms of the celestial emperors he begins the incantations for summoning the spirits while watching the smoke rising from the censer. If the smoke rises straight up, then it is the Yellow Thearch descending first, if the vapor flowed east, it is the Azure Thearch descending first, and so on. If the smoke was scattered and disordered then it is the spirit maidens arriving first. Kneeling, the adept intones five incantations, invoking in turn the five directional Thearchs, beginning with the east:

> I respectfully request the descent of the azure emperor 蒼帝 of the east, *Lingweiyang*,[44] lord of the Green Sprout nine-pneumas heaven, the high perfected kings, the green-waisted jade maidens and the various spirit officials of the eastern domain.

After completing the invocations for all five Thearchs, the adept concludes with a formula directed at the masters who are the mythical initiators of the lineage:

> I respectfully request the descent of Emperor Yu of Xia of Patterned Mandate 文命,[45] the Perfected of the five sacred and numinous mountains, the spirit officials of waterways and of the four great rivers, the terrestrial transcendents, jade maidens, master Lüli 角里 and the various spirit officials (3.6b2).

Each Thearch is greeted with two kowtows. When all the spirits have assembled, the adept again offers wine and lights incense. He now proceeds to announce the reason for the ceremony, beginning with a humble introduction.

> I, so-and-so, am a person of flesh, born of the womb, a descendent of dried bones, was born and raised in the world of mire, and am [just] filthy pneumas crawling and collecting in the dirt. My accumulated guilt is as deep as the rivers and sea; the flaws I embrace are deep and heavy. Since I reached the

---

44 This is the one of the five arcane names of the celestial Thearchs used in the *Array*.
45 This epithet for Yu appears in *Shiji* 2.49; Nienhauser 1994: 21. It may be based on the chapter "Virtues of the Five Emperors" (*Wudi de* 五帝德) in *Dadai liji* 大戴禮記. The "Dayu mo" 大禹謨 chapter of the *Shangshu* includes the line "*wenming* [patterned commands] were spread through the realm" 文命敷於四海. Kong Anguo's commentary does not understand Wenming as a name but explicates it as "patterned virtue and instructional commands" 文德教命; the line thus means "his patterned virtue and the commands of his instructions were spread throughout the realm" (*Shangshu zhengyi* 4.22b in SSJZS 134b). Although he had studied with Kong Anguo, Sima Qian apparently followed another line of interpretation.

age of cognition 有識,[46] I have reverently admired the great Dao, and wished
to perfect my pneuma. This would be my greatest delight, but as my essences
and spirits are slight and meager, I have not been able to communicate with
that which is above. I always maintain my heart and concentrate on goodness
(*shouxin nianshan* 守心念善).[47] Should I dare to violate and transgress [the
rules] I especially fear that [even if] I were to advance by as little as a silk
thread or a hair's breadth, I would fall down to the nine springs. But heaven
had willed that I would fortunately be granted a view of the Lingbao writs.
This perfect scripture is magnificent; it was secreted in a dark tower. I, therefore, do not dare to carry it without caution, or to wear it without permission,
lest I harm the perfect law (3.6b6–7a).

Humans are thus naturally coarse in body and behavior, but they can be
redeemed by the possession of the *Lingbao* scriptures and talismans, which can be
obtained by correctly following this very procedure. The adept continues by ver-
balizing the physical performance, and reiterating the symbolic value of the silks
as proofs of his contract with the Thearchs:

Today I perform a purification rite and a summoning sacrifice for the five
monarchs and the various lords and respected elders, in order to certify my
contract with the spirits (*ding shenqi*) 定神契. The pledge of vermilion and
green is the bond of the oath joining us. It is effective and worthy of trust.
I promise not to divulge it [the text]. Even to those cherished by heaven and
beloved of earth, transmission of the text can only be once in forty years. It is
clear in the law that there can be neither propagating nor transmission [of the
text] in the middle [of this period].

The adept now pronounces the results derived from possession of the talismans.
Beginning with the apotropaic function of the talismans, which, as we will see in
the next chapter, had been their original use, he proceeds to enumerate a series of
increasingly numinous effects. The talismans thus will not only ward off beasts
and demons, but will cause the expulsion of the three worms and eventually lead
to longevity.

---

46 This term refers to a developmental stage, but although used often in the Daoist texts as well as in
    general writings, rarely given a specific age. In *Santian neijie jing* this age is given as 7 *sui* (DZ
    1205: 1.6b; Bokenkamp, *Early*, 217), which is also the age when the earliest registers were
    bestowed on children in the Celestial Master community.
47 This line probably alludes to the type of practice discussed in the *Xiang'er Commentary*:

>   The essences may be compared to the waters of a pond and the body to the embankments
>   along the side of the pond. Good deeds are like the water's source. If these three are all com-
>   plete, the pond will be sturdy. If the heart does fix itself on goodness (*xin buzhuan shan* 心
>   不專善), then the pond lacks embankments and the water will run out (*Xiang'er zhu* S 6825,
>   lines 329–31 in Ōfuchi, *Tonkō dōkyō zurokuhen*; Bokenkamp, *Early*, 114).

   The accumulation of goodness in this context refers to maintaining the precepts.

I, so-and-so, aspire to be a recluse in the forest and have no desire for glory. Wearing the talismans when climbing mountains will allow me to go anywhere I wish without hindrance. Metal and stone will be crushed for me. When collecting herbs, they will not disappear from me. Traveling vertically up to the heaven or horizontally across the earth, I will go wherever I desire. [These talismans] make the mountain sprites immediately submit, [and cause] wolves and tigers to flee and retreat. They will enable me to command ghosts and spirits. I will live long and have lasting vision. Numinous pneuma will protect me while deviant fiends will lose their lives. Diseases and poisonous beasts will not appear before me, and the *Wangliang* demons will flee far away. This is because I receive the support of the heavens above and the aid of the numinous pneumas. My [bodily] spirits shall long preserve my body, causing the three corpses to fade away. This is the flowing mercy of the grand Thearch. The masses [of other spirits] cannot compete with its provision of vast salvation (*hongji zhi shi* 洪濟之施) (3.7a6–7b2).

At this point the adept may add specific requests. With a second offering of wine and lighting of incense, the Thearchs are sent off with a set of incantations which parallel the summoning formulas. Thus end the instructions for the *jiao* rite.

There are several important points to note in this ritual. First, we should consider the symbolism of the colored silks that envelop the five Lingbao talismans on their respective mats. A piece of Southern Harmonious Cinnabar Silk (*nanhe danzeng* 南和丹繒) is torn (*lie* 裂) and spread on each mat, and a roll of Emerald Grove Silk (*pilin zhibo* 碧林之帛) is cut (*ge* 割) and placed upon it. The talismans are then placed between these two layers of silk on their respective mats. According to the instructions, this act effects an "offering of fidelity" (*xiaoxin* 效信) between the spirits and the adept.

This terminology is significant as it resonates with the terms used to describe the act of "breaking the tallies" by which ancient rulers gained allegiance of their vassals. As I discuss in more detail in the following chapter, such allegiance was made when a talisman was split in two (*pofu* 剖符) with each party in the contract receiving a tally (*qi* 契) as guarantee. Similarly produced documents were carried by royal envoys, and functioned as credentials (*xin* 信). This ritual act should, therefore, be seen in the context of the intimate links between royal symbols of investiture and Daoist initiation rites, as shown by Anna Seidel.[48] I argue that rather than symbolizing the ritual act of bloodletting, as suggested by the commentary, the colored silks, which enveloped the talismans, were themselves talismans. I suggest, following Seidel, that these silks are emblematic of the "River Chart" and "Luo Writ" (*Hetu luoshu* 河圖洛書), which were green and red, respectively.[49]

48 Seidel, "Imperial Treasures."
49 Seidel, "Imperial Treasures," 310.

In ancient mythical narratives, these charts functioned as emblems of heaven's mandate. The symbolism of their inclusion in the transmission ritual is thus an emulation of the receipt of the imperial mandate. As I discuss in greater detail in the following chapter, the *Lingbao* talismans are here elevated to cosmological status, superseding the ancient talismanic charts. While this talismanic complex may be seen as emblematic of the contract between master and disciple, it is more importantly a mark of the authority conferred on the disciple by possession of the *Lingbao* talismans.

The second major point in this ritual procedure is the sacrifice of the goose which is offered to the spirits. This act harks back to the blood sacrifice of the *fangshi*, the popular cults, and the imperial rituals. This part of the procedure was omitted in the later developments of the ritual, while the bloodless oath of fidelity using the silks became emblematic of the Daoist ritual. The new understanding of the colored silks as replacing the physical victim should thus be seen as directly influenced by criticisms of blood sacrifice.

This new understanding of the silks lent itself to the title of the rite, and was inscribed into the mythographic narrative that opens the *Array of the Five Talismans*. Having completed the compilation of the *Celestial Writ of the Five Talismans of Lingbao* (*Lingbao wufu tianwen* 靈寶五符天文), the Great Yu performed a rite named "Southern Harmonious Cinnabar Silk" as he secreted one copy of the text before his apotheosis.[50] Southern Harmonious Cinnabar Silk thus became a synecdoche for the whole ritual, implying a pure, bloodless rite.

The same understanding of the colored silks signifying bloodless ritual was adopted by Ge Chaofu into the ritual system of the Lingbao scriptures, exemplified by the ritual program presented in the *Jade Instructions in Red Script*.[51] The second *juan* of this text contains the "Jade Instructions for an Offering Rite for Summoning the Perfected of the Five Thearchs of Numinous Treasure of Primordial Commencement" (元始靈寶五帝醮祭招真玉訣), which is an expansion of the *jiao* rite of the *Array of the Five Talismans*.[52] At the core of the rite we find the emplacement of the Five Talismans, here coupled with the Five Perfected Writs (*Lingbao wupian zhenwen* 靈寶五篇真文):

> Tear a five foot long piece of southern harmonious cinnabar silk and place it on the altar. Set the "Five Perfected Writs" and "Five Talismans" on it. Cut a

---

50 DZ 388: 1.6b8.
51 *Taishang dongxuan lingbao chishu yujue miaojing* 太上洞玄靈寶赤書玉訣妙經 DZ 352. It is a commentary to *Five Tablets in Red Script* (*Yuanshi wulao chishu yupian zhenwen ianshu jing* 元始五老赤書玉篇真文天書經 DZ 22). These two texts may be considered the fundamental among the Lingbao scriptures. Liu Xiujing's catalogue lists the *Five Tablets in Red Script* as the first of the Lingbao scriptures (here entitled *Taishang dongxuan lingbao wupian zhenwen chishu* 太上洞玄靈寶五篇真文赤書), followed by the *Jade Instructions* (entitled *Taishang dongxuan lingbao yujue* 太上洞玄靈寶玉訣). The section *Wupian zhenwen* in DZ 22 is a revision of the *jiao* rite in the *Array*. DZ 352 provides ritual instructions for it.
52 DZ 352.2.20a8–28b5.

five foot long piece of emerald grove silk and cover the Writs and Talismans… The talisman placed between the cinnabar and green is considered to be the covenant of cut hair and smearing blood 令符處丹青中以為落髮歃血之盟.

As I discussed above, the original intent of the silks in the *Array* was said to symbolize "offering of fidelity." In this rewriting of the ritual, the exegesis presented in the commentary to the *Array*, which clearly differs from the ritual instructions, has now become the explicit meaning of the rite. The colored silks have replaced the bloodletting of the ancient rites of fealty. Even clearer is the gloss to this passage in the *Jade Instructions*:

> Azure is a substitute for hair, and cinnabar is a substitute for a blood smearing oath. The Perfected do not wound the spirits [of the body] or deplete their virtue. Therefore use the [the silks] to substitute for it.[53]

青以代髮, 丹以代歃血之誓. 真人不傷神損德, 故以代之.

The ritual procedure in the *Jade Instructions* still includes an offering of a wild goose, but it was no longer a central aspect of the rite as it was in the *Array*. When Liu Xiujing formulated the transmission of the Lingbao scriptures in the middle of the fifth century, he based it on the ritual procedure of the *Jade Instructions*, citing it verbatim in his *Transmission Rites of Lingbao*. He did not, however, include the offering of the goose in the ritual. The oath of cinnabar and azure has become the core of the transmission rite.[54]

The transmission ritual of the five Lingbao talismans thus marks a major transition in the development of Daoist ritual. While the early set of instructions clearly required a blood sacrifice for summoning the celestial deities, this was rejected in the later developments of the rite. The red and green silks, which originally served as talismanic emblems symbolic of receiving heaven's mandate, came to be seen as replacing the blood oath. This does not, however, mean that the talismans should be seen as a sacrifice. Rather, this ritual indicates a vastly different understanding of the relationship forged by ritual.

In his study of this rite, Kristofer Schipper suggests that it presages what was to become the standard Daoist ritual program. He argues that the ritual is structured around the prayer offered by the practitioner while receiving the talismans. This prayer is enveloped by two ritual stages, which are identical but in reverse order. Incense is lit and wine is offered during the summoning of the spirits, and when they are sent off. The formulaic incantations at these complementary stages are identical, save for exchanging the phrase "respectfully invite X Thearch" with

---

53 DZ 352.2.23a1.
54 DZ 528.1b9–2a5.

"I have troubled X Thearch." The structure of the *jiao* rite may be schematically summarized as:[55]

(A) Installation of the sacred area and donning vestments,
(B) Summoning of the spirits, composed of two stages:
B1, externalizing the bodily spirits,
B2, descent of the celestial spirits.
(C) Wine offering (with incense)
(D) Prayer
(C*) Wine offering (with incense)
(B*) Sending off the spirits:
B*1: calling back the bodily spirits,
B*2: ascent of the celestial spirits.
(A*) Dispersal of the altar.

Schipper further argues the structure of this rite corresponds to a more generalized form of Daoist ritual which he has elsewhere elaborated as consisting of four great "articulations":

(1) Installation of ritual area, which is a creation of perfect world, in which all spatial and temporal categories are integrated. The basic markers of the ritual area are the five Lingbao talismans, or, more precisely, the Perfect Writs (*zhenwen* 真文), which are a development of these talismans in the *Five Tablets in Red Script* and the *Jade Instructions*.

(2) Fast (*zhai* 齋), which Schipper defines as the passage in this created closed universe.

(3) Offering (*jiao*), which celebrates the covenant with the spirits.

(4) Dispersal of the ritual area, which entails the ritual oblation of talismans and scriptures.[56]

Schipper argues that the "sacrifice of writings" marks the climax of the ritual process:

[T]he ritual area – where, for a moment, all the powers of the universe have been concentrated and materialized in the sacred *True Writs* – is, at the final moment of the dispersal, consumed in a great blaze… This represents an incredible shortening of time with respect to the temporal cycle of the cosmos and allows the world to benefit from the spiritual force released by this action.

---

55 Schipper "Reihō," 225–26.
56 Schipper, *Taoist Body*, 76–7.

Schipper suggests that this "sacrifice of writings" is unique to Daoist ritual, and should extend our conception of sacrifice.[57]

As I discuss in the following chapter, Daoist texts were indeed perceived as emanations of the transformative and creative pneumas of the cosmos. Talismans were considered closest in form to the primordial *qi*. Schipper suggests that the emplacement of the talismans is more than a consecration of the ritual area, but a recreation of the universe. Their transformation by fire is, thus, a completion of a cosmic cycle of creation and destruction. Schipper's analysis is accepted by Kenneth Dean, who also stresses the importance of the oblation of the five writs:

> The recitation of scriptures within the re-created universe of the sacred space established by the placement of the Five True Talismanic writs, followed by a burning of these talismans represents an acceleration of the process of revelation and return, and is thus the engine of merit making in the ritual.[58]

Schipper's analysis of Daoist ritual as culminating in "sacrifice of texts" is not applicable to the *jiao* rite of the *Array*. While he is correct regarding the creative power of talismans in the *Array*, there is nothing equivalent to the "sacrifice of texts" in the *jiao* rite of the *Array*.

At the end of the rite the talismans were to be transmitted to the practitioner, and they were neither destroyed nor sacrificed. This rite rather exemplifies the ritual transmission by which Daoist lineages were constructed and maintained. Charged by the descent of the Thearchs, the talismans would now function as efficacious protective devices. Two other elements in the ritual program, the oath in cinnabar and azure and the offering of a wild goose, also cannot be reconciled with the notion of sacrifice as defined by Schipper, but need to be explained by reference to older forms of sacrifice and communication.

Schipper argues that the sacrifice of scripture replaced the older cultic practice of blood sacrifice.[59] There is, however, a qualitative difference between the two types of sacrifice. Schipper interprets Daoist ritual as a process by which the universe is re-created by placing the texts and is de-constructed by their oblation. Blood sacrifice, however, was never understood to have a creative function within the rite. Sacrificial practice was central to the ancient Chinese polities, from the Shang, through the Zhou and the dynastic imperial states.[60] Discussions of sacrifice in early China focus on two complementary aspects. First, sacrifice was perceived

---

57 Schipper, *Taoist Body*, 90; Kenneth Dean, *Taoist Ritual and Popular Cults of Southeast China* (Princeton: Princeton University Press, 1993): 47.

58 Dean, *Taoist Ritual*, 48.

59 See also Dean, *Taoist Ritual*, 181.

60 Catherine Bell provides a discussion of various interpretations of sacrifice in *Ritual Perspectives and Dimensions* (New York and Oxford: Oxford University Press, 1997): 111–13. For a more specific study of sacrifice in the Chinese context, see Michael Puett, *To Become a God: Cosmology, Sacrifice, and Self-Divinization in Early China* (Cambridge: Harvard University Asia Center, 2002).

as necessary sustenance for the ancestors, thereby securing their beneficence and favorable mediation in support of the living members of the family. Second, sacrifice was discussed as a primary factor for determining the legitimate hierarchic power relationship in society.

Most modern scholarship on sacrifice interprets it from the perspective of the principle of *do ut des* (I give, in order that you should give), that is a belief in the reciprocity of gift giving. Michael Puett has shown that sacrifice is better understood as a series of transformations of sacralization and desacralization between the sacrificer, the victim, and the respective divine powers. Puett focuses on the transformative power of the sacrifice, which, more than nourishment, is necessary to transform the dead into ancestors.[61] In the imperial sacrificial system of the Qin and early Han, the centralization of sacrifice in the person of the king was linked to the active quest for immortality by the First Emperor of Qin and Han emperor Wu. Thus, the imperial project was expressed in the cultic realm in the centralization of sacrifice which in turn was to transform the emperor himself into a divine being.[62] Opponents of these imperial claims for divinization stressed the function of ritual as leading to proper social and ecological cohesion. Nevertheless, in all of these discussions, there is an underlying assumption of sacrifice as a medium of communication between the human realm and that of the spirits. There is also an underlying assumption that the spirits, from the personal ancestral spirits to the high gods, require physical sustenance. These assumptions were rejected by the Daoist lineages, which instituted pure offerings in place of flesh offerings.

The burning of scripture cannot therefore be seen simply as replacing the older practice of blood sacrifice, but as a new conceptualization of the role of ritual. As we saw above, the understanding of the colored silks as replacing blood sacrifice came by a gradual process. In the *Array of the Five Talismans*, blood sacrifice is an integral part of the ritual, and colored silks were to wrap the talismans. While the commentary to the rite explains the symbolism of the silks as replacing the blood and hair used in traditional oaths, I argue the silks may have originally symbolized the red and green River Chart and Luo Writ. When the silks do come to be understood as replacing the blood smearing rites of oath taking, they do not replace the sacrifice of the goose. When the sacrifice is finally abandoned it is not replaced by another rite. The use of silks and the sacrifice of the goose are thus not functionally equivalent, as may be implied by the rhetoric of later commentators and codifiers. While the ritual form of oath taking may have been retained, the actual concept of what the ritual does is therefore fundamentally different.[63]

As evidence for his hypothesis, Schipper has located another reference to a sacrifice of a wild goose in a method entitled "Ingesting Bamboo Shoots with

---

61 Puett, *To Become*, 51–52.
62 Puett, *To Become*, 237–45.
63 See also Cedzich's note in Michel Strickmann, *Chinese Magical Medicine* (Stanford: Stanford University Press, 2002): "although it is true that the Taoists replaced the people's sacrifices to the 'vulgar' gods by written communication with the invisible hierarchies (and did so quite intentionally), it is questionable whether the burning of documents can therefore be considered 'sacrifices'" (288 n.29).

Avian Flesh appended" (*Shi zhuxun, hongfu fu* 食竹筍鴻脯附).[64] The instructions
are followed by a short verse:[65]

> A great goose, a thousand-year-old bird,
> With its meat, you may summon the celestial perfected.
> The five thearchs taste the lunar floreate,
> They array their seats as guests in empty space.

While sharing key terms with the *jiao* rite of the *Array of the Five Talismans*, this
passage does not resolve the problem of the sacrifice of the goose. Rather, it is
added evidence of the complex relationship between Daoist practices and their
antecedents. It seems that the poem is describing a practice in which celestial deities can be enticed by flesh. As we have seen, this understanding of sacrifice is typical for the imperial rites as well as the popular rituals, which Daoism criticized.

According to the commentary appended to the poem, the goose was an emblem
of the moon and the bamboo shoots were symbolic of the sun. As in the case of the
colored silks, this explanation seems to be a reformulation of an older practice,
which was thereby assimilated into the Daoist concept of "pure" offerings.

The source for the oblation of texts should therefore be sought elsewhere. The
most likely source is the petitioning rite of the Celestial Masters. This rite culminated in the completion of written forms, inscribed in triplicate, addressed to the
Three Offices of heaven, earth, and water. One was placed on a mountaintop,
a second was buried in the earth, and the third cast into a flowing stream.[66] This rite
may, in turn, have been inspired by, and perhaps modeled on, the imperial *feng* (封)
sacrifice wherein the emperor buried a set of texts so that the covenant between
him and heaven, as evidenced by the receipt of heaven's mandate, was sealed.[67]

---

64 Schipper, "Reihō," 224; this practice is listed among several methods for ingesting lunar, solar,
and astral pneumas collected in the twenty-third chapter of *YJQQ*, DZ 1032: 23.17b:

> One who ingests the solar and lunar floreate essences should always obtain bamboo shoots to eat,
> they are the embryonic forms of solar efflorescence. It is also named Great Brightness (*daming* 大
> 明). One should also always eat avian flesh; feathered birds are the embryonic form of the moon.
> (月胎之羽鳥; this phrase seems corrupt; as it is supposed to parallel the line concerning the sun,
> I translate it accordingly). It is also named Lunar Egret (*yuelu* 月鷺). If you wish to ingest solar
> and lunar [essences] you should ingest these things, as their pneumas respond and activate them.

65 The provenance of this method is unclear. As a comment on the term "goose" (*honglu*) is attributed
to the Perfected of Grand Void (Taixu zhenren 太虛鎮人), which is an epithet of Master Redpine
in the Shangqing system, the passage may be from a Shangqing source. A note appended to the
verse states it was an ancient fisherman's song. While this may allude to the "Old Fisherman" song
of the *Chuci*, it probably implies a source in a local tradition, and not a Daoist revelation. The verse
and the accompanying passage seem, therefore, to be of different sources.

66 See the discussion in Strickmann, *Chinese*, 1–23, and Cedzich's notes to this section, especially
286 n.8, n.12, 287 n.14, and 288 n.20.

67 On the development of the *feng* sacrifice and differing perceptions of this rite during the Han, see
Mark Edward Lewis, "The Feng and Shan Sacrifices of Emperor Wu of the Han" in Joseph
McDermott, ed. *State and Court Ritual in China* (Cambridge University Press, 1999).

Whether these rites may be interpreted as a "sacrifice of scripture" awaits further analysis. Here it will suffice to say that the *jiao* rite of the *Array* is not an example of the text-centered rites which came to distinguish Daoism. Rather, it is representative of an older tradition, in which blood sacrifice was the main form of offering to the spirits.

Later branches of Daoism found means to accommodate flesh offerings within the developed *jiao* ritual programs. However, at the early stage of development of the *jiao* rite, exemplified by the transition from the *Array* to the *Five Tablets in Red Script*, we find an abandonment of the sacrificial aspect of the ritual. One expression of this shift is the change in nomenclature of the Five Thearchs in the *Five Tablets in Red Script*. In the latter text the arcane names of the five Thearchs are revealed to be no more than the personal name of the Five Ancients, which are primordial emanations of the five phases.[68] Here it will suffice to note that while the rite of the *Array* is still indebted to the imperial ritual system with its sacrificial practices, the later reformulation of this rite divorces the five Thearchs from the imperial ritual system. The Thearchs come to be seen as manifestations of the Dao, and hence beyond the need for material sustenance.

V   Abhorrence of blood in Shangqing Daoism

In Celestial Master texts, the rejection of blood rites is predicated on the rejection of sacrificial ritual as a means of communication. We find far a deeper sense of abhorrence of blood in the instructions presented by Wei Huacun to Yang Xi (probably dating to the 360s): "Gentlemen who cultivate the Dao wish to not see blood and flesh. Seeing and avoiding them is not as good as not seeing them at all".[69]

Wei Huacun's teachings bridge the early Celestial Masters and the fourth century Shangqing lineage. The following example, a citation from *Secret Instruction for Ascending to Perfection*, a compilation of Shangqing practices by Tao Hongjing, presents a reformulated transmission rite for the "Nine-fold Reverted Cinnabar" (*Jiuzhuan dan* 九轉丹), which was among the alchemical methods most revered by Ge Hong:

> To receive this scripture all must ascend an altar and make a contractual oath by ripping silk and proffering gold … Transmission requires purification.

---

68   Raz, "Imperial Efficacy," 107–8.
69   TPGJ 58.383. This is based on a dialogue preserved in *Zhen'gao*: "She asked: 'Do you abhor blood?' He replied: 'I certainly do.' She said: 'Supposing there is blood along the path, as you abhor it what would you do?' He replied: 'I would avoid it.' She then said: 'Avoiding it is good, but not as good as never even seeing blood.'" (DZ 1016: 1.6b7). This is the first teaching presented to Yang Xi in Wei Huacun's hagiography as preserved in the *Taiping guangji*. This editorial choice by the compiler of the hagiography probably represents the author's attitude that the initial and primary distinguishing feature of Daoist practice is its renunciation of all bloody practices. In the *Zhen'gao* this teaching is recorded among the earliest encounters between Yang Xi and his teacher.

The use of gold and jade rings as a contract replaces the oath of cutting hair and smearing blood.[70]

This passage recasts the methods advocated by Ge Hong into the discourse of bloodless rites. These passages demonstrate that both the Celestial Masters and the early Shangqing lineage rejected blood rites, and that this understanding extended to initiation rituals. A similar explanation is also found in a late Shangqing text, the *Flying Feathered Scripture*, in its discussion of transmission rites:

> This esoteric treasure is a restricted text of the Most High. It is the essential instruction for perfection … Previously, smearing the mouth with blood and lavish altars, cutting hair and establishing a covenant constituted the oath of faith for not divulging [the secret teaching]. Later sages considered smearing the mouth with blood an injury offending against the living pneuma, and saw cutting hair as a transgression offending against the body. They cautiously replaced blood letting oaths with two ounces of gold, and used thirty-two feet of soft azure silk instead of the contracts requiring injury to the hair.[71]

Indeed, Daoist transmission and ordination rites described in late Six Dynasties compilations, such as Lu Xijing's *Transmission Rites of Lingbao* (*Lingbao shoudu yi* 靈寶授度儀) and the *Radiant Codes of the Four Culmens* (*Siji mingke* 四極明科), while providing details of the altar arrangements, invocations and offerings required for the receipt of various texts, clearly exclude blood sacrifice.[72]

VI   Transmission narratives

So far in this chapter we have looked at rituals of transmission. Although these ritual instructions and descriptions may be more prescriptive than descriptive,

---

70 *Secret Instruction for Ascending to Perfection* (*Dengzhen yinjue* 登真隱訣 DZ 421) originally consisted of twenty juan. The extant version in the Daozang includes only three. The passage cited here is not in the current *Dengzhen yinjue* but preserved in TPYL 671.1a–2a. While the provenance of this passage is problematic, and how much it reflects early Shangqing ideas may be debatable, it certainly reflects the same shift in the procedure and symbolism of transmission rites. Even if it is a later understanding (but still prior to the sixth century) of these changes, it does not conflict with my hypothesis.

71 *Dongzhen taishang feixing yujing jiuzhen shengxuan shangji* 洞真太上飛行羽經九真昇玄上記 DZ 1351.10a1–8. 此太上禁書內寶為真之要訣也…先歃血累壇剪髮立盟為不宣泄之信誓也. 後聖以歃血犯生氣之傷剪髮違位毀之犯. 謹以黃金二鎰代割血之信, 青柔之帛三十二呎當割髮之約. Robinet, *Révélation*, vol. 2, 195 dates this text to approximately the seventh century.

72 *Taishang dongxuan lingbao shoudu yibiao* 太上洞玄靈寶授度儀表 DZ 528, composed by Liu Xiujing, provides detailed instructions for the transmission of the Lingbao scriptures. *Taizhen yudi siji mingke jing* 太真玉帝四極明科經 DZ 184 was compiled in the fifth or sixth century and represents an attempt to integrate the Lingbao and Shangqing ritual and scriptural lineages; Robinet, *Révélation*, vol. 2, 428–30.

such rituals were certainly performed, and they are critical to our understanding of the formation of lineages, and to the self-perception of lineages. In this section I turn to an examination of narratives of transmission, which was a way for lineages to define themselves rhetorically.

In discussing the transmission of specific texts, such as the *Array of the Five Talismans*, we need to distinguish the transmission of the text as a whole, as described in sources external to it, from the tales of transmission of particular teachings or scriptures within the text itself. In the case of the *Array*, the former type narratives describe the transmission of a coherent text, entitled *Lingbao jing* or *Wufu jing*, at specific stages of redaction. Narratives of the second type are embedded in the text itself and describe transmissions of discrete texts and practices. By their inclusion in the *Array* the authors of the text claimed them as part of their heritage. I discuss both sets of narratives in the following pages.

There are a number of distinct tales of transmission in the *Array*. These tales serve two purposes: to demonstrate the antiquity of the teachings contained in the *Array*, while delineating the correct lineage of transmission by which it arrived at its present state (that is, the state of the text after its compilation in the late third or early fourth centuries). This authorial intent is reflected in the selection and manipulation of the tales of transmission which, as we shall see, often conflict. As the text is a composite of various earlier materials with their own respective transmission tales, the compilers tried to manipulate these diverse traditions to cohere into a grand narrative. This attempt was not totally successful as there is not a single and clear tale of transmission of the *Array of the Five Talismans*. Various texts and practices are said to have been transmitted from a variety of masters to different disciples and it is not always clear how the particular text or practice mentioned is related to the *Array of the Five Talismans* itself. These tales may be conveniently divided into four categories:

1   A brief note attached to a specific text or practice. In form, this is the simplest type. However, it is also the easiest to manipulate by simply providing another note. A possible path to follow in these cases is to track particular practices and texts through the specific content in order to check possible links.
2   Transmission and reception of teachings mentioned in a particular person's biography. Here the focus is usually the person, and the social context in which s/he operated. The practices and texts may not be related except by association with this person.
3   A history of transmission of a particular teaching. As the focus here is on the text or practice, there may be multiple lineages of transmission mentioned. This category is especially problematic as it often seeks to construct a unitary image of a teaching by obfuscating the multiplicity of versions and lineages. However, as is the case with the tales in the *Array*, this type often retains early versions and conflicting images as its author/s tries to negotiate rival visions of the teaching.

4   The most developed tale is a history of a teaching with cosmogonic and mythic origins that completely override the human lineage of transmission. This type often includes remnants of all the above categories in a carefully crafted fiction. This is the hardest type to untangle as often the rivalries and variants included in the third type are smoothed out and omitted from the grand vision formulated.

A concept which may be of use here is *historiola*, a term used in studies of Egyptian and Hellenistic magic to refer to an abbreviated narrative incorporated into a magical spell.[73] Basing his analysis on Austin's Speech Act theory, David Frankfurter discusses the *historiola* in relation to both ritual and myth. He argues that uttering *historiola*e in a ritual context directs their "narrative" power into this world. Even when the specific context of a *historiola* is unclear, it always seems to be an application of mythical lore to a "real world" situation. Despite the variety of contexts in which the *historiola* was used, Frankfurter is able to demonstrate a number of links between the narratives and the ritual contexts in which they appear. Although Frankfurter's analysis is based on studies of Egyptian magic, some of these contexts are remarkably similar to those we find in Daoist texts, such as the notes appended to talismans, and even to extended narratives.

Three features of *historiolae* seem to me particularly important: (1) the ritualist identifies himself as a god; by collapsing the boundaries between the human and mythical dimensions the *historiola* is effective not by analogy or precedent, but by becoming dynamically real within the ritual context; (2) the *historiola* may be, or may include, an account of the genesis and initial use of a specific incantation within it, which is then used by the ritualist in a ritual context or written on an amulet; (3) the *historiola* may account for a substance used in the accompanying ritual.[74]

In relation to myth, Frankfurter describes the *historiola* as a distinct level of discourse, one which applies or directs cosmic power, while myth remains the general "framework." This model encompasses a creative process wherein "(1) an abstract set of concepts and relations that might crystallize around or into (2) certain figures, names, places, or folklore motifs according to a culture's current circumstances, and they come into being within (3) a variety of performative settings according to a variety of forms that range from priestly liturgy to scribal mythography to *historiolae*, drama, sculpture or painting." While the mythical fragments in the *historiola* are often traceable to known "myths" it is quite obvious that some *historiolae* do not refer to overarching macro-myths at all, but are compilations and syntheses of diverse lore. "The *historiolae* 'are' the myths,

---

73   David Frankfurterr "Narrating Power: The Theory and Practice of the Magical *Historiola* in Ritual Spells," in Marvin Meyer and Paul Mirecki, eds. *Ancient Magic and Ritual Power* (Leiden: Brill, 1995): 457–76.

74   Frankfurter, "Narrating," 469, citing Jørgen Podemann Sørensen, "The Argument in Ancient Egyptian Magical Formulae," *Acta Orientalia* 45 (1984).

rather than derivative of them, and the canonical myths which scholars appeal to are literary contrivances, masking the diversity and even incoherence of the actual traditions." The *historiola*, therefore, is recognizable as it adapts known motifs and elements, which provide authority and power, while deliberately blending them to create new meaning. "The specific terms, symbols, and motifs do not themselves constitute 'myth' but rather the *authoritative discourse of precedent* in a given region at a certain time – a discourse that would certainly change over time".[75] The creative process that Frankfurter describes for the *historiola* proves similar to the creative process by which texts, such as the *Array of the Five Talismans*, were formed.

First, as mentioned in the Introduction, the final section of the *Array of the Five Talismans* is an originally independent text, entitled *Scripture of the Perfect One*. A comparison of the mythical narrative of transmission and the rituals advocated in the main text of the *Array of the Five Talismans* and the *Scripture of the Perfect One* shows that these two texts were compiled by utterly different lineages. The main figure in the *Array of the Five Talismans* is the flood-hero Yu, who is in fact credited with transcribing the Lingbao talismans and secreting them at Mt. Bao, which is by Lake Tai, on the south-eastern coast. This was the ancient state of Wu. Following the fall of the Han, the warlord Sun Quan established himself as ruler of Wu. The narrative continues to describe the discovery of the Lingbao talismans and associated text in Mt. Bao. Several motifs in the narratives of the *Array of the Five Talismans* reveal that it was composed in the kingdom of Wu.[76] The purpose of the narrative is to authenticate the Offering *jiao* ritual, which is the focus of the text.

In contrast, the main figure in the narrative of the *Scripture of the Perfect One* is the Yellow Thearch. This narrative makes no reference to the Lingbao talismans or to the *jiao* ritual. As the locus of the teaching is Mt. Emei in Sichuan, this text was probably initially composed by a lineage based in that region.[77]

These two narratives were evidently composed within different lineages, with distinct cosmological and ritual programs. Significantly, neither of these narratives refers to Laozi, who is associated with a few minor practices.[78] The legitimacy and authority sought by the lineages that composed both texts did not, therefore, depend on what has come to be a defining mark of Daoism, the deified Laozi. Rather, both lineages defined themselves through ancient sages, imperial pedigree, and Han era *fangshi*.

Our discussion of the *jiao* ritual and its commentary reveals a further stage in compilation, and evidence for further divergence among the lineages involved in

---

75 Frankfurter, "Narrating," 474.
76 For details, see Raz, *Creation*, 181–85.
77 For details, see Raz, *Creation*, 156–80.
78 Two teachings are attributed to Lord Lao in *juan* 2: (1) the *Lingbao* [Method] for Ingesting the Essences of the Five Numinous Herbs; a comment by Yue Zichang refers to Confucius (j2, #1), (2) *Lingbao Method of the Three Heavens* (j2, #2); the third *juan* lists a Yang Life Talisman of Upper Profundity of the Nine Heavens which is said to have been transmitted from Laojun to the Elder of Most High (j3, #16).

the compilation of the *Array of the Five Talismans*. We saw above that there is a clear distinction in the ritual transmission of the *Lingbao* talismans described in the verse and accompanying instructions the *Array of the Five Talismans* and the understanding of the rite presented in the commentary. This distinction should alert us to the possibility that the instructions and commentary were composed by different lineages. Indeed, we find that the transmission narratives associated with each passage also indicate different lineages.

The verse is attributed to Yue Zichang 樂子長, whose name is attached to most of the other textual elements in the *Array of the Five Talismans*.[79] He is, however, unknown outside of this text, and all later hagiographic references to him are based on the *Array*. Yue Zichang is said to have received the instructions for this ritual procedure from his master, Han Zhong 韓眾, who should probably be identified with the well known practitioner of esoteric arts of the Qin and early Han, one of the three Masters of Esoterica (*fangshi* 方士) dispatched by the First Emperor of Qin to the isles of the transcendents in search of potions for evading death (不死之藥).[80] Yue Zichang and Han Zhong are the two main figures in the lineage with which the compiler of the *Array of the Five Talismans* identified. The text compiled by this lineage was known to Ge Hong, who refers to it in his *Baopuzi*.[81]

The lineage mentioned in the commentary is different. The most intriguing question is who the name Ling refers to. Most scholars agree that Ling should be identified with Zhang Daoling, the first Celestial Master.[82] The Little Lad of the Eastern Sea is the Azure Lad, who is mentioned in Ge Hong's *Inner Chapters* as well as in archaeological material that pre-dates the Shangqing revelations.[83] In

79 Yue Zichang is associated with the following methods in the *Array*: (1) he inscribes the names of the "Scripture of Transcendents Imbibing the Pneuma of all Heavens of the Five Directions" transmitted by Master Luli to Hua Ziqi (1.11a); (2) receives "The Essential Instructions of the Numinous Treasure" from the Transcendent of Huolin (1.15b7); (3) receives and reveals both "Upper Array of the Numinous Treasure" and "Texts for Controlling and Managing" (3.3a2); (4) Receives the oral instructions of the full *jiao* rite from the Transcendent of Huolin (3.3a3); (5) Verse composed by Yue Zichang, and written by King Fu Chai of Wu (3.7b4). A large number of the methods and teachings listed in chapter 2 are attributed to Yue Zichang; (6) Five Herbs method, citing *Xiaojing shoushenqi* (2.2a5); (7) "Lingbao Methods of the Three Heavens" (2.2b1); (8) "Diverse Lingbao Methods [for Ingesting] Sesame" received from the Transcendent of Huolin (2.4a8). These may include the following seven methods listed in 2.4b3–7a2; (9) "Methods of the Perfected Received by Yu" (2.9b2); (10) "Yue Zichang's method for processing sesame paste" (2.24b9); (11) "Yue Zichang's method for ingesting sesame" (2.25a4); (12) "Yue Zichang's method for ingesting date kernels" (2.36a5).

80 *Shiji* 6: 252, 258, see Nienhauser, *Grand Scribe's Records*, 145, 150; Han Zhong here is written with a variant graph 韓終. The other two were Master Hou 侯先生 and Scholar Shi 石生. It is in this context that the prophecy concerning the fall of Qin is first encountered. The prophecy was included in a set of charts and registers brought back by Scholar Lu from his journey across the seas.

81 For a discussion of these references, see Raz, *Creation*, 134–42.

82 Lü Pengzhi, *Tangqian*, 79 n.4.

83 Ge Hong lists "Talismans of the Little Lad of the Eastern Sea" as necessary for expelling the hundred dangers when crossing seas and waterways (*BPZ* 17.7a7–9; Wang Ming, 307). By the mid

the Shangqing revelations he appears as one of the major deities communicating with Yang Xi.[84] Elsewhere in the *Array of the Five Talismans* we are told that a version of the Five Talismans was transmitted by the Little Lad of the Eastern Sea to a Mr. Ling. The references to Zhang Ling and the Little Lad of the Eastern Sea may hint at the historical association of Shangqing Daoism with Celestial Master Daoism.

Turning to transmission narratives external to the *Array of the Five Talismans*, we also find hints at divergent lineages, and probably variant texts with similar titles. Most importantly, these variants occur within the same group of families, alerting us to the fact that we should take the rhetoric of secrecy very seriously.

Lu Xiujing included the *Array of the Five Talismans* in his Catalogue of the *Lingbao* Scriptures, and described it as follows:

> *Taishang dongxuan lingbao tianwen wufu jingxu*, one *juan*. Currently of two *juan*, anciently it was of one scroll. In the past, Yu of Xia had extracted the various texts of the Lingbao scriptures to produce this *juan*, and secreted it in the northern face of Mt. Laosheng. Yue Zichang received it from the Transcendent of Huolin and subsequently circulated it in the world. The Transcendent Duke [Ge Xuan] received this text during his lifetime and divided it into two scrolls. At present, people sometimes divide the text into three scrolls.[85]

Clearly aware of the problematic nature of this text, Lu Xiujing was trying to account for discrepancies in size and content of different versions. As *juan* were not of a standard size, Lu's statement regarding differences in the numbers of *juan* is no more than an indication that there were different versions of the text. While adopting the transmission tale found in the beginning of the third *juan* of the *Array of the Five Talismans*, he also included a reference to Ge Xuan, Ge Hong's

fourth century, the Little Lad of the Eastern Sea had achieved deification paralleling that of the Daoist higher deities. A mortuary document, dating to 361 CE, names him as witness and expediter at the end of a list of funerary goods. The document was found in a tomb near *Guihuayuan* 桂花園, the north gate of Changsha, in 1953, and first reported in *Wenwu cankao ziliao* 文物參考資料 1955.11; further reports in (1) "Jin Zhou Fangming qi Panshi yiwuquan kaoshi" 晉周芳命潘氏衣物券考釋, *Kaogu tongxun* 考古通訊, 1956.2: 95–99; (2) "Changsha liangjin nanchao sui mu fajue baogao" 長沙兩晉南朝隋墓發掘報告, *Kaogu xuebao* 1959.3: 75–103. Discussed briefly in an overview of "records of funerary objects" by Hong Shi 洪石, "Dongzhou zhi jindai mu suochu wushu jiandu jiji xiangguan wenti yanjiu" 東周至晉代墓所出物疏簡牘及其相關問題研究, *Kaogu* 2001.9: 59–69. Translated in Albert E. Dien, "Turfan funeral Documents," 31.

84 Paul Kroll, "In the Halls of the Azure Lad," *JAOS* 105 (1985): 75–94; Kamitsuka Yoshiko 神塚淑子, "Hōshu seitōkun omegutte – Rikuchō jōsei Dōkyō no ikosatsu" 方諸青童君をめぐって— 六朝上清派道教の一考察 *TS* 76 (November 1990): 1–23; Campany, *To Live*, 350, 355–6.

85 P 2256, lines 20–24, see Ōfuchi Ninji, *Tonkō dōkyō zokorukohen*, 727: 太上洞玄靈寶天文五符經序一卷. 右[今]二卷, 舊是一卷. 昔夏禹列出靈寶經中眾文, 為此卷. 藏勞盛山陰. 樂子長於霍林仙人邊, 遂行人間. 仙公在世時所得本是分為二卷 今人或作三卷; cf. Ōfuchi, *"On Ku,"* 40. I follow Ōfuchi's suggested emendations, reading "currently 今" for "right 右."

granduncle, who is not mentioned in the *Array of the Five Talismans* itself.[86] Lu credits Ge Xuan with producing a version in two *juan*, which would therefore pre-date Ge Hong.

The title given the text by Lu Xiujing includes the term "Cavern of Profundity" (*dongxuan* 洞玄). This term first appeared in the *Lingbao* scriptures, and was used by Lu Xiujing as a marker for the *Lingbao* scriptures.[87] The use of the term in the title here does not indicate any change in content, but is merely a modification of the scripture's title to fit Lu's list. However, Lu's text may not be entirely the same as the current Daozang version. Lu Xiujing does not explain how the text was transmitted between Ge Xuan's time and his own, but we may get a glimpse of this in the writing of another of the great Daoists of the period, Tao Hongjing, whose *Declarations* contains a partial record of the textual transmissions within the Ge-Xu clan.

The records of textual transmission in *Zhen'gao* seem to indicate that at least two versions of the *Lingbao* talismans and texts were transmitted contemporaneously. The earliest record of a transmission of these texts is Yang Xi's receipt of a scripture entitled *Lingbao wufu* from Liu Pu 劉璞 in the sixth year of the *Yonghe* era (350), when Yang Xi was 21 years old. The previous year, Yang Xi had received, from persons unknown, the Talismans for Controlling Tigers and Leopards of Central Yellow 中黃制虎豹符.[88]

Liu Pu was the elder son of Wei Huacun 魏華存 (251–335), who posthumously became Yang Xi's major teacher and transmitter of Shangqing teachings.[89] A daughter of Wei Shu, Education Minister (*situ* 司徒) of the Jin, Wei Huacun is said to have set her intention on attaining transcendence. Her practices included ingestion of sesame powder (*huma san* 胡麻散) and *fuling* pills (茯苓丸), along with methods of breath control (*tuna qiye* 吐納氣液). She wished to live in seclusion, but was forced by her parents to marry Liu Wen of Nanyang, by whom she had two sons, Pu and Xia 瑕. The family migrated south with the great wave of northerners who fled the fighting and invasions of the central plains. At some point after migrating south, she began to receive visitations from spirits, who identified themselves as Perfected from the Shangqing Heaven. She completed

---

86 Ge Xuan is mentioned in a note in DZ 388: 2.22b, which is probably an impossible-to-date interpolation.

87 Ōfuchi Ninji, "The Formation of the Taoist Canon," in Holmes Welch and Anna Seidel, eds. *Facets of Taoism* (New Haven and London: Yale University Press, 1979): 253–67. See also Ōfuchi Ninji, *Dōkyō shi no kenkyū* 道教史の研究 (Okayama: Okayama daigaku kyōzaikai shoseki, 1964): 268.

88 DZ 1016: 20.12a2: 楊先以永和五年已酉歲受中黃制虎豹符六年康戌又就魏夫人長子劉璞受靈寶五符.

89 Wei Huacun's hagiography is preserved partially in *TPGJ* 58, *TPYL* 678.6a–8a and citations in DZ 421; see the detailed analysis in Robinet, *Révélation*, vol. II: 399–405; Despeux, *Immortelles*: 51–67. On the continued reverence to Wei Huacun, see Edward Schafer, "The Restoration of the Shrine of Wei Hua-ts'un at Lin-ch'uan in the Eighth Century" *Journal of Oriental Studies* 15 (1997): 124–137, who translates the stele inscription to Wei Huacun composed by Yan Zhenqing 顏真卿 (709–784) in 769, *Jin zixu yuanjun lingshang zhen siming nanyue furen Wei furen xiantan beiming* 晉紫虛元君領上真司命南嶽夫人魏夫人仙壇碑銘 (*Quan Tangwen* 340.17–22).

her instruction after sloughing off her physical form at the age of 83.[90] According to her hagiography it was at this stage that she encountered Zhang Ling, the first Celestial Master, and received new versions of rites of the Celestial Masters. This hagiographic account reflects the fact that much of her teaching is concerned with recasting Celestial Masters ritual,[91] and we may accept Tao Hongjing's note that Wei Huacun had been a Libationer (*jijiu* 祭酒) of the Celestial Masters.[92] As Robinet argues, Lady Wei clearly played a role in linking the Celestial Masters with the Shangqing movement.[93]

It is unclear whether the transmissions of the *Lingbao wufu* and Central Yellow Talismans were progressive grades within a structured initiation process. However, we should recall that, according to the prefatory section of the third *juan*, a version of the Five Talismans was said to have been transmitted by the Little Lad of the Eastern Sea to Mr. Ling. The instructions for using the talismans include the following formula:

> Embracing the Lingbao talismans when entering rivers and crossing chasms, the Thearch of the North will open a path [for me], krakens and dragons will guard and follow me, water sprites will be startled; I will live for long and have enduring sight, and have eternal joy and heavenly blessings.... Wearing these talismans when climbing mountains, the mountain sprites will flee far. The Great Thearch of Central Yellow (*Zhonghuang taidi* 中黃太帝) will be my support, and tigers, leopards, and the hundred beasts will not dare block me. [As I climb] Towering cliffs and deep caves then the earth pneumas will not interfere. Deviant demons will submit and die; the *Wangliang* demons will retreat to their homes.[94]

The formula includes a reference to the Great Thearch of Central Yellow who will protect the wearer of the talismans from tigers and leopards. This reference resonates with the Talismans for Controlling Tigers and Leopards of Central Yellow received by Yang Xi prior to receiving the *Lingbao Wufu*.

The Little Lad of the Eastern Sea was to become a major deity in the Shangqing pantheon, named Azure Lad 青童, or more regally: Lord of the Golden Porte of

---

90 In the terminology of the Shangqing hagiography she "transformed her body by borrowing a sword" (*tuojian hoaxing* 託劍化形; in TPYL 678.7b the phrase is "using a method for hiding her radiance her borrowed form was transformed by a sword" (*yong zangjing zhifa tuoxing jianhua* 用藏景之法託形劍化).

91 See, in particular her teaching on Entering the Oratory 入靖 preserved in Tao Hongjing's *Dengzhen yinjue* 登真隱訣 DZ 421: 3.1a–5a, which is subtitled "Oral Instructions Told by Master Zhang of the Three Heavens of Correct Unity to the Lady of the Southern Marchmount" 正一三天法師張諱告南嶽夫人. Tao comments that these instructions were transmitted after both personages had already attained Transcendence. However, this Ritual is clearly a reworking of the older Celestial Master rite. See Cedzich, "Das Ritual der Himmelmeister."

92 *Dengzhen yinjue* DZ 421: 3.5b7.

93 Robinet, *Révélation*, vol. 1, 52, 59; vol. 2, 399–405.

94 DZ 388: 3.2a9–2b10.

the Eastern Sea 金闕東海君. If, as most scholars agree, the name Ling does indeed refer to Zhang Ling, the first Celestial Master,[95] then this section of the *Array* may well be a remnant of the *Lingbao Wufu* which was transmitted among the Celestial Masters. The transmission of the *Lingbao wufu* by Wei Huacun's son, Liu Pu, to Yang Xi suggests that, a decade before the first Shangqing revelations, Yang Xi was initiated into a Daoist lineage related to the Celestial Masters.

The reference to Zhang Ling in the *Array of the Five Talismans*, linking the Little Lad of the Eastern Sea with the Celestial Masters, fits well with the early lineage of Shangqing, which emerged among families associated with the Celestial Masters. It is probably this version of the *Lingbao Wufu* which is referred to in another passage in the *Declarations of the Perfected*:

> Yang [Xi] wrote down a *Lingbao wufu* of one fascicle. Originally, this was in the hands of Ge Can 葛粲 of Jurong. At some time during the *taishi* era (465–471 CE) Ge showed this to Master Lu [Xiujing]. Lu had already propagated the *Red Writ in Perfect Script* 真文赤書, the *Man-bird* [chart] and the *Five Talismans* (*Renniao wufu* 人鳥五符). [As] he had transmitted and spread them widely he did not want to have another revelation of a divergent source. He therefore presented Ge with valuable silks and obtained the text. He kept it hidden and locked away. Master Gu [Huan] heard about this and desperately sought to see it. Consequently, Lu did not allow it to be seen. He only transmitted it to Sun Youyue 孫游嶽 of Dongyang and to his female disciple Mei Lingwen 梅令文. When Lu died they returned the text to Xu Shubiao 徐叔摽 of Mount Lu, who later revealed it. When Xu died, it came into the hands of Lu Huaiwen 陸環文.[96]

Tao Hongjing is criticizing Lu Xiujing for suppressing the original manuscript by Yang Xi, which was originally in the possession of Ge Can, an otherwise unknown descendent of the Ge clan. Lu Xiujing, who had also received a different set of scriptures, considered this text to conflict in some way with the textual revelations which he was intent on propagating, namely the *Five Tablets in Red Script*.

Conclusion

In the first part of this chapter we examined the ritual construction of lineages, focusing on the shift from blood oaths to "pure" covenants. We saw that this shift is closely related to the rejection of the sacrificial cultic system, and entails a

95 Max Kaltenmark "*Ling-pao* 靈寶: note sur un terme du Taoisme religieux," in *Mélanges publiés par l'Institut des Hautes Études Chinoises* (Paris 1960): vol. II, 559–88. 1960; Robinet, *Révélation*, vol. 1, 72–73. This narrative is embedded in Zhang Ling's hagiography in *Shexian zhuan*, see Campany, *To Live*, 349–56. Kobayashi does accept this identification, but does not discuss the issue further. Kobayashi, *Rikuchō*, 104, n.30.
96 DZ 1016: 20.2b1; Strickmann, *Mao Shan*, 58–9.

different conception of divinity. Indeed, the rejection of blood is one of the primary determinants of Daoist lineages.

In the second part of the chapter we investigated transmission narratives, and the rhetorical construction of lineages. Focusing on a single text, the *Array of the Five Talismans*, we noted that there were at least three distinct lineages involved in the composition of different sections of the text. We also noted that there were at least two distinct lineages which transmitted texts associated with the Five Talismans. The internal hints cohere with the records of textual transmission included in Tao Hongjing's *Declarations of the Perfected*, which indicate that at least two versions of the *Lingbao* talismans and texts were transmitted contemporaneously in the Jiangnan region.

3 Talismans

The power of inscription

The Sons of Heaven all are essential treasures of the Five Thearchs. Each has its moment of inception; they succeed each other, arising in accord with the sequence of epochs. They must possess the talismans and ledgers of the spirits and numina; then the various spirits will aid and assist them and cause the inauguration of the throne and the establishment of the way. All rulers should place charts and registers (*tulu* 圖錄) at their side, and thereby rectify themselves.[1]

天子皆五帝精寶, 各有題 序次運相據起. 必有神靈符紀, 諸神扶助, 使開階立遂, 王者當置圖錄坐旁, 以自正.

Introduction

Talismans have been ubiquitous in Daoist practice since the emergence of the earliest Daoist communities in the second century CE. Daoist scriptures and ritual manuals from all periods and lineages list vast numbers of talismans and provide detailed illustrations and instructions for their production and use. Talismans are used for healing rites, for exorcism, as apotropaic devices, and as emblems of authority. Talismans are the first device deployed by Daoist priests in order to demarcate sacred space, preparing it for the emplacement of the altar. Through the ritual, the various documents employed by the priests are stamped or inscribed with talismans in order to authenticate and activate the pronouncements and locutions. As the ritual progresses, the priest repeatedly burns talismans, transforming them into the cloudy medium that will transport their power to the realms of the spirits and deities. The most powerful and efficacious of talismans do not require material form, as the priest inscribes them in the air with precise hand movements, while controlling his breath and visualizing his journey to the celestial court. Talismans are indeed the most efficacious of Daoist devices. In this chapter, I focus on the question: why are talismans so

---

1 Chunqiu yankongtu 春秋演孔圖, collated in IS. 18.2, WSJC 2.581; originally cited in TPYL 76.355a, *Chuxueji* 初學記 9.

central in Daoist practice, and why are they perceived to be charged with such numinous power?

Daoists did not invent the use of talismans. As with the other practices discussed in this book, the history of talismans extends back into the Warring States era, and possibly earlier. Evidence from this era, both textual and material, shows that talismans were used as symbols of fealty and authenticity at the highest political levels while in the common religion of the period talismans were used for healing and exorcism. The use of talismans in Daoist ritual is descended from both of these early practices. Along with charts and registers, talismans were part of the imperial bureaucratic apparatus that became the model for Daoist cosmology and ritual. Daoists also adopted the use of talismans of apotropaic, exorcistic, and healing traditions of early China. Daoists, however, soon came to perceive talismans as more than apotropaic devices and signs of power. The cloudy forms of talismanic script were perceived as manifestations of the primordial pneumas of the cosmos, and talismans were described as the very engines of cosmogenesis. This chapter traces these developments.

To pre-empt a complex argument, my analysis of talismans focuses on the terms "true form" (*zhenxing* 真形) and "true name" (*zhenming* 真名) that are used in medieval Daoist texts to denote the esoteric and primordial shapes and names of mountains, spirits, gods, scriptures, and all things of the world. While these terms provide us with an emic understanding of talismans, I suggest that, analytically, the efficacy of talismans is based on the power inherent in "inscription." This notion refers to the efficacy inherent in the ability to inscribe and name the things of the world, which grants power over those things being named and portrayed. As this notion, however, is applicable to several other types of documents, such as charts, registers, and contracts, I introduce two other notions that distinguish the efficacy of talismans: recognizability and signification.

By using these complementary terms, I refer to fact that, while talismans are incomprehensible in mundane linguistic terms, they are recognizable as emanations of the Dao itself. Simply put, my argument is that talismans used as pragmatic devices, as political marks of authority, in healing, exorcism, and apotropaic practices, depend for their significance on external referents, and may be usefully analyzed according to Charles Sanders Peirce's categories of symbol, index, and icon.[2] These pragmatic talismans may be iconic, indexical, or symbolic signs of contractual obligations or infused with power that is external to the device itself. Daoists, of course, continued to use talismans for pragmatic purposes, but they

---

2   Peirce himself did not provide a single, coherent presentation of his analysis of signs. I find Naomi Janowitz' concise presentation particularly useful: (1) Icon is "a sign which would possess the character which renders it significant, even though the object may have no existence." Icons are not arbitrary… but have a formal resemblance to the entities they represent. (2) Index is a sign that is linked to what it represents by a "pointing" relationship, and needs to be in spatio-temporal congruity with that object. (3) Symbol is a sign that has an arbitrary relationship to what it represents, and is based solely on accepted social convention. Naomi Janowitz, *Icons of Power: Ritual Practices in Late Antiquity* (University Park: Pennsylvania State University Press, 2002): xxii–xxiv.

infused their own talismans with far greater significance – or, perhaps, a quality beyond significance.

Daoist talismans were themselves perceived as primordial cosmogonic forces. They do not have external referents and were not perceived as representing anything other than themselves. That is, the talismans are self-referential, and perceived as actual inscriptions of primordial emanation of *qi*. The efficacy and power of talismans stem from their actual participation in cosmogenesis. This understanding of talismans was based on several ancient myths and practices, but eventually coalesced around the Lingbao talismans. In the second half of this Chapter, I trace the changing notions regarding the Lingbao talismans, which transformed from one of many apotropaic devices in early texts to having a critical function in Daoist cosmogony and cosmology. These talismans, or writs in talismanic script inspired by them, came to be seen as the primordial emanations of the Dao in the initial moments of inception, as the original true forms and names of all things.

Part I: Efficacious terminology

The use of talismans and amulets was not, of course, restricted to Chinese religions, but was ubiquitous in late antiquity among Jews, Christians, and adherents of Greco-Roman religions. Such coincidence of practice, temporality, and, most importantly, the range of traditions in which we find the use of talismans, allows for comparative analysis. Scholars of these Hellenistic and medieval Western traditions often categorize the use of talismans and amulets as "magic." More recently, scholars of late antiquity have come to realize that the term "magic" originated in polemical debates about correct religious practice, and that the label "magic" is problematic and fraught with connotations and implications derived from such polemics.[3] Nevertheless, as has recently been shown by several scholars of Western traditions, these polemical debates are not about the efficacy of the practices decried as "magic" but rather about the appropriate wielding of power.[4] While we do not find a term equivalent to magic in texts from early medieval China, we do find debates about efficacy and proper ritual agency. Thus, while I do not use the term magic in my analysis, insights from studies of Western traditions may be helpful for understanding and analyzing the Chinese material.

Official histories report that talismans were among the core practices of the earliest Daoist movements. In fact, according to these reports it was due to the efficacious talismanic healing practice of Zhang Jue that adherents flocked to the Taiping

3 A particularly useful survey of studies and bibliography is provided in the "Introduction" to Scott Noegel, Joel Walker, and Brannon Wheeler, eds. *Prayer, Magic, and the Stars in the Ancient and Late Antique World* (University Park: Pennsylvania State University Press, 2003); Janowitz, *Icons of Power*; Don C. Skemer, *Binding Words: Textual Amulets in the Middle Ages* (University Park: Pennsylvania State University Press, 2006).
4 Janowitz is particularly succinct and useful on this point; Janowitz, *Icons*, 1–17.

movement.[5] Zhang Ling, the first Celestial Master, is said to have "fabricated talismans and writings with which he deluded the people."[6]

These reports were, of course, critical of the Daoists and their practices. However, we should note that the historians did not doubt the inherent efficacy of talismans. Rather, they criticized the fabrication of talismans (*wei fuzou* 為符祝 or *zaozuo fushu* 造作符書). Unlike the talismans, and other omens, deployed by the rulers to authenticate their rule, these talismans were not "natural" and did not represent the true patterns of nature. The official historians criticized the Daoists as rebels who fabricated talismans in order to fool the population.

This point is clear in the following report about the rebel leader Dai Yi 戴異 who:

> obtained golden seals, but they were without marks or characters. Consequently, he offered sacrifice at the well together with Long Shang of Guangling. He produced talismanic writings [or talismans and writings] and styled himself Great Superior Luminary. He was subdued and executed.[7]

The point here is that the seals Dai Yi obtained lacked any markings, and therefore could not function as signs of any type. He then resorted to manufacturing talismans and writings to support his claim. These, however, were patently false, which may explain his quick demise. We should emphasize, however, that this critique assumes the existence of "real" seals, talismans, or other objects, that carry true signification.

I POWER OF INSCRIPTION

By "inscription," I refer to the efficacy inherent in inscribing names and forms, which grants power over the things named and portrayed. This notion was central to imperial power, providing the ruler with legitimacy and authority and allowing him to claim the support of the spirits. The passage cited at the beginning of the chapter, from the *Chunqiu yankongtu*, a weft-text associated with the *Spring and Autumn Annals*, identifies the ruling emperors with the essence of the Five Thearchs, who are themselves manifestations of the five phases. Appearing in the world in accord with the epochal sequence of the phases, the human rulers are thus defined as embodying the cosmic patterns. Their rise is authenticated by talismans, ledgers, charts, and registers (*fu* 符, *ji* 紀, *tu* 圖, *lu* 錄), terms that represent different modalities for inscribing the world. Not mere symbolic regalia, these documents were essential for understanding and controlling cosmic power. These different textual modalities were adapted by Daoists to become crucial devices in

---

5 "The leaders of the Taiping movement grasped a nine-node staff, made talismans and incantations, instructed the ill to knock their heads and confess their faults and gave them talismanic water to drink." 太平道師持九節杖, 為符祝, 教病人叩頭思過, 因以符水飲之; *Dianlue* 典略 cited in SGZ 8.264, HHS 75.2436; also HHS 71.2299.

6 HHS 75.2435: 造作符書以惑百姓.

7 HHS 7.316: 戴異得黃金印, 無文字, 遂與廣陵人龍尚等共祭井, 作符書, 稱太上皇, 伏誅.

the Daoist ritual systems, and particularly the bureaucratic ritual of Celestial Master Daoism.

The power of inscription, however, was not limited to imperial documents and authority. We find that this power was wielded by Masters of Esoterica. In Chapter 1, we saw that Tang Gongfang's early proof of power was his ability to capture rats by inscribing a gaol on the ground.[8] Similar practices are mentioned in Li Yiqi's 李意期 hagiography:

> If someone needed to travel a long distance quickly, Li Yiqi would give him a talisman and write something in vermilion underneath both arms. [After describing the remote and wonderful places they traveled to] Li would model what they described in dirt; it would correspond in all respects to what they had seen, only it was in miniature, and then in a moment it would vanish… When Liu Bei wanted to attack Wu he summoned Li with proper respect and inquired about the auspicious and inauspicious [aspects of his plan]. Li did not reply but asked for paper and brush. He drew troops, horses and weapons on several dozens of sheets and then ripped up and destroyed each of them in his hands. He then drew a great man, dug a hole and buried the paper in the hole…. [After suffering a great defeat at the hands of Wu] in anger and shame Liu Bei developed an illness and died. Now the meaning [of Li's action] was clear to all. His drawing of a great man and burying it was meant to convey the death of Liu Bei.[9]

Li Yiqi is able to affect change through inscription. He could cause others to travel instantaneously by inscribing talismans. He could then draw the images that they had seen on their journey. His response to Liu Bei's inquiry is intriguing in combining the production of images with performance. The powers of inscription these practices exemplify are traceable to ancient mythical clusters that asserted claims of legitimacy, authority, and control that extended beyond the human realm to encompass spirits and natural forces.

The primary myth expressing the notion of true forms and shapes is the narrative of Yu casting bronze tripods on which were representations of all harmful demons. The narrative is embedded in a speech preserved in the *Zuozhuan*:

> Anciently, the realm of Xia possessed virtue. The faraway regions made representations of their anomalies 遠方圖物; the nine shepherds presented metals [of their regions]. Tripods were cast [with] images of the anomalies

8   See Chapter 1 for details.
9   I follow the composite translation in Campany, *To Live*, 228–30, 437–8. Campany suggests Li Yiqi may be another example of adepts surnamed Li affiliated with the Celestial Masters. Note that this event is recounted at the end of Liu Bei's biography in the SGZ 32, which contains long and elaborate discussions of prophecies and weft-texts by members of the Yang Hou lineage who persuade Liu Bei to take the throne. In discussing Li's practices Campany refers to the technique of inscription relating it to "miniaturization" and the system of correspondences between the macrocosm and microcosm.

象物. All anomalies were represented to allow the people to know the spirits and other deviations. Hence, people traveling through rivers and marshes, hills and forests did not encounter the harmful creatures, and the *limei* and *wangliang* were unable to encounter them. Their use enabled harmony of those above and below, and the attainments of heaven's blessings.

Yu's tripods became a major iconic and narrative trope in discussion of legitimacy and power. For instance, in the late fourth century BCE, Zhang Yi 張儀, counselor to the King of Qin, advised the king to attack the state of Han 韓 so as to be near the tripods kept at the ancestral temple in the Zhou capital of Luoyi. Zhang's main argument was that by "attaining the tripods and seizing the charts and registers [you] can hold the son of heaven hostage to command all under heaven, and the whole world will submit."[10]

In his speech, Zhang Yi associated the tripods with charts and registers (*tushu*). While here these terms refer to administrative documents, maps and lists of names that marked the territory and population under control by the person possessing them, the terms are clearly linked to the ancient mythical cluster of intrinsically powerful inscriptions, the River Chart and Luo Writ 河圖洛書. The pragmatic emblems of office are thus linked with the symbolic and mythic regalia, and shared in the same mythology of forms and names.

In the changing polities of the late Warring States, the general population began to receive names and titles. While marking the people as legally autonomous, the inscription of these names in registers subordinated them to the ruler. By possession of these registers, and recording the names and residences of the subordinate population, officials gained their status as intermediaries of the ultimate authority. Mark Lewis argues that the registers and maps became metonyms for the ruler's authority, and concludes that inscription marked subjection. He continues: "these written depictions of population and territory came to magically embody the objects that they represented".[11]

Whether administrative charts and registers in the pre-imperial period were talismans possessing intrinsic magical power, as suggested by Lewis, remains debatable. However, by the late Han, the charts and registers had transcended the pragmatic symbolism of office holdings, and had become emblems of power. This is best demonstrated by examining the role of charts in the weft texts in which the authority of the ruler is fully dependent on the texts he possesses, and the attitude towards these charts in contemporary texts. One example, from a late Han stele inscription, exemplifies the notion of charts and writs, not as administrative documents, but as emblems of rule. Closely following the weft texts, the Han Chi 韓敕 stele relates the failure of both the First Emperor of Qin and of Xiang Yu to their irreverence to the charts and writs:

10 *Shiji* 70.2282.
11 Lewis, *Writing,* 26.

Qin and Xiang caused disorder, did not revere the charts and writs, turned their back on the Way and betrayed Virtue, distanced themselves from the sagely carriage, ate coarse grains and died at Shaqiu.[12]

秦項作亂不尊圖書倍道畔德, 離敗聖輿, 食糧亡于沙丘

II EARLY TALISMANS

The use of talismans in Daoism is derived from ancient ceremonies of political fealty as well as uses of talismans in apotropaic and healing practices.[13] Appointment of an official was always accompanied by the receipt of title and seals of office. The seals were inscribed with the name of the office and were to validate official documents. Worn by the official at his waist, the seals were emblems of power and authority.[14] Along with seals of office, authority was bestowed on the officials by the granting of talismans.[15] Made of bamboo, wood or bronze, silk, or paper on which contracts were written, a talisman (*fu*) consisted of two split halves (*pofu* 剖符). Each party in the contract received a tally (*qi* 契) as guarantee. Military appointments, too, were confirmed by the bestowal of signs of authority. The most famous of these were the "copper tiger tallies" 銅虎符.[16] A general received half of a tiger tally from the ruler, which allowed him to master and mobilize troops. The tallies were inscribed with the conditions and limits of the general's authority. Tallies allowed transit through border passes and into the

---

12 "Han Chi bei" 韓敕碑 in *Jinshi cuipian* 9; Nagata Hidemasa 永田英正, Kandai sekkoku shûsei 漢代石刻集成 (Kyoto, Dôhôsha, 1994), vol. I, 124–26, vol. II, 89–93. The First Emperor of Qin died at Shaqiu (near modern Guangzong county, Hubei) while on his fifth tour of the realm, during the seventh month of 211 BCE; *SJ* 6.264; Nienhauser *The Grand Scribe's Records*, vol. 1, 154; Denis Twitchett and Michael Loewe, eds. *The Cambridge History of China, vol. 1: The Ch'in and Han Empires, 221 BC–AD 220* (Cambridge: Cambridge University Press, 1986): 68, 81. Xiang Yu was Liu Bang's main rival during the civil war which ensued following the collapse of the Qin. He finally committed suicide in the twelfth month of 202 BCE; Xiang Yu's biography is *Shiji* 7, for a concise summary of the civil war, see Twitchett and Loewe, *Cambridge*, 111–19.

13 For examples in the Mawangdui medical texts, see Harper, *Early Chinese*, 167, 301 (MSI.E.273), 354 (MSIII.83–4). For examples in the Shuihudi 睡虎地 texts see Liu Tseng-Kuei 劉增貴, "Qinjian "rishu" zhongde chuxing lisu yu xinyang" 秦簡‘日書’中的出行禮俗與信仰 *BIHP* 72.3 (2001): 503–41, esp. 522–26.

14 Li Xueqin, *Eastern Zhou and Qin Civilizations*, trans. by K.C. Chang (New Haven: Yale University Press, 1985): 399–417.

15 The Han dictionary *Shuowen jiezi* provides the following definition: "Talisman is authentication. According to Han regulations, use a six-inch long bamboo strip, divide it and then match the parts together." 符信也. 漢制, 以竹長六寸, 分而相合 (1987: 5A.5b).

16 Lothar von Falkenhausen, "The E Jun Qi Metal Tallies," in Martin Kern, ed. *Text and Ritual in Early China* (Seattle: University of Washington Press, 2005): 79–123, esp. 85–89. Despite their early provenance the *Shiji* claims these tallies were reputedly an innovation by Han emperor Wen, who in his second year "for the first time produced copper tiger tallies and bamboo envoy tallies for the ministers and officials of the state." 始與國守相為銅虎符, 竹使符 (*Shiji* 10.424; Nienhauser, *The Grand Scribes Records*, vol. 2, 166). Perhaps the point is that emperor Wen systematized a variety of ancient tallies.

ruler's inner chambers. Periodically, the officials and generals would return to the capital to "match tallies" (*hefu* 合符) with the ruler and thus prove their continuing allegiance.[17] The mythical antecedents for these were the ceremonies in which the ancient sages "matched tallies" with the spirits as symbols of authority.[18]

As these examples show, early *fu* 符 were bipartite talismans. The imagery on the talismans was less important than the artifact itself. This is not the case with the talismans that appear in the Eastern Han and in later Daoism. First, Daoist *fu* in the medieval were not bipartite. Rather, they were perceived as exact facsimiles of celestial models. Indeed, as we will see below, the talismans produced by Daoist masters were perceived as sharing in the same ethereal yet substantial quality of cosmic patterns.[19] Thus, rather than evidence of contractual obligation, they function as signs of authority. Moreover, the glyphs become far more important than the artifact on which they are inscribed. This indicates a shift in the function of *fu* from an artifact signifying a contract between parties to an esoteric sign indicating power over the entity signified.

III   EASTERN HAN TALISMANS

The official histories do not provide much in the way of describing actual practices. However, recent examinations of archaeological evidence marshaled by Anna Seidel, Wang Yucheng, Zhang Xunliao, and Liu Zhaorui have cast much light on Han period talismanic practices and the continuities between these and Daoist practices.[20] Wang Yucheng has actually labeled the talismans inscribed on the jars, bottles and stones in Eastern Han tombs as "Daoist talismans" 道符.[21]

---

17 In 196 BCE Liu Bang, the first Han emperor, gathered his followers and relatives to reward their support. After the emperor "split tallies and distributed fiefs" 剖符行封, the vassals "swore allegiance which was recorded in cinnabar on iron tallies, placed in a golden casket in a stone chamber, and preserved in the ancestral temple." The ceremony was sealed by the sacrifice of a white horse. *Shiji* 8.384; *Hanshu* 1B.60, 1B.81 作誓丹書鐵契, 金匱石室, 藏之宗廟; cited in Seidel, "Imperial Treasures," 311. This classic description was reformulated into a Daoist myth that conjoined the empire and the Celestial Masters, and even claimed superiority of the Daoist revelation over the mundane administrative system. According to the fifth century *Inner Explanations of the Three Heavens*, sixteen years after the revelation of Lord Lao to Zhang Daoling (i.e. in 157 CE), Zhang made a covenant with the Han emperor at court using "the blood of a white horse as contract and iron tallies inscribed in cinnabar as verification." Standing before the Three Offices of Heaven, Earth and Water, and the Great Year General (Jupiter) they swore together to always employ the Correct Law of the Three Heavens. DZ 1205: 1.6a6 以白馬血為盟丹書鐵券為信; Bokenkamp, *Early*, 216; Seidel, "Imperial Treasures," 315.

18 Seidel, "Imperial Treasures," 311–14 provides several examples collated from the weft texts.

19 See also John Lagerwey, *Taoist Ritual in Chinese Society and History* (New York: Macmillan, 1987): 153–66.

20 Besides the studies mentioned above, other recent relevant studies include: Nickerson, *Taoism*, Lian Shaoming 連邵名, "Kaogu faxian yu zaoqi fu" 考古發現與早期符 *KG* 1995.12: 1125–30; Liu Zhongyu 劉仲宇, "Daofu suyuan" 道符溯源, *Shijie zongjiao yanjiu* 1994.1: 1–10; Wang Yucheng 王育成, "Donghan daofu shili" 東漢道符實例, *Kaogu xuebao* 1991.1: 45–56.

21 Wang, "Donghan daofu," 282.

Zhang Xunliao has questioned the very definition of Daoism and its early history.[22] A full treatment of these critical questions is beyond the scope of this chapter, but as my analysis reveals important differences between Eastern Han talismans and Daoist talismans, I would argue great caution before adopting either Wang's use of "Daoist talismans" or Zhang's historical reconstruction.

Among the best examples for continuities between Han era and Daoist practices and terminology is the ordinance jar unearthed in the tomb of Cao Bolu 曹伯魯, dating to the second year of *yangjia* 陽家 (133 CE) and inscribed with a short text and two red talismans.[23] The inscription provides a rare clear glimpse into beliefs and practices pertaining to the relations between the living and the dead during the Han:

> [Date]…the Envoy of the Celestial Thearch 天帝使者, on behalf of the family of Cao Bolu diligently removes danger and expels odium, making them a thousand *li* distant. Odium [using] great peach [wood] will not stay, [ ] [ ] reaching to the place of ghosts. …The living possess nine, the dead possess five, the living and the dead take distinct paths, separate from each other by a myriad *li*. From today I will for long protect their descendants, their longevity will be as of gold and stones and to the end they will not have misfortune. In order to prove their oath, they use divine medicinals to secure the tomb and seal it with the Yue Stamp of the Yellow Spirit (*Huangshen yuezhang* 黃神越章). In accord with the rules and regulations 如律令.[24]

The obvious continuities in terminology between this text and Daoist practices have been analyzed by Anna Seidel, Zhang Xunliao, and Wang Yucheng.[25] The

22 The most comprehensive study to date is Zhang Xunliao and Bai Bin, *Zhongguo daojiao kaogu* 中國道教考古 (Beijing: Xianzhuang shuju, 2006); Bai Bin, "Religious Beliefs as Reflected in the Funerary Record," in John Lagerwey and Pengzhi Lü, eds. *Early Chinese religion: the Period of Division (220–589 AD)* (Leiden: Brill, 2010): 989–1073. Based on their analysis of "vessels for dissolving (demonic) infusion" 解注器 Zhang and Bai suggest that Celestial Master Daoism first formed in the central regions, centered on Luoyang and Chang'an, during the reign of emperor Ming (57–75 CE). It then expanded west, southwest, and south in successive stages. One branch passed through Hanzhong and into Sichuan to develop into the Way of the Five Pecks of Rice around the time of emperor Shun (125–44). A second branch passed through Anhui province and expanded into the lower reaches of the Yangtze in Jiangsu and other areas in the southern coast. This branch was the basis for the expansion of Daoism during the Six Dynasties period. A third branch followed the Silk Road to the west during the late Han and Three Kingdoms period and developed in the Xining district of Qinghai Province. During the Jin and Sixteen Kingdoms period this branch expanded significantly in the Gansu area, especially in Dunhuang.
23 Found in 1972 at Zhujiabao 朱家堡 in Huxian 戶縣 county, Shaanxi. See Zhuo Zhenxi 禚振西, "Shaanxi huxian de linagzuo hanmu" 陝西戶線的兩座漢墓, *Kaogu yu wenwu* 1980.1; idem. "Caoshi zhushuguan kaoshi" 曹氏朱書罐考釋, *Kaogu yu wenwu* 1982.2: 88–91; Wang Yucheng, "Donghan daofu," 45–50. Anna Seidel, "Traces of Han Religion, In Funeral Texts Found in Tombs" in Akizuki Kanei 秋月觀映, ed. *Dōkyō to shukyō bunka* 道教と宗教文化 (Tokyo: Hirakawa, 1987): 23–57; Zhang and Bai, *Zhongguo*, vol. 1, 109 ff.
24 Seidel, "Traces."
25 Seidel, "Traces,"; Zhang Xunliao, "Donghan"; Wang Yucheng, "Donghan tiandi shizhe lei daoren yu daojiao qiyuan" 東漢天帝使者類道人與道教起原, *Daojia wenhua yanjiu* 16 (1999): 181–203.

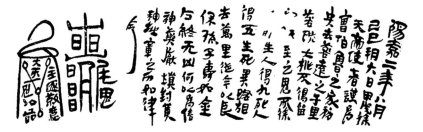

Figure 3.1 Cao Bolu talismans.

formula "in accord with the rules and regulations" remains a basic element in Daoist petition through the Six Dynasties to the present. By the fourth century, the Celestial Thearch, the deity by whose authority the documents were issued, was replaced by the "Newly Emerged Lord Lao of the Most High" in tomb ordinances associated with Celestial Master Daoism.[26]

Another element that reveals continuity between Han religious practice and Daoist practice is the Yue Stamp of the Yellow Spirit. Seals bearing the inscription *Huangshen yuezhang* are the most common seal among extant late Han seals.[27] In the early fourth century, Ge Hong describes the use of Yue Seal of the Yellow Thearch.[28] Thus, the Yue Stamp of the Yellow Spirit that appears in funerary contexts during the Han, was, by the early fourth century, used to produce seals for

26 Nickerson sees this change as a mark of "the commencement of the early Daoist liturgical tradition when the religion of the grave-securing writs was subsumed under the revelation of the deified newly emerged Laozi to the first Celestial Master, Zhang Daoling." Another major contrast between the proto-Daoist exorcist tradition and Daoist soteriology indicated in the terminology of the Daoist tomb ordinances was the change in destination of the dead who are said to return to the Three Heavens rather than stay secure in their tombs. Nickerson, 1996: 180.

27 There are also examples of inscriptions of *Huangshen* 黃神 only. Liu Zhaorui 留昭瑞, "Lun 'Huangshen yuezhang' jiantan huangjin kouhao ji xiangguan wenti" 論"黃神越章" 兼談黃巾口號 的意義及相關問題, *Lishi yanjiu* 1996.1: 125–32; Lu Yixing 陸錫興, "'Huangjun faxing' zhuzi kemingzhuan de tansuo" "黃君法行" 朱字刻銘磚的探索, *KG* 2002.4: 85–8; Wang Yucheng, *Daojiao fayin lingpai tan'ao* 道教法印令牌探奧 (Beijing: Zongjiao wenhua chubanshe, 2000): 12–13 lists 22 exemplars of seals with *Huangshen yuezhang* and another 6 inscribed with *Huangshen yuezhang tiandi shen* (see p.20–21 for illustrations).

28   The ancients who entered mountains all wore it at their side. It is four inches wide and has 120 characters. If one uses it to produce clay stamps, and places these some hundreds of paces around in the four directions around one's location, then tigers and wolves would not dare encroach. Not only does it ward off tigers and wolves, but if one is in the mountains and rivers near a temple of blood-drinking demons which cause misfortune, one can use it to seal the earth to cut off their path and they would not return to be spirits.

Ge Hong adds a short anecdote about a great turtle that dwelt in a pool of the Shitou 石頭 river. This turtle could produce demonic visions and spread disease. Dai Bing 戴昞 of Wu used this seal to produce hundreds of stamps which he then threw into the pool. The turtle finally floated up, and was killed. The illnesses were then cured. *Baopuzi* 17.313; Ware, *Alchemy* 298–9.

apotropaic use. By the thirteenth century, a seal with the same name was used to stamp documents to be submitted to heaven during the performance of a ritual.[29]

The first talisman next to the inscription on the Cao jar is divided into two parts. On the top, a *tu* 土, with two graphs of sun (*ri* 日) within it; on the bottom, arrayed from right to left are the graphs *wei* 尾 above *gui* 鬼 (which may represent *kui* 魁, the bowl of the dipper); in the center the graph for moon (*yue* 月), and three graphs of sun 日 drawn vertically.

This composition is explicated by Wang Yucheng to be an emblematic representation of the content of the inscription.[30] Demonstrating that the top part of the talisman is the graph 旹, which was used in the Han as an alternative graph for time (*shi* 時), Wang suggests its meaning here is the timeliness of death as part of the natural process. The graphs for sun and moon are emblematic of the distinction between the realms of the dead, affiliated with the moon and *yin*, and of the living, affiliated with the sun and *yang*. The graphs *wei* and *gui* represent the lunar lodges "Tail" and "Ghost." The former, composed of nine stars called "nine sons" (*jiuzi* 九子), is associated with the harem. The latter, composed of five stars, is said to be in charge of sacrifice and rituals, and in particular funerary rites (*zangsi cisi* 喪死祠祀).[31] Wang suggests that *wei* and *gui* are thus emblematic of the nine stars of "Tail" associated with procreation and the five stars of "Ghost" associated with correct ritual. This, then, is a graphic representation of the sentence "The living possess nine, the dead posses five, the living and the dead take distinct paths" in the inscription. While the "Tail" asterism secures the family's descendents, the "Ghost" ensures the dead are secure in their realm.

The second talisman on the Cao ordinance jar exemplifies the function of *Taiyi* as an apotropaic deity in the common religion of the late Warring States and early Han. Li Ling has shown that it may in fact be an example of the design on the Taiyi spear (太一鋒) described in the *Shiji*.[32] The talisman is enclosed by a design shaped like the seal-script form of 允 (permit, grant). Within this form there is a Y-shaped pattern composed of three small circles in a triangular formation above a fourth circle. The circles are linked by single black lines in a form typical of star charts. Within the upper portion of the Y is inscribed 大天一; on the left is inscribed 主逐敦惡, and on the right 鬼以節. Wang Yucheng interpreted this inscription as "Making a tally with *Taiyi* and *tianyi* in charge of pursuing demonic spirits".[33] *Taiyi* is associated with three stars, which are labeled *Tianyi*. These two figures should be seen in context with the *Taiyi* spear described in the *Shiji*:

> When attacking Nanyue, [the emperor] offered prayer to *Taiyi*. On a banner attached to a pole of non-fruiting jujube he drew the sun, moon, northern

29 Michel Strickmann considers this change to mark the distinction between diffuse occultism and formal Daoism; *Chinese Magical Medicine*, 191; for more examples of later uses, see 140–41, 179.
30 Wang Yucheng "Donghan daofu," 46–8.
31 *Shiji* 27.1298, 1302.
32 Li Ling "Archaeological," 17, 19, fig.10 on 37; Monica Drexler, "Schriftamulette *fu* auf zwei Grabvasen der Östlichen Han-Zeit," *Monumenta Serica* 49 (2001): 242–44.
33 Wang Yucheng, "Wenwu," 269.

dipper and the Ascending Dragon, representing an image of the three stars of *Tianyi*, thereby making a *Taiyi* spear. It was called the Numinous Banner. The Grand Scribe raised and pointed it in the direction of the state to be attacked while praying for victory.[34]

Another example that reveals intriguing continuities with later Daoist practice is a talisman and incantation found at Shaojiagou 邵家溝 (Jiangsu).[35] Wang Yucheng has shown that the talisman and the incantation are closely related in content, and are complementary in their exorcistic function. While the incantation is relatively clear, the form of the talisman has raised some debate. Wang argues that the star chart represents the six stars of the Southern Dipper, and that the graphs above should be read "Lord of the Talisman" *fujun* 符君. Liu Lexian argues persuasively that the image is that of the Northern Dipper with its seven stars, and the graphs should be read as "Lord of the Northern Dipper" *Beidou jun* 北斗君.[36]

The incantation is directed at the ghost that is associated with a specific day of death, *yisi* in this case. This ghost, which may be seen as a transformation of the

Figure 3.2 Shaojia gou talisman

34 *Shiji* 28.1395; *Shiji* 12.471.
35 Reported by Jiangsu sheng wenwu guanli weiyuan hui, "Jiangsu gaoyou shaojiagou handai yizhi de qingli" 江蘇高郵邵家溝漢代遺址的清理 KG 1960.10: 20–21. Drexler, "Schriftamulette," 238; Wang, "Wenwu," 279; Csikszentmihàlyi, *Readings*, 164–6; Zhang and Bai, *Zhongguo*, vol. 1, 252.
36 Liu Lexian 劉樂賢, "Shaojiagou Handai mudu shang de fuzhou ji xiangguan wenti" 邵家溝漢代木牘上的符咒及相關問題 (Taipei: Zhongguo wenhua daxue shixuexi, 1999).

deceased itself, causes illness if it is unsettled and it must therefore be kept away from the living:

> As for one who dies on an *yisi* day, his ghost name is Tianguang. The Spirit-commander of the Celestial Thearch, already knows your name. Let disease be removed 3000 *li*. If you have not departed, the Southern Mountain … will come and swallow you. Hurry, in accord with the rules and commands."

> 乙巳日死者, 鬼名為天光. 天帝神師已知汝名, 疾去三千里, 汝不既去, 南山, 給-- 令來食汝. 急如律令.

The authority that issues this command is the Commander of Spirits of the Celestial Thearch. The tomb also included a clay stamp 封泥 inscribed with "Envoy of the Celestial Thearch" 天帝使者 that may be proof of authentication of the command. The request, or command, is followed by a threat that, were it not obeyed, the offending spirit would be devoured by the spirit of South Mountain. We should note first the importance of knowing the true names of ghosts and spirits in order to control and exorcize them. Second, this particular ghost is correlated to the day of death, indicating the incorporation of time into the bureaucratic ritual realm. The talismans used in funerary contexts, the imagery on the Taiyi spear, and the clay seal all exemplify the power inherent in representation and naming. The correct image, drawn precisely, brings about change in reality itself. This efficacy is precisely what I refer to as "the power of inscription."

IV   TALISMANS IN DAOIST PRACTICE

Wang Yucheng's explications of talismans are ingenious and intriguing, yet they beg the question of the talismanic form itself. If, indeed, talismans are written forms of incantation, why do they need to be so convoluted and abstruse? If talismans can be parsed intelligibly as complete and cogent written locutions, why were they were not written this way in the first place?

Wang certainly demonstrates that talismans and incantations may be mutually explicable. Indeed, instructions for applying talismans often specify that they are to be accompanied by an incantation. Hence, according to Wang's hypothesis, we may assume that, however inscrutable the talisman may appear to be, it carries the same meaning as the oral formula. In other words, Wang assumes that the enunciated words of a formula and the inscribed representation of a talisman carry similar meanings in different formats. This is indeed a valuable insight to recall when we look at talismans that contain designs which are not as easily explicable. However, this hypothesis seems to over-rationalize the notion of the power of inscription exemplified by the talismans. This is especially true for Daoist talismans.

Daoist notions concerning the origins of talismans and talismanic writing reveal that their power was due precisely to their incomprehensibility. They are emanations of rarefied *qi*, far nearer the primordial creative process than regular human writing, and express truths that the human script cannot fully replicate.

Regular script is thus no more than "traces" of the original patterns. Talismans are therefore pure signification – and do not signify anything beyond themselves. We find a hint of this in Ge Hong's notions of the origin of talismans:

> Master Zheng said that the talismans transmitted from Laojun are all celestial patterns (*tianwen* 天文). Laojun could communicate with the spirit-luminaries and the talismans were transmitted by the spirit-luminaries. Nowadays when people use them they are rarely efficacious because many errors have entered later copies during the long history of their transmissions. Moreover, if one's faith [in their efficacy] is not sincere, then their application will not succeed. Like ordinary writing, if there are mistakes in talismans, not only are they not beneficial, but they will cause harm... But, nowadays, the graphs of the talismans are unreadable, and mistakes cannot be perceived. Therefore, nobody realizes they are incorrect.[37]

There are several points to note here. First, talismans are defined as "celestial patterns" and clearly distinguished from ordinary writings (*shuzi* 書字). Second, the correct forms of talismans originated with spiritual beings, and were transmitted into our world by Lord Lao.[38] Third, the efficacy of talismans depends on the precise inscription of the correct form. Even the slightest deviation from the original form may be dangerous. Fourth, unqualified faith in the efficacy of the talisman is necessary. Unlike regular writing, the efficacy of the talisman is not in legibility, but, on the contrary, in the precise inscription of incomprehensible patterns.[39] Thus, the efficacy of the talismans is not in legibility or comprehensibility, but in adherence to their original form – which is said to be "celestial."

The notion of "celestial writing" underlies the detailed discussion on the origins and types of writing preserved in the *Declarations of the Perfected*. In response to Yang Xi's query as to why the celestial Perfected do not themselves write, the Lady of Purple Tenuity provides a complete theory of the evolution (or devolution) of writing as a process paralleling the cosmogonic differentiation. At the earliest stage of the differentiation of the Dao, "the sinking effulgences of the void profundity, there is no path by which they can be sought; the words emanate in empty space, there is no thing by which they can be traced." These flashes of light and tones float freely in the void and gradually coagulate into actual signs, the "visible traces of writing [which are] are nothing more than wielding shapes on

---

37 Wang, BPZ, 19.335, Ware, *Alchemy*, 313.
38 Laojun, Lord Lao, is one of the epithets used for the deified Laozi. As discussed in Chapter 1, the deification of Laozi was a complex development and the understanding of this divine figure varied across cultural strata and among Daoist groups. Ge Hong himself seems not to have seen Laozi as a cosmic deity, but as a successful practitioner. The precise understanding of Laozi in this passage is unclear.
39 As evidence for the incomprehensibility of talismans, Ge Hong tells of Jie Xiang 介象, who alone could "read talismanic writing" (*du fuwen* 讀符文) and discern mistakes. No one since has had the same ability (Wang, BPZ, 19.336, Ware, *Alchemy*, 314).

paper and tablet." The lecture continues with a more detailed description of the development of script and appearance of texts in the human realm:

> When the five colors first sprouted was the moment the patterns of script were determined. To perfect human interaction and to distinguish *yin* and *yang* then appeared the flying celestial writings in all directions of the Three Primordials and Eight Nodes (*sanyuan bahui* 三元八會).[40] There were also eight bright radiant cloud-seal dragon glyphs 八龍雲篆明光之章. Later, at the time of the two luminous sovereigns they elaborated the script of the Eight Nodes and made Dragon and Phoenix graphs. Examining the cloud seal traces they accordingly made Brahma writings. The two ways thus diverged, perfection was damaged and the easy [path] was followed. The root and branches were separated. Thus were made the sixty four types of script…

> The script of the Three Primordials and Eight Nodes is the most perfect of all scripts. It is the progenitor of all created patterns and graphs. The cloud-seal of bright radiance [script] arose from this root ancestor. It was the beginning of writing. Now, the script of the Three Primordials and Eight Nodes is only used by the eminent perfected and pure transcendents of the luminous supreme culmen. The Cloud-seal of bright radiance graphs are today seen in the talismanic script of the spirits.[41]

This passage, dating to the original Shangqing revelations of the mid 360s, was meant to explain specifically the emergence of the Shangqing scriptures. However, it was adopted by later Daoist authors, beginning with Lu Xiujing to explain the emergence of all Daoist scriptures. The obscure terminology was adapted to explicate the developed scriptural and ritual corpora and the arrangement of the texts within the Daoist canon of the late Six Dynasties and Tang. Thus, Lu Xiujing introduced a typology of all texts into Twelve Categories (*shier bu* 十二部). The first category "Basic Scriptures" (*benwen* 本文) is defined as "Celestial Writings" transcribed into human script.[42] "Divine Talismans," the second category, are defined as "the patterns of dragon graphs and phoenix designs, the letters of numinous traces and talismanic writings."[43] I discuss the incorporation of the Shangqing theory of scriptural emergence into Lu Xiujing's textual categories at the end of this chapter. Here, suffice it to say that, according to the theory enunciated by Yang Xi, talismanic

---

40 The precise referent of this term is unclear. I discuss it further at the end of this chapter.

41 DZ 1016: 1.8a2–9a2. See Lothar Ledderose "Some Taoist Elements in the Calligraphy of the Six Dynasties," *Toung Pao* 70 (1984): 246–78. For further analysis of the relationship between the celestial and human scripts.

42 The Twelve Categories follow the listing of texts in Lu Xiujing's Lingbao catalogue as preserved in Song Wenming's *Tongmen lun* P 2256, see Ōfuchi, *Tonkō dōkyō zurokuhen*, 727; ZHDZ, vol. 4, 511. This list of Twelve Categories is cited in DJYS DZ 1129: 2.14b4–24a and YJQQ DZ 1032: 6.20a–23a.

43 DJYS DZ 1129: 2.15a3; YJQQ DZ 1032: 6.20b7.

writing is not meant to be legible or comprehensible. On the contrary, the power inherent in talismans derives from their direct linguistic inaccessibility.

On the other hand, the incomprehensibility of the talismanic writing is not nonsensical. The actual designs on the talismans are inspired by, and based on, recognizable patterns, such as pre-Qin seal-script, stylized forms of regular graphs, and representations of humanoid or animal figures.[44] The common cloud-like forms, which are pervasive in talismanic designs, are suggestive of the primordial pneumas within which the talismans were generated. The patterns of talismanic writing are therefore simultaneously suggestive of meaning while defying complete comprehension. This principle of recognizability, I suggest, provides the talismanic patterns with their ultimate significance.

In his study of Egyptian and Greek amulets, David Frankfurter reaches similar conclusions regarding the comprehensibility of talismanic writing and the relationship between the graphic forms of talismans and the spells associated with them.[45] Beginning with a basic contrast between the sacred aspect of Egyptian hieroglyphic script on the one hand, and the Greek phonetic script on the other, Frankfurter analyzes the different religious cultures entailed by this dichotomy. Thus, while Greek amulets and spells were fundamentally embedded in oral performance and replicated direct speech, Egyptian amulets and writing were the core of ritual performance. More importantly, Frankfurter explores the convergence of these two traditions in the Graeco-Egyptian synthesis that characterizes Hellenistic and Roman periods. Two basic talismanic forms appeared during this period. Both types demonstrate that comprehensibility was superseded by notions of power. One type of amulet was composed of geometric arrays of vowels. This was "a striking development in the use of writing, that the vowels – originally a revolutionary contribution to the phonetic alphabet – could become concretely powerful as visual symbols." Phonetic signs were thus used as emblems of power, carrying non-linguistic significance. In similar fashion, the use of strings of vowels in spells was "intended to transcend not only writing but speech itself, whether through the deliberate composition of spiritual sounds or as a mimesis of actual glossolalia".[46] A second type of writing on amulets involved the use of *charaktêres*, small designs and figures without a source in any known alphabet, yet employed in such a way that a "meaning" (albeit unutterable) is implied in their sequence or arrangement. These *charaktêres* functioned not as "artificial" writing, but as "sacred" writing, in the sense of heavenly books, whose contents would be intelligible only to deities, angels or the enlightened. The impact of hieroglyphic script on this tradition was critical, as "these incomprehensible yet

---

44 See the categorizations of pre-Han, Han and Daoist talismans in Wang Yucheng, "Donghan daofu"; idem, "Luelun kaogu faxiande zaoqi daofu" 略論考古發現的早期道符, *KG* 1998.1: 75–81; idem, "Wenwu suojian zhongguo gudai daofu shulun" 文物所見中國古代道符述論, *DJWH* 9 (1996): 267–301.

45 David Frankfurter, "The Magic of Writing and the Writing of Magic: The Power of the Word in Egyptian and Greek Traditions," *Helios* 21.2 (1994): 189–221.

46 Ibid, 200–2.

mysterious signs might, in the more general context of heavenly books and writing, function as a prototype or archetype for a body of sacred characters that was magical in presence but lacked referential meaning." Thus, hieroglyphs were used on amulets, and many figurative *charaktêres* have been shown to derive from traditional hieroglyphs.[47]

I suggest that the principle of recognizability is also at work with the amulets and spells examined by Frankfurter. In a world of general illiteracy, in the Hellenistic Mediterranean as well as in traditional China, the sacred power inherent in writing was due more to belief in the efficacy of accessing and inscribing secret names and formulae than in legibility. Moreover, the use of ancient scriptural forms on Daoist talismans is comparable to the adaptation of Egyptian hieroglyphs in Hellenistic amulets. Simultaneously incomprehensible yet recognizable as efficacious script, these emblems of ancient wisdom were intrinsic signs of power.

V   True forms and true names

If talismans are indeed intrinsic signs of power, how do they signify and what do they signify? I suggest that this signification is explained through the Daoist notions of "true form" and "true name." Elaborating on the ancient and imperial notions of inscribing forms and names, we find Daoist texts referring to charts, talismans, or names that express the inherent, hidden, and real aspect of the things of the world. Several medieval Daoist texts use "true form" and "true name" to refer to the intrinsic and essential form of things, as they are truly within or as they are beyond their mundane appearance.[48]

The importance of knowing the true names of spirits is continued in the *Demon Codes of Nüqing*, a text dating to early Celestial Master Daoism, which includes chapters devoted to apotropaic and exorcistic practices. Introducing a list of demon names, the text states:

> Now, I record their true names and order you to know them. Once you know a demon's name its deviance will not dare come forth. Calling a demon's name three times will cut off the demonic pneuma.[49]

Perhaps the best known example for the term "true form" is the *Charts of the True Forms of the Five Marchmounts*. This text, which probably originated among the Masters of Esoterica, was considered one of the most efficacious devices of all by Ge Hong, and was eventually incorporated into the Daoist canon as one of the *Sanhuang* scriptures. Ge Hong reports that simply possessing these talismans

---

47 Ibid, 205–8.
48 Kristofer Schipper, "The True Form: Reflections on the Liturgical Basis of Taoist Art," *Sanjiao wenxian* 4 (2005): 91–113.
49 *Nüqing guilü* 女青鬼律 DZ 790. For an introduction to this text, see Lai Chi-tim, "The *Demon Statutes of Nüqing* and the Problem of the Bureaucratization of the Netherworld in Early Heavenly Master Daoism," *TP* 88 (2002): 252–81.

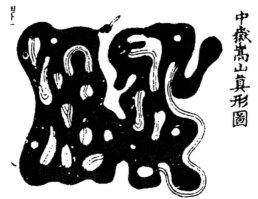

中嶽嵩山真形圖

Chart of the True Form of the Central Marchmount Mt. Song

青城山一名天國山

Chart of the True Form of Mt. Green Citadel (Qingcheng shan)

Figure 3.3 Charts of the true form of the five Marchmounts.

Source: *Dongxuan lingbao wuyue guben zhenxing tu* (DZ 441).

protected the home from demonic incursions. Wearing these talismans on their bodies, Daoist masters were protected from all dangers, natural and demonic, when they entered mountains to seek herbs, minerals, and esoteric knowledge.[50]

These charts may originally have been no more than apotropaic devices for adepts actually entering mountains, but when they were incorporated into the Shangqing scriptures, they were accorded far greater efficacy. According to the *Preface and Discourses on the Perfect Forms of the Five Marchmounts*, a text associated with the Shangqing lineage:

> The Perfect forms of the five marchmounts are the images of mountains and waters. They are configuration of the tortuous and labyrinthine peaks … If

50 Wang, *Baopuzi*, 19.336–37, 17.300.

you possess the Perfect form of the eastern marchmount, you will command men and spirits, your life will be at peace and you will attain longevity ... If you possess the *Perfect forms of the five marchmounts* in their entirety, you will ascend to heaven and traverse the earth, and you will circulate throughout the four directions.[51]

The efficacy of the charts is here extended far beyond protection of the traveler. Indeed, the charts now defined as the intrinsic and essential aspects of the sacred mountains grant access to the internal realms of the Marchmounts through meditation. Daoist scriptures and epigraphic materials reveal two basic variants of the "true forms." The first type are labyrinthine maps of the inner realm of each mountain, indicating watercourses and caverns.[52] Similar charts are also included for the "assistants" of the Marchmounts: mounts Qingcheng, Lu 廬山, Huo 霍山, and Qian 潛山.[53] The inclusion of these mountains reflects both the historical circumstances of the Southern Dynasties, which had no direct access to any but the southern Peak as well as specific significance of each of the mountains. Mounts Huo and Qian had both functioned as the southern Marchmount during the Han.[54] The inclusion of both of these mountains as assistants to Mount Heng in the *Charts of the Perfect Forms of the Five Marchmounts* indicates that Daoists were aware of these various identifications and attempted to elide the differences by including both. Mount Qingcheng, which became central to Celestial Master Daoism after the third century, was subsumed under the persona of the Elder of Qingcheng 青城丈人, who was described as "in charge of all terrestrial transcendents, the superior officer of the five marchmounts, and chief of all the officials".[55] Similar charts are also found in the *Scripture of Man-Bird Mountain*.[56]

The second type of charts, also found on steles and mirrors, are abstract emblems that represented the mountains in a purely symbolic form.[57] Although

51 *Wuyue zhenxing xulun*, DZ 1281, 21b–22a; cited in *Yunji qiqian* 79.1a and DZ 441.1a.
52 See the charts in *Wuyue guben*, DZ 441, 8b–25b, and *Lingbao wuliang durenshangqing dafa* 靈寶無量度人上經大法, DZ 219, 21.16a–22b.
53 *Wuyue zhenxing xulun*, DZ 1281, 24a–25a; cited in YJQQ DZ 1032: 79.3b–4a and DZ 441, 3b–4a. The assistant mountains are also mentioned in the transmission rite compiled by Tao Hongjing, *Taogong chuanshou yi* 陶公傳授儀 in Ōfuchi, *Tonkō dōkyō zōkurokuhen* (Tokyo: Fukubu shoten, 1979): 721–22, and ZHDZ, vol. 4, 521–3.
54 James Robson, *Power of Place: The Religious Landscape of the Southern Sacred Peak* (Nanyue 南嶽) *in Medieval China* (Cambridge: Harvard University Asia Center, 2009): 116; Robson follows the complex debates about the proper location of the southern marchmount through the Six Dynasties.
55 *Wuyue zhenxing xulun*, DZ 1281, 24a; cited in YJQQ DZ 1032: 79.3b3, DZ 441, 3b1.
56 The *Scripture of Man-Bird Mountain* is preserved in two nearly identical versions, DZ 434 *Xuanlan renniao shan jingtu* 玄覽人鳥山經圖 and YJQQ DZ 1032: 80.19b–20a.
57 See *Sanhuang neiwen yibi* 三皇內文遺秘, DZ 856, 11b–13b. These talismanic representations are found on several late imperial steles and mirrors. For steles, see Edouard Chavannes, *Le T'ai chan: Essai de Monographie d'un Culte Chinois* (Paris, E. Leroux, 1910): 415–24 (for steles dating

labeled charts, the actual figures are no more than iconic emblems that do not bear any reference to mountains.[58]

Another example for the use of "true form" is found in the *Annals of the Sage, The Undifferentiated Primordial Luminary Thearch*.[59] This hagiography portrays Laozi as a manifestation of the formless Dao, and presents various transformations and permutations by which the body of Laozi appears. The practitioner is to meditate on these manifestations while realizing the ultimate ineffable reality:

> A student of the supreme Dao should realize the true form. Although the true form is fathomless, contemplating it would suffice to obtain good fortune. For a student who does not know his source is like an infant who has lost his mother. If you are able to know the mother then you will know the child. Once you know the child you will be able to maintain the mother.[60] What is the mother? It is the existent within the nonexistent. This is the Dao.[61]

The metaphor of mother and child relationship between the ultimate Dao and manifested cosmos is a core metaphor in the *Daode jing*.[62] As discussed in Chapter 1, during the Han and through the Six Dynasties, Laozi had come to be identified with the Dao and perceived as a cosmogonic figure.[63] Contemplation of the Dao thus becomes a contemplation of the transformative process by which Laozi emerges from the formless Dao and proceeds to manifest the universe.

The *Annals of the Sage* continues to describe the attainment resulting from correct visualization, meditation, and realization of the true form of the Dao:

> If you are able to penetratingly perceive the body of that without body, and to inscribe and imagine the true form, that pattern which is unique, that is to

---

to 1378, 1614, 1682; the last is reproduced in Kiyohiko Munakata, Sacred mountains in Chinese Art (Champaign: Krannert Art Museum, University of Illinois at Urbana Champaign, Urbana University of Illinois Press, 1990): 113; and Little, *Taoism*, 358–9, for a stele dating to 1604; and on several mirrors excavated from tombs dating from the Han to the Qing, see Cao Wanru and Zheng Xihuang, "Shilun daojiao de wuyue zhenxingtu," *Ziran kexueshi yanjiu* 1987.6: 52–7; and Li Jinyun, "Tan Taicang chutu de wuyue zhenxing jing," *Wenwu* 1988.2: 177–8. The most extensive study is Zhang and Bai, "Jiangsu mingmu chutu he chuanshi gu qiwu suojiande daojiao wuyue zhenxingfu yu wuyue zhenxingtu," in *Zhongguo daojiao kaogu*, vol. 6, 1751–1833.

58 On the cosmographic significance of these various mountains, see Gil Raz, "Daoist Sacred Geography" in John Lagerwey and Lü Pengzhi, eds. *Early Chinese Religion: Part Two, The Period of Division* (Leiden and Boston: E.J. Brill, 2010): 1399–1442.

59 *Hunyuan huangdi shengji* 混元皇帝聖紀, preserved in YJQQ DZ 1032: 102.1a–6a.

60 This line cites *Laozi* 52 of the received version.

61 DZ 1032: 102.4b–5a.

62 Citing *Daode jing* 1 and 52 of the received version.

63 Seidel, "Divinisation"; Schipper, "Taoist Body" HR 17 (1978): 355–86; Livia Kohn, *The God of the Dao*.

imagine attentively in accord with your mind, then you will receive blessings and recompense. If you contemplate this in your mind, and within your mind increase and advance you will spontaneously attain the Dao. This is the meaning of the phrase: "If you think of the Dao, the Dao will think of you."[64]

This passage links the contemplation of the true form of Laozi, the formless Dao in its transformation, with attainment of the Dao. The significance of the "true form" here is the merging of the manifested form of Laozi with the undifferentiated and ineffable process of the Dao. The contemplation of the "true form" thus allows the practitioner to transcend his own limited form as it appears in the microcosm, and to merge with the cosmic process. Of particular interest is that this visualization of the true form of Dao is presented as a gloss on the final line of this passage: "If you think of the Dao, the Dao will think of you." The proximate source for this line is a line from the *Commands and Admonitions*, a third century Celestial Master text: "If you think of the Dao, the Dao thinks of you; if you do not think of the Dao, the Dao will not think of you."[65] Stephen Bokenkamp suggests that this phrase was a slogan of the early Celestial Masters.[66]

The *Scripture of the Jade Pendant and Gold Ring* presents a practice in which talismans are both ingested and used for meditation. Proper practice leads to the appearance of the "true form" of the Thearchs after the talismans are deployed correctly:

> There are the charts with golden names of the thearchs, their graphs are arrayed in jade clarity. If you attain and receive these instructions, keep silent as you cultivate and revere them. If you contemplate and visualize them day and night, then within three years the true forms will descend and you will spontaneously fly and ascend.[67]

有金名帝圖, 列字玉清, 得授此訣, 日夕存念, 不出三年, 真形克降, 自然飛騰也

Each of the talismans in this text is said to express the "secret tones and esoteric names" 秘音內諱 of the celestial spirit it represents. The talismans enable the adept to summon the celestial spirits, who will manifest their true forms. Finally, the adept will be able to ascend to the celestial realms. For example:

64 YJQQ DZ 1032: 102.6a.
65 *Dadao jia lingjie* in DZ 789: 15a, 子念道, 道念子; 子不念道, 道不念子也.
66 Bokenkamp, *Early*, 61.
67 *Taishang yupei jindang taiji jinshu shangjing* 太上玉佩金璫太極金書上經 DZ 56; P. 2409 preserves a fragment, published in Ōfuchi, *Tonkō dōkyō zurokuhen*, vol. 1, 366–70. An early version of the text was probably in circulation prior to the Shangqing revelations, Robinet, *Révélations*, vol. 1, 213–18.

Jade Pendant of Yang-radiance Talisman of the Secret Tones and Esoteric Name of the Celestial-*hun* Essence of Limitless Longevity and Supreme Bestower of Good.

This is the pneuma of yang-radiance, of limitless longevity and supreme bestower of good who rules the perfected inner spirits within the Bright Hall. Inscribe it in azure on white silk and wear it on your body. Also, inscribe the talisman on paper, and ingest it on your day of destiny and on the eight nodal-days while meditating on the perfected within the Bright Hall. After three years you will see the perfect form. You will spontaneously know the superior tones of the nine heavens and obtain the writs of the nine heavens. The Thearch-lord will descend to you, the eight effulgent spirits of your body will lift your form and you will ascend beyond the nine heavens.[68]

上上禪善无量壽天魂精祕音內諱玉珮陽明之符, 則上上禪善无量壽天陽明之氣, 主明堂中真內神. 青書白絹, 佩身. 又書白紙, 本命, 八節日服之, 內思明堂中真. 三年則者钫見真形, 自然明知九天上音, 得九天之書也, 帝君下降, 八景舉形, 上昇九天之上也.

We should emphasize here that the talisman is the coagulated form of the ethereal *qi*, and is to be perceived simultaneously as the ultimate shape and name of the deity. That is, the talisman unites the true shape and true name. By emphasizing the unity of shape and sound in the form of the talisman, the author claims that it embodies the primordial *qi* prior to the emanation of the most basic categories of existence. The actual practice associated with the talismans harks back to the ancient apotropaic uses, but the attainment promised here is far beyond the protective or healing efficacy imagined in earlier uses of talismans.

Part II: the Five Talismans of the Numinous Treasure

The most important talismans in medieval Daoism are, arguably, the five Lingbao talismans. As discussed in Chapter 2, the transmission of the Five Talismans was developed into the earliest Daoist *jiao* ritual, which came to form the basis for the synthesis of the pure rites of the Daoists. The significance of the Lingbao talismans themselves developed from one of many apotropaic devices for those entering mountains to the ultimate cosmogonic symbols, which appeared prior to all things and from which emanated the Lingbao scripture, all other scriptures, and in fact the cosmos itself. Tracing these developments allows us a view of the development of Daoism, how Daoists distinguished their practice from other traditions, competition among Daoist lineages, and finally, a unified vision of Daoism with the Lingbao talismans at the core.

68 DZ 56.10b.

I   Early apotropaic use

Aside from the references in the *Array of the Five Talismans*, the earliest references to the *Lingbao* talismans is in Ge Hong's *Inner Chapters*, which describes them as one of many alternative protective devices used by masters entering the mountains. Interestingly, Ge Hong refers to the *Lingbao* talismans themselves as "Laozi's Numinous Treasure Talismans for Entering Mountains" *Laozi rushan lingbaofu* 老子入山靈寶符. In Chapter 11, "Medicinals for Transcendence" (Xianyao 仙藥) Ge Hong discusses the procedures for entering mountains and collecting the efficacious herbs needed for the production of elixirs. The *Lingbao* talismans are crucial for this process: "Without long purification in extreme concentration and without wearing Laozi's Numinous Treasure Talismans for Entering Mountains at one's side, one will not be able to view these [herbs] in this life."[69]

Further on in the chapter, Ge Hong describes a ritual for entering mountains in which these talismans are crucial. After selecting a proper day and hour for entry, the adept is to wear the *Lingbao* talismans while leading a white dog and holding a white rooster. One should then place salt and "Mountain-opening" talismans on large rocks while holding Wu hops in one's hand. The mountain spirits will then be satisfied and allow the adept to gather the efficacious herbs.[70]

The *Lingbao* talismans are only one set of similar devices reported by Ge Hong. In Chapter 17, "Climbing [mountains] and Fording [rivers]" (Dengshe 登涉), he lists several sets of talismans for entering mountains, many of them also said to have been transmitted by Laozi or associated with Chen Anshi, a famous *fangshi* of the Qin-Han era. These talismans are extremely efficacious, their provenance is ancient, and, as noted above, they are "celestial patterns transmitted from deities." Yet, Ge Hong does not ascribe cosmological status to talismans. As with the talismans used in Celestial Master rites, there is no hint that talismans are themselves cosmological agents.

II   Defining the cosmos

While maintaining the basic apotropaic function, the authors of *Array of the Five Talismans* presented the *Lingbao* talismans as emblems of the five phases, and even as unique manifestations of cosmic power. As we saw in Chapter 2, the *jiao* rite, which is the core ritual of the *Array of the Five Talismans*, grants the performer far higher attainment then mere protection in the mountains.

The five Lingbao talismans are provided in the third chapter of the *Array of the Five Talismans*. They are listed sequentially beginning with east in the sequence of mutual production, and named "Lingbao Talisman [confirming] the Mandate of the East," and so on.[71] The term used here to name the talismans is not simply

---

69 BPZ DZ 1185 11:2a 非久齋至精及佩老子入山靈寶五符亦不能得見此輩也; Ware, *Alchemy*, 179.
70 BPZ DZ 1185 11:9b; Ware, *Alchemy*, 185.
71 DZ 388: 3.9b–11b. The talisman of the center is named "Lingbao Talisman [confirming] the Mandate of the Center *wuji* 戊己"; *wuji* are the celestial stems associated with center.

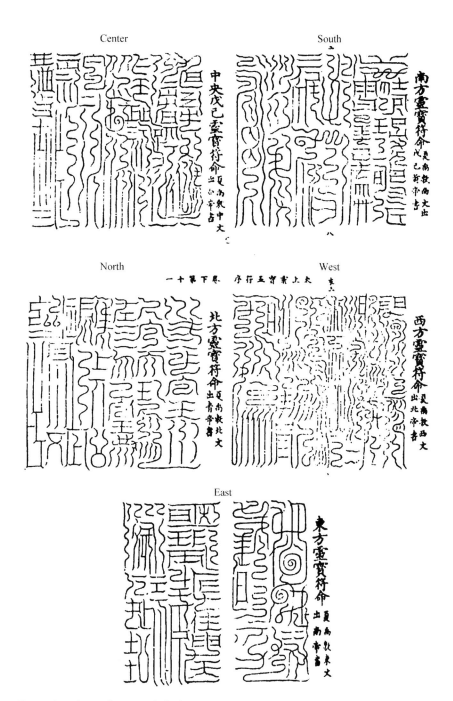

Figure 3.4 Five Talismans of Lingbao.

Source: *Array of the Five Talismans* (DZ 388).

fu but *fuming* 符命, which I translate as "Talisman [confirming] the Mandate." This was the title of the collection of portents used by Wang Mang to prove his legitimate claim to the imperial throne. The 42 chapters of this compendium listed various auspicious objects.[72] The first of these portents was a white stone, round at the top and square at the bottom, signifying heaven and earth, which had an inscription in red: "Announcing that Mang, Lord who pacified Han, will be emperor."[73]

Each of the *Lingbao* talismans is preceded by a short note expressing the progression along the production cycle. The first says: "Yu laid out the East writ from which will emanate the writing of the Southern Thearch 夏禹敷東文出南帝書." The remaining notes follow the same formula. The first thing to note here is that the talismans are termed writ (*wen* 文) and writing (*shu* 書). These terms resonate with description of other emblematic texts and auspicious objects, such as the River Chart and as the *fuming* of Wang Mang. Second, while the text does not explicate these notes and how they reflect the actual use of the talismans, these brief notes imply that Yu is the ultimate guarantor of the mandate. He is the one who reveals each talisman in turn. As each talisman is the emblem of the respective ascendant phase and of the directional Thearch, Yu is thus managing the entire cycle of phases and their associated rulers. Third, the talismans produce each other sequentially, representing and ensuring the continuity of the natural patterns.

The narrative that describes the appearance of the Lingbao talismans is a history of decline, which begins with an idyllic description of "profound antiquity" (*xuangu* 玄古) when all the patterns of nature were harmonious:

> Living beings held onto the Way in their actions, and responded to heaven's intent. Heaven and humanity harmonized pneumas… At that time men's years amounted to ninety thousand years. Later they began to study the ways of transcendence and ascended to heaven. This may be called "ultimate transformation in accord with one's heart"; it may be called "ultimate non-method of instruction and transformation." This teaching, too, was without a trace.[74]

Following this harmonious idyllic past, human history begins to decline with "the minute examination of all natural signs and the creation of hexagrams which imaged the myriad things... This was the cause for the rise of concerns."[75] This veiled critique of the evolution of the divinatory system of the *Book of Changes* is intriguing precisely because it is phrased in terms of signs that are simulacra of natural patterns.

The *Array* continues with a historical narrative that is a traditional account of the five ancient Thearchs, beginning with Xuan Yuan 軒轅, the Yellow Thearch, who

---

72 For the compilation and categories of portents, see *Hanshu* 99B.4112–3.
73 *Hanshu* 99A.4078: 告安漢公莽為皇帝.
74 DZ 388: 1.1a.
75 DZ 388: 1.a10 相自然諸兆卦象萬物···有事興與此兆矣.

pacifies the realm. The *Array* closely follows the texts of the "Records of the Five Thearchs," the first chapter of Sima Qian's 司馬遷 *Records of the Historian* (*Shiji* 史紀).[76] Continuing to the reign of Thearch Ku, the text interpolates into this well known narrative the transmission of three texts, the *Perfected Numinous Scripture of the Nine Heavens*, the *Perfected Treasure Talismans of the Three Heavens*, and the *Perfected Gold Writ of the Nine Heavens*. These texts are described as revealing the workings of heaven and earth and all categories of the things the world, from the movements of sun and moon to the types of rock and minerals. Thearch Ku, however, was unable to understand these texts, so after revering them he secreted them at Mount Zhong, to "await a later meritorious sage."[77]

> The narrative continues to describe in detail Yu's flood quelling work. And, it is at the culmination of this civilizing process, when Yu is offering sacrifice to the Celestial Consort, that he obtains the texts that had been secreted by Thearch Ku. Yu then personally wrote down the profound essentials of perfected numina and gathered the treasured writs of the celestial bureaus. He ordered and organized them by sections and numbers. He distinguished the methods of practicing the five colors by determining their directions and naming their Thearchical appellations. The original name of the most high was *Lingbao Five Talismans in Celestial Script* 靈寶五符天文.[78]

This narrative places the five Lingbao talismans, and related texts, in the context of a cosmological narrative and embeds their appearance in the well known story of Yu's conquest of the flood, yet there is no claim that the talismans are themselves cosmogonic factors. While the talismans and associated texts are said to reflect cosmic order, they are not the creators of the order itself.

III   Cosmogenesis

The *Array of the Five Talismans* inspired the scriptural and ritual production of the following centuries in several ways. The most significant impact of the text was arguably the elaboration of the five Lingbao talismans into the Perfect Writs, which are at the core of the Lingbao revelations. The talismans are now seen as primordial emanations of the original pneumas that emerged from the unitary Dao prior to all things. In fact, cosmogonic narratives in several Lingbao scriptures indicate that the talismans produced the cosmos through a continued process of emanation, with the Lingbao scriptures serving as a type of blueprint for the cosmos itself. Perhaps the earliest of these narratives is found in the *Five Ascendant*

76 *Shiji*: 1.3.10; Nienhauser, *Grand Scribe's*, vol. 1, 2. This passage should also be compared with *Dadai liji* "Wudi de" 五帝德 7:1a.
77 DZ 388: 1.4a.
78 DZ 388: 1.6b.

Talismans of Perfect Unity.[79] This text is among the earliest Lingbao revelation texts, and may well pre-date the texts compiled by Ge Chaofu. Intriguingly, while the text is in the voice of Lord Lao and does not refer to an author, other Lingbao texts refer to it as composed by Zhang Daoling, the first Celestial Master.[80] The original *Scripture of the Five Ascendant Talismans* consisted of one chapter, but the Daozang version is divided into two.[81] The second chapter includes instructions for three rituals, which are reformulations of older ritual practices, such as carving effigies, the use of hallucinogenic herbs, and astrological divination. These practices are recast within a new ritual discourse of visualization, and a rather crude grafting of Buddhist cosmology. In the first chapter, before the ritual instructions, the text provides the basic definition for the term *Lingbao* and for the Five Talismans that are at the core of the new ritual and cosmology. The text begins with a cosmogonic statement:

> Lord Lao said: at the inception of primordial chaos (*hundun* 混沌), at the source of the subtle and marvelous, prior to the opening of heaven and earth, the self-generated Perfect Writs of Lingbao already existed, the image of that prior to the high lord.

> I am the abyssal gateway of the great way of Lingbao; those that received their essential marvelous [power] became the spirits of heaven, earth, and man. Upon the separation of the limpid and turbid pneumas of the Five Talismans, I emerged.[82]

Both explicitly and by allusion to and citation of the *Daode jing*,[83] the author of this passage equates the talismans with the Dao. The talismans are prior to the separation of the limpid and turbid pneumas. Lord Lao and the essential spirits of

---

79 *Taishang wuji dadao ziran zhenyi wuchengfu shangjing* 太上無極大道自然真一五稱符上經 DZ 671. A Dunhuang manuscript, P 2440 *Lingbao zhenyi wuchengjing* 靈寶真一五稱經, preserves an early version of the text and includes several important variants. For the text, see Ōfuchi, *Tonkō dōkyō zurokuhen*, 10–22. For a study of the text and a comparison of the two versions, see Gil Raz, *Ritual and Cosmology: Transformations of the Ritual for the Eight Archivists* (M.A. Thesis, Indiana University, 1996). For the ritual scheme in this text, see Gil Raz, "Time Manipulation in Early Daoist Ritual" *Asia Major* (2005): 27–65. For a color illustration and brief discussion, see Little, *Taoism*, 201–203; Ishii Masako 石井昌子, "Reihō kyō rui" 靈宝経類 in *Kōza tonkō* 4: *Tonkō to chūgoku dōkyō* 講座敦煌 4: 敦煌と中国道教 (Tokyo: Daitō, 1983): 164–67.
80 *Taishang dongxuan lingbao benxing suyuan jing* 太上洞玄靈寶本行宿緣經 DZ 1114.5b; *Taiji zuo xiangong qingwen shang* 太極左仙公請問經上 S 1351, Ōfuchi, *Tonkō dōkyō zurokuhen*, 86, lines 35–7. I discuss these texts further in Chapter 5.
81 P 2440 is not divided into chapters. The Lingbao catalogue refers to the text as consisting of one *juan*; see Ōfuchi Ninji, "On Ku Ling-Pao-ching," 37.
82 DZ 671: 1.1a; these lines are absent from P 2440.
83 Direct citations from *Daode jing* include "image of that prior to the high lord" describes the Dao in 4, "subtle and marvelous" describes the attainment of ancient masters of Dao; "marvel" (*miao*) describes Dao in 1, "subtle" (wei) describes Dao in 15. Sima Qian describes Laozi's own words as "subtle and marvelous" (*Shiji* 63.2156).

the cosmos all owe their existence to the talismans. The text continues to define the talismans as:

> The five self-generating ascendant talismans correspond above to the five planets; they manage and summon the contracts with the five dippers. Below, they give form to the five marchmounts, as they are of the same root of the five phases. In the center, they treasure the five viscera, the roots of the five ways.[84]

After presenting the Five Talismans, in order, with their complete correlates, the text reiterates the cosmogonic significance of the talismans:

> The five ascendant spontaneous talismans of the most high numinous treasure, were generated before heaven; they transformed together with the pneuma of the Dao. They are the perfection of my Dao. Subsequently were generated heaven and earth. The myriad spirits of heaven and earth all return to *Lingbao*… The Perfect Writs of Lingbao are the root of the Dao.[85]

The *Five Ascendant Talismans* is among the earliest of the Lingbao revelation texts, which appeared circa 400 CE, and represents an early attempt at the synthesis that was to become a major characteristic of the Lingbao scriptures. The talismans in this text are named "Ascendant" and their form is wholly different from the Lingbao talismans of the *Array of the Five Talismans*. The *Five Ascendant Talismans* is thus probably an attempt to supersede and replace the Lingbao talismans. Nevertheless, the ritual scheme and cosmology of the *Five Ascendant Talismans* are still based on the Han era five phase cosmology and *fangshi* practices. The main ritual in the text is a ritualized divination method that entails the deployment of the Five Talismans, another set of talismanic representations of the eight trigrams, and a set of twelve figurines marking the twelve celestial stems, carved from a hallucinogenic root. This spatial alignment was aligned with a temporal marker, the East Well constellation. As I have shown elsewhere, this ritual emplacement was a recreation of the moment of the rise of the Han dynasty.[86] This rite is followed by another ritualized divination method that incorporates a psychoactive herb and the six *jia* 六甲, an ancient divinatory scheme based on the sexagesimal cycle. Finally, the text presents a unified ritual system entitled "twenty four charts." These charts are all mentioned in *Baopuzi*, as well as other early sources. While the significance of this ritual scheme remains unclear, it does represent an effort at systematizing and integrating diverse practices into a unified system. Alongside the Han cosmology and the *fangshi* techniques, the text also introduces basic Buddhist concepts, particularly the spatial cosmology of the ten

---

84 DZ 671: 1.3a; P 2440, lines 14–15.
85 DZ 671: 1.11a; P 2440, lines 147–51.
86 For details, see Raz, "Time Manipulation."

directions.[87] This, however, is not a substantial change to the cosmology of the ritual system.

IV   The Perfect Writs of the Lingbao scriptures

The synthesis of the *Five Ascendant Talismans* did not move beyond the Han cosmological assumptions. While the text did equate the Five Talismans with the Dao, and provided them with a cosmogonic role, the actual cosmology was still the traditional five phase cosmos. In the next stage of Lingbao revelations, we find far more complex cosmogony and cosmology, first elaborated in the two complementary texts, the *Five Tablets in Red Script* and the *Jade Instructions*. The system introduced in these two complementary texts was further expanded into a cosmogonic narrative that encompassed several other Lingbao scriptures, all of which were perceived as having emanated from original writs that appeared as cloud-seal scripts floating in the primordial and ineffable unity of the Dao.

The *Five Tablets in Red Script* and *Jade Instructions* were directly inspired by the *Array of the Lingbao Talismans*. The ritual instructions in these two texts are to a large degree an expansion and elaboration of the *jiao* ritual in the *Array* adapted to the grand cosmological vision of the Lingbao system.[88] Rather than

---

87 The Buddhist impact in the Dunhuang version is far more explicit as the spirits of the directions are named Buddhas and bodhisattvas. These titles were expurgated from the Daozang version, see Raz, "Ritual and Cosmology."

88 The section "Numinous Treasure Official Titles of the Five Ancients of Primordial Beginning" (*Yuanshi wulao lingbao guanhao* 元始五老靈寶官號) (DZ 22.1.31a–35a) is a rewriting of the passage in the section "Official Titles" of the *Array* (DZ 388: 1.14b10–15b6) amalgamating the correspondences of the five sprouts with the planets and Marchmounts. DZ 352.2.4a–13b3 is an expanded version of the methods for ingesting the pneumas of the five directions. The section "Jade Instructions for *Jiao* rite for summoning the Perfected by the Five Thearchs of Lingbao of Primordial Commencement" ("Yuanshi lingbao wudi jiaoji zhaoshen yujue" 元始靈寶五帝醮祭招真玉訣) in DZ 352.2.20b–28b is a rewriting of the *jiao* rite of the *Array*. While closely following the instruction for *Jiao* rite of the *Array*, several significant differences need to be noted:
(1) The ritual involves two sets of talismans: the Five Lingbao talismans and the Five Perfect Writs in Red Script (赤書五篇真文). The use of two sets of talismans is maintained in the transmission rite of the Lingbao scriptures in Lu Xiujing's *Taishang Dongxuan Lingbao shoudu yi* 太上洞玄靈寶授度儀 DZ 528.1b–2a and in DZ 411.2a. Both texts cite DZ 352 as their source, which in turn cites the *Array*.
(2) Unlike the rite in *Array*, the ritual in the *Jade Instructions* is to be performed once every three years and repeated three times. That is, a complete ritual cycle consists of three *jiao* in nine years. The rites are to be held on certain auspicious dates, defined as Days of Establishing Ruler (*Jianwang zhiri* 建王之日): in spring, on *jiayin* 甲寅 and *yimao* 乙卯 days; in summer, on *dingsi* 丁巳 and *bingwu* 丙午; in 'four seasons', on *wuchen* 戊辰, *wuxu* 戊戌, *jiwei* 己未, and *jichou* 己丑 days; in autumn, on *gengshen* 庚申 and *xinyou* 辛酉 days; and in winter, on *guihai* 癸亥 and *renzi* 壬子 days.
(3) The ritual is to be performed on a mountain where a "tall altar" (*gaotan* 高壇) is established. The ritual space is bordered by ropes with five doorways made of bamboo through which the Thearchs will enter. Each doorway is marked with a plaque inscribed with the name and attributes of the respective Thearch. Four doorways are set at the cardinal directions, and the fifth doorway, by which the Thearch of the center will enter, is marked at the direction of the Ruler of the season

became manifest spontaneously in the Void Cavern (*Kongdong* 空洞) in the primordial darkness before the emergence of the Worthy of Primordial Commencement (Yuanshi Tianzun 元始天尊), and the subsequent differentiation of heaven and earth and the radiances of sun and moon.[92]

The five tablets are identified with five Ancients, with each tablet said to be the "style name" (hao 號) of the directional Ancient. We should also note that each of the tablets is labeled as a different type of text: the eastern writs are "stanzas" (*zhang* 章), the south are "records" (*jin* 衿), the center are "books" (*shu* 書), the west are "tablets" (*pian* 篇), and the north are "writs" (*wen* 文).[93] The texts themselves are provided in the scripture in stanzas in cloud script. Rather than continuing the tradition of the Lingbao talismans, these titles show that Ge Chaofu aimed at integrating the bureaucratic imagination of Celestial Master Daoism into the cosmogonic vision introduced in the *Array of the Five Talismans* and further developed in the *Five Ascendant Talismans*.

The text provides the Jade Tablets in talismanic script, with each tablet divided into four verses. Following each tablet, short notices describe, but do not translate, the contents of each verse, also specifying the number of graphs in each verse and the total number of graphs in the tablet. More importantly, these descriptions further reveal the bureaucratic imagination that informs this text. Each tablet represents the offices under the Ancient who administers the respective direction, and the verses within the tablets are bureaucratic documents produced by offices in charge of specific affairs. Thus, we find that the first office in each direction is in charge of the high gods (east), divine transcendents (south), previous lives on the Jade Tablets of the divine transcendents (center), transcendent pneumas (west),

---

92 DZ 22: 1.1b1.

93 Names of the Five Ancients and Titles of their respective texts:

Direction	Ancient	Text
East	Azure Numinous Primal Elder of the Floreate Grove of Tranquil Treasure 安寶華林青靈始老	*Spirit-generating perfection treasuring Stanzas of the Cavern of Profundity* 生神寶真洞玄章
South	Cinnabar Numinous Perfect Elder of Glorious Yang of Brahma Treasure 梵寶昌陽丹靈真老	*Heaven-penetrating from the Southern Clouds Treasure-Numinous Writ* 南雲通天寶靈衿
Center	Primordial Elder of Primordial Numinosity of jade treasure 玉寶元靈元老	*Numinous Book of the Nine Heavens of Cavernous moisture of the Treasure Kalpa* 寶劫洞湝九天靈書
West	Bright Numinous Luminous Elder of the Golden Porte of Seven Treasures 七寶金門皓靈皇老	*Subtle chapter of the bright cavern of golden perfection* 金真寶明洞微篇
North	Dark Elder of Five Numina of Flourishing and Extinction from the Lunar Singularity of Cavernous Yin 洞陰朔單鬱絕五靈玄老	*Treasured Bright writ of the perfection-generating primordial spirit* 元神生真寶明文

and Perfected (north). The second office in each direction is responsible for the relevant stars, constellations, and their temporal correlates. The third office in each direction administers ghosts and demons. In the south, we find the office of Feng 酆, the Daoist netherworld, which was developed in response to the complex Buddhist netherworld.[94] In the west, we find the office in charge of the Six Heavens, the mundane realm ruled by demons according to Celestial Master Daoism.[95] The fourth office in each direction administers the aquatic spirits (see Table 3.1).[96] Each note reiterates that these graphs are all "self-generated" by the Ancient in charge of the respective direction.[97]

Each note ends by providing alternative titles to the text. One set of alternative titles is based on the Slips of the Eight Awes (*baweice* 八威策), while a second set of alternative titles refers to "divine incantations" (*shenzhou* 神呪). The inclusion of these titles reveals more about Ge Chaofu's effort at synthesis. The term "divine incantations" may well be related to the sectarian movement that arose during the early fifth century, which was one among several efforts at reforming Celestial Master Daoism. As I discuss this group in detail in the following chapter, suffice it here to say that the inclusion of this term as an alternative title to the Jade Tablets effectively collapses the *Divine Incantations* into the system of the Jade Tablets, and thus effectively erases this challenge.

The Slips of the Eight Awes was an ancient apotropaic device, which is mentioned in both the *Array of the Five Talismans* and in Ge Hong's *Inner Chapters*. Like the five Lingbao talismans, this was one of the many devices that offered protection for those entering mountains, and not the most efficacious:

> When a superior Master enters the mountains he should grasp the *Inner Writ of the Three Luminaries* and the *Charts of the Perfected Forms of the Five Marchmounts*. He can thus summon the mountain deities wherever he is, and in accord with the 'spirit registers' 鬼錄 summon and request the aid of the [spirits] of the local shrines, mountain officials and protectors of the home. Then, the anomalies of wood and stone and the mountain and river sprites would not dare come and test him.

> The next best device (其次) is to place seventy-two 'sprite-securing' talismans 精鎮符 [around one's location]. One should then produce the emblems

---

94 Fengdu, located in the far northwest, was introduced in the Shangqing scriptures as the locus of the bureaucratic administration of the Three Bureaus, who judged the souls of the dead. *Declarations of the Perfected*, Chapters 5 and 15–16, preserve detailed descriptions of the geography of Fengdu, and especially of its current residents, many of whom were historical figures and relatives of the elite families who patronized Yangxi. Sandrine Chenivesse, "Fengdu: cité de l'abondance, cité de la male mort," *Cahiers d'Extrême-Asie* 10 (1998): 287–339; Stephen R. Bokenkamp, *Ancestors and Anxiety*, 33 ff. *et passim*.

95 See my discussion of Lu Xiujing's *Abridged Codes* in Chapter 5.

96 Table 3.1 and the following discussion is based on DZ 22: 1.7b–29b.

97 The east tablet is said to be by the Celestial Worthy of Primordial Commencement.

Table 3.1 Verses of the Five Tablets

East: (120 graphs)
Alternative title: "Plaque of Divine Incantations of Eight Awes from Eastern Mountain"
東山神呪八威策文

Offices: (1) Charts and registers for Evaluating Divine Transcendents of the Primordial Tower of the Nine Heavens in charge of Summoning the High Lords of the Nine Heavens (24 graphs).
(2) Eastern Floreate Hall in Purple Tenuity Palace in charge of Astral Office and rectifying celestial measures (32 graphs).
(3) Hostels of the Officers of Spirits of the Eastern mulberry in charge of controlling the ghosts and demons and rectifying the pneumas of the nine heavens (32 graphs).
(4) Jade tower in north-east jade gateway of the Nine Heavens in charge of controlling the aquatic Thearch of the eastern ocean and the flood calamities of the great kalpa and summoning the kraken-dragons and all matters of the aquatic deities (32 graphs).

South: (152 graphs)
Alternative titles: "Slips of Eight Awes of Red Thearch" 赤帝八威策文; "Divine Incantations of the Nine Heavens" 九天神呪

Offices: (1) Hostel of Cavernous Yang of Nine Heavens in charge of golden names on the charts and registers of the divine transcendents of the Nine Heavens (32 graphs).
(2) Cinnabar Tower of the Three Pneumas in charge of summoning astral offices, clarifying the measures, and rectifying the celestial divisions (32 graphs).
(3) Controller of Northern Feng and Rectifier of ghostly pneuma (40 graphs).
(4) Controller of aquatic Thearch of the South Ocean and the flood calamities of the great transformation and summoning the kraken-dragons and all matters of the aquatic deities (40 graphs).

Center: (144 graphs)
Alternative titles: "Slip of Yellow Thearch's Awesome Power" 黃帝威靈策文; "Great Incantation of the Yellow Spirit" 黃神大呪

Offices: (1) Jade Treasure Dark Tower of Grand Darkness in charge of the previous lives on the Jade Tablets of the divine transcendents and confirming their transcendent pneuma (40 graphs).
(2) Controller of astral offices and rectifying the celestial measures (40 graphs).
(3) Controller of North Thearch and Rectifier of celestial pneuma verifying ghostly essence (16 graphs).
(4) Controller of aquatic Thearch of the Central Ocean, waters of the four springs, calculations of the overflowing flood calamities, and summoning the aquatic deities and all matters of the kraken-dragons (48 graphs).

West: (136 graphs)
Alternative titles: "Eight Awes Writ for Summoning Dragons" 八威召龍文; "Divine Incantation of West Mountain" 西山神呪

Offices: (1) Unadorned Numinous Palace of the North Carriage of the Nine Heavens in charge of summoning the transcendent pneuma (48 graphs).
(2) Dark Window of the Gold Pylon in charge of controlling the White Thearch's astral offices, rectifying and clarifying the celestial measures (24 graphs).

(*continued*)

Table 3.1 Verses of the Five Tablets *(continued)*

      (3) Controller of ghostly pneumas of the Six Heavens (16 graphs).
      (4) Controller of aquatic Thearch of the West Ocean and the myriad sprites
         of the seas, summoning the cloud dragons in order to protect against flood
         calamities (48 graphs).

North: (120 graphs)
Alternative title: "Eight Awes Writ for Controlling Celestial [Spirits]" 八威制天文;
                "Divine Incantation of North Mountain" 北山神呪
Offices: (1) Book of the North Carriage of Flourishing Singularity Limitless Mystic
         Primordial in Purple Tenuity in charge of all charts and registers of the
         Perfected (40 graphs).
      (2) Book of the Celestial Northern Mystic Primordial Dipper in charge of
         controlling the Northern astral offices and rectifying the celestial pneuma
         (32 graphs).
      (3) Controller of celestial demons and myriad ghosts of the North Thearch
         (24 graphs).
      (4) Controller of aquatic Thearch of the North Ocean, administrator of the
         myriad sprites of the seas, summoning kraken-dragons in order to carry the
         body (24 graphs).

of the Hundred Depravities 百邪之章 and the twelve Embracing the Primordial Seals of the Ruby red Bureau 朱官印包元十二印, and use them to seal the four sides of their dwelling. Then, the Hundred Depravities would not dare enter. The next best device is to grasp the Tallies of the Eight Awes and wear the Jade Slips of Laozi 執八威之節佩老子玉策, then the mountain sprites can be commanded. Who would then dare to cause them harm?[98]

Ge Hong refers again to the same talismans, or very similar ones, among a list of other protective devices for venturing into mountains:

One may also employ the Tiger Pace of the Seven Stars, Jade Spirit Talismans, Talismans of the Eight Awes and Five Ascendants 八威五勝符, Li'er's Talismans of Great Peace, Seals of Central Yellow Floreate Canopy, Sulphurous Powders 石流黃,[99] burnt horns of oxen and goats, or erect Lord of the Western Marchmount's Talismans for Constraining Mountain [spirits]. These are all efficacious.[100]

This reference is particularly intriguing, as it suggests that talismans of the Eight Awes and the Five Ascendant Talismans were used together. The latter term may well be a variant of the better known Lingbao talismans, and perhaps

---

98 Wang, *Baopuzi* 17.300–01, Ware, *Alchemy*, 282.
99 The more common term for sulfur is *shiliuhuang* 石硫黃. See Ho Peng Yoke, "*Alchemy*," 167.
100 Wang, *Baopuzi* 17.312, Ware, *Alchemy*, 295.

the source for the talismans at the core of the Lingbao scripture *Five Ascendant Talismans* discussed above.[101] This connection may help explain the close relationship between the Slips of the Eight Awes and the Lingbao talismans that we find in the *Array of the Five Talismans* and further developed in the Lingbao scriptures of the late fourth and early fifth centuries.

Among the many talismans found in *Array of the Five Talismans* is the "Writ of the Most High of the Three Heavens for Subduing Krakens, Dragons, Tigers, Leopards, and Mountain Sprites" 三天太上伏蛟龍虎豹山精文.[102] An appended note mentions that it is also named "Writ of the Eight Awes." The accompanying text explains this is a protective talisman, to be employed when entering mountains:

> A Daoist [should] carry this writ in his sleeves when entering mountains. The hundred beasts and demonic creatures will merely walk by your side as you proceed. Grasping this writ in your hand, the hundred beasts, mountain demons and poisonous creatures will retreat a thousand *li*.

While Slips of Eight Awes is given as an alternative title, it was probably the earlier name of the device. By naming it "Writ of the Three Heavens" the author of the *Array of the Five Talismans* placed the practice within the cosmology of the Three Heavens linking it to the other practices listed in the text. Most importantly, the Slips of Eight Awes was thus subordinated to the five Lingbao talismans. We find a similar strategy of incorporation in the *Five Tablets in Red Script* and the *Jade Instructions*. Not only are the alternative titles of the Jade Tablets clearly related to the Slips of Eight Awes, but an entire section in the text is devoted to this device.

The second *juan* of the *Jade Tablets* lists several efficacious methods. The first device in this chapter is the "Lingbao Writ of the Eight Awes from the Most High Cavern of Mystery for Subduing Krakens, Dragons, Tigers, Leopards, and Mountain Sprites." This title is clearly a reworking of the title in the *Array of the Five Talismans*. Here, moreover, the status of the Eight Awes is elevated as they are said to have appeared together with the Perfect Writs of Primordial Commencement within the Red Heaven at the cosmogonic moment of emanation.[103] The text then provides several practices and talismans related to the Eight Awes. Among these are two complementary talismans, the Yang Life Talisman of Great Simplicity of the Nine Heavens 九天太素陽生符, also known as the Dragon Script of Eight Awes 八威龍書, and the Yin Life Talisman of Great Darkness of the Three Heavens 九天太玄陽生符.[104] These two talismans are

101 DZ 671 and P 2440.
102 DZ 388: 3.12b5.
103 DZ 22: 2.1a '太上洞玄靈寶召伏蛟龍虎豹山精八威策文'與 '元始餘篇真文' 同出於赤天之中.
104 These talismans are also derived from the *Array of the Five Talismans* DZ 388: 3.13a–14a which includes four talismans: (1) Yang Life Talisman of Upper Profundity of the Nine Heavens 九天太玄陽生符, (2) Missing – probably complementary to (1), (3) Yang Life Talisman of Upper

defined as complementary: "the two pneumas of yin and yang, the essence of sun and moon."[105] These two talismans are so efficacious that, if a woman would ingest the former, she would be assured of rebirth as a male, and if a male ingested the latter in the next life he would be a woman![106]

The instructions for the first talisman state that after a purification of a hundred days one should enter the chamber and meditate on the sun's essence. If one is able to ingest and swallow it, then one would be as long lived as the sun, and coeval with heaven and earth. By contemplating the numinous and meditating upon the true forms one would spontaneously be able to fly. The instructions for the second talisman are similar, except for replacing moon for sun. The instructions continue:

> A Daoist master who wishes to escape by means of a corpse (*shijie* 尸解) should inscribe this in black lettering on a wooden sword. He should hold it to his breast and lie down. Promptly, this blade would take on his human form, and die.[107]

The practices associated with the Slips of Eight Awes clearly hark back to the traditions of the *fangshi* and do not entail the complex cosmology presented in the *Five Tablets in Red Script*. The inclusion of these practices not only reveals the reliance of Daoists on these older traditions, but, more importantly, the essential erasure of these practices by their very inclusion within a ritual system that makes far higher claims of efficacy.

The *Five Tablets in Red Script* includes several other apotropaic talismans, such as a set of twenty talismans for protection during the imminent catastrophes as predicted by the eschatological system of "Yang-nine hundred and six" (*yangjiu bailiu* 陽九百六), which predicted a series of cataclysmic floods culminating in complete destruction of the current cosmos.[108] These talismans, too, are an elaboration of a set of two talismans in the *Array of the Five Talismans* named "Flying Talismans of Long Peace from the Kings of the Nine Heavens":

> Persons of the Dao wear these in order to ensure that the thousand toxins of the Yang-nine hundred and six do not attach to their bodies.[109]

The talismans in the *Five Tablets in Red Script* are to be deployed in accord with the five directions, with four talismans in each direction protecting against different cataclysmic formulations. By employing these talismans, the practitioner

---

Profundity of the Three Heavens 三天太玄陽生符, (4) Yin Life Talisman of Upper Profundity of the Three Heavens 三天太玄陰生符.

105 DZ 22: 2.3b.

106 DZ 22: 2b–3a 女吞此符復生為男身... 男人吞此符後化為女子. These parallel attainments are not mentioned in the *Array* which specifies that (3) is for males and (4) is for females (see note 104).

107 This is slightly different from the instruction for talismans (3) and (4) in the *Array*.

108 The numerology of the system is explained in the preceding pages DZ 22: 2: 4a–8b.

109 DZ 388: 3.12a–b.

will bring salvation to the "physical body of students of the Dao,"[110] protect the state and preserve the seed people,[111] and their bearer will be spontaneously generated in the new *kalpa*.[112]

Most importantly, all these various talismans are said to have emerged together with the Perfect Writs:

> The Jade talismans of the Five Ancients and Three Primordials of Primordial Commencement, the Jade Tablets Perfect Writs of Lingbao, and the Talismans of Great and Small Kalpa cycles all emerged together at the Purple Tenuity Palace on Jade Capitoline Mountain in Supreme Mystic Capital. These writs secure (gu 固) the heavens and the pneumas of three primordials. Use them to ward off the calamities of great and small Yang-nine and great and small hundred and six kalpa concatenations. They will cross over the body of the student [of the Dao], whose names were previously inscribed in gold in the Mystic Capital. All those who get to see and wear these writs will avoid great calamities and become sage lords and seed-people. All will ascend to heaven in broad daylight to have audience at the upper palaces of the Mystic Capital. Even if their merit is incomplete they will attain release from their corpse and transmigrate. When they attain transcendence, they will in accord with the cosmic cycles sink and float, and will bind their karma with the perfected.[113]

While the text and ritual system of the *Five Tablets in Red Script* is obviously based on the *Array of the Five Talismans*, the Lingbao talismans themselves are here reduced to an auxiliary role and subordinated to the Perfect Writs. As noted by Stephen Bokenkamp long ago, each of the talismans of the *Array* are here divided into two parts and introduced as distinct talismans.[114] Like the talismans in the *Array*, the sequence here also follows the production cycle of the five phases, but describes the production of the succeeding talisman as "transformative generation" (*huasheng* 化生), an originally Buddhist term that refers to spontaneously generated entities.[115] Thus, the talisman of the east:

> Talisman of the Azure Thearch of the East, Celestial Writs of the Nine Heavens transforms to generate the pneuma of the Red Thearch.[116]

---

110 *Xuezhe renshen* 學者人身 DZ 22: 2: 9a1, 9b2, 10b7, 11a10, 12a10, 13a3, 14a6, 15b8, 16a10.
111 *Anguo cun zhongmin* 安國存種民 DZ 22: 2: 9b1, 10a2.
112 佩之即得化生始分之中DZ 22: 2: 10b1, 12a5, 14a1.
113 DZ 22: 2.17a–b: "bind their karma" 結緣 is a Buddhist term referring to forming a karmic bond with a Buddha, for rebirth in Pure Land, or future salvation.
114 Bokenkamp, "Sources."
115 DDB lists numerous examples, see (http://www.buddhism-dict.net/cgi-bin/xpr-ddb.pl?q=%E5%8C%96%E7%94%9F).
116 DZ 22: 1.10b8.

The pneuma of minor yang transforms and generates great yang. The three pneumas of cinnabar heaven manage the minor kalpa of *si* 巳 and the great kalpa of *wu* 午.

V Inner sounds and self-generated jade graphs

Another important Lingbao scripture, the *Inner Sounds and Self-Generated Jade Graphs of All Heavens*, introduces yet another set of celestial writs, which are also known as "Secret Language of the Great Brahma" 大梵隱語.[117] The text begins with a cosmogonic narrative detailing the emergence of celestial script from the primordial pneuma and proceeding to the emanation of the cosmos:

> The jade graphs of the celestial writs are the congealed flying profound pneumas to form numinous patterns. They merged with the eight nodes to form tones, and harmonized with the five harmonies to form verses. When the great epochal cycle (*dayun* 大運) was initiated there was spontaneous tintinnabulation and a divine wind arose in the void, penetrating sounds echoed and reverberated. These graphs blazed above all the heavens and illuminated within the great murk. They transformed together with the Draconic Han eon, proceeding through the Red Clarity eon to the Extended Vigor eon.[118] They were smelted with water and fire through cycles of life and death.[119] They continued to exist though a billion kalpas. They unfurled as the eight limits in the abyssal node, and were implanted as the numinous glow in the sun. The two principles grasped them in order to separate, the three radiances grasped them in order to be distinguished, the superior sages employ them in order to shine forth, the five marchmounts treasure them in order to become numinous.

---

117 *Taishang lingbao zhutian neiyin ziran yuzi* 太上靈寶諸天內音自然玉字 DZ 97.

118 Draconic Han (*longhan* 龍漢), Red Clarity (*chiming* 赤明), and Extended Vigor (*yankang* 延康) are names of cosmic epochs introduced in the Lingbao scriptures. The sequence here differs from the sequence given in other Lingbao scriptures, in which Extended Vigor precedes the Red Clarity epoch. The epoch of Draconic Han is within the primordial Dao, prior to the separation of the primordial Dao. It was during this epoch that the Celestial Worthy coalesced within this formless void. Although formless, this epoch is described in positive terms. At the end of this era there is collapse (*pohuai* 破壞). The subsequent epoch of Extended Vigor is described as "dark and murky" 幽冥. In the following Red Clarity epoch, radiant light emanated again, and, with the appearance of the Perfect Writs of Lingbao, the cosmos took form. These descriptions are found in the Lingbao scriptures *Taishang zhutian lingshu duming miaojing* 太上諸天靈書度命妙經 DZ 23.2a, *Taishang dongxuan lingbao zhihui zuigen shangpin dajie jing* 太上洞玄靈寶智慧罪根上品大戒經 DZ 457.12a. On the one hand, the invention of these ancient epochs responds to the incredibly vast temporal imagination of the Buddhist sutras, with its cycles of *kalpas* and *yugas*. On the other hand, stylistically these names resonate with the imperial Chinese reign titles. Also, note that the Draconic Han simultaneously refers to the Milky Way and to the Han dynasty. Bokenkamp, *Early*, 399 discusses these epochs in the context of the *Scripture of Salvation* (*Duren jing* 度人經).

119 "Life and death" 生死 is the standard Chinese translation for the Indic Buddhist term *samsara*. The reference here is simply to the endless cycle of transformation.

All attain them in order to live. The state reveres them in order to be peaceful. Rare indeed is the great model; illustrious indeed is the eminent worthy! Within, produced through non-action were the roots of heaven and earth.

If you obtain them you will not die, if you revere them you will exist for long, if you treasure them the perfected will descend to you, if you cultivate them you will become a divine transcendent. You will cross over death, and while your skeleton will be in the long night, your living *hun*-soul will be refined in the vermilion palace. These marvelously transformative writs emerged by self-generation. If adulterated they will not be muddied, if left still they cannot be any purer, if damaged they will not be destroyed, if destroyed they return to life. Eminently wondrous in the great void, they are the ancestors of the myriad thearchs, their awesome efficacy in the vast remoteness 恢廓 is difficult to put in words.[120]

The text then proceeds to present each writ of the four cardinal directions. The titles of the writs reiterate that the celestial script is simultaneously the "inner sounds" and the "self generated jade graphs." Each writ consists of 64 graphs that encode the names and functions of eight heavens at each direction; eight graphs to a heaven. While the number of graphs at each direction is an obvious reference to the hexagrams of the *Book of Changes*, the actual functions of the heavens expresses a complex amalgamation of Daoist, imperial bureaucratic, and Buddhist ideas.

Each writ is followed by a list of the eight heavens in the respective direction, with a systematic and formulaic listing of their residents officials, beginning with pentachromatic jade youths, brocade-wearing jade maidens,[121] and officials under the jurisdiction of the talismans of the five Thearchs (of each heaven). The list of officers at each direction includes merit-scribes 功曹 of nirvana 滅度 and of rebirth 更生, and a host of registrars and inspectors. The number of officials at each of these bureaucratic posts is 32, thus creating a numerologically resonant cosmos, in which the number of heavens corresponds to the numbers of officials at each post within the grand, complex, all encompassing scheme.

The text continues by providing an explanation, perhaps better understood as translation into mundane script, of the eight graphs of each heaven. These graphs inscribe (*shu* 書) complex cosmological structures, which, like their earthy imperial models, are simultaneously architectural edifices as well as bureaucratic functions. For example, the graphs of the first heaven in the east are explicated as:

The first, second, and third graphs inscribe the towers of the mystic capital. These writs are used to rectify the temporal measures of heaven and earth, which are in charge of summoning the crowd of perfected and great deities of

---

120 DZ 97: 1.1a–b.
121 "Brocade-wearing" 繡衣 was a synecdoche for officials since the Han dynasty.

the ten directions. The fourth and fifth graphs inscribe the thearch's tower southern extremity 遊臺南軒, which is in charge of divine transcendents who were self-generated within the void nullity. The sixth, seventh, and eighth graphs inscribe the gates of sun and moon, which are in charge of the rays that penetrate the nine abysses, and open the bureaus of the long night.[122]

These explanations of the writs are followed by precise instructions for preparing and ingesting the graphs on appropriate days. The graphs of the first heaven in the east are to be used hence:

> On the ten *zhai* days of each month inscribe in vermilion the first, second, and third graphs and ingest them, while facing the ascendant direction and incanting the proper formula. In a hundred days the myriad spirits will arrive for audience. On the fifteenth and thirtieth days of each month inscribe in vermilion the fourth and fifth graphs and ingest them, while facing east and incanting the proper formula. If you ingest them for twenty four years, you will live as long as the divine perfected, and from *samsara* you will ascend to roam at the Thearch's towers. On the days of the first and last quarter of the month 上下弦望,[123] inscribe in vermilion the sixth, seventh, and eighth graphs and ingest them while facing the moon. In eight years the innards of your body will glow, your face will become golden, and from *samsara* you will ascend to the hostels of sun and moon, where you will be refined and attain transcendence.[124]

These ritual instructions reveal an intriguing amalgam of practices. First, despite the cosmogonic status of the writs, they are to be ingested as the ancient talismans used for healing. The efficacy of the writs is understood in abstract terms as unifying sound and form. More than iconic forms, the writs are of the actual substance of the complex entities they represent. More precisely, they are not representational signs, but objects that share in the very substance of the abstruse cosmological truths they represent in ritual events. Second, the set of ten *zhai* days mentioned here is part of the newly formulated Lingbao ritual system, which merged ancient indigenous Chinese ritual notions with the Buddhist rite of *uposatha*. The Buddhist rite was performed on six days of each month (8, 14, 15, 23, 29, and 30) and consisted of a recitation of the monastic code (*pratimoksa*) by the monks and nuns followed by individual confessions of sin.[125]

---

122 DZ 97: 1.5b–6a.
123 More precisely the seventh, eighth, twenty-second, and twenty-third days.
124 DZ 97: 1.6a.
125 Michel Soymié, "Les dix jours de jeûne du taoïsme," in *Yoshioka Yoshitoyo hakase kanri kinen Dōkyō kenkyū ronshū* 吉岡義豐博士還紀念道教研究論集 (Tokyo: Kokusho kankōkai, 1977): 1–21; Lü Pengzhi, *Tangqian daojiao yishi shigang* 唐前道教儀式史綱 (Beijing Zhonghua shuju, 2008): 129–40; idem. "Daoist Rituals," in John Lagerwey and Lü Pengzhi, *Early Chinese Religion: the Period of Division (220–589 AD)* (Leiden: Brill, 2010): 1284–88; Sylvie Hureau, "Buddhist

The Lingbao formulation recast the Buddhist repentance rite in bureaucratic terms, and added four more days (1, 18, 24, and 28) to a total of ten. According to the *Five Tablets in Red Script*, on each of these ten days the respective directional deities inspect the merits and faults of mortals and ghosts under their jurisdiction. They thus dispatch their celestial officers to descend into the world to inspect and evaluate the faults, sins, and merits of people and spirits. For example, on the first day of the month, the great sage lords of the north-west, including the ultimately perfected deities, the Limitless High Lord of the Great Dao, and the Perfected Luminous Elder regularly meet at the Purple Tenuity Palace at the north-west Jade Capitoline Mountain in the Mystic Capital to hold a *zhai* to worship the celestial writs (奉齋朝天文). On that day, they dispatch the officers under jurisdiction of the Big Dipper, the interrogators of the Three Bureaus, and the Inspectors of the Four Departments to descend and circulate in the human realm and assess the merits and offenses of the people.[126]

The fifteenth day is associated with the east. At the head of this host are deities associated with early Celestial Master Daoism, the Limitless Great Dao of the Three Heavens of Great Purity, Mystic, and Primordial, the Supreme Mystic Elder, and Most High Lord Lao.[127] Also included here are the 1,200 Officers, the bureaucratic apparatus of Celestial Master Daoism,[128] and the Latter Sage Thearch-Lord of the Golden Pylons (*Jinque housheng dijun* 金闕後聖帝君), who is Lord Li, the messianic figure introduced in the Shangqing scriptures.[129]

A great convocation of the celestial deities is held on the thirtieth day of each month.[130] The list begins with a dizzying array of terms strung to name the limitless, pervasive, primordial, without peer, Lord of the Dao. Along with terminology culled from the *Daode jing*, the name includes the term Contractual Authority of Orthodox Unity, the name favored by the community of Celestial Master Daoism. The host of spirits includes the Celestial Master deities mentioned above. Also included in this list are the Lord of Spirit Treasure 神寶君, Lord of Perfected Treasure 真寶君, and Lord of Numinous Treasure 靈寶君.[131] These three lords are introduced in the Lingbao scriptures as original revelators of the three scriptural corpora, namely the Three Sovereigns (*San Huang* 三皇), Shangqing, and Lingbao, that were synthesized into a single canon, entitled Three Caverns. I discuss the complex development of this notion and its place in the emergence of a

Rituals," in *Early Chinese Religion: the Period of Division (220–589 AD)* (Leiden: Brill, 2010): 1213–27.

126 DZ 22: 3.1a.
127 DZ 22: 3.2a–b.
128 For details on this cosmic bureaucracy Ursula-Angelica Cedzich, "The Organon of the Twelve Hundred Officials and Its Gods," *Daoism: Religion, History and Society* 1 (2009): 1–95.
129 His hagiography is *Shangqing housheng daojun lieji* 上清後聖道君列紀 DZ 442; translated in Bokenkamp, *Early*, 339–66.
130 DZ 22: 3.5b–8a.
131 DZ 22: 3.7a.

Daoist orthodoxy in Chapter 5. Suffice it here to note that the list of Lords also includes a fourth one, Lord of Celestial Treasure 天寶君.

Returning to the *Inner Sounds and Self-Generated Jade Graphs*, the text continues by describing the appearance of the eight graphs of each heaven in the four directions. At the end of each directional section, the Celestial Worthy instructs the Great Lord of the Dao about the cosmogonic aspect of the 64 graphs. For example, in the case of the southern heavens:

> At the initiation of the Red Clarity epoch, the pneumas of the eight heavens divided equally among the cinnabarine southern heavens. Each heaven possessed eight graphs, to a total of sixty-four tones. Within all the heavens there were innumerable hidden tones of the great Brahma secret sounds. A practitioner of the Way of the Celestial Lords of the Three Pneumas must wear these tones at his belt and recite these stanzas as he comes and goes.[132]

The passage continues with precise instructions for meditation and recitation, which are reiterated at each direction. The text thus brilliantly combines a complete ritual meditative program aligned with a complex cosmogony emanating from the secret Brahma language, which unites graphs and tones in complete synesthesia. On the one hand, this synesthetic vision is meant to reproduce the formless and undefined unity, within which signs were simultaneously visible and audible, or more precisely, before visibility and sound emerged as distinct phenomena. The practitioner is to attain this perception by contemplating and ingesting the talismans. The purpose of this discourse, and its associated practices, is to undermine and confound mundane sensual perceptions thus allowing the meditator to attain heightened awareness and enter an altered state of consciousness.

VI Liu Xiujing's scriptural categories

Many of the texts produced by various Daoist lineages were compiled into a canon by Lu Xiujing, and organized into Three Caverns. Alongside the canonization of scriptures, which I discuss in the following chapter, Lu also introduced a typology of texts. As described by Song Wenming in his *Tongmen lun*, in organizing the Lingbao scriptures Lu Xiujing "collated the body and its applications and distinguished among the intertwining branches, to compile twelve types."[133] The twelve textual modalities are: (1) Original source of the scriptures 經之本源, (2) divine talismans, (3) jade instructions, (4) numinous charts, (5) lists and registers, (6) injunctions and precepts, (7) awesome rites, (8) recipes, (9) techniques, (10) biographies, (11) verses, (12) memorials and petitions. This division of Daoist texts into twelve types continued as one of the basic editorial methods of later Daoist canons.

---

132 DZ 97: 3.27b.
133 P 2861, ZHDZ 4.511a; 總括體用, 分別雜貫, 合有十二種.

The first among these twelve categories, that is the source of all Daoist scriptures, which Lu Xiujing named "original source of the scriptures," is none other than the Celestial Scripts of Lingbao, also known as the "Self-generated celestial books in the script of the eight nodes" 自然天書八會之文, with 1,109 graphs in total. Lu arrived at this number by simply adding up the numbers of graphs claimed in four different Lingbao texts to be the primordial source of all Lingbao scriptures. We should note that this total number is not found in any of the Lingbao scriptures themselves. Lu Xiujing introduced these four groups of graphs without mentioning the titles of the texts, only referring to numbers of graphs, which he follows with a description of the efficacy of this particular set of graphs.

First among these were 668 graphs, which Lu Xiujing described as the "original root of the three powers (heaven, earth, and humanity), they produced heaven and established earth, they brought forth humanity and the spirits. They are the root of the myriad things. The so-called way of heaven, way of earth, and way of spirits, all refer to this." These graphs are introduced in the *Five Tablets in Red Script* as the original Perfect Writs that constituted the primordial form of the text.[134]

Next are the 256 graphs that Lu Xiujing described as:

> discoursing on the measures and times of all heavens; on the names, positions, and titles of the great sages and perfected transcendents, the locations of their administrative offices, bureaus, citadels, and towers; the transformations of the divine transcendents, their hierarchical rankings and the types of demons that follow them; the lives, deaths, and karmic cycles of humans and spirits.

These graphs are introduced as the "Spontaneous Celestial Script of the Secret Tones of the Great Brahma" in the *Inner Sounds and Self-Generated Jade Graphs*, and Lu's summary indeed corresponds to the content of the text.[135]

Next were 64 (the text mistakenly had 63) graphs that Lu described as:

> the titles of the primordial essences of the five directions, to be ingested by those who seek transcendence, to refine their spirits and transform their bodies; this is a method for ascending in broad daylight.

The source for this set of graphs is the section entitled "Names of all Heaven from the Scriptures of the Most High Perfect One of the Luminary Person" in the third *juan* of the *Array of the Five Talismans*.[136] While this section appears to include only 60 graphs, Wang Chengwen argues that these graphs encode the invocations of the five directional sprouts, which are given in the subsequent

---

134 See Table 3.1 for details.
135 DZ 97; see above for details.
136 DZ 388: 3.14b–15b.

narrative of the Yellow Thearch's quest.[137] Indeed, the terms used to describe these graphs summarize the instructions of the text.

Finally, there are the remaining 121 graphs that were "absent, and without elaboration into sound."[138] These graphs must be in the texts that Lu Xiujing listed as "not yet appeared."

Song Wenming's commentary on Lu Xiujing's categories is particularly instructive. He begins with a detailed history of the emergence of script from the primordial patterns, which is based on the Shangqing narrative we saw above, but also includes citations from Lingbao scriptures. He ends by linking this Daoist theory of textual emergence to the better known history of writing that developed in the late Warring States and Han. Song Wenming labels the first category "Original Patterns" (本文) and divides his discussion into two parts. The second rubric, "function" (應用), is a summary of Lu Xiujing's analysis of the 1,109 original graphs. The first rubric, "transformations of patterns" (變文), which concerns us here, is a history of script, which Song Wenming divides into six distinct moments. The initial moment describes the primordial generation of script. Song Wenming begins by quoting the passage from *Declarations of the Perfected* cited above:

> When *yin* and *yang* separated, there appeared the pneumas of the Three Primordials and Eight Nodes which coagulated (成) into the script (書) of the flying celestials (*feitian* 飛天).[139] These were also inscribed into the Eight Dragon Cloud-seal of bright radiance graphs.[140]

Song then turns to exegesis of this passage, explicating the process of transformation, as well as explaining its abstruse terminology:

> The script of the Three Primordials and Eight Nodes transformed and pervaded all by its recitation.

Song continues by explicating the word "pattern" (*wen* 文) as referring to both "division" (*fen* 分) and "ordering principle" (*li* 理):

> As these scriptures emerged, the two principles were divided and the myriad things were thereby ordered. These scriptures are the warp and woof of heaven and earth, hence they are named "pattern."

---

137 DZ 388: 3.21a–b; Wang Chengwen, 王承文, *Dunhuang gu lingbao jing yu jintang daojiao* 敦煌古靈寶經與晉唐道教 (Beijing: Zhonghua shuju, 2002): 694–95.

138 The text mistakenly has 123 graphs.

139 This term may possibly refer to *devas* or *asparsas*. The term is used in Buddhist texts to designate celestial beings who protect the buddha-lands; DDB (http://www.buddhism-dict.net/cgi-bin/xpr-ddb.pl?98.xml+id%28%27b98db-5929%27%29).

140 P. 2256, lines 84–5; ZHDZ vol. 5, 512a; cf. DZ 1016: 1.8b2.

Returning to the passage from the *Declarations*, Song quotes the words of the Lady of Purple Tenuity:[141]

> Now, the script of the Three Primordials and Eight Nodes is only used by the eminent perfected and pure transcendents of the luminous supreme culmen. The Cloud-seal of bright radiance graphs are today seen in the talismanic script of the spirits.

To explicate this passage, Song Wenming quotes the *Wentong Lue* 文統略 [Principles of Writing, Abridged], a no longer extant text by Lu Xiujing:

> When the undifferentiated primordial divided, it separated into three powers, these are named the three primordials. Once the three primordials were established, the five phases appeared together. Three and five are eight, and these are referred to as the eight nodes. They are prior to writing. Next there appeared the eight bright radiant cloud-seal dragon glyphs. These self-generated flying dark pneumas congealed to form patterns, each graph the size of a ten-foot square 丈, that were inscribed in the midst of the not yet formed heaven. The two principles relied upon them in order to unfurl, the three radiances rely upon them in order to illumine, the hundred spirits rely upon them in order to transform, and creatures treasure them in order to live.

In these lines, Lu Xiujing is recasting the passage from the *Inner Sounds and Self-Generated Jade Graphs* cited above, which attributed these cosmogonic functions to the jade graphs. The ultimate source for these lines, however, is the well known verse from *Daode jing* 39 that celebrates the numinous efficacy of the One. Clearly, these lines reiterate the numinous primacy of the celestial writs.

Song Wenming next turns to a discrepancy between Lu Xiujing's understanding of the sequence of events and the words of the Lady of Purple Tenuity, which are quoted from the *Declarations*:

> The Three Primordial and Eight Nodes is the progenitor of all established patterns and graphs, the eight dragon cloud-seal arose from this root ancestor. It was the beginning of writing.[142] Master Lu, however, has already clarified that the Eight Nodes [script] was first, and the Eight Dragon [script] was next. If the latter was already present in the midst of the not-yet formed heaven, how can the former take form after the separation?

---

141 Intriguingly, Song Wenming refers to this passage as originating in *Traces of the Perfected* (*Zhenji* 真迹), a collection of Shangqing material compiled by Gu Huan 顧歡 (420–83) that preceded Tao Hongjing's *Declarations of the Perfected*.

142 DZ 1016: 1.8b9. Again, intriguingly, Song Wenming attributes these lines to *Traces of the Perfected*.

To clarify this matter, Song Wenming now turns to the Lingbao scriptures. He begins by citing the *Five Chapters in Red Script*: "The five numinous treasure talismans and Perfect Writs in red script emerged before the primordial beginning."[143] Song concludes somewhat confusedly:

> Hence, the three primordials must not be the three primordials associated with three powers, and the five phases are not the five phases of heaven and earth. These, then, must refer to the three primordials of the Elders of Three Treasures (*Sanbao zhangren* 三寶丈人). The three primordials were followed by the five virtues. They should not be confused 容關 with the three primordials and five phases that emanated after the separation of the three powers. How can this be said?

> The *Life Spirits of the Nine Heavens* says: "Of the myriad things of heaven and earth, were it not for the nourishment by three pneumas and the guidance of the nine primordials, none could exist."[144] It also says: "The three pneumas are at the head of heaven and earth, the nine primordials are the root of the myriad things."[145] Therefore we can surmise these three pneumas existed prior to the opening of heaven and earth and before the appearance of the three powers.

Song Wenming ends this first section by defining "cloud-seal" as "inscribing and composing cloud script" 撰集雲書. Such are the square graphs of the *Five Chapters* and the arrays of eight graphs of the *Inner Sounds*. The second moment, according to Song's scheme, is the elaboration of the Eight Nodes into the Dragon-Phoenix patterns, which are also known as Terrestrial Writings 地書. This probably means that this form of script is no longer celestial, but found in the mundane world. Song glosses the word "writing" (*shu* 書) with the homonym "to unfold" (*shu* 舒). He then explicates how these ancient scriptural forms were used as "writing":

> [Writing] unfolds and spreads over all matters and forms, hence it means to unfold. Henceforth stage the profound sages used writing in order to describe the celestial patterns.

The following stages listed by Song Wenming accorded with well known moments in the history of writing as codified since at least the Han dynasty.

---

143 DZ 22: 1a10.

144 *Dongxuan lingbao ziran jiutian shengshen zhangjing* 洞玄靈寶自然九天生神章經 DZ 318.2a5; *Lingbao ziran jiutian shengshen sanbao dayou jinshu* 靈寶自然九天生神三寶大有金書 DZ 165.2a4, the original line has "the myriad transformations of heaven and earth.... Nine pneumas."

145 DZ 318.2a6, DZ 165.2a5, the original has "The three pneumas are the revered of heaven and earth."

Among the earliest and perhaps best known is Xu Shen's 許慎 formulation in his "Postface" to the *Shuowen jiezi* 說文解字:[146]

> Third, during the era of the Yellow Thearch 軒轅, Cang Jie 蒼頡 while relying on the power of the dragon and phoenix collected the patterns of bird tracks and made the ancient patterns, thus creating the ancient forms. Fourth, the ancient script was transformed into great seal-script by Archivist Zhou 史籀 during the Zhou.[147] Fifth, the great seal-script was transformed into small seal-script by Cheng Miao 程邈 during the Qin.[148] Sixth, small seal-script was transformed into clerical script 隸書 by Xu Yang 盰陽 following the Qin.

While these latter four stages follow the traditional understanding of the history of script as formulated by Xu Shen, we should emphasize that the first stage in the traditional narrative is Fu Xi's observation of the celestial images (象) and terrestrial models (法), and his composition of the trigrams. This is followed by Shennong's 神農 use of corded ropes. Xu Shen history of script is thus a history of sagely discovery, beginning with perceiving and emulating natural patterns, and proceeding through further stages of refinement. Song Wenming replaces this history of human sagely discovery with a series of pre-cosmic self-generated graphs which emerge within the undifferentiated Dao, inspired by the narrative of descent in the *Declarations*, its development in the Lingbao scriptures, and its codification in Lu Xiujing's works.

Song Wenming concludes this section with a passage summarizing the history of script, beginning with the second stage, which is when the primordial unity was broken. He resumes his discussion by returning to the passage from the *Declarations* cited above:

> Therefore, it was in the second moment, while the seal-script bright radiant glyphs existed, that the Brahma script was formed to accord with it 順形.[149] The branches broke and flowed apart spreading through the thirty-six heavens and to all the regions in the ten directions. The currently transmitted scriptures all use the clerical script to explicate the celestial writings. These are confused and yet they flourish.

Song Wenming thus reiterates the primacy of the celestial writs of Lingbao, which appeared in the pre-existent primordium. It was only in the second stage of their transformation, when the graphs formed into cloud-seals, that the Brahma script appeared. Initially, the Brahma script is said have accorded with the

---

146 *Shuowen jiezi* 說文解字 15a. For a summary of Xu Shen's historical presentation, see, Mark E. Lewis, *Writing and Authority in Early China* (Albany: SUNY Press, 1999): 273 ff. For Xu Shen's own theory of script, see Françoise Bottero, "Revisiting the *wén* 文 and the *zì* 字: The Great Chinese Character Hoax," *Bulletin of the Museum of Far Eastern Antiquities* 74 (2002): 14–33.

147 Traditionally dated to King Xuan 宣 (r. 827–780 BCE) of the Zhou.

148 In Xu Shen's narrative this transformation is associated with Li Si 李斯.

149 In the *Declarations* passage the subject of this action are the two Luminous Lords (DZ 1016: 1.8b 4).

seal-script. But, later the unity of the script disintegrated, leading to the fragmented scriptural system of the contemporary world. As the Brahma script is associated with Buddhism, we may surmise that this linguistic collapse is also reflected in the religious sphere. Nevertheless, the narrative of six transformations linking the primordial graphs with the contemporary clerical script creates a linear history that ensures the authenticity, legitimacy, and superiority of Daoist scriptures over all other writings.

The theory and history of script formulated by Song Wenming was accepted by later compilers and codifiers. The seventh-century *Great Principles of the Profound Teaching* [*Xuanmen dayi* 玄門大義] follows the *Tongmen lun* closely in its discussion of the Twelve Categories. The passage cited above is quoted almost verbatim in the section on "celestial writings" 天書.[150] The passage also appears in the eighth-century compendium *Pivot of Daoism* [*Daojiao yishu* 道教義樞] and the Song era encyclopedia *Seven Slips from the Cloudy Satchel* [*Yunji qiqian* 雲笈七籤].[151] The talismanic source of all writing, and, most importantly,

---

150 *Dongxuan lingbao xuanmen dayi* 洞玄靈寶玄門大義 DZ 1124.7a8–ba4. As suggested by Chen Guofu (*Daozang*, p. 3–4) and demonstrated by Ōfuchi Ninji, *Dōkyō to sono kyoten* 道教とその經典 (Tokyo: Sōbunsha, 1997): 225–30, the current *Xuanmen dayi* in 1 *juan* is probably a remnant of an original 20 juan *Xuanmen dalun* 玄門大論 that is listed in the *Daozang quejing mulu* 道藏闕經目錄 DZ 1430: 1.20a2 (also listed is *Dongxuan lingbao xuanmen dayi* DZ 1430: 1.112b7, without specific size). See also Schipper and Verellen, *Taoist Canon*, vol. 1, 439.

151 The following discussion, cited in both *DJYS* 2 and *YJQQ* 7, provides several opinions after citing the *Daomen dalun* 道門大論 for the definition of "celestial writing" (*Tianshu* 天書) which in turn was based on the *Zhen'gao* passage as well as Lingbao materials:

> When *yin* and *yang* first separated, there appeared the pneumas of the Three Primordials, Five Virtues and Eight Nodes which coagulated (*cheng* 成) into the script of the flying celestials (*feitian* 飛天, possibly referring to devas). Later it was inscribed into the Eight-Dragon Cloud-seal of bright radiance graphs.

The text then debates the terminology: (1) Citing Lu Xiujing:

> the three primordials are the three elements (*sancai* 三才, heaven, earth and man; *DJYS* mistakenly has 二才); once they are established, the five phases emerge together. Once the five phases are in position, the three and the five harmonize. This is called the Eight Nodes. This is the source for the various scripts.

(I follow *DJYS* 2.17a8 for *yuan* 元.) (2) Citing *Chishu yupian* (DZ 22: 1a10), the *Lingbao chishu wupian zhenwen* emerged before the primordial beginning. Hence, the Three Primordials are not the three elements, and the Five Virtues cannot be the five phases. The former must then refer to the pneumas of the Elders of Three Treasures (*Sanbao zhangren* 三寶丈人; referring to the Elder of Celestial Treasure, the Elder of Lingbao and the Elder of Spiritual Treasure who are, respectively, the ancestral pneumas (*zuqi* 祖炁) of the Celestial Treasure Lord, the Lingbao Lord, and the Spiritual Treasure Lord). The three pneumas spontaneously generated the five virtues. Hence the *Jiutian shengshen zhang* 九天生神章 says:

> None of the myriad transformations of heaven and earth would have been produced were it not for the nourishment by the three pneumas or the guidance of the nine pneumas. The

the perception that the Daoist scriptures are transformations of primordial celestial graphs thus became orthodoxy.

Conclusion

Our discussion in this chapter traced the development of ideas regarding the efficacy of talismans from their earliest attested uses as apotropaic devices, on the one hand, and as icons of authority on the other. In both cases, the use of talismans assumes an efficacy, or sacrality, that expresses power that is beyond mundane linguistic limits. The actual graphic forms operate through principles of recognizability, that is the recognition that the forms are meaningful although not necessarily comprehensible, and inscription, which is the power inherent in inscribing names and forms which grants power over the things named and portrayed.

In Daoist texts of the medieval era these principles become explicit in the notions of "true names" and "true forms." Moreover, Daoists developed cosmogonic narratives in which the emanation of the cosmos from primordial unity of the Dao to the manifested world is literally paralleled, perhaps even presaged, in the evolution, or rather devolution, of script from primordial graphs self-generating in the void to the mundane script used in the human realm. The Daoist scriptures are thus perceived as literally inscribing the world. The power of inscription inherent in the scriptures and talismans is now claimed by the Daoist master who can produce talismans, penetrate the true forms and true names of the powers beyond the mundane world, and, through ritual, access, the primordial Dao itself.

three pneumas are revered by heaven and earth, the nine pneumas are the root of the myriad things (citing *Lingbao ziran jiutian shengshen sanbao dayou jinshu* 靈寶自然九天生神三寶大有金書 DZ 165.2a4).

Therefore, we can surmise these three pneumas existed prior to the emergence of heaven and earth and before the appearance of the three elements. (3) Master Song 宋法師 suggests the Three Primordials are the pneumas of (a) Grand Without-Origin Eminent Jade Luminosity of the Chaotic Cavern (*Hundong tai wuyuan gaoshang yuhuang* 混洞太無元高上玉皇), (b) Grand Without-Origin Supreme Jade Void of Red Chaos (*Chihun tai wuyuan wushang yuxu* 赤混太無元無上玉虛), (c) Primordial Supreme Jade Void of Mysterious Penetration of Dark Silence (*Mingji xuantong yuan wushang yuxu* 赤混太無元無上玉虛); the five virtues are the five conjunctions of the three primordials, namely: *shaoyin, taiyin, shaoyang, taiyang,* and harmonious center (*he* 和) (DZ 1129: 2.17a7; DZ 1032: 7a–8b). While the *YJQQ* attributes the passage to the *Daomen dalun,* the *DJYS* does not provide a source. Meng Anpai 孟安排, the compiler of *DJYS* mentions *Xuanmen dayi* as a major source of inspiration for his own work, but so massive that few students can study it (DZ 1129, Preface 4b2–6). It seems therefore that *Daomen dalun* and *Xuanmen dayi* are alternative titles for the same text.

4 The Yellow and the Red
Controversies over sexual practice

> Do not dwell together with ritual masters and Daoists who are of the Yellow and Red; when lying down, at rest, when sitting, or standing; do not mix with them, nor share food and drink with them. If they are Daoists of the Cavern of Spirits or Cavern of Perfection, then you may travel with them.[1]

In previous chapters, we saw how various lineages debated and negotiated a range of practices, and how this complex set of interactions gradually led to merger and synthesis and an emergence of a self-conscious unity among lineages. More specifically, the rejection of blood rites by which certain lineages consciously defined themselves as distinct from the sacrificial practices of traditional religion came to be accepted by various lineages to form one basis for the new religious tradition. The establishment of "pure" rituals of initiation and transmission, and the communal rituals that developed from these by which Daoist lineages distinguished their own practices, were based on a conceptually new vision of divinity and a different cosmology than traditional religion. This new vision of divinity, which was not based on deified humans but on the Dao itself as an active force that acted through manifestations, led to new conceptualizations of the relationships among members of the Daoist community on the one hand, and between humans and the spirit realm on the other. Both of these relationships were modeled on textual transmission between masters and disciples, which were extended to textual guarantees and bureaucratic models that formed the new modes of communication between humans and deities. In Chapter 3, we saw how Daoists came to see their texts as actual cosmogonic agents whose existence was prior to all things, and which in fact generated all things in the world. The previous chapters

---

1 P 2403, published in ZHDZ, vol.4.98a–b. This Dunhuang manuscript is a fragment of *Taishang lingbao weiyi dongxuan zhenyi ziran jingjue* 太上靈寶威儀洞玄真一自然經訣, a text not extant in the Daozang. First identified by Ōfuchi Ninji, the Dunhuang manuscripts P 2356, P 2403, and P 2452 are remnants of a Lingbao text listed in Lu Xiujing's Lingbao catalogue as *Taishang taiji taixu shangzhenren yan taishang lingbao weiyi dongxuan zhenyi ziran jingjue* 太上靈寶威儀洞玄真一自然經訣. See Ōfuchi, *Tonkōdōkyō mokurokuhen*, 77–9; idem *Tonkō zurokuhen*, 86; idem, "On Ku," 53; Schipper and Verellen, *Taoist Canon*, 239. Published in ZHDZ: vol. 4, 97–100. Wang, *Dunhuang*, 33 ff. focuses on this text.

have demonstrated ways in which the debates among Daoist lineages over effi-cacy gradually led to the acceptance and merger of different practices in ever growing ritual and scriptural syntheses. In this chapter, I examine a contrasting development – the gradual rejection and erasure of sexual practices from the emerging Daoist synthesis.

Variously known as "merging pneumas" (*heqi* 合氣) or "the Way of the Yellow and Red" (*huangchi zhidao* 黃赤之道), sexual ritual was an integral part of the complete initiation process in the early Celestial Master community. The Daoist lineages that emerged in the fourth and fifth centuries explicitly and vehemently rejected sexual initiation rites. Moreover, as the passage cited above indicates, these lineages came to identify Celestial Master Daoism itself with sexual ritual, and hence to reject Celestial Master Daoism. This passage from the Lingbao scripture *Awesome Rites of Lingbao* 靈寶威儀 hints at a vision of a new commu-nity, which was to exclude those Daoists identified simply as "yellow and red" while allowing the adherents of the Lingbao ritual code to mix with Daoists identified by their textual affiliation with the Cavern of Spirits and Cavern of Perfection. I discuss this vision of community further at the end of this chapter.

While much of this may have been no more than rhetoric, texts composed within Celestial Master lineages in the fifth century also reject sexual practice. Indeed, it was precisely the rejection of sexual ritual that distinguished these so-called "reformist" Celestial Master groups from the earlier community. While these "reformist" movements may have been short lived, their impact was long lasting in that the emerging Celestial Master synthesis of the fifth and sixth cen-turies excluded sexual rites. On the other hand, the rejection of sexual initiation rites may also help explain why Celestial Master texts and rituals were excluded from the synthesis of the Three Caverns envisaged in the Lingbao scriptures, and as developed by Lu Xiujing. I discuss these and other Daoist efforts at integration and systemization in the next chapter; suffice it here to say that comments regard-ing the exclusion of sexual initiation rites are among the most explicit in the various efforts at formulating Daoist orthodoxy.

This chapter begins with an examination of early records of sexual practices, dating back to the Warring States and early Han. This is followed by an examina-tion of the sexual initiation rite in early Celestial Master Daoism. Although there are numerous references to this practice, the actual details of the sexual rites are not at all clear. In this section, I focus on the *Initiation Rite of the Yellow Book*. This is a Celestial Master ritual manual, which was probably composed in the late fourth century in response to critique of the sexual initiation rite. Thus, while the text includes early material and shows obvious parallels with other Celestial Master texts, it presents a reformulated ritual form, already indicative of the attempts by Celestial Masters to recast their rite. I then turn to an examination of the criticism and rejection of the sexual rites, and by extension of Celestial Master Daoism, including various reformulations within the tradition of Celestial Master Daoism. The examination of the controversies surrounding sexual ritual will allow us a glimpse of far more antagonistic debates among Daoist lineages than we have seen so far. Finally, I examine the rise of monastic and celibate communities that became the main vehicle for Daoism in the following centuries as the Celestial Master communities declined.

Sexual practices in early China

Generally labeled in Chinese as "Methods of the Bedchamber" (*fangzhong shu* 房中術), sexual cultivation techniques were among the cultivation techniques (*yangsheng* 養生) that were prevalent in early China prior to the rise of organized Daoist communities in the second century CE. As one of the primary purposes of these techniques was ensuring conception, securing pregnancy, and the birth of sons, these techniques were transmitted both within lineages of practitioners of esoterica as well as among the general public. These practices remained popular throughout the medieval period, and are well documented in contemporary sources. Manuals of sexual techniques are listed in the bibliographic chapters of the official histories from the Han to the Tang. All of these texts were lost in China at some time after the tenth century, but fragments were collected into Tamba Yasuyori's 丹波康賴 (911–95), *Ishimpō* 醫心方 [*Prescriptions from the Heart of Medicine*].[2] These fragmentary collations are now known to be descendants of a tradition extending far back into the Warring States era. The earliest texts now available are the several manuscripts of sexual manuals discovered among the texts unearthed in Mawangdui in 1973. These texts, dating to the third century BCE, demonstrate the antiquity of the tradition of sexual cultivation techniques and shed new light on the links between this tradition and Daoist practices in medieval China.[3]

Manuals of sexual cultivation are sometimes labeled Daoist in modern studies.[4] We should note, however, that the tradition of sexual cultivation was prior to the rise of Daoism, and continued to develop separately. There was clearly interaction between the traditions, but we should not conflate them. Some Daoist lineages that emerged in the early medieval period explicitly criticized the techniques

---

2 The *Ishimpō* fragments were discovered and reintroduced into China by Ye Dehui 葉德輝 (1864–1927) in the early twentieth century (*Shuangmei jing'an congshu* 雙梅景闇叢書 (Changsha, 1903), and brought to the attention of Western scholarship by Robert van Gulik's *Sexual Life in Ancient China*. A more recent collation of the *Ishimpō* fragments is included in Li Ling 李零, *Zhongguo fangshu kao* 中國方術考 (Beijing: Dongfang, rev. edn, 2000): 501–27.

3 The sexual manuals unearthed at Mawangdui have been studied and translated by Donald Harper, "The Sexual Arts of Ancient China as Described in a Manuscript of the Second Century B.C." *HJAS* 47 (1987): 539–93; idem., *Early*. Some of these texts are included in Douglas Wile, *Art of the Bedchamber* (Albany: SUNY Press, 1992), which also provides translations of the popular Bedchamber manuals and some texts of sexual inner alchemy.

4 See, for example, van Gulik who characterized these texts as Daoist, and described their attitude to sexual practice:

   The Daoist speculations on the magical power of the sexual union applied to both man and woman. Although there were some Daoist adepts who selfishly concentrated on strengthening their own vital force by tapping that of their woman-partners, disregarding their health and sometimes even harming it, the general principle was that both partners should share in the benefits accruing from the sexual discipline

   (van Gulik, *Sexual Life*, 84)

advocated in the bed chamber manuals, while other lineages adopted and adapted these practices. Some Daoists, such as the authors of early Celestial Master texts who criticized specific techniques of sexual cultivation, introduced techniques of sexual cultivation into their ritual system. Later Daoists condemned these very practices. As Daoists were indeed very concerned with sexual practices, we need to be very careful about simplistically labeling specific practices and texts as Daoist. We need to carefully examine Daoist scriptures, and distinguish the different attitudes toward sexual practice in the context of specific ritual programs.

As summarized by Donald Harper, the goal of sexual cultivation in the early texts of sexual cultivation was to "generate vapor (*qi*) and essence (*jing* 精), which the man absorbs and stores in his body".[5] These texts are androcentric, and while there is some concern for female orgasm, this is not so much in the interest of pleasure for the female as for the critical role that absorbing the female essence had for the benefit of the male practitioner.

The main practice advocated in the bedchamber manuals was essence retention, and its reversion into the body, in order to ascend the spinal column and replenish the brain. In medieval texts, this practice came to be known as "returning the essence to replenish the brain" (*huanjing bunao* 還精補腦). While this term does not appear in the Mawangdui texts, Harper shows that the notion of essence retention is clearly present in these texts.[6] Wile and Harper agree that the term *jing* as used in these texts does not refer to semen but rather to a refined form of *qi*.[7] The brain (*nao* 腦), in the medical theory prevalent in early China, was not perceived as a locus of the mind or consciousness, but rather as the main site for the production and dispersal of bone marrow.[8] Replenishing the brain thus referred to augmenting and strengthening the skeletal structure of the body.

Essence retention could be achieved by two basic techniques, either by withdrawal from the woman, withholding ejaculation, and reverting the essence internally; or by preventing ejaculation at the point of orgasm by pressing a point between anus and scrotum or constricting the buttocks, causing the essence to reverse its path internally. Inspired perhaps by van Gulik, who coined the term *coitus reservatus* to describe the practice of essence retention,[9] Joseph Needham went on to label the former technique of orgasmic cultivation as *coitus conservatus*, while he labeled the latter *coitus thesauratus*.[10] Douglas Wile labeled this latter technique "retrograde ejaculation." Whether the techniques included orgasmic or non-orgasmic cultivation, the main point was activating the essence during

---

5   Harper, *Early*, 136.
6   Harper, *Early*, 138.
7   Wile, *Art*; Harper, *Early*, 138.
8   Ted Kaptchuk, *The Web that has no Weaver: Understanding Chinese Medicine* (New York: McGraw-Hill Professional, 2000): 351–2; Paul Unschuld, *Huang Di Nei Jing Su Wen: Nature, Knowledge, Imagery in an Ancient Chinese Medical Text* (Berkeley: University of California Press, 2003): 139.
9   van Gulik, *Sexual Life*, 47.
10 Needham, *Science*, vol. 5, part 5, 177–79.

the sexual act, withholding ejaculation and reversing the flow of the essence internally to nourish the body.

As Donald Harper and Douglas Wile have provided us with excellent translations of the Mawangdui manuals, and of several of the later sexual manuals, I will only provide a brief example of one such manual, the *Zidu jing* 子都經, which is extant only in fragments in the *Ishimpō*. Attributed to Wu Zidu 巫子都 and purportedly a teaching presented to Han emperor Wu, the text was probably composed after the third century.[11]

According to the opening narrative, Han emperor Wu observed Zidu by the river Wei, and noticed he had an "extraordinary pneuma extending more than ten feet above his head." Asked by the emperor, Zidu claimed he received instruction in sexual methods from Lingyang Ziming:

> The art of *yin* and *yang* is a secret of the bed chamber. I, your servant, should not openly speak about it. Those who can practice this are few, and I dare not divulge it. I received this teaching from Lingyang Ziming when I was sixty-five years old and have practiced this art for seventy-two years. All those who seek life should seek that which provides life. If one covets women for their beauty, and expends his force to emit [semen], the hundred blood vessels will be damaged, and the hundred ailments will all arise together.[12]

Another fragment of the text is cited in a section devoted to "curing illnesses":

> The way for making one's vision bright: at the moment you are about to ejaculate lift your head, hold your breath, and call out loudly, gazing to the left and right. Contract your abdomen, reverting the essence and pneuma, causing them to enter into the hundred vessels. The method preventing deafness: at the moment you are about to ejaculate, inhale a large breath, clench your teeth, hold your breath, causing a humming sound in your ears. As before, contract your abdomen and cause the pneuma to circulate throughout the body until it becomes very strong. Even in old age, you will not be deaf. The way to harmonize the five viscera, regulate digestion, and curing the hundred illnesses: when about to ejaculate, expand your abdomen by intentionally filling it with *qi*. After contracting, the essence will disperse and return to the hundred vessels.

The main interest in this passage is the health of the male practitioner, with little interest in the female. The main practice is indeed retention of the essence by controlling the moment of ejaculation, causing the flow of essence to reverse itself and circulate through the male body. While there is little interest in the female's

---

11 *Ishimpō*, vol. 5, chapter 28, 2b; collated in Li, *Zhongguo fangshu kao*, 512–4; translated in Wile, *Art*, 104. Wu Zidu is anachronistically introduced as Imperial Son-in-law 駙馬都尉, a title that was first bestowed upon He Yan 合晏 (d. 249) by Cao Cao.

12 *Ishimpō*, vol. 5, 2b; Li, *Zhongguo fangshu kao*, 512.

health or pleasure, the passage continues to reveal a great deal of interest in the female anatomy:

> [Follow a rhythm of] nine shallow and one deep [thrusts] between the "zither strings" and the "wheat teeth." The correct *qi* will return, while the noxious *qi* will depart....[13]

The terms "zither strings" *qinxian* 琴絃 and "wheat teeth" *maichi* 麥齒 are part of a nearly standard terminology that appears throughout the sexual manuals as designations for locations within the female genitals.[14] The former is usually associated with shallow penetration, and the latter with the next level of depth. This is considered the optimal level for sexual practice, where "harmony of yin and yang is attained." Penetrating to deeper levels of the vagina is harmful to both the female and male. Significantly, these terms appear already in the Mawangdui manuscripts. In the "Discussion of the Culminant Way Under Heaven" (*Tianxia zhidao lun* 天下至道談), "wheat teeth" is the sixth point mentioned in a list of twelve parts of the female genitalia,[15] and both terms appear on a diagram of female genitals in the text "Recipes for Nurturing Life" (*Yangsheng fang* 養生方).[16]

The text continues by explaining that the purpose of sexual practice is not only to conserve the male's essence, but to accumulate the female essence as well:

> The way of *yin* and *yang* is to treasure the semen.[17] If one can cherish it, then one's nature and allotment can be preserved.[18] After ejaculating, one should collect the female's *qi* in order to replenish oneself. "Re-establishing by nine" means practicing inner breath nine times. "Pressing the one" means applying pressure with the left hand below the genitals in order to revert the essence and return the semen. "Collect the female's *qi*" by "nine shallow and one deep." Place your mouth next to the enemy's mouth. Exhale and inhale through the mouth, subtly drawing in the two pneumas. Swallow them, and with mental concentration cause them to descend to the abdomen, thereby strengthening your penis.[19]

---

13 *Ishimpō*, vol. 5, 26b–27a; Li, *Zhongguo fangshu kao*, 513; Wile, *Art*, 104.

14 Wile, *Art*, 236 n 73, 243 n 129.

15 Harper, *Early*, 436.

16 Harper, *Early*, 359–60, the diagram is on 362.

17 This is one of few specific references to semen *jingye* 精液 in these texts, which generally refer to essence *jing*.

18 Wile translates the compound *xingming* 性命 simply as life, but we should note that this compound incorporates two distinct aspects that together comprise a person's life: *xing* refers to the innate nature with which a person is born, and *ming* refers to the allotment of life bestowed upon him. While these two terms are critical for understanding Chinese notions of human life, the multivalent understandings and complex debates about them are beyond the scope of this book. See, for example, the several essays in Christopher Lupke, ed. *The Magnitude of Ming: Command, Allotment, and Fate in Chinese Culture* (Honolulu: University of Hawai'i Press, 2005).

19 *Ishimpō*, vol. 5, 27a–b; Li, *Zhongguo fangshu kao*, 513; Wile, *Art*, 104.

We should note that the female is here labeled enemy (*di* 敵), exemplifying an inherent ambivalence toward sex and particularly about the woman's role.[20] On the one hand, females are the source for nourishing the male and, in the *Ishimpō* texts, the instructors in sexual arts. Yet, they are also competitors for the benefits that accrue to the one who absorbs the other's *qi*. Sex is like a battle, which for the uninitiated male who cannot control ejaculation is depleting and dangerous, for "women can be vampires who may take away a man's essence".[21] The sexual manuals therefore teach the male methods for conserving his essence and for absorbing the female sexual energies.

As exemplified by the excerpts from the *Zidu jing*, retention and reversion of the essence were the basic practices in the traditions of sexual practice described in the bedchamber manuals since the Han dynasty. Writing in the early fourth century, Ge Hong referred to these techniques in his summary of sexual practice:

> There are over ten schools of sexual techniques: some seek to fill and save the damaged and depleted, some seek to heal all illnesses, some seek to absorb yin in order to replenish yang, some seek to increase their years and prolong their lives. Their most essential point is returning the essence to nourish the brain. [This method was transmitted by the Perfected by word of mouth and was not written down]. Though one may ingest medicines, without knowledge of this essential point, one will not gain longevity. One cannot totally cut off yin and yang [sexual intercourse], for if *yin* and *yang* do not merge then one will have illness due to blockages, and due to many illnesses arising from depression and celibacy one will die early. Freely indulging in one's desires will also lead to diminishing one's years. Only by achieving a harmony through regulation may one be without loss. If one does not receive methods by oral instruction not even one in ten thousand may practice this without inflicting death on oneself. People like the Mystic [maiden], Unadorned [maiden], Zidu, Rongcheng zi, and Pengzi 彭子 may have made a rough record of this but to the end they did not commit its essentials to paper.[22]

Ge Hong refers to the best known practitioners of sexual techniques in early China. Their names, and texts associated with them, are mentioned in several hagiographic, historical, and bibliographic accounts. Rongcheng 容成 is men-

20 Wile, *Art*, 45 is particularly incisive on this point.
21 Schipper, *Taoist Body*, 147.
22 Wang, *Baopuzi*, 8.150; Ware, *Alchemy*, 140. The passage continues to emphasize the importance of receiving oral instruction form a teacher and the superiority of alchemical practice:

> Those intent on seeking 'non-death' exert themselves seeking this. I received my master Zheng's instructions and I record them in order to show future believers in the Dao. This is not my personal opinion. I indeed have not yet received the full instructions. Biased Daoists (一塗道士) sometimes concentrate only on the methods of sexual intercourse in order to control the spirits and do not produce the great elixirs of gold and cinnabar – this is extreme stupidity.

tioned among the earliest masters of sexual practices. The Mawangdui manuscript *Ten Questions* (*Shi Wen* 十問), a set of 10 interviews between mythical rulers and sages, includes a dialogue between the Yellow Emperor and Rongcheng, who expounds on breathing techniques and preservation of pneuma.[23] In the Han hagiography *Liexian zhuan*, Rongcheng is said to be an ancient master who was the Yellow Emperor's teacher. His practices are described as "replenishing and guiding" 補導 and "extracting essence from the mystic female" 取精於玄牝. His essential teaching is defined as the "valley spirit does not die" 谷神不死.[24] Intriguingly, these practices are closely associated with the terminology of the *Daode jing*.[25] Several masters of esoteric arts are said to have followed Rongcheng's "methods of managing females" 御婦人術, which consisted of "tight control and non-ejaculation, returning the essence to replenish the brain."[26] A text associated with Rongcheng, *Rongcheng's Way of Yin* 容成陰道 in 26 scrolls, is listed in the section on sexual arts in the *Hanshu* bibliographic chapter.[27]

The Mystic Maiden (Xuannü 玄女) and Unadorned Maiden (Sunü 素女) are often mentioned together as instructresses in sexual techniques. While absent from the early manuals unearthed at Mawangdui, their names are listed among the most important of sexual practitioners in post Han sources. Aside from mentioning their practicing here, Ge Hong also lists a *Xuannü jing* 玄女經 in his bibliographic chapter.[28] A text by the same title is listed in the bibliographic chapter of the *History of Sui* as part of *Sunü midao jing* 素女秘道經, and a *Prescriptions of Sunü* (*Sunü fang* 素女方) is listed separately.[29] These texts are no longer extant, but extensive sections are preserved in Chapter 28 of *Ishimpō*.[30]

In his assessment of the sexual manuals, Robert van Gulik saw *coitus reservatus* as evidence for an enlightened and egalitarian sexuality.[31] Charlotte Furth criticizes van Gulik for viewing "*coitus reservatus*, the key technique taught by the bedchamber manuals, as evidence for a traditional Chinese understanding of sex as the domain of the erotic, with fulfillment of pleasure for men and women as its central, if not sole, purpose". Furth argues that these manuals "were not 'about'

23 Harper, *Early*, 393–399; idem, "Sexual Arts," 546.

24 DZ 296: 3.7a, Kaltenmark, *Lie-sien*, 55–60.

25 Jao Tsung-I 饒宗頤, "'Chuan Laozi shi' Rongcheng yishuo gouchen" '傳老子師'容成遺說鈎沉, *Beijing daxue xuebao* 1998.3, rpt. in *Jao Tsung-I ershi shiji xueshu wenji* 饒宗頤二十世紀學術文集 (Taipei: Xinwenfeng, 2004): vol. 5, 105–18.

26 握固不瀉還精補腦. *Houhanshu* 82B.2740 for Ling Shouguang 泠壽光, 82B.2750 for Gan Shi 甘始, Dongguo yannian 東郭延年, and Feng Junda 封君達.

27 *Hanshu* 30.1778.

28 Wang, *Baopuzi*, 19.333.

29 *Suishu* 隋書 "Jingji zhi" 34.1050.

30 These fragments were fully translated by van Gulik, *Sexual*, 135 ff.; Douglas Wile, *Art*, 85–100.

31 Summarizing the teachings of the Bedchamber manuals, van Gulik wrote:

   [these texts] are primarily manuals of normal conjugal sexual relations… against the background of the polygamic family system…lay great stress on the necessity of a man understanding the sexual needs and the sexual behavior of his womenfolk…importance of making the woman reach orgasm during every coitus is constantly stressed.

pleasure or women simply as objects of desire, but about what medieval Chinese understood as serious goals of life and death, linking health, spirituality and social purpose."[32] Furth stresses that these manuals view sex as a "microcosmic human re-enactment of primary creative processes."[33] With the added evidence of the Mawangdui manuscripts, van Gulik's interpretation is even less sustainable.

Most importantly, we should be careful about distinguishing the tradition of the bedchamber manuals from the Daoist texts that appeared in medieval China. Neither van Gulik nor Furth examined the various sexual practices described, advocated, and discussed in Daoist scriptures. Hence, while Furth is correct in pointing out that the traditional bedroom manuals were male-centered and viewed the female as a repository of *yin* essence, we find similar criticism in several Daoist texts. As Schipper points out in reference to van Gulik's work, "...this is not true Daoism. It is a mistake to look for Daoism in the idea of 'nourishing yang at the expense of yin'."[34]

While several Daoist lineages adopted sexual techniques into their ritual programs, they tended to explicitly oppose the methods of "collecting yin." For example, the hagiography of Lord Pei, which dates to the first half of the fourth century, introduces a variant of sexual practice in which a male and female practice together, both retaining their fluids and reverting them to nourish the brain. This practice, we are warned, is secret and is distinct from the mundane practices that focus on male attainment:

> This practice allows men and women to gather living pneuma and nourish their essence and blood together. This is not the exoteric method which focuses on 'plucking yin to augment yang.'[35]

使男女並取生氣含養精血. 此非外法專採陰益陽也

The practice is performed in an oratory (*jing* 靖), and begins by the participants focusing their thoughts through apophatic techniques ("first forget forms and all things" 先須忘形忘物) and preparatory incantations:

> Then the male contemplates his Kidney to secure his essence, and refines the pneuma to ascend up the spine and return to the *niwan*. This is called

32 Charlotte Furth, "Rereading van Gulik: Sexuality and Reproduction in Traditional Chinese Medicine," in Christina K. Gilmartin *et al.*, eds. *Engendering China: Women, Culture and the State* (Cambridge: Harvard University Press, 1994) criticizes van Gulik for his optimistic view of Chinese sexual practices as envisioning "a robustly connubial heterosexual marriage bed" with "an enlightened *ars* erotica which... places a high valuation on male responsibility for female pleasure" (128).

33 Idem: 130–1.

34 Schipper, *Taoist Body*: 149.

35 *Qingling zhenren Peijun zhuan* 清靈真人傳, preserved in the encyclopedia *Yunji qiqian*, (*YJQQ* 105.3a4–5). Robinet considers Pei Xuanren 玄仁 and his practices to be a part of distinct revelation which was a precursor to the Yang Xi revelations. The extant text is based on an earlier hagiography, probably dating to the early fourth century; Robinet, *Révélation*, 1: 55; 2: 375–84.

Returning to the Primordial (*huanyuan* 還元). The female contemplates her heart and nourishes her spirits, refining her fire to become still. She causes the pneuma of her breasts to descend to the Kidney, and rise up the spine, and to reach the *niwan*. This is called Transforming to Perfection (*huazhen* 化真). Cultivating this in the cinnabar chamber, in a hundred days one will penetrate to the numinous realm. If one practices this for a long time one will spontaneously attain perfection, live long and transcend. It is a way of non-death.

The main point here is the joint and complementary practice in which both the male and female cultivate their respective essences through meditative techniques. There is no explicit description of sexual contact in this practice, but the instructions for concentration and reversion of the essence share the terminology of sexual cultivation techniques, and imply a practice of withholding orgasm.

In summary, we must remember that the tradition of sexual practices pre-dated the rise of institutionalized Daoist communities. These practices remained popular even while Daoist lineages advocated their distinctive sexual practices. Condemnation of the tradition of bedchamber manuals is found in the earliest texts of Celestial Master Daoism. Indeed, the condemnation of specific aspects of sexual cultivation was a critical part of the process by which Celestial Master Daoism distinguished and separated itself from other contemporary traditions.

Sexual rites in the way of the Celestial Master

The earliest extant text of Celestial Master Daoism, the *Xiang'er Commentary*, presents a clear awareness of the tradition of sexual cultivation, and severely criticizes the practices and techniques associated with the very texts discussed above:

> The Dao teaches people to congeal their essences and form spirits. Today, there are in the world false practitioners who craftily proclaim the Dao, teaching by means of texts attributed to the Yellow Emperor, the Mystic Maiden, Gongzi, and Rongcheng. They say that during intercourse with a woman one should not release the essence, but, through meditation return its essence to the brain to fortify it. Since their spirits and hearts are not unified, they lose that which they seek to preserve.[36]

The *Xiang'er Commentary* clearly identifies the practitioners of these "false" teachings who claim to possess the Dao. This assertion, of course, identifies them as close rivals. The practice of essence retention is "false" because these practitioners do not harmonize their intention, the heart, and their internal spirits.

36 *Xiang'er zhu*, lines 87–9; Bokenkamp, *Early*, 87.

The reference to "congealing essence" is particularly significant, and seems to allude to the practice actually advocated by this text:

> If, once one has congealed one's essences and formed spirits, there are excess yang pneumas, one should strive to cherish the self and, shutting the heart, cut off longings. It is not permissible to arrogantly deceive yin.[37]

This passage seems to imply that, by retaining his essence, the male practitioner may accumulate too much yang. This excess yang may not be tempered with yin essence "borrowed" from a female through sexual cultivation techniques. This is a rather strange perspective on the practices we saw above, not found in the texts themselves. Is this merely a polemic by the author of the *Xiang'er Commentary*, or perhaps a hint at interpretations of the practice unknown to us?

The sexual practice advocated in the *Xiang'er Commentary* seems to be based on a notion that essence is to be preserved within the body, not by withholding ejaculation and absorbing the female essence, but rather by controlling sexual desires. It is not quite clear what this method is, but the following passage may offer an intriguing hint:

> Those who know how to preserve within the black have the power of the Dao ever resident within them. They do not 'borrow' from others, since needing to have it given to you is not as good as keeping it to yourself. Those who practice the *Classic of the Mystic Maiden* and the methods of Gongzi and Rongcheng all wish to borrow. But what creditor exists who will loan? So they receive nothing.[38]

The criticism is clearly aimed at the practice of absorbing female essence, precisely the type of practice we found in the *Zidu jing*. The extant fragment of the *Xiang'er Commentary* does not provide a clear description of the practice it advocated. Nevertheless, implicit in these passages is the notion that the practice followed by the community did include some form of essence retention. These direct references to specific texts and techniques indicate that the Celestial Masters themselves were engaging in similar practices and were, therefore, particularly intent on defining the correct sexual practice.

While it is quite clear that the practices of the early Celestial Master community included some sexual rituals, extant sources do not allow for a complete reconstruction of the rite. From scattered references, many based in polemical texts condemning this practice, we may speculate that there were two distinct practices. The first, about which we know a little more, was an initiation ritual in which a male and female adept together received a register of spirit-generals. A second practice seems to have been sexual cultivation technique, perhaps particularly

---

37 *Xiang'er zhu*, lines 92–3; Bokenkamp, *Early*, 88.
38 *Xiang'er zhu*, lines 430–2; Bokenkamp, *Early*, 125. I have no further information on Gongzi.

aimed at securing pregnancy and birth. It is unclear whether these two practices were related, and it seems that most sources conflate them.

Our most important source for the Celestial Master initiation ritual is the *Initiation Rite of the Yellow Book* (hereafter, *Yellow Book*).[39] Several scholars have studied this important text, yet the relationship between this text and the early Celestial Master community remains unclear. The titles of several other texts also contain the term "Yellow book" (*huangshu* 黃書), a term which may be a marker for sexual practices. Closely related to the *Yellow Book* is a text entitled *Dongzhen huangshu* [*Yellow Book of the Cavern of Perfection*].[40] According to *Dongzhen huangshu*, Laozi transmitted the *Yellow Book* in eight chapters to the first Celestial Master.[41] The text goes on to list eight titles that seem to be sections of the *Yellow Book*; perhaps a progression of texts to be presented along a graded process of initiation: (1) "Red pneuma" 赤炁, (2) "Three pneuma" 三炁, (3) "Nine talismans" 九符, (4) "Seven talismans" 七符, (5) "Mystic Register" 玄籙, (6) "Complete in Chaos" (*Huncheng* 混成), (7) "Central Edict," with three sections (*Zhongzhang* 中章三), (8) "Spirit register" 神籙.[42]

These two texts need to be distinguished from two other texts, *Dongzhen taiwei huangshu tiandijun shijing jinyang sujing*, DZ 81, and *Dongzhen taiwei huangshu jiutian balu zhenwen*, DZ 257.[43] While there are possible hints at sexual practice in DZ 257, the focus of DZ 81 is talismanic. These two closely related texts are probably remnants of an earlier *Taiwei huangshu* 太微黃書, which is said to have originally included eight *juan*.[44] The reference to eight *juan*, as well as the clear distinction made in DZ 81 between the teaching of *Taiwei huangshu* and the "minor method of the Yellow and Red" 非黃赤之小術 (11a7), probably hints at a composition which postdates and responds to the Celestial Master ritual.[45]

---

39 *Shangqing huangshu guodu yi* 黃書過度儀 DZ 1294.
40 *Dongzhen huangshu* 洞真黃書 DZ 1343.
41 DZ 1343.2a1, 7b5. The purported date for this transmission is problematic as these two passages differ in dating the event. In 2a1 the text has "First year of the *Han'an* era, *renwu*, second year, *guiwei* day" 漢安元年壬午二年癸未; The first year of the *Han'an* era (142) was *renwu*. It is unclear what "second year" refers to here. In 7b4 the text states the transmission was in the first year of the *Han'an* era, first month, tenth day, at noon. The *Dadao jialing jie* states the initial revelation of Laozi was in the "First year of the *Han'an* era, first day of fifth month" (DZ 789.14a9).
42 DZ 1343.2a1. In 7b5 the text lists the "Mystic Register" and "Complete in Chaos" charts and book 圖書 after mentioning the *Yellow Book*. Elsewhere in the text, some of these titles are mentioned as sections within the *Yellow Book*: "Spirit register" (13b6), "Mystic Register" (7b1, 13b6), "Central Edict" (8a4, 13b6), "Complete in Chaos" (13b6). The *Zhen'gao* mentions the methods of "Complete in Chaos" together with "Yellow Book with the Red Borders" 用混成及黃書赤界之法 (DZ 1016: 6.4b.7). In their note to this passage Yoshikawa and Mugitani refer to *Laozi* 45, not realizing that in this context "Complete in Chaos" must refer to a title related to the *Yellow Book*; Yoshikawa and Mugitani, *Shinkō kenkyū*, 222 n.70.
43 洞真太微黃書天帝君石景金陽素經 DZ 81 and 洞真太微黃書九天八籙真文 DZ 257.
44 DZ 81 corresponds to the title of the seventh and DZ 257 to the eighth of the list in DZ 257.2 a6–b3.
45 Tao Hongjing comments that there were two versions of *Taiwei huangshu* in circulation, one attributed to Dai Meng 戴孟 (active in the Eastern Han, during emperor Ming's reign, 57–75 CE),

Further complicating the provenance of the *Yellow Book* is the fact that there were several texts circulating with similar titles. The *Declarations*, for instance, lists an *Essentials for Longevity of the Yellow Book with the Red Borders* (*Huangshu chi changsheng zhi yao* 黃書赤界長生之要). Tao Hongjing notes that this text was inscribed by Xu Mi, and was originally in the Du household.[46] He differentiates it from another text entitled *Inner Perfection According to the Yellow and the Red* (*Huangchi neizhen* 黃赤內真) and attributed to Juanzi 涓子.[47] As we noted earlier in the chapter, an early set of practices, affiliated with Pei Xuanren 裴玄仁, also included sexual cultivation. Lord Pei's hagiography reports that he received a *Yellow Book of the Grand Primordial of the Upper Pivot of Four Pneumas* (*Siqi shangshu taiyuan huangshu* 四氣上樞太元黃書) in eight *juan*.[48] The complex relationships among these various texts are still subject to scholarly debate, and perhaps may not be resolved without further textual discovery.[49] Nevertheless, these references demonstrate that several texts with similar titles, and probably similar practices, circulated contemporaneously among different Daoist lineages.

Daoist sources refer to the initiation rite of Celestial Master Daoism as "The Way of the Yellow and Red" (*Huangchi zhi dao* 黃赤之道), but this term is found almost exclusively in polemical tracts which criticize this practice.[50] By the fourth century, this label was used pejoratively to designate the Celestial Master tradition itself. The significance of the term Yellow and Red (*huangchi* 黃赤) is unclear. This compound is found neither in the *Yellow Book* nor in the closely related *Dongzhen huangshu*, and it appears only once in the *Demon Codes*, a Celestial Master text compiled during the third and fourth centuries, without a clear explanation. Based on the verses that include this term, Zhu Yueli suggests that red and

and another written in the hands of Yang Xi and Xu *pater et fils*, of which only the eighth juan, a table of contents, was in circulation (DZ 1016 14.6b8–9). For details, see Isabelle Robinet, *Révélation*, vol. 2, 307–10; Schipper and Verellen, *Taoist Canon*, 191–2. Zhu Yueli argues that DZ 257 and DZ 81 were probably composed after 370, and that DZ 81 may in fact postdate Tao Hongjing (Zhu Yueli, "Huangshu kao," 168–5).

46 DZ 1016: 5.2a10.
47 DZ 1016: 5.2b10; Yoshikawa and Mugitani, *Shinkō kenkyū*, 178, 181 n.23, referring to DZ 184.1.
48 DZ 1032: 105.8b9.
49 Zhu Yueli 朱越利 argues that the Yellow Book affiliated with Lord Pei is different from the *Taiwei huangshu*. He suggests that the original text was a fourth-century *Huangchi jing* 黃赤經. This text was changed to *Huangshu* between 420 and 518. The current DZ 81 is the seventh *juan* of the *Huangshu*, while DZ 1343 is the eighth *juan* (Zhu, "Huangshu kao," 168–175; idem. *Daozang fenlei jieti* 道藏分類解題 (Beijing: Huaxia, 1996). Wang Ka considers the current *Huangshu* (DZ 1294) and DZ 1343 to correspond to one *juan* each of the original Six Dynasties text of eight *juan*. He argues that DZ 81 is a *Shangqing* text, related to the *Huangchi neizhen*. Robinet suggests that as it is mentioned in *Zhen'gao* but not referred to as part of Yang Xi's revelations it must be earlier than the Yang Xi revelations (Robinet, *Révélation*, vol. 2, 307–310).
50 The *Scripture of Divine Incantations from the Cavernous Abyss* states: "Daoists should wholeheartedly uphold the followers of the Three Caverns. They should not travel together with Daoists of the Yellow and Red. If you are among male or female Daoists of the Yellow and Red, then you should establish a separate parish 自別立治" DZ 335: 10.8a10. See also the citations from the *Declarations of the Perfected* (*Zhen'gao* 真誥, DZ 1016) discussed below.

yellow refer, respectively, to sun and moon, and by extension to husband and wife.[51] While suggestive, the use of sun and moon in these verses does not warrant such an interpretation.

Another explanation of the term is found in a Shangqing scripture, the *Embryonic Essence of the Ninefold Alchemical Superior Transmutations*, which defines "yellow and red" as follows:

> Yang pneuma is red, it is called Profound Cinnabar. Yin pneuma is yellow, it is called Yellow Essence. When yin and yang merge the two pneumas descend, the essence transforms and the spirit congeals. [If this moment] corresponds to the nine heavens above, then the pneumas of the nine heavens descend and fill the cinnabar field and coagulate together with the essence, knotting together in the "gate of destiny." [This process] require nine transitions to produce the ninefold elixir. The transformation above and coagulation below are completed in a human.[52]

This text, however, does not refer to the practice of the Celestial Masters, but describes the formation of the fetus during conception. The terminology of the text is borrowed from the alchemical tradition, and the practice advocated here is a meditative reversal of the gestation process, by which the practitioner could unknot the knots and return to the unformed state. This text is clearly based on a cosmology that is very different from that we find in Celestial Master texts. Little wonder, then, that the color associations of red and yellow differ from those we find in the relevant Celestial Master scheme.

The *Dongzhen huangshu* explicitly refers to the male pneuma as white and the female pneuma as yellow.[53] Most importantly, as I discuss in detail below, the focus of the rite in the *Yellow Book* is in fact on three colored pneumas: azure, yellow, and white. Rather than referring to male and female *qi*, the term Yellow and Red probably refers to titles of texts, the *Yellow Book* and the *Red Pneuma*. Among the texts

---

51 Zhu Yueli, "Huangshu kao," 181; citing the following verses:

> How can one say: with great learning can one attain transcendence, attain great peace and cross over to become a Perfected? The sun and moon will be arrayed like comets, the pneumas of the Dao of 3,5,7,9 will shine/spread through the nine provinces like fathers and brothers, are those unified by contract, their hearts harmonized, with their intentions all as one, their way follows the scripture/guideline, the great essentials of the Yellow and Red preserve longevity. 豈可言何不少學得神仙, 太平過度為真人, 日月列布如流星, 三五七九道憑明, 分布九州 若父兄, 皆同一契心合幷, 義各如一道引經, 黃赤大要守長生.
>
> (DZ 790: 5.2b1–4)

> "The way of heaven is vast, faithful and self-producing; coming at dawn and departing at evening, heaven and earth last long; consider the sun as husband, and the moon as wife, the intercourse of celestial pneuma, what is it like?" 天道蕩蕩, 信自有; 且來暮去, 天地久; 一日為夫, 月為妻; 天 氣交接, 等何如? (DZ 790: 5.2b7–8).

52 *Shangqing jiudan shanghua taijing zhongji jing* 上清九丹上化胎精中記經 DZ 1382.2b–3a. Robinet, *Révélation*, vol. 2, 171–4. Not cited in the extended quote in YJQQ 29.4a–6b;

53 DZ 1343.1b2, 8a2, 15a6, 7b1: "If you can practice according to the Mystic Register, the pneumas will be chaotic and mixed, the yellow and white pneumas can together kill or can give life."

associated with the *Yellow Book*, the *Dongzhen huangshu* lists a text entitled *Red Pneuma* 赤炁.[54] The transmission of this text seems to be the first step in the initiation rite.[55] Among the injunctions in the *Demon Codes*, to be discussed below, we find the following: "Do not recklessly transmit the *Red Pneuma* to commoners."[56]

The term Yellow and the Red should therefore be understood as "the *Yellow Book* and the *Red Pneuma* register."[57] Indeed, the purpose of the ritual is the receipt of a document entitled *Contractual Commands in Yellow Script* (*Huangshu qiling* 黃書契令), which seems to be a register of the spirit-generals that the initiates receive during the rite. This document is mentioned in both the *Yellow Book* and the *Dongzhen huangshu*,[58] as well as in polemical texts that critique this practice. Importantly, a burial document dating to 433 CE, found in a tomb of a Daoist named Xu Fu 徐副, refers to him as Libationer of Daiyuan Parish, recipient of Contractual Commands in Yellow Script 祭酒代元治黃書契令徐副.[59]

Perhaps even more important is that the social significance of the rite also remains unclear. Kristofer Schipper has argued that the sexual rite was the ordination by which members of the early Celestial Master community attained the registers of 150 spirit-generals, the highest level of initiation of ordinary members of the community. Schipper argues that this ordination was conferred on a couple, man and woman, rather than on individual adepts and was attained through the unifying of the couple's registers during the rite of the *Yellow Book*.[60] Some have seen this initiation rite as a marriage rite.[61]

Members of the Celestial Master community progressed through a series of initiations in which registers, lists of spirit-generals under the command of the adept, were bestowed on them. At the earliest stage, at the age of six or seven, the child received the protection of a single general. At the age of 12, the adept received registers of 10 generals. This was followed by a register of 75 generals. Unfortunately, the earliest documentation extant for these progressive initiation ranks dates to the fourth century, and may therefore not quite correspond to the proceedings in the early community. These registers of spirit-generals were

---

54 DZ 1343.2a2.
55 DZ 1343.12b9, 7b6, 15a–b. The latter reference is a complex verse describing the initiation and transmission rite that includes the lines: "transmit the Red Pneuma, and then the Book" 過赤炁某書…度赤炁, 次度某書.
56 DZ 790: 3.3b6; Kleeman, "Daoism," 23.
57 The *Zhen'gao* lists several texts whose titles include the terms yellow and red. In these cases too, the title seems to refer to the color of the text and the script.
58 DZ 1294: 3a9, 23b8, 24a3; DZ 1343.12b7.
59 Wang Yucheng 王育成, "Xu Fu diquan zhong tainshidao shiliao kaoshi" 徐副地券中天師道史料考釋, *Kaogu* 1993.6, 571–75.
60 Schipper, *Taoist Body*, 148–49; for a detailed study, see Kristofer Schipper, "Taoist Ordination Ranks in the Tunhuang Manuscripts," in Gert Naundorf, Karl-Heinz Pohl, Hans-Hermann Schmidt, eds. *Religion und Philosophie in Ostasien: Festschrift für Hans Steininger zum 65 Geburtstag* (Würzburg: Königshausen und Neumann, 1985): 127–48, esp. 131–5.
61 For example, Bokenkamp calls this rite a marriage rite (*hunyin yishi* 婚姻儀式) in his "Tianshidao hunyin yishi."

presented to both males and females, with the spirits on male registers named "transcendents" 仙 and those on female registers named "numinae" 靈. The clearest presentation of this procedure is in Dunhuang manuscript S 203, which is a remnant of a Celestial Master *Protocol for the Transmission of Registers and Parishes* (*Zhengyi fawen dulu duzhi yi* 正一法文度籙度治儀).[62] This text includes a liturgy and a set of petitions and documents for receiving the registers in their appropriate sequence. These invocations are pronounced by either male or female initiates, who request a register of transcendents or numina, respectively:

> So-and-so is without a register, and has concentrated his/her heart on revering the Dao and has carefully cultivated goodness, now requests the troops and clerks of one general of the superior transcendents or superior numina.

> So-and-so having worn at the belt the child's register of one general of the superior transcendents or superior numina, is a mortal who has concentrated his/her heart on revering the Dao and has practiced and cultivated in sincerity, who cherished the Dao and wished to progress; having grown older, now requests the troops and clerks of ten generals of the superior transcendents or superior numinae.

After presenting the requests for the register of 75 generals, the text continues with the following:

> So-and-so having worn at the belt the register of seventy five generals of the superior transcendents or superior numinae … now requests the troops and clerks of one hundred and fifty generals of both offices, the superior transcendents or superior numinae.[63]

How were the initiates to receive the full complement of 150 generals? Most scholars agree that this was to be attained through a sexual or conjugal ritual, which would unite the two registers.[64] In this text, however, the request is a bureaucratic document and there is no hint of a sexual or conjugal rite that would unite the two registers.

The dual system of transcendents or superior numina is mentioned in several texts associated with Celestial Master Daoism, albeit dating to the fourth and fifth centuries.[65] Nevertheless, Lü Pengzhi speculates that these gendered registers may well have been part of the Celestial Master community since the late Han.

---

62 The text is published in Ōfuchi, *Tonkō zurokuhen*, 880–4. I follow Lü Pengzhi's critical edition and study, "Tianshidao shoulu keyi"; I was greatly aided by John Lagerwey, "Zhengyi Registers."
63 Lü Pengzhi, "Tianshidao," 141–2.
64 Schipper, "Taoist Ordination"; Lagerwey, "Zhengyi Registers"; Lü Pengzhi, *Tangqian*, 197.
65 See Lü Pengzhi, "Tianshidao," 89–101; Lagerwey, "Zhengyi Registers."

Be that as it may, the dual registers are mentioned in the sixth section of the *Yellow Book*, in a preparatory meditation in which the presiding priest externalizes his bodily spirit-officials: "officials of both the superior transcendents and superior numinae: merit officials upright envoy of Correct Unity yin-yang living pneuma that cures illness, envoys of the left and right officers, and yin and yang spirit-clerks."[66]

There is, however, no reference to registers in the *Yellow Book*, or in the closely related *Dongzhen huangshu*. Rather, this was a rite of initiation, which, according to the opening lines of the *Yellow Book*, all members of the Celestial Master community were to undergo before the age of twenty.[67] Performed together by a pair of initiates, male and female, under the instruction of a master, the ritual includes a complex choreographed intercourse. The stated purpose of the rite is the transformation of the initiates into "seed people."

Nor is there is any indication that the rite in the *Yellow Book* was a "marriage" ceremony. The *Dongzhen huangshu*, on the other hand, explicitly states that the rites it advocates are for husband and wife.[68] While sharing some terminology with the *Yellow Book*, the purpose of the practices in *Dongzhen huangshu*, with its complex numerology and hemerology, appears to be a calendrical device to select auspicious days for intercourse to ensure the continuing health, and ensure pregnancy.

The initiation rite of the *Yellow Book* needs to be understood in the context of the ritual and cosmology of contemporary Celestial Master texts. Most importantly, the ritual expresses the basic hope of Celestial Master Daoism, a bureaucratic salvation within an eschatological framework of imminent calamity. This hope is encapsulated in the following vow, which is repeated by the initiates at several points during the ritual:

> Together, we uphold the Way and Virtue. We wish (*yuan* 願) to be released from investigation by the Three Bureaus and released from the [celestial] net and [terrestrial] web; that we be erased and removed from the death records, and that our names be inscribed for longevity on the jade registers. We will cross over and ford (*guodu*) the nine calamities and become the seed people of the next world.[69]

---

66 DZ 1294.2b9–10.

67 DZ 1294.1a1. The text literally states: "Disciples receiving the Dao at their master's parish should not be over the age of twenty." The text continues by stating that, if a person older than 20 was about to "receive the Dao" but had not yet been initiated, he should also undergo this rite. This presumably refers to new converts to Daoism.

68 DZ 1343.1a6, 15a5. Lin Fu-shi 林富士, "Luelun zaoqi daojiao yu fangzhong shu de guanxi" 略論早期道教與房中術的關係, BIHP 72.2 (2001): 250 notes that DZ 1343 and DZ 1294 diverge precisely on this point. While the rite in the former was restricted to married couples, the rite in the latter was an initiation rite, possibly a rite of passage to adulthood, and not restricted to married couples.

69 DZ 1294. 6b10; see also 3b7, 5b9, 6a7, 8a3.

共奉行道德, 願為臣妾解除三官考逮解脫羅網. 撤除死籍著名長生玉曆, 過度九厄得為後世種民

The basic purpose of the ritual is therefore salvation, not merely from the mundane limits of time, but, more importantly, from the catastrophes at the imminent end of the epoch. This salvific hope was based in the bureaucratic vision, which was a basic organizing principle of Celestial Master Daoism. This bureaucratic vision entailed a tripartite cosmology of the Three Bureaus: heaven, earth, and water. These Offices were populated by a host of administrators, officials, clerks who were in charge of life and death registers. The bureaucratic ranks extended to the ranks of the communal priests, who communicated with the various extra-human officials through written messages delivered during visualized audiences that were modeled on the imperial system.

A second key notion mentioned in the vow is that of the seed people. This notion was part of the eschatological vision underlying the emergence of Celestial Master Daoism, which appeared during the social and political turmoil of the second century. The fall of the Han was viewed as a cosmological crisis. The continuing disorder of the succeeding era of disunion, the Three States and the Northern and Southern Dynasties, was added proof that a cataclysm, which would cleanse the world, was imminent.

Third, the vow includes the term *guodu* 過度 which I translate "cross over and ford." This term is, of course, part of the title, in which I render it as "initiation." This term has to be understood in the context of the characteristics distinguishing Daoist initiations from those of the seekers of transcendence. Daoist initiations led to higher realms of realization and higher status and greater power within a systematic bureaucratic cosmos, and ultimately to a return to the Dao. The use of the term *guodu* here conflates the meanings of "initiation" and "crossing over:" the initiation rite will literally allow the initiates to cross over to the next world where they will become seed people of a new humanity.

The key terms "seed person" (*zhongmin* 種民) and "release from the web and net" (*jietuo luowang* 解脫羅網) are critical in Celestial Master Daoism. We find them, for instance, in one of the earliest extant Celestial Masters texts, the *Demon Codes of Nüqing*.[70] This text reveals how the bureaucracy of the Three Heavens, the eschatological vision, and the rite of Merging Pneumas were merged in a grand salvific program:

> The lords of the Three Bureaus will select the seed people from among those who employed 'merging pneumas' to the total of 18,000. From the past till

---

70 *Nüqing guilu* 女青鬼律 DZ 790. Difficult to date with precision, the current text is a compilation impacted by later authorial and editorial manipulations, probably compiled from several different sources. Lai Chi-tim surveys several opinions dating the original *Demon Codes* between the third and fourth centuries, Lai Chi-tim, "The *Demon Statutes*." Adrianus Dudink tentatively suggests this is a third-century compilation, Schipper and Verellen, *Taoist Canon*, 127. For an extensive analysis, see Kleeman, "Daoism in the Third Century."

the present only a few [were selected], the great quota is yet unfilled so you should exert yourself, change your heart and transform your innards to become a Perfected of the Dao. If you receive oral teaching from a master to become a worthy and make wearing my tallies and contracts a priority, then you will get to see the spirit transcendent princes of Great Peace and the Five Thearch Lords will transmit the secret words to you. Esteeming the pneumas of the Dao of three, five, seven, and nine, they will dwell in [your] clear and subtle Mt. Kunlun. You will soon see the Three Heavens enter your body, you will be released from the web and net and will reverence Lord Lao.[71]

The importance of sexual cultivation techniques in the service of salvation and transcendence is reiterated elsewhere in the *Demon Codes*:

Your longevity will emerge from your intention. As soon as you cherish the [practice] 'three, five, seven, nine,' your pneumas will be rectified, and you will become a seed person, you will be released from the web and net, and your body-spirits will in broad daylight ascend and fly to the celestial halls.[72]

The term "three, five, seven, nine," which appears in both the *Demon Codes* and in the *Yellow Book*, refers to a breathing technique used in sexual practice. The significance of the ritual, however, extends beyond debates on sexual techniques. The ritual procedure of the *Yellow Book* must be read in the context of Celestial Master ritual and mythography. The ritual is based on a cosmogony in which the procreative function of *yin* and *yang* is a secondary, and not a primary, stage of cosmogony. In these cosmogonic narratives, *yin* and *yang*, whose interaction leads to the manifestation of the familiar world, appear in the cosmos in a later stage of a complex cosmogony. Indeed, a careful reading of the ritual procedure reveals that the ritualized intercourse is not, in fact, the climax of the ritual procedure. The climax of the rite is the production of a perfected being within the body of the initiate. The ritualized intercourse that follows the production of this homunculus is the first stage in the ritual reconstruction of the cosmos.

The cosmogony developed by the Celestial Masters was an elaboration of the famous, but obscure, passage in chapter 42 of Daode jing: "The Way produced One, the One produced Two, the Two produced Three, and the Three produced the myriad things." This passage has been interpreted in various ways, with yin and yang often taken to be the "Two." Even if that were correct, the "Two" is the third stage of the cosmogony. Authors in the Celestial Master tradition have, however, interpreted this passage in more complex ways. One of the earliest extant texts of

71 DZ 790: 5.1a: 三宮主者擇種民, 取合炁者萬八千, 從來至今有幾人, 大限未足子勤身, 改心易腸道真人, 師受口訣以見賢, 佩吾券契一為先, 得見太平神仙君, 五帝主者傳秘言, 三五七九道气尊, 治在清微昆侖山, 近見三天入人身, 解脫綱羅拜老君.
72 *Nüqing guilü* 女青鬼律 DZ 790: 5.3b2: 子之長生出子心. 三五七九一為親, 唯炁大正, 為種民, 解脫羅網. 具身神白日高飛入天堂.

the Celestial Masters, the *Commands and Admonitions for the Families of the Great Dao*, of the mid third century, provides this account:[73]

> The Dao bestows itself by means of subtle pneumas. They are of three colors, associated with the Mystic, Primordial, and Inaugural pneumas. The mystic is azure and formed heaven, the inaugural is yellow and formed earth, the primordial is white and formed the Dao. Within the three pneumas, the Dao controls all above and below and is the father and mother of the myriad things.[74]

There is no reference at all to *yin* and *yang* in this cosmogony. Rather the Dao spontaneously generates three colored pneumas, whose interaction eventually produces the world. Importantly, these emanations are within the primordial unity of the Dao, which is still "undifferentiated chaos."

An even more complex cosmogony is provided in the fifth century *Inner Explanations of the Three Heavens*, a text I discuss in the next chapter as one of the "reformist" Celestial Master texts.[75] According to this text, the primordial Dao, "self-actualizes"[76] into the cosmos through a series of transformations. The initial transformation produces the Elder of the Way and the Power, a primordial form of Laozi. The primordial unity then generates three pneumas, the Mystic, Primordial, and Inaugural. The text emphasizes the unity of these three pneumas, which were "intermingled in undifferentiated chaos." In the next cosmogonic stage, these pneumas transformed to produce the Mystic and Wondrous Jade Maiden. After the generation of the Jade Maiden, the undifferentiated pneumas coalesced within her, transforming and producing Lord Lao. The culmination of the cosmogonic process is the transformation of Lord Lao himself, the cosmic form of Laozi. Lord Lao emanates the mystic, primordial, and inaugural pneumas, which eventually become, respectively, the heavens, water, and earth.[77]

The cosmogonic narratives of Celestial Master Daoism thus elaborate on the emanation of the formless Dao into three. These self-generated and transformative colored pneumas thus precede the formation of yin and yang, and the resulting procreation through sexual conjoining. These three primordial colored pneumas are visualized and internalized in the *Yellow Book* repeatedly in various sections of the rite. The three pneumas are first mentioned in section 9, which is devoted to visualizing the three pneumas and their colors:

---

73 *Dadao jia lingjie* 大道家令戒 in *Zhengyi fawen tianshijiao jieke jing* 正一法文天師教戒科經正 DZ 789.12a–19b; transl. in Bokenkamp, *Early*, 165–85. For the dating, see p. 150.

74 DZ 789.12a6–10: Bokenkamp, *Early*, 165–6.

75 *Santian neijie jing* 三天內解經 DZ 1205; the first chapter is translated in Bokenkamp, *Early*, 204–29. As this text explicitly celebrates the rise of Liu Yu (356–422) and the establishment of the Song dynasty in 420 it must have been written shortly thereafter; see Bokenkamp, *Early*, 150.

76 Borrowing Bokenkamp's translation for *ziran* 自然.

77 DZ 1205: 1.2a5–b8; Bokenkamp, *Early*, 207–8. See Chapter 5 for a fuller analysis.

Contemplate the perfectly azure pneuma of the Supreme (*Wushang*), the per-fectly yellow pneuma of the Mystic Elder (*Xuanlao*), and the perfectly white pneuma of the Most High (*Taishang*); these three pneumas together are one, indistinct (*hundun*) and shaped like an egg, [in it] the five colors all mixed. Cause this [complex vision] to descend to your Cinnabar Field.[78]

無上炁正青, 玄老炁正黃, 太上炁正白, 三炁共為一, 混沌狀似雞子, 五色混黃, 下詣丹田.

The ritual procedure of the *Yellow Book* consists of a long series of complex movements and breathing exercises, incantations, and visualizations, which are described in detail in the 20 sections of the text. The male and female initiates perform symmetrical and complementary actions in reverse directions. For instance, in circulating the pneumas through the body, the male proceeds by making the pneumas ascend on the right and descend on the left, while the female proceeds by first causing the pneumas to descend on the left and then ascend on the right.

Sections 1–13 of the procedure are preparatory, and include instructions for entering the ritual space and summoning the body gods through meditation, visualization, and breathing exercises. These gods include spatial and temporal categories, such as days and directions, various bureaucratic categories, and spir-its, which are emanations of the Dao. The most important are the Three Pneumas. Sections 14–17, the core of the rite, culminate in a production of a homunculus within the body of the initiate, followed by ritualized intercourse. The remain-ing sections, 18–20, describe the ritualized exit from the ritual space, which includes the "Announcement of Merit" (*yangong* 言功), in which the initiate thanks the gods which participated in the rite and requests their promotion in the celestial ranks.

Section 14 begins with an exercise called Releasing the Knots and Ingesting in which the master undoes the disciples' clothes and belts and loosens their hair. This is followed by a rite named Ingesting Life and Exhaling Death (食生吐死), in which the couple sit side by side facing the ruling direction, with legs stretched, the male on the left and the female on the right. They inhale slowly through the nose, and, lowering their heads, they swallow the air. They lie down together and shut their eyes, while slowly exhaling the "dead pneuma" through the mouth. The following series of ritual exercises has to be understood as an ascent through increasingly rarified cosmological structures and cosmogonic stages. In section 15, the couple creates the cosmological schema known as the Nine Palaces through a complex choreography of hands and feet.[79] The climactic part of the ritual is

---

78 DZ 1294. 5b8–10.

79 This section has been analyzed in Marc Kalinowski, "La transmission du dispositif des neuf palais sous les Six Dynasties," in Michel Strickmann, ed. *Tantric and Taoist Studies*, vol. 3 (Bruxelles, Institut Belge des Hautes Études Chinoises, 1987): 773–811.

described in sections 16–17, during which a perfected being, named Peach Vigor (Taokang 桃康), is produced within the bodies of the initiates. The generation of the homunculus is followed by a highly ritualistic and choreographed intercourse.

Section 16, named Treading the Meridians (*nieji* 躡紀, 11a10–21b8) includes a series of exercises, beginning with a complex set of massages following various paths along the body, performed alternately by the male on his female partner. This is followed by the female massaging her male co-initiate, following the same sequence but in reverse.

In the next exercise, Contemplating the Three Pneumas (*si sanqi* 思三氣), the initiates lie prone and meditate on the three pneumas penetrating and circulating through their bodies:

> Meditate that *Wushang*, perfect azure is on the left; *Xuanlao*, perfect yellow, is to the right; and Taishang, perfect white [is at the center]. They penetrate (貫) our bodies, our six *jia*, five viscera, and our stems and branches (birthdates). Ascending on the left and descending on the right, they circulate through the whole body. They return and administer within our Cinnabar Field below, and above ascend to Mt. Kunlun.

> 思神左无上氣正青, 右玄老氣正黃, 太上氣正白, 貫臣妾身六甲五藏支干間. 左上右下, 周帀一身. 還治臣妾下丹田中, 上昇崑崙山.[80]

This exercise resumes the process of re-integrating the Three Pneumas in the individual body. After visualizing the Three Pneumas and circulating them through the body, the initiate finally lodges them in the two centers of the body, the Cinnabar Field below and Kunlun above.

In the next exercise, called Contemplating the One Palace (*Si yiguan* 思一官), the initiates visualize the colored pneumas of four temporal periods which precede the separation of the Dao into the manifested cosmos. These are the mystic primordial azure pneuma of Great Clarity (太清), the white pneuma of Great Simplicity (太素), the red pneuma of Great Inception (太初), and the yellow pneuma of Great Beginning (太始). The visualization of the temporal eras is followed by visualizing the colored pneumas of the five viscera: liver (azure), lungs (white), heart (red), spleen (yellow), and kidneys (black). Each pneuma is visualized as circulating the palace of the One, within the lower Cinnabar Field, and inhabited by a Perfected Lord who controls it.[81] These nine pneumas express the temporal and spatial unity, which underlies the manifested cosmos.

---

80 12b10–13a2; "administer" translates the word *zhi* 治. This was an important term in Celestial Master Daoism, referring to the 24 administrative centers, sometimes translated as "parishes," which structured the community.

81 Males should visualize the circulation of pneumas ascending on the left and descending on the right; females visualize the circulation of pneumas as ascending on the right and descending on the left (14a2).

While the technical terminology mentioned in this exercise seems to supersede the cosmogony of the *Commands and Admonitions* discussed above, it in fact harkens back to an earlier cosmogony, that of the Han weft texts. According to the *Yiwei qianzoudu* 易緯乾鑿度:

> There was Great Transformation, there was Great Inception, there was Great Beginning, there was Great Simplicity. Great Transformation was prior to the appearance of pneuma. Great Inception was when pneuma first appeared. Great Beginning was when form first appeared. Great Simplicity was when material first appeared.

> 有太易, 有太初, 有太始, 有太素. 太易者, 未見氣也. 太初者, 氣之始也. 太始者, 形之始也. 太素者, 質之始也.[82]

In the cosmogony of the *Yellow Book*, we find that the Great Transformation, *Taiyi* 太易, of the weft text was replaced with Great Clarity, *Taiqing* 太清, the high heaven of the early Daoist tradition, common to both the Celestial Masters and to the alchemical tradition of Ge Hong. As in the Celestial Master cosmogony found in the *Commands and Admonitions*, here too *yin* and *yang* appear at a later stage in the cosmogony.

Once the various visualizations and breathing exercises have been completed, the ritual enters the climactic stage, which consists of three parts: preparation for visualizing the homunculus, the production of the homunculus, which is immediately followed by ritual intercourse. The first section is called Guiding Oneself 自導. The male begins by massaging his female partner in three movements, again summoning the Three Pneumas. First, with the left hand proceeding from left breast to foot, while incanting: "Left Wushang." Second, with the right hand proceeding from right breast to foot, while incanting: "Right Xuanlao." Third, with left hand proceeding from forehead down to lower Cinnabar Field, while incanting: "Taishang". Each movement is repeated three times. The procedure is repeated with the opposing hand.

The final movement in this section is unclear. The technical terms used here are not explicated. Similar usages elsewhere in the text suggest that *kui* 魁

---

82 *Yiwei qianzoudu* 易緯乾鑿度 in Nakamura and Yasui: 1A.24; 1A.38. See also the succinct description in the *Xiaojing goumingjue* 孝經鉤命決 which adds a fifth stage, "Great Culmen" and incorporates the five stages into a cosmogony called "Five Epochs":

> Prior to the separation of heaven and earth there was Great Transformation, there was Great Inception, there was Great Beginning, there was Great Simplicity, and there was Great Culmen. These are the Five Epochs. When form and simulacra have not yet separated, this is Great Transformation. When primordial pneuma first sprouts, this is Great Inception. At the first buds of pneuma and form, this is Great Beginning. When form changes and possesses shape, this is Great Simplicity. When material form is complete, this is Great Culmen. The five pneumas gradually change, this are the Five Epochs. 天地未分之前, 有太易, 有太初, 有太始, 有太素, 有太極, 是為五運. 形象未分, 謂之太易. 元氣始萌, 謂之太初. 氣形之端, 謂之太始. 形變有質, 謂之太素. 質形已具, 謂之太極. 五氣漸變, 謂之五運. (Nakamura and Yasui, 5.76).

"dipper-bowl" refers to the penis head and that *qi* 起 refers to erection.[83] Then, with the right hand, the male massages the lower Cinnabar Field of the female, reaching the Gate of Life (生門). With the right hand he opens the Golden Gate (金門), while holding the Jade Stalk (玉籥) with his left hand he marks (*zhu* 注) the Gate of Life. The terminology here is very simple: "gate of life" refers to the vaginal opening, "golden gate" refers to the labia, and "jade stalk" refers to the penis.[84] Then, with the left hand, the man rubs the woman's Kunlun (probably navel), and with his right hand he massages her Gate of Destiny (*Mingmen* 命門), horizontally and vertically. He incants three times:

> Water flows east, the clouds return west.
> Yin nurtures yang, the pneumas are subtle.
> The mystic essences and dark fluids
> Ascend to audience to the Master's gate.

Referring to himself and his companion as spiritual beings, the male describes the procedure in the following incantation:

> The spirit-male "holds onto the gate," the jade maiden "opens the door." The accompanying pneumas follow *yin*, these pneumas will spread over me.[85]

The phrase "holding the gate" refers to essence retention and "opening the door" refers to the vagina.[86] The second couplet refers to the male absorbing the female pneumas, as they bathe him. The corresponding incantation by the female (*Yi*) refers to the cosmological symbolism of yin and yang:

> Yin and yang diffuse transformation; the myriad beings are irrigated and born. Heaven covers and earth supports; let the pneumas diffuse through my body.[87]
> 陰陽施化, 萬物滋生, 天覆地載, 願以氣施妾身

The word I translate here as "diffuse" (*shi* 施) is often used in sexual manuals to describe ejaculation. Here, it refers to the fecund powers of *yin* and *yang*, and the intermingling of the pneumas is here perceived as a sexual act through which life comes into existence. At this point, the pair has ascended through temporal

83 "The riding dipper-bowl rises, do not receive the Three-Five, the dragon proceeds above" 乘魁起, 不受三五, 龍行上 (14a). Similar phrases appear in 16a1 (for the male massage) and 16a3 (for the female massage): "yang rises, riding the dipper-bowl…" 陽起乘魁.
84 Li Ling 李零, "Donghan weijin nanbeichao fangzhong jingdian liupai kao" 東漢魏晉南北朝房中經典流派考. Zhongguo wenhua 15/16 (1997): 151.
85 DZ 1294.14a2.
86 Li Ling, 1997: 151; Lin Fu-shi, "Luelun zaoqi daojiao yu fangzhong shu de guanxi" 略論早期道教與房中術的關係, BIHP 72.2 (2001): 253; Zhang Chaoran 張超然, "Rudao yu xingdao: Zhao Sheng yixi tianshi jiaotuan de huangchi jiaofa" 入道與行道: 趙昇一系天師教團的黃赤教法, *Taiwan zongjiao yanjiu* 3.1 (2003): 20.
87 DZ 1294.14a3.

cycles to the creative aspect of *yin* and *yang*. But there has been no penetration or mingling. Rather, we have the male absorbing yin, and possibly reverting his own essence, while the female also absorbs both pneumas.[88]

The next section entitled Male and Female Incantations 甲乙祝法 (14b6–18b2) begins with the male and female placing their individual endeavors in a cosmological context, indicating the cosmic status of the initiates and their ritual act while marking the relative positions of the male and female. The male incants:

> I wish to ride the celestial net and enter the terrestrial web, the four seasons and five phases will position themselves. The Perfected are unshaken, they hold onto the net and web. The five pneumas of themselves descend; the dark and the yellow return. My five viscera spontaneously become radiant.

The female incantation begins with the line "I wish to rest on the earth and support heaven, harmonize yin and yang," and continues with "the four seasons…" as the male. Again, the male grasps his penis and, summons the Three Pneumas, and while thrice marking (*zhu*) to left, right, and center he requests that they eradicate all calamities. Now the two initiates together incant:

> Initiate and companion, beg to have initiation. We will together uphold the Way and Virtue. We beg for long life, for lasting vision, and to become seed people.

The next incantation describes the production of the homunculus Peach Vigor (Taokang). Again, marking the center, incant thrice:

> Left Wushang, Right Xuanlao, and Taishang, the three pneumas together produce within my body, in chaos (混沌) become one. This being is named Peach Vigor, he resides in the Northern Extremity. He is styled Zidan (子丹), his clothes are of the five colors, and he wears a red turban and great cap. His bed of gold and jade, flanked by five-colored rails and curtains of pearl and jade, stands precisely in the Gate of Destiny (*mingmen*). Spirit-man and jade maidens stand as servants at both sides. The yang pneuma turns to the left, yin pneuma proceeds to the right. Above they reach [the heaven of] Great Purity (太清), below they reach the bottomless. They constantly roam through the nine palaces, five viscera, and six store houses. Commanding the various spirits on the registers, Taokang summons them by name and does not let them escape. He is always in my body, and with me will become transcendent.[89]

---

88 Zhang Chaoran also emphasizes that these passages imply non-ejaculation (20).
89 DZ 1294.14b6–15a2.

左無上，右玄老，太上，三气共生臣妾身混沌為一.名曰桃康，舍止北極，
號曰子丹，衣服五色赤幘大冠，金床玉榻，五色欄干珠玉斗帳，正當命門.
神男玉女侍兩邊. 陽氣左轉，陰氣右旋，上至太清，下至無下. 常游九宮，
五藏六府之間. 領錄群神案錄，召名不得逋亡. 長在我身興我俱仙.

With the production of the homunculus within the initiates' bodies, the ritual reaches its climax. The initiates have returned to the primordial moment of emanation, when the three pneumas were one – the undivided Dao.

The following sections began the descent back to the world of the myriad things, which was manifested through the intermingling of yin and yang. Lifting his head, the male inhales the living pneuma through the nose, to the rhythm of three, five, seven, nine. The male (*Yang*) incants: "I practice the Way of Heaven," and the female (*Yi*) incants: "I practice the Way of Earth."

The male now enters the Gate of Life. Stopping half way, he incants: "Lord Liu and Lord Niu (柳君妞君) and the myriad spirits are born. I wish to shake the heavens and rock the earth. The five lords are each spontaneously sincere." The female incants: "Lord Liu and Lord Niu are in the Cinnabar Field store house. I wish to rock the earth and shake the heavens. The five spirits in my body are each spontaneously solid." The male now "advances to the deepest abyss." The rite continues with a series of deep and shallow thrusts, accompanied by incantations and visualizations. The rite ends through a further set of massages with numerical and directional correlates, and finally a ritual dismissal of the participating corporeal spirits.

The first thing to note here is that the ritual instructions do not refer to the receipt or transmission of registers. Rather, this rite leads to the generation of a homunculus, which, in turn, ensures the transformation of the initiates into seed people. This ritual protocol is not, in fact, describing the rite of "merging pneumas" that was the rite of unifying the registers. Nevertheless, the ritual presented here clearly coheres with the cosmological, salvific, and eschatological premises we find in other Celestial Master texts. It is probably a reformulated ritual program, composed in response to criticisms of the early ritual.

Daoist critique of sexual rites

As mentioned above, the Way of the Yellow and the Red came to define the Celestial Masters. In distinguishing themselves from the Celestial Masters, the new Daoist movements that appeared in the fourth and fifth centuries often did so by explicitly criticizing the sexual practices of the Celestial Masters.

However, even earlier than condemnation of the ritual, we find criticisms of improper use of the rite of Merging Pneumas in the Celestial Master text *Demon Codes of Nüqing*. While these may not necessarily be due to the rite of Merging Pneumas as presented in the *Yellow Book*, they clearly indicate the potential abuse of the sexual initiation rites. Chapter 3 of the *Codes* includes a set of 22 injunctions and four extended disquisitions in the voice of the Celestial Master concerning proper behavior.[90] Several of the injunctions are concerned with proper sexual behavior, which needs to conform to the communal codes, including some that specifically deal with sexual initiation rites:[91]

> #10: Do not transmit the Way to a young virgin in order to enter her vagina, damaging her spirits and hurting the pneumas; thus acting in opposition and without the Dao.

> 不得傳道童女, 因入生門傷神犯氣, 逆惡無道. (3.2a9)

> #21: Do not recklessly transmit the red pneuma to commoners, and with your mouth, hands and heart seek to have intercourse, thus abandoning the Dao, turning your back on your master, and without the teaching.

> 不得以赤炁忘傳俗人, 口手胸心更相交接, 委道自叛師主無法 (3.3b6)

Not only do these injunctions indicate the potential abuse of the sexual initiation rites, but they also allow us to question whether the rite Merging Pneumas was a marriage rite to be performed once, or an initiation ritual that could be performed several times and with different partners. Similar problems of abuse and improper practice are raised in the following passage:[92]

> On a day [you perform the technique of] 3,5,7,9, be careful to practice living pneuma. You must rely on my charts and diagrams, and not offend the three pneumas. Then you may transform to a transcendent. Among the people, they should never know the true names of the father and mother of the Dao. Hence they are commoners. Among Daoists, if one knows the Contract and Commands of Yellow Book, but does not know the twenty-four spirits, then he is a sham.[93]

With such potential for abuse, it is little wonder that the new movements that arose in the fourth century were careful to distinguish themselves and their prac-

---

90 For a full translation and study of these injunctions, see Kleeman, "Daoism."
91 Other injunctions that deal with sexual behavior are: #8: "Do not engage in fighting, slander, drunkenness, illicit sex 淫色" (3.2a6); #10: "Do not engage in homosexual activity" 不得反男為女 陰陽倒錯 (3.2a9); #11: "Do not engage in sex in the open air, thus offending the three radiances" (3.2b3).
92 Compare to the following: "Men and women under–heaven who already know the 3,5,7,9 way of longevity, if you do not rely on my method but practice evil and act licentiously, then upon your death you will be placed before the evil men [for punishment]" (DZ 790: 3.5a 2).
93 DZ 790: 3.4a8–5a.

tices from the disturbing sexual rites. Nevertheless, the critique we find in these later texts is not about improper performance, but a condemnation of the rite itself.

The most vehement attack on the sexual practices of the Celestial Master tradition is found in early *Shangqing* teachings of the mid fourth century, which clearly distinguish between their own Superior Way of Shangqing and the Lower Ways of Celestial Master Daoism. This is undoubtedly because Wei Huacun and the Xu family were all followers of Celestial Master Daoism. Yang Xi repeatedly warns Xu Mi from continuing his practices of sexual cultivation. Among the earliest explicit criticisms of the sexual practices of the Celestial Masters are several passages in the *Declarations of the Perfected*:

> The Way of the Yellow and the Red is a method for mixing pneumas. Zhang Ling received it in order to spread [the teachings] and transform [the people]. It is just one method for producing offspring, it is not a matter for the perfected…Zhang Ling received this in order to instruct the people. He did not practice it for his own transformation and ascent… Sexual yearning is known as yellow and red, the superior way is known as esoteric writings.[94]

Another passage, in the voice of the Lady of Purple Tenuity, states:

> As for the Yellow Book with Red Borders, although it contains the secret essentials of longevity it is in fact a lower technique of obtaining life. It is not the method spoken of by the gentlemen of the upper palaces in their radiant floating chariots. This way is merely for nourishing and cultivating life, it is not the superior way. If you embrace the perverse pneuma and simultaneously practice the esoteric writings, it will certainly suffice to inscribe you in the Water Bureau and summon you to judgment of the Three Bureaus.[95]

The Shangqing scriptures reformulated the sexual practices of the Celestial Masters in two ways. First, the joint practices were recast into individual practices in which a male practitioner could refine his own essences to produce a perfected homunculus within his own body. Second, the practice of "merging pneumas" was recast into a "pure" marriage rite, named "pairing radiances" (偶景), between male adepts and female deities.[96] However, for our purposes, the transformation of the joint sexual practice into an individual meditation technique is most important.

---

94 DZ 1016: 2.1a4–5; cf. Stephen R. Bokenkamp, "Declarations," 178.
95 DZ 1016: 2.1b2–9.
96 The importance of this teaching in the Shangqing revelations is evidenced by the fact that the "pure" marriage rite occupies most of the first chapter of the *Zhen'gao*, (for a partial translation, see Bokenkamp, "Declarations," 166–79); and that passages criticizing the Way of the Yellow and the Red are in the voices of three revelators: Qingxu zhenren, Ziwei furen, and Ziyang zhenren (DZ 1016: 2.1a1–2.2a10).

A key document of this tradition is the *Upper Scripture of Purple Texts Inscribed by the Spirits*.[97] According to this text the human body contains the spirits of the Three Primes (*sanyuan* 三元), the primordial pneumas which emanated from the Dao. Each of these spirits is visualized as a newborn baby. Within the Gate of Destiny, the navel, dwells the most important of these entities, the Grand Sovereign of the Mystic Pass. The text goes on to define the Gate of Destiny as the navel, and the Mystic Pass as the passageway that joins the placenta to the viscera at the moment of birth. This passageway contains a Palace of Life, and it is here that the Grand Sovereign dwells. He holds a talisman bearing his own image with which he mixes and pours the primal pneumas to replenish the fetus and restore the placenta. The name of the Sovereign is Taokang (Peach Vigor).[98]

The homunculus generated by the conjoined initiates during the rite of Merging Pneumas is now said to be part of the original complement of corporeal spirits – and it is not produced through sexual ritual. In fact, the text explicitly criticizes those Daoists who practice the way of recycling the seminal essences, cycling the Yellow and the Red, without knowing the name of the sovereign and possessing the talisman. The text continues by emphasizing individual meditative practice:

> Those Daoists who regularly, when lying down at night, envision the Grand Sovereign and perform the incantations according to this method and who swallow the talisman at the new moon in order to foster the growth of the fetus and essences will achieve transcendence. There is no need to bother about techniques performed by man and woman together for cycling augmenting essences. Moreover, intercourse with a woman for the purpose of rising to the heavens and recycling pneumas in order to become a Celestial Transcendent, are methods more treacherous than fire and water.[99]

The impact of the Shangqing criticisms of Celestial Master sexual practice was so great that the various attempts at reforming Celestial Master that appeared during the fourth and fifth centuries all vehemently rejected the Way of the Yellow and the Red. We have already seen in the Introduction that this was one of the perverse ways which Kou Qianzhi sought to extirpate from the Daoism.

Another sectarian movement that arose during this time was associated with the millenarian tract *Scripture of Divine Incantations from the Cavernous Abyss*, which prohibited its followers from mixing with Daoists of the Yellow and Red:

> Daoists should whole-heartedly revere the followers of the Three Caverns. They should not travel together with Daoists of the Yellow and Red. If there

---

97 *Huangtian shangqing jinque dijun lingshu ziwen shangjing* 皇天上清金闕帝君靈書紫文上經 DZ 639, translated in Bokenkamp, *Early*, 307–31.

98 DZ 639.11a7–12a4, Bokenkamp, *Early*, 326–7; see also Bo Yi 柏夷 (Stephen Bokenkamp), "Tianshidao hunyin yishi 'heqi' zai shangqing lingbao xuepai de yanbian" 天師道婚姻儀式 "合氣" 在上清靈寶學派的演變, *Daōjia wenhua yanjiu* 16 (1999): 241–8.

99 DZ 639.13a8, Bokenkamp, *Early*, 330–1.

are among you, male or female Daoists of the Yellow and Red, then you should establish a separate parish.[100]

The institutional and ritual aspects of the community envisaged by the authors of the *Divine Incantations* were clearly reformulations of the Celestial Master community. Among the most important scriptures listed in the *Divine Incantations* was the *Celestial Contracts and Regulations of the Yellow Book* (*Huangshu qiling* 天上黃書契令),[101] which was not to be confused with the mundane *Yellow Book*:

> From today the *Celestial Contracts and Regulations of the Yellow Book* and scriptures are superior. No longer accept the Yellow and Red and Purple Palace that is current in the world.[102]

The most significant and lasting challenge to the Way of the Celestial Master was the attempt of the Lingbao scriptures to construct a new Daoist community that would replace the Celestial Masters while integrating various scriptural and ritual lineages into the scriptural and ritual scheme of the Three Caverns. One expression of this vision is presented in the *Awesome Rites of Lingbao*. We noted that the passage cited at the head of this chapter excluded the Celestial Master adherents while incorporating those Daoists affiliated with the textual categories of Cavern of Spirits and Cavern of Perfection. A commentary in the voice of Ge Xuan, the Transcendent Duke, embedded in the text defines these categories:

> The Cavern of Perfection consists of thirty-nine stanzas. The Cavern of Spirits, also known as Cavern of Transcendence 洞仙, is the *Celestial Writs of the Three Sovereigns of the Most High*. The Cavern of Mystery 洞玄 is Lingbao [scriptures]. The Three Caverns of Upper Purity are the most revered of all books.[103]

After defining the terms, the text continues in the voice of the Dao, contrasting the superiority of the Master of the Three Caverns with Celestial Master Daoists on the one hand, and Buddhists on the other. Importantly, this contrast is explained in karmic terms:

> People in the world have karmic bonds from past lives 宿緣. One who attains to be a Ritual Master of the Lingbao Scriptures and who makes offerings to the Most High Three Caverns is a thousand times superior than a Daoist of

---

100 *Dongyuan shenzhou jing* DZ 335: 10.8a10.
101 Also known as the *Celestial Occult Yellow Book* 天玄黃書 (20.9b).
102 DZ 335: 20.18b. Compare DZ 335: 20.22b1–5 which distinguishes between the "worldly Yellow Book" 世間黃書 and the *Celestial Huangshu qiling* 天上黃書契令; DZ 335: 20.20b which states that "those who vainly receive the inner and outer Yellow Book and Purple Palace, are but small Daoists" 空受內外黃赤紫府, 小小道士.
103 P 2403, ZHDZ, vol. 4, 98b.

the Yellow and Red and a hundred times better than an arhat. An arhat is one who has attained spiritual communication and extinction 滅度.[104]

The text continues by describing the necessity of "forming hidden bonds with worthies" and accumulating merit through repeated birth, until attaining the level at which one can receive the Lingbao scriptures. Importantly, the text reiterates that the Lingbao scriptures should be transmitted in accord with the correct ritual to "Daoists, Sramana, and kings."[105] This text thus hints at a missionary effort meant to convert adherents of other teachings in order to create a new community.

We find similar rhetoric in other Lingbao scriptures. For example, the *Instructions for Holding Lingbao zhai by the Perfected of the Grand Culmen*, which is among the earliest manuals for conducting the Lingbao *zhai* ritual, excludes Celestial Master Daoists from participating in the rite:

> When conducting a Lingbao *zhai*… even if only a single person in the house has received the scriptures, anyone among the rest of the household who wishes to, may listen to the ritual. If there is a libationer present of the yellow and red and of the great one 黃赤太一祭酒 who wishes to view the ritual, he may listen and observe the great transformative rite, but he may not share your seat.[106]

As I discuss further in the next chapter, the *Instructions for Holding Lingbao zhai* should best be seen as a ritual manual that was composed specifically for the purpose of converting Celestial Master Daoists. This passage refers to two situations in which Lingbao ritual masters may find themselves conducting a ritual. The preceding lines specify the ritual ranks of performers of the rite. The line immediately prior to the passage specifies that adherents should be ranked according to their receipt of the Lingbao scriptures. While only those who have received the scripture can actually perform in the ritual, non-initiated may observe the ritual. Members of a particular household may listen if at least one member of the house is initiated. And, most pertinently for our discussion, a Celestial Master libationer can watch the proceeding, but cannot participate in the ritual itself. The text clearly envisages a ritual hierarchy distinct from that of Celestial Master Daoism, here defined through two ritual markers, the Yellow and the Red and Great One.

Conclusion

The tradition of sexual cultivation is, arguably, the most controversial of cultivation practices, both in medieval China and in modern scholarship. The numerous

---

104 Ibid.
105 P 2403, ZHDZ, vol. 4, 100b.
106 *Taiji zhenren fu lingbao zhaijie weiyi zhujing yaojue* 太極真人敷靈寶齋戒威儀諸經要訣 DZ 532: 20b.

references in early sources, the texts found at Mawangdui, and those preserved in the *Ishimpō*, reveal the antiquity and continuity of this tradition. However, we should be wary of conflating these practices with the sexual techniques adopted by the early Celestial Master tradition.

Writing in the early fourth century, Ge Hong saw the practice of "reverting the essence to replenish the brain" at the core of the tradition of sexual cultivation. While providing several reasons for sexual practice, he stresses the importance of ensuring the healthy circulation of *qi* within the body. The texts Ge Hong mentions, and this very practice, were specifically mentioned in the *Xiang'er Commentary* as false. Yet the early Celestial Master community clearly adopted sexual cultivation techniques in its rites of initiation. While our current state of knowledge does not allow for a full reconstruction of this rite, we may be certain that it was practiced throughout the Six Dynasties, and continued into the Tang despite the heavy criticism in Shangqing and Lingbao texts, and within the Celestial Master tradition itself.[107]

We may well ask the reason for the vehement rejection of sexual cultivation. Scholars have generally tended to associate the criticism of sexual practice with Buddhist influence.[108] While this may be true in the Lingbao scriptures, which consciously adapted Buddhist notions, it does not explain the particular vehemence we find in the Shangqing scriptures. If sexual initiation was really necessary to attain the complete register of 150 spirit-generals, then Buddhist criticism does not seem sufficient as an explanation for the wholesale rejection of this rite.

I suggest that we may find a hint for this rejection in the reformulated rite as presented in the *Yellow Book*. This ritual is no longer about receiving registers, but about a quest for transcendence, which is far beyond the protection provided by the hierarchy of registers. Like the recast sexual practices in the Shangqing scriptures, which wholly internalized the act, this text, too, focuses on producing a perfected self within the body of the practitioners. While in this rite the male clearly practices essence retention, as in the old tradition of sexual cultivation, the female also shares in the practice. On the one hand, this continues the egalitarian tradition of early Celestial Master community; on the other hand, the rite empha-

---

107 There is some evidence that sexual practices continued into the late Tang. According to DZ 1237 *Sandong xiudao yi* 三洞修道儀 by Sun Yizhong 孫夷中, composed 1003 (Schipper and Verellen, *Taoist Canon*, 973):

> A boy of seven is known as *Lusheng dizi* 祿生弟子; a girl of ten is known as *Nansheng dizi* 南生弟子. First, they receive instruction from a Master, they take on Three Precepts, and Five Precepts. Eventually they quit eating meat (止葷血). From this point they can no longer marry. When they reach adulthood, males are known as *Qingzhen dizi* 清真弟子, females are known as *Qingxin dizi* 清信弟子. Now in accord with the code, they purify and together practice the "sexual rite of the yellow and the red" 常依科齋戒兼行黃赤交接之道
>
> (3a6–b1)

108 Wang Chengwen, *Dunhuang*, 437.

sizes the internalization of the practice, as in the Matching Radiances advocated in the Declarations of the Perfected. In Chapter 2 we saw that the rejection of blood rites in Celestial Master Daoism was extended to total abhorrence of blood in the Shangqing teachings of Wei Huacun. Taken together, we may perhaps speculate that the Shangqing teachings, as expressed by Yang Xi, view the ideal body as a closed system, self-sufficient unto itself for attaining transcendence.

While the criticism in Shangqing and later Celestial Master texts is perhaps best seen as recasting the Celestial Master tradition and cleansing it of sexual practice, the criticism we find in the Lingbao texts, as in the opening passage, and indeed in the *Scripture of Divine Incantations*, marginalizes members of the Celestial Master community, who are defined by this practice. In both of these textual traditions, we find attempts to integrate the various scriptural and ritual traditions current in the late fourth and early fifth centuries within a unified canon, the Three Caverns. While the two textual traditions differed as to which scriptures were to be in the Caverns, they were in agreement about the rejection of early Celestial Master scriptures and rites.

5 Creating orthodoxy

Let us begin our discussion of Daoist orthodoxy with three passages describing the origins of Daoism. According to the "Treatise on Buddhism and Daoism" (*Shilaozhi* 釋老志) of the *History of the Wei*:

> As for the source of Daoism, it emerged from Laozi.[1]
>
> 道家之原, 出於老子

According to Lu Xiujing's *Abridged Codes of the Daoist Community*:

> The Most High was appalled that things were like this and hence bestowed upon the Celestial Master the Way of Covenantal Authority of Correct Unity with its prohibitions, precepts, statutes, and codes.[2]
>
> 太上患其若此, 故授天師正一盟威之道, 禁戒律科.

According to the section "Origins of Daoism" 道教所起 in the encyclopedia *Yunji qiqian*:

> The learning of contemporaries is mostly shallow. They only recite the *Daode* and do not know about the Perfected Scriptures, so they say Daoism arose from Zhuang Zhou and began with "Below the Pillar" (Laozi)....[3]
>
> 今人學多浮淺, 唯誦 '道德', 不識真經, 即謂道教起自莊周, 始乎柱下.

These three passages present different visions of Daoist history as told by Daoist authors. Rather than discount the narratives from which these passages are culled as mythical imaginings, I suggest that we take them very seriously as

---

1   *Weishu* 魏書 114.3048.
2   DZ 1127.1a; Nickerson, "Abridged," 347–59.
3   *Yunji qiqian* DZ 1032: 3.3b.

reflections of Daoist history. Of course, these passages cannot be taken as representing the social reality of medieval Daoism. Rather, they are representative of the debates and changing self-perceptions of Daoists during this period. On the one hand, these narratives reveal a growing sense of a Daoist identity, and attempts at integration of various Daoist lineages. On the other hand, these narratives reveal complex strategies of distinction as Daoist lineages negotiated their distinct identities as they presented themselves to the readers of these narratives.

In the preceding chapters, we traced debates about various practices as they were adopted, adapted, and reformulated by various lineages, which were often in competition. Some of these debates were internal. In such debates, different lineages debated correct practices while recognizing similarities and differences among themselves. Other debates were external, in which Daoist lineages criticized groups, practices, and notions, which they excluded from their emerging synthesis. External debates, for instance, include the rejection of blood rites. The debates concerning the efficacy of talismans and the development of these devices into cosmogonic writs exemplify internalist debates.[4] As we saw in our examination of sexual practices in Chapter 4, internalist arguments could turn to externalist arguments. While the early Celestial Master community debated the correct sexual technique, later lineages rejected these practices totally. In fact, in some cases, the rejection of sexual practice entailed the rejection of Celestial Master Daoism.

Nevertheless, it is precisely in these debates that the various lineages found commonality, which, by the fifth century, led to attempts at developing an integrated scriptural and ritual system. Indeed, there were several attempts at integration, but it was Lu Xiujing's efforts at establishing orthodoxy that were eventually accepted by later compilers of Daoist canons during the Tang and Song. Even the *Zhengtong Daozang*, completed in 1583, despite its radical changes in the arrangement of texts that incorporate hundreds of scriptures of later Daoist lineages, is still, at least rhetorically, based upon the Three Caverns (*sandong* 三洞) that formed Lu's canon.[5]

Lu's project of creating orthodoxy by integrating various Daoist scriptures, lineages, and ritual schemes, however, was neither the only nor the first such project. There were several other efforts at determining Daoist orthodoxy in the late fourth century and through the fifth and sixth centuries. Some attempts, exemplified by the Lingbao scriptures of the late fourth and early fifth century, attempted to integrate

---

4   The distinction between internal and external arguments is similar to the notions of "intrinsic" and "extrinsic" developed by Robert Campany in his analysis of medieval hagiographic narratives:

> intrinsic [meaning] are rationales for practices or norms that explicitly explain and justify the practices in terms of their benefits, properties, and functions or in terms of their authoritative origins… Extrinsic meanings or functions pertain when practices or norms have the effect… of associating practitioners with certain values and dissociating them from others. Campany, *Making Transcendents*, 41–2.

5   For a comprehensive summary of these developments, see Schipper and Verellen, *Taoist Canon*, 5–39.

several scriptural and ritual traditions into a coherent whole. Other attempts, such as Kou Qianzhi's efforts at creating a reformed Celestial Master ecclesia, were more exclusive. In fact, it is arguable that such attempts at orthodoxy began with the earliest Daoist lineages. These early attempts, however, were not integrative but exclusionary.

While determining the preferred scriptures and ritual schemes, creators of orthodoxy also construct histories, with historical narratives that provide ancient and genealogical authority to the scriptures and rituals. In this chapter, I examine several different attempts at creating Daoist orthodoxy during the fifth century, examining various historical narratives, canon construction, and ritual systemizations that indicate, on the one hand, attempts at integration of the tradition in the face of external challenges, and, on the other hand, competition among lineages within the tradition.

Before delving into the relevant texts, however, we should ask whether "orthodoxy" is indeed an appropriate term for the process we are examining here. Etymologically, the meaning of orthodoxy is "right belief." Perhaps not coincidentally, the Chinese term closest in meaning and use to orthodoxy is *zheng* 正, which was explicated by the Han philologist Xu Shen 許慎 as: "to stop, to stand firm and be content with one principle or high authority, and hence to be restrained by it."[6] The word *zheng* already appears in Shang oracle bones where it signifies "successful targeted action."[7] While Xu Shen's etymological basis for his explanation may be wrong, his definition does reflect the full moral signification that the word acquired by the Han dynasty.[8] *Zheng* thus comes to mean "upright" and "correct" in a moral sense. The metaphor of uprightness is clearer when compared with words used to define improper or illicit teachings or practices, such as "deviant" *xie* 邪, "overflowing" *yin* 淫, and "bent" *qu* 曲.[9]

It is in this terminological context that we need to place the term *zhengyi* 正一, the preferred label of Celestial Master Daoism for its own teaching. Translatable as Orthodox Unity, this term reflects the vision of the Celestial Master as representing the correct teaching of the Dao, the ultimate one. Later Daoist lineages did not adopt the label *zheng* to describe their own teachings, nor was it used in the various texts I discuss below to signify orthodoxy. Nevertheless, as we have seen in the preceding chapters, and will see in this chapter, Daoist texts are concerned with defining correct practice and teachings; in short they are about orthodoxy. While I argue that the term orthodoxy is useful as a term for analysis, I would not use the term "heresy" to describe the teachings rejected by the emerging Daoist orthodoxy.

---

6   Cited in Chi-yun Chen, "Orthodoxy as a Mode of Statecraft: The Ancient Concept of *Cheng*" in Kwang-Ching Liu, ed. *Orthodoxy in Late Imperial China* (Berkeley: University of California Press, 1990): 28.
7   Ibid.
8   Ibid: 31–52.
9   John B. Henderson, *Construction of Orthodoxy and Heresy: Neo-Confucian, Islamic, Jewish, and Early Christian Patterns* (Albany: SUNY Press, 1998): 21.

Orthodoxy and canon formation

In a comparative study of orthodoxy, John Henderson cogently argues that ortho-doxy is a dynamic process, never entirely closed or fixed. Orthodoxy arises in response to what was later called heresy or heterodoxy by the emerging ortho-doxy. Indeed, careful examination of contemporary sources often reveals "a fluid situation in which emerging orthodoxies could hardly be distinguished from emerging heresies." Even more pertinently, Henderson notes that the "determina-tion of orthodoxy would seem to be more dependent on historical vicissitudes than on any comprehensive religious revelation or inescapable theological logic."[10] A similar point is made by Bart Ehrman, who notes the "widespread diversity of early Christianity, but also the blurred boundaries between what counted as ortho-doxy and heresy..."[11]

Significantly, both authors note that the creation of orthodoxy requires a concomitant construction of heresy. Rather than dispensing with the category of heresy as a subjective label applied by the dominant orthodoxy, both Ehrman and Henderson note that heresies are determined through debates within tradi-tions as groups negotiate their different interpretations of practice and teach-ings. Thus, the creative act of canonization and systemization is also an exclusionary process, by which the creators of orthodoxy determine which narratives, texts, practices, and genealogies are correct and which are deemed incorrect. We will find precisely these strategies in our examination of Daoist orthodoxy below.

In his analysis of the creation of the Christian canon, Ehrman provides a useful summary of the factors that led to the victory of the "proto-orthodox" Christians in creating Christianity in their vision.[12] Among these were: (1) Claims for ancient roots that precede rival scriptures, insisting that the scriptures of Judaism pre-dicted Jesus and the church. (2) The rejection of contemporary practices of Judaism allowed their particular form of Christianity to be a universal faith. (3) An insistence on church hierarchy, invested with authority that determined correct belief, proper liturgy and worship, and the books which were considered scrip-tural authorities. (4) The proto-orthodox were in constant communication with one another, determined to establish a worldwide communion. They were inter-ested not only in their own communities, but also in other communities and wished to spread their version of the religion throughout the world.[13] Among the most important factors that aided the victory of the proto-orthodox was the close

10 Henderson, *Construction*, 39.
11 Bart D. Ehrman, *Lost Christianities: the Battle for Scripture and the Faiths we Never Knew* (New York: Oxford University Press, 2003): 178.
12 Ehrman uses the term proto-orthodox to designate the "form of Christianity that endorsed the beliefs and practices that eventually came to dominate the religion toward the middle of the third century" (Ehrman, *Lost*, 7).
13 Ehrman, *Lost*, 179–80.

relationship between this group and the imperial centers at Constantinople and, especially, Rome.[14]

While we will find similar factors in the Daoist case, it is particularly instructive to note the differences between the so-called "proto-orthodox" camp in early Christianity and Daoists. Most importantly, we should note at the outset that Daoists never created an ecclesiastical institution and orthodoxy as coherent and powerful as did the orthodox Christian church. This may well be due to the fact that it is difficult to assert a particular Daoist lineage as proto-orthodox. While the Way of the Celestial Master is certainly central to the emergence of Daoism, it cannot be simply claimed as "proto-orthodox" Daoism. First, as noted in the Introduction, the Celestial Master tradition is not as coherent and continuous as the texts claim. While we lack details, it seems that the community that left Hanzhong was shattered during the third century,[15] and that various groups claiming allegiance to the Way of the Celestial Master coexisted contemporaneously during the fourth century. We find little evidence of cohesion or solidarity among adherents of Celestial Master Daoists. Indeed, we find rival claims for orthodoxy in fifth century texts associated with different Celestial Master lineages, such as the texts associated with Kou Qianzhi, Lu Xiujing, or Master Xu, the author of the *Inner Explanations of the Three Heavens*,[16] that I examine below.

Moreover, the attempts at integration and orthodoxy expressed in the Lingbao scriptures explicitly reject Celestial Master Daoism. An early effort by Lu Xiujing to create a reformed Celestial Master ecclesia, his *Codes for the Daoist Community*, was followed by his efforts to systematize the scriptures and rituals in accord with the cosmological scheme of the Three Caverns, which excludes the Celestial Master texts and practices. We should here recall Ehrman's reminder that, in the case of early Christianity, "not even the parameters of proto-orthodoxy were hard and fast… They evolved over time, with new boundaries occasionally being set up and old ones shifted accordingly".[17] As evidenced by Lu Xiujing's own efforts, the constant shifting of boundaries in Daoism was, as we will see, far more complex.

Henderson notes several important distinctions between the European situation, in which the Catholic orthodoxy was created, and the Chinese realm. While Henderson refers to the formation of Neo-Confucian orthodoxy, particularly the Cheng-Zhu 程朱 school, during the late imperial era, the points he raises are even more pertinent to the circumstances in medieval China and the emergence of Daoism. Indeed, it may well be that the strategies formulated by Neo-Confucian authors were modeled upon efforts at creating Daoist orthodoxy half a millennium

14 Ehrman, *Lost*, 174–79, *et passim;* Brown, *Rise*, 54–92; Henderson, *Construction*, 40–8.
15 Bokenkamp, *Early*, 152, 177, 185n6. See Introduction for further details.
16 *Santian neijie jing* 三天內解經 DZ 1205.
17 Ehrman, *Lost*, 136.

earlier. Henderson summarizes the differences between the Chinese case and the Catholic case in the following terms:

1   There was no central ecclesiastical authority comparable to the ecumenical councils or Papacy, which could state authoritatively what constitutes "right doctrine."
2   Neo-Confucians placed more emphasis on practice than on doctrine. This is, indeed, what we find in the Daoist texts as well. However, as I have argued in the Introduction, debates on practice entail debates about meaning.
3   Political support and motivation – The Neo-Confucian ascendance was closely affiliated and determined by the relationship of its teachings, and personal ties of scholars, to the imperial courts of the Song, Yuan, Ming, and Qing. It is, however, important to note that the Cheng-Zhu orthodoxy was attained over centuries of debates among distinct Neo-Confucian schools.[18] Daoists never attained such support, though, as we will see below, not for lack of trying.
4   Certain lineages and practices, which were later categorized as orthodox, appeared earlier than the "orthodoxy," and were co-opted into the emerging orthodoxy. We must remember that orthodoxy is a creative process. As a lineage claiming orthodoxy emerges, it has to negotiate its claims in the context of rival claims made by contemporary and earlier lineages.

A particularly intriguing consequence of such competing claims for authority is the development of strategies for asserting temporal primacy. Among the most important claims made in Daoist texts is asserting ancient, indeed primordial, pedigree. Such claims were at the core of the discourse on talismanic writing we discussed in Chapter 3. Daoist claims for ancient authority are more complex than those made by Christian authors. Daoist authors envisioned distinct temporal stages, referring first to the primordial moments of emanation and, second, to the recent historical context of the appearance of the text in the contemporary age. Daoist authors thus asserted their authority based on being doubly prior. First, Daoists claimed their particular text, or texts, existed at the primordial moments of creation. Different lineages thus produced ever more complex cosmogonies in order to accommodate these claims. Second, Daoists also asserted that their particular texts were revealed into the contemporary world earlier than those of their competitors. These two claims for temporal primacy are particularly important in understanding the structure of the Lingbao textual corpus.

The Lingbao textual corpus, as listed by Lu Xiujing, consisted of two basic divisions. In his *Preface to the Lingbao Catalogue*, Lu states his primary motivation was to expunge the forgeries that had become mixed with the true scriptures. Basing himself on an "ancient catalogue" (*jiumu* 舊目), Lu complained that the

---

18 Henderson, *Construction*, 69–84, *et passim*.

forgeries were transmitted indiscriminately along with true scriptures, that some circulating texts were not listed in the catalogue, and that the "ancient and new" texts amounted to 55 scrolls. The "ancient catalogue" may well be a rhetorical trope used by Lu for legitimating his project. Nevertheless, Lu set out to establish the authentic Lingbao canon:

> I now list the scriptures of the ancient catalogue, [indicating] those already revealed, as well as those matters transmitted to the Duke Transcendent.[19]

The extant remainder of Lu's catalogue, as preserved in Song Wenming's *Tongmen Lun*, is indeed divided into two basic divisions. The first division, consisting of ten parts in thirty scrolls, is defined as "ancient scriptures of the Celestial Worthy." The second division is described as "new scriptures that provide precepts, and essential instructions, and explanations for correct practice that had been received by Transcendent Duke Ge."[20]

As the former textual group is heavily impacted by Buddhist cosmology and terminology, while the latter is indebted to Celestial Master material, Kobayashi Masayoshi has suggested that the two textual divisions reveal two distinct authorial hands. Kobayashi argues that the former textual group, which he labels the Celestial Worthy lineage, were authored by Ge Chaofu, who is part of what he calls the Way of the Ge family, that extends from Ge Xuan (traditional dates 164–244), through Ge Hong, to Ge Chaofu. Kobayashi further argues that due to the obvious impact of Kumarajiva's (344–413) Buddhist translations on these texts, their composition must postdate Kumarajiva, who arrived in China in late 401. Kobayashi argues that the *Five Tablets in Red Script*, which he views as the first Lingbao text, may indeed have been written at that time. The more developed Celestial Worthy texts, Kobayashi argues, were composed at about 420. The texts of the second textual corpus, labeled "Transcendent Duke corpus" by Kobayashi, are characterized by a reverence to the *Daode jing*, usually entitled *Five-thousand Graphs*, and by the important role of Celestial Master Zhang Daoling in the revelation and transmission of the Lingbao texts. Kobayashi argues these texts were produced around the year 424 by a "Three Caverns Celestial Master lineage" 天師道三洞派 .[21] It is not quite clear what social reality this category reflects.

In his study of the Lingbao scriptures, Wang Chengwen points out that the "New" texts cite and refer to the "Ancient" texts. He, thus, also argues that the "New" texts were compiled later, as elaborations and explanations of the "Ancient" texts.[22] Wang does not elaborate as does Kobayashi on the possible authorship of the different texts.

19 DZ 1032: 4.6a.
20 P 2861, ZHDZ vol. 5: 510b, 510c; Ōfuchi, "Ku Ling-pao."
21 Kobayashi, *Rikuchō*, 162–78.
22 Wang, *Dunhuang*, 99–107.

Stephen Bokenkamp argues that these two divisions do not reflect different authorial voices, but a coherent temporal imagination.[23] The Ancient Scriptures had been revealed by the Celestial Worthy in primordial times. As they were in existence prior to human affairs, they do not refer to mundane historical affairs. Such references are found in the New Scriptures, which are said to have revealed directly to Ge Xuan, the Transcendent Duke, during the Wu dynasty. Among the most detailed narratives of this revelation of the Lingbao scriptures is preserved in a fragment of the *Awesome Rites of Lingbao* 靈寶威儀:

> Xu Laile 徐來勒, the Perfected of Great Culmen, appeared on Mt. Kuaiji at noon on the first day of the first month of *jimao* year and transmitted [the Three Caverns] to Left Transcendent Duke of the Great Culmen, Ge Xuan, also named Xiaoxian. On Mt. Tiantai, Xuan transmitted [the Three Caverns] to Zheng Siyuan, the Sramana Zhu Falan and Shi Daowei, and to Sun Quan 孫權 (182–252), the ruler of Wu. Later, on Mt. Maji, Siyuan transmitted the teachings to Ge Hong, grand-nephew of the Transcendent Duke, styled Master Embracing the Unhewn, the author of the *Inner and Outer books…* Master Embracing the Unhewn, on the third day in the third month of the sixth year of the *Jianyuan* era (349), on Mt. Luofu, transmitted the [teachings] entrusted over generations to his disciples.[24]

The fictive lineage given in this narrative is mentioned in several other Lingbao scriptures,[25] and was accepted as authoritative in the Daoist history presented in the *Yunji qiqian* encyclopedia. Resonating with the narratives of lineage we saw in Chapters 1 and 2, the significance of this narrative is in the inclusion of Buddhists and the ruler of Wu among the disciples of Ge Xuan. The narrative alludes to several important themes and tropes in the Lingbao mythology and cosmology. First, the narrative explains the appearance of the texts of the Three Caverns in the world through the mediation of the Perfected Xu Laile, first of the three Perfected, who are said in the Lingbao scriptures to have revealed the texts to Ge Xuan. While the narrative creates a clear transmission through Zheng Siyuan to Ge Hong, the disciples also include two Buddhists and Sun Quan, who declared himself emperor of Wu in 222. The allusion to Sun Quan indicates the importance of seeking political support, here hinting that the Wu dynasts were indeed privy to the revelation. The presence of the Buddhist disciples, of course, indicates the superiority of the Daoist teachings. In a more developed version of this narrative,

---

23 Stephen Bokenkamp, "The Silkworm and the Bodhi Tree: The Lingbao Attempt to Replace Buddhism in China and Our Attempt to Place Lingbao Taoism" in John Lagerwey, ed. *Religion and Chinese Society* (Hong Kong: Chinese University Press; Paris: EFEO, 2004): vol. 2, 7.

24 P 2452; ZHDZ vol. 4, 100c.

25 For example, *Dongxuan Lingbao Yujing shan buxu jing* 洞玄靈寶玉京山步虛經 DZ 1439.

Ge Xuan and his Buddhist and Daoist disciples are attached through karmic bonds.[26]

The first of the New Scriptures is the *Array of the Five Talismans*. While the *Array of the Five Talismans* was in fact a major inspiration for the Lingbao revelations, it is here included as one of the fundamental texts in the secondary revelation. On the other hand, as we saw in Chapter 2, the *jiao* rite of the Array was reformulated into the central rite of the *Five Tablets in Red Script* and the *Jade Instructions*, the first and second scriptures in the list of Ancient Scriptures. Moreover, as we saw in Chapter 3, the Lingbao talismans of the *Array of the Five Talismans* are elaborated in the Lingbao scriptures into the talismanic origins of all scriptures, and indeed of the world itself.

Perhaps even more importantly, by situating the New Scriptures associated with Ge Xuan in the recent past, the author can discuss and contrast the Lingbao teachings with rival contemporary teachings, Daoist and Buddhist. Thus, the Celestial Master teachings can be subtly rejected by asserting that Zhang Daoling in fact received the Lingbao teachings. For example, the *Questions of Duke Transcendent* [*Xiangong qingwen* 仙公請問],[27] one of the "new" Lingbao scriptures states:

> The Eminent Laozi said: As for what is prior in the Dao, nothing approaches the *zhai*. There are numerous methods of *zhai*, and they are for the most part the same, but the one with the most merit is the Lingbao *zhai*. There are few in the world who can study it. Those who study it are all masters of the Great Vehicle, who have in previous lives accumulated blessings, and who are nearing transcendence. There is also the *zhai* method of the Three Heavens, which is similar to the Lingbao method.
>
>   The Duke Transcendent replied: The method of the Three Heavens is a method that was transmitted to the Celestial Master, Master of the Teachings of the Three Heavens, it is named the *Scripture for Instructions in the Teachings* (*Zhijiao jing* 旨教經). This is clearly a secondary teaching. This method is fully elaborated in the *Five Ascendants Writs of Lingbao* 靈寶五稱文. But, because this celestial writing is all encompassing and marvelous, it is incomprehensible to mundane worthies. Only superior transcendents and perfected whose profundity equals that of the most high can penetrate this teaching.[28]

26 *Taishang dongxuan lingbao benxing suyuan jing* 太上洞玄靈寶本行宿緣經 DZ 1114: 3a–5a. For a translation and study, see Stephen Bokenkamp, *Ancestors and Anxiety*, 158 ff.
27 This text is listed in Lu Xiujing's *Catalogue* as *Xiangong qingwen* 仙公請問 經 in two parts. The first part is not preserved in the Daozang. Ōfuchi identifies Dunhuang manuscript S 1351, *Taiji zuo xiangong qingwen shang* 太極左仙公請問經上, as the first chapter of this text, and *Taishang dongxuan lingbao benxing suyuan jing* DZ 1114 as the second chapter. Ōfuchi, *Tonkō moko-rokuhen*: 66, *Tonkō zurokuhen*, 86; idem, "On Ku," 54; Taoist Canon, 239. Wang, *Dunhuang*, 86–158, focuses on this text.
28 S 1351, in ZHDZ, vol. 4, 119c. My translation is indebted to Bokenkamp, "Prehistory of Laozi," 412.

A parallel passage in the second chapter of the scripture includes the lines:

> In studying the Dao, nothing is prior to *zhai*. Among *zhai*, none surpass the Lingbao *zhai*. Its methods are eminent and marvelous, and should not be revealed in the mundane realm…. In the past, when the Perfected of Orthodox Unity [Zhang Ling] studied the Dao he received the Lingbao *zhai*. After his Dao was complete, he said this *zhai* was the most eminent…. When one first begins to study, one is at the stage of the Small Vehicle. But one who reveres the profound scriptures of the Three Caverns is called a master of the Great Vehicle. First, he saves others, and later saves himself.[29]

Zhang Daoling is thus effectively detached from the older Celestial Master teachings, labeled here as the Small Vehicle, and claimed as one of the recipients and transmitters of the Great Vehicle, the teachings of the Three Caverns. I discuss this passage further at the end of this chapter.

I suggest that we should understand the division of the Lingbao scriptures into two temporal corpora as a complex rhetorical strategy. On the one hand, the Ancient Scriptures claim primacy over all other revelations, both ancient and recent. On the other hand, the New Scriptures provide an explanation for the appearance and transmission of texts and practices prior to the revelation of the Ancient Scriptures around the year 400. Thus, any skeptical claims as to the origins of these revelations are thwarted. Practices and notions, which were the actual antecedents for the complex cosmological and ritual programs of the Lingbao scriptures, can thus be relegated to partial and incomplete revelations as the complete teachings are fully revealed in the Ancient Scriptures. The temporal distinction thus provides internal legitimacy and authenticity to the Lingbao revelations.

Constructing history

As illustration of the debates on practice by which Daoist lineages distinguished themselves from other traditions and from each other, I now return to the passages describing Daoist history cited above. The practice, or perhaps discourse, under debate here is the self-perception of Daoists as they negotiate their identity.

We may start by contrasting the three perceptions of Daoist origins cited above. The first is from the *History of the Wei*, completed in 554, the first official history to include a chapter devoted to Buddhism and Daoism. While the Buddhist section of the Treatise is a relatively coherent historical narrative, the Daoist section is essentially a hagiography of Kou Qianzhi, and the opening narrative I examine below is culled from Daoist scriptures. As we saw in the Introduction, the term *daojiao* was used in the *Treatise* and in Kou's *Laojun yinsong jie jing* as a designation for Celestial Master Daoism, probably in response to the challenge of the

---

29 DZ 1114.5a–6a.

Lingbao scriptures. Here, I show that this attitude is found in the historical vision of the *Treatise*.

The second quote is from Lu Xiujing's *Codes for the Daoist Community*. This passage asserts that Daoism originated with the revelation of Lord Lao to Zhang Daoling, who was bestowed with the title Celestial Master, and the establishment of the ecclesia, here named Covenantal Authority of Orthodox Unity with its injunctions and bureaucratic forms of communication.

The date of the *Codes for the Daoist Community* is unknown. I argue that it must have been composed before Lu's Catalogue of the Lingbao Scriptures, which was compiled in 437. In the preface to this catalogue, which is preserved in the *Yunji qiqian*, Lu introduces himself as Disciple of the Three Caverns (*Sandong dizi* 三洞弟子), indicating that this catalogue, too, was, at least conceptually, part of a canon of the Three Caverns. The historical narrative of the preface, which is indebted to the cosmology and mythology of the Lingbao scriptures, describes three moments of revelations in the historical past. The first is the secretion of texts by the Great Yu, the second is Lord Lao's revelation to the Celestial Master, and the third is the Transcendent Lord Ge Xuan's transmission of texts at Mt. Tiantai.[30] The first of these moments, while clearly based on the narrative of the *Array of the Five Talismans*, actually refers to the entirety of the Lingbao corpus in its nascent talismanic form. The third refers to several narratives in the Lingbao scriptures that describe the revelation of the scriptures to Ge Xuan. The actual wording of the second moment refers to "descent of the perfected" (降真), which seems to imply that the revelation to the Celestial Master was actually of Lingbao scriptures and not of the texts associated with the Way of the Celestial Master. This revelation is superseded by the final revelation of the Lingbao scriptures. In short, the preface to the Catalogue of the Lingbao Scriptures, as well as the catalogue itself, is clearly at odds with the historical narrative and ritual formulation of Lu's *Codes for the Daoist Community*. I discuss Lu Xiujing's changing perceptions of Daoism in detail later in this chapter.

The third quote is from an imperially sponsored Daoist *summa*, the *Yunji qiqian* that was compiled by Zhang Junfang 張君房 and presented to Song emperor Ren in 1027. The sources of the narrative I discuss here, however, are all from Six Dynasties scriptures. As I discuss below, the historical vision of Daoism presented in this text is best interpreted as a response to the histories presented in reformist Celestial Master texts composed in the fifth century, such as Lu's *Codes for the Daoist Community*, the *Inner Explanations of the Three Heavens*, or the *Treatise* associated with Kou Qianzhi. These texts present different idealized views of Celestial Master Daoism. However different these views were, they agreed that the Way of the Celestial Master was unique and did not explicitly seek to integrate with other Daoist scriptural and ritual traditions.

The three passages thus express different visions of Daoism, which Daoists wished to present to their imperial sponsors. The three passages clearly reflect

---

30 YJQQ DZ 1032: 4.4b.

how Daoists viewed their own beginnings. Yet, these visions are clearly at odds. The *Treatise* asserts the primacy and uniqueness of Laozi, the *Codes of the Daoist Community* claims the centrality of the Celestial Master, and the "Origins of Daoism" follows the cosmogonic mythologies developed in the Lingbao scriptures and explicitly rejects the primacy of Laozi and undercuts the Celestial Masters. Intriguingly, however, the *Treatise* and the "Origins of Daoism" agree on the earliest set of revelations in the human realm, as is apparent in the opening passage of the *Treatise*:

> As for the source of Daoism, it emerged from Laozi. In his own words, he was born prior to heaven and earth, and thereby supports the myriad things. Above, he dwells in the jade capital, and is the ancestor of the divine kings; below, he is at the purple culmen, and is the chief of the flying transcendents. With a thousand changes and myriad transformations, his virtue is non-virtue; he takes form in response to stimulus, he extinguishes his traces and is forever transforming. He instructed the Yellow Thearch at Mt. Emei, taught Di Ku on Mt. Mude, the Great Yu heard his instructions on longevity, and Yin Xi received his teachings on the Way and Virtue. As for the scriptures for ascending to the mystery and pacing in flight that are written on cinnabar in purple lettering, and the marvelous discourses from the numinous cavern that [resonate like] jade-stones and radiant as gold, they are beyond count.[31]

> 道家之原, 出於老子. 其自言也, 先天地生, 以資萬類. 上處玉京, 為神王之宗; 下在紫微, 為飛仙之主. 千變萬化, 有德不德, 隨感應物, 厥迹無常. 授軒轅於峨嵋, 教帝譽於牧德, 大禹聞長生之訣, 尹喜受道德之旨. 至於丹書紫字, 昇玄飛步之經, 玉石金光, 妙有靈洞之說, 不可勝紀.

Seemingly a clear and straightforward narrative describing the emergence and basic cosmology of Daoism, this passage, in fact, collapses a complex religious history of some four centuries into a few brief lines. The narrative manipulates an earlier mythology in order to incorporate the Lingbao scriptures, the Shangqing revelations, and other texts, which are all unnamed, into a grand vision of Celestial Master Daoism that paradoxically rejects much of the early Celestial Master tradition.

The first line introduces the ancient sage Laozi as the originator of Daoism, and the source of all the Daoist texts. This is, however, not the ancient human philosopher but a primordial manifestation of the Dao. As we saw in Chapter 1, this was a new perception of Laozi that developed during the Han. This primordial vision introduces the transmission of Daoist teaching from Laozi to a series of ancient culture heroes, the Yellow Emperor, Di Ku, and the Great Yu.

The source for this set of transmissions is the *Array of the Five Talismans*. As we saw in Chapter 2, however, in the *Array of the Five Talismans* the transmission

31 *Weishu* 魏書 114.3048.

to the Yellow Thearch, on the one hand, and to Di Ku and Yu, on the other, constitute two distinct narrative traditions emanating from lineages that can be distinguished by their practices, cosmology, and locality. The narrative of Di Ku and Yu forms the opening of the *Array*, and is focused on the transmission of the Five Lingbao Talismans into the human realm. This narrative was composed by a lineage based around Lake Tai and Mt. Bao. The narrative of the Yellow Thearch, on the other hand, is from the *Scripture of the Perfect One*, an independent scripture that was probably composed by a lineage centered in Mt. E'mei.[32] This narrative does not in fact refer to the Five Lingbao Talismans. Rather, it is focused on the teaching of the Three Ones and the Perfected One. Moreover, neither Laozi nor Zhang Daoling are mentioned in these two transmission narratives.

The distinct narratives and practices of the *Array of the Five Talismans* are conflated in the *Treatise*. On the one hand, by conflating these narratives and placing them alongside the narrative of transmission of the *Daode jing* to Yinxi, the *Treatise* implies that the ultimate teaching is in fact Laozi's *Daode jing*. On the other hand, by eliding all references to the Lingbao talismans and teachings, the *Treatise* also erases the Lingbao tradition from the history it presents. The final line of the passage refers obliquely to the Lingbao scriptures. The reference to "pacing in flight" may be to the practice of "pacing the void" (*buxu* 步虛), which was at the core of Lingbao practice.[33] The emergence of these scriptures in the "numinous cavern" 靈洞 may also be an oblique reference to the Lingbao scriptures.[34] Nevertheless, these revelations are all superseded by the recent revelation to Kou Qianzhi, as detailed in his *Laojun yinsong jiejing*, which, as we saw in the Introduction, called for cleansing of *daojiao* from the "false methods of the three

---

32 See Introduction for details.

33 A Lingbao scripture devoted to "Pacing the void" is *Dongxuan lingbao yujing shan buxu jing* 洞玄靈寶玉京山步虛經 DZ 1439. For studies of this text, see Stephen Bokenkamp, "The 'Pacing the Void Stanzas' of the Lingbao Scriptures," unpublished M.A. Thesis, University of California Berkeley, 1981; Liu Yi, "Lun gu lingbao jing 'shengxuan buxu zhang' de yanbian" 論古靈寶經 '昇玄步虛章' 的演變, in Florian Reiter, ed. *Foundations of Daoist Ritual* (Wiesbaden: Harrassowitz, 2009): 189–205. Since the Tang, this rite became central to Daoist ritual. For Tang, see Edward Schafer, "Wu Yün's 'Cantos on Pacing the Void'," *Harvard Journal of Asiatic Studies*, 41 (1981): 377–415. For modern performance see Kristofer Schipper, "Study of Buxu: Taoist Liturgical Hymn and Dance," in Tsao Peng-yeh and Daniel P.L. Law, eds. *Studies of Taoist Rituals and Music of Today* (Hong Kong: Society for Ethnomusicological Research in Hong Kong, 1989): 110–120.

34 The term appears in several Lingbao texts in a generic, non-technical sense. In the *Twenty-four Charts of Lingbao* (*Dongxuan Lingbao ershisi sheng tujing* 洞玄靈寶二十四生圖經 DZ 1407) the term appears in a verse celebrating the "Mountain-opening Chart for Collecting Herbs" 採芝 開山圖 where it simply refers to "numinous caverns that open once in a myriad kalpas" (14b). Significantly, the Twenty-four Charts are arrayed cosmologically in three sections (*bu* 部), which are also entitled "caverns." The first section is entitled "cavern of heaven" (dongtian 洞天), the second is entitled "cavern of profundity" (dongxuan 洞玄), and the third is entitled "cavern of numinae" 洞靈 (cited in YJQQ DZ 1032: 80.14; also cited in *Taixuan bajing lu* 太玄八景錄 DZ 258, a later rewriting of the *Twenty-four Charts of Lingbao* from a Shangqing perspective).

Zhangs."[35] The *Treatise* continues by collapsing the teachings bestowed upon Zhang Daoling and the Lingbao scriptures.[36] This finally allows the *Treatise* to claim supremacy for the revelations received by Kou Qianzhi, which are described in full detail in the following pages of the *Treatise*.

The dismissal of Lingbao and the primacy of Laozi presented in the *Treatise* is directly challenged in the section "Origins of Daoism" from *Yunji qiqian*:

> In seeking the source of Daoist scriptures and declarations, we find they arose during the era of the three Primordials (*sanyuan* 三元). In accord with their source, they sent down their traces which formed the five virtues. Combining three and five, thus were formed the eight nodes. The graphs of the eight nodes were formed out of marvelous pneumas…. As for the currently circulating Lingbao scriptures, they were transmitted by the Celestial Perfected Luminary Person to Xuanyuan, the Yellow Thearch, on Mount E'mei. The Celestial Perfected Luminary Person also transmitted them to Di Ku at the tower of Mude. Yu of Xia caused their descent to Mount Zhong. King Helü stealthily viewed them at Juqu. Later, the likes of Ge Xiaoxian and the disciples of Zheng Siyuan transmitted it from master to disciple in an unbroken line. As for Laozi's *Daodejing*, it is a supplement to the texts of the great vehicle. It is a scripture of the three auxiliaries (*fu* 輔) and is not included in the teachings of the three caverns. The learning of contemporaries is mostly shallow. They only recite the *Daode* and do not know about the perfected scriptures, so they say Daoism arose from Zhuang Zhou and began with "Below the Pillar" (Laozi).… It is clear from the above that the scriptures of the Daoists are not limited to the *Five-thousand* (graphs, i.e. *Daode jing*) alone.[37]

> 尋道家經誥, 起自三元; 從本降迹, 成於五德. 以三就五, 乃成八會. 其八會之字, 妙氣所成… 今傳 '靈寶經'者, 則是天真皇人於峨嵋山授於軒轅黃帝. 又天真皇人授帝嚳於牧德之臺, 夏禹感降於鍾山, 闔閭竊闚於句曲. 其後有葛孝先之類, 鄭思遠之徒, 師資相承, 蟬聯不絕. 其老君 '道德經', 乃是大乘部攝, 正當三輔之經, 未入三洞之教. 今人學多浮淺, 唯誦 '道德', 不識真經, 即謂道教起自莊周, 始乎柱下 … 由此明道家經誥, 非唯 '五千'.

---

35 *Weishu* 114.3051.
36 *Weishu* 114.3048:

> When Zhang Ling received the Dao on Heming, he was transmitted the Petitioning Writs of the Twelve-hundred Celestial Officers 天官章本千有二百, which he transmitted to his disciples, so that these practices flourished. The methods of fast, offering, obeisance, and reverence 齋祠跪拜 were all complete. The Three Primordials and Nine Offices, one hundred and twenty officials, and all the spirits were all integrated and governed 統攝. He also named kalpic epochs, just like the Buddhist scriptures. Their names were *Yankang*, *Longhan*, *Chiming*, and *Kaihuang*. At the end of each epoch, he said heaven and earth would totally collapse. These books had numerous restrictions and secrets, and those who were not followers could not even glimpse them.

37 *Yunji qiqian* DZ 1032: 3.2b-4a.

This passage is based on Lingbao cosmology, which as discussed in Chapter 3, described the emanation of the cosmos as a series of cosmogonic transformations of primordial talismanic scripts. This narrative emphasized that the most eminent deity, the Celestial Worthy of Primordial Commencement, and the Lingbao scriptures appeared within the primordial Dao prior to the manifested world. This time before time is here referred to as the Three Primordials. These temporal moments are also identified as incomprehensibly ancient deities, each of which transmitted the scriptures of one of the Three Caverns. Significantly, these texts are also labeled "scriptures of the great vehicle," adopting the Chinese Buddhist translation term for *mahayana* as a category of superior texts.

The passage here, however, incorporates a later canonic category, Four Auxiliaries (*sifu* 四輔): (1) *Taixuan jing*, which include the *Daode jing* and its commentaries, (2) *Taiping jing*, (3) *Taiqing jing*, alchemical texts, and (4) *Zhengyi*, texts of the Celestial Master. I discuss this more expansive view of the Daoist canon, and Daoism itself, in the concluding chapter. Here suffice it to say that, while this categorization is more inclusive, it is still based on the supremacy of the Three Caverns. This passage stresses the secondary nature of the *Daode jing* and criticizes the misguided notion that the origins of Daoism are the ancient philosophical classics.

The passage provides more detail adapted from the *Array of the Five Talismans*, but, like the *Treatise*, it also conflates the distinct narratives in order to hide the early distinctions in the tradition. The passage then provides the idealized lineage, beginning with Ge Xiaoxian, better known as Ge Xuan, and his disciple Zheng Siyuan, Ge Hong's teacher, as recipients of the teachings. Interestingly, while Ge Xuan indeed has an extremely important role in the Lingbao scriptures, he is not therein explicitly described as having transmitted the *Five Talismans*. Ge Hong does not refer to Ge Xuan in his *Baopuzi*, but he does say that he received the Five Lingbao Talismans and associated texts from Zheng Siyuan. As the Lingbao talismans were not central to Ge Hong's practice, the fact that he does not refer to Ge Xuan as transmitting them may not be particularly significant. It is likely that Ge Xuan had indeed transmitted the talismans along with the other teaching he transmitted to Zheng Siyuan.[38]

Most importantly, however, the passage from the *Yunji qiqian* explicitly states that the texts referred to in these early narratives were in fact the Lingbao scriptures. As we saw in Chapter 3, this shift in referent from the Lingbao talismans to the Lingbao scriptures is based on the narratives found in the Lingbao scriptures.

The Three Caverns

Lu Xiujing's canon incorporated three distinct textual corpora that he arranged in Three Caverns: the Cavern of Perfection (*dongzhen* 洞真) constituted the canon of Shangqing scriptures, the Cavern of Mystery (*dongxuan* 洞玄) constituted the canon of Lingbao scriptures, and the Cavern of Divinity (*dongshen* 洞神)

---

38 On Ge Hong's relationship and attitude to Ge Xuan, see Campany, *To Live*, 157 ff.

constituted the canon of Sanhuang 三皇 scriptures. Lu's epithet Disciple of the Three Caverns is in fact a response to the title Master of the Great Teaching Three Caverns (*Sandong dafa shi* 三洞大法師) bestowed upon Ge Xuan in the Lingbao scriptures.[39] The concept of the Three Caverns originated in the Lingbao scriptures.

The label Three Caverns in not as straight forward as it may appear at first glance. The term Three Caverns as a label for a textual canon seems to resonate with *Tripitaka*, the Three Baskets of the Buddhist canon, translated as Three Treasuries (*sanzang* 三藏) in Chinese. It is, however, unlikely that the Daoist notion of Three Caverns was based on the Buddhist canon. Firstly, the Three Baskets of the Buddhist canon are *sutra*, *vinaya*, and *abhidharma*. While certain Daoist texts reveal evident borrowing, even wholesale adaptation, of various Buddhist texts, the Daoists did not adopt the Buddhist textual categories. The earliest attempt to compile the various Buddhist texts current in China was undertaken by Dao An 道安 (312–85) in 374. This catalogue, *Zongli zhongjing mulu* 總理眾經目錄 [*Classified Catalogue of Scriptures*] was not divided into the Three Baskets, and did not include *vinaya* and *abhidharma* as textual categories. A Buddhist canon based on the textual divisions of the Three Baskets did not appear until the end of the fifth century.[40] Thus, at the time that Ge Chaofu, and other authors of Lingbao scriptures, were formulating their notions of the Three Caverns, there was not a Buddhist catalogue that could serve as a model.

Most significantly, the notion of the Three Caverns should be seen as an elaboration of the familiar cosmogony in *Daode jing* 42. The Three Caverns are thus the Three that emerge from the One. Indeed, the Lingbao scriptures clearly state that the ultimate source of the scriptures is within the unitary Void Cavern. As mentioned in Chapter 3, the *Five Tablets in Red Script* describes the spontaneous emanation of the primordial Jade Tablets of the Five Ancients within the Void Cavern in the primordial darkness prior to all existence.[41] In the *Scripture of Divine Stanzas Born in the Self-Generated Nine Heavens*, discussed below, the Void Cavern is the locus wherein the nine transformative pneumata are hidden prior to their emergence and emanation of the cosmos.[42] Moreover, these nine pneumata are themselves products of three primordial caverns, the Great Cavern (Dadong 大洞), the Cavern of Mystery, and the Cavern of Divinity, that are described as consecutive eons in a complex cosmogony. The *Yunji qiqian* describes Void Cavern in the following terms:

> Primordial pneuma, which is within the indistinguishable and beyond the abyssal darkness, was born in the Void Cavern. Within the Void Cavern, it

---

39 *Taishang dongxuan lingbao zhenyi quanjie falun miaojing* 太上洞玄靈寶真一勸戒法輪妙經 DZ 346.2b.

40 For a brief survey of these developments, see Sylvie Hureau, "Translations, Apocrypha, and the Emergence of the Buddhist Canon," in John Lagerwey and Lü Pengzhi, eds. *Early Chinese Religion: the Period of Division (220–589 AD)* (Leiden: Brill, 2010): 758–60.

41 DZ 22: 1.1b1.

42 *Dongxuan lingbao ziran jiutian shengshen zhangjing* 洞玄靈寶自然九天生神章經 DZ 318.1b10–2a1.

was produced in great nullity. Great nullity transformed and the three pneumas illumined therein. The three pneumas were undifferentiated. By generating within the great emptiness they established the cavern; by relying on the cavern they established non-existence; by relying on non-existence they produced existence; by relying on existence they established the void. The transformations of void nullity are self-generation within emptiness. The first pneuma is named inaugural, the middle pneuma is named primal, and the third pneuma is named dark. Dark pneuma was produced within the void, primal pneuma was produced within the cavern, and inaugural pneuma was produced within the nullity. Hence one produced two, and two produced three. Three transformed and gave birth until reaching the nine darknesses. Upon reaching nine, the process reverted to one, and entered into the perfection of the Dao. The clear pneuma formed heaven, the turbid pneuma congealed into earth, and the middle pneuma harmonized and formed humanity. The three pneumas divided and separated, thereby giving life to the myriad transformations. The sun and moon arrayed their radiances and the five planets blazed forth. The superior three heavens were produced by the purity of the three pneumas, their emptiness is beyond non-existence, and their limit is without limit.[43]

Void Cavern is therefore a metaphorical description for the undifferentiated unity of the Dao. It is within this cavern that the primordial transformations occurred. This cosmological metaphor should remind us of the significance of "caves" in the emerging Daoist lineages. First, the most important talismanic writs were said to have been discovered in caves. The main narrative of the *Five Talismans of Lingbao* describes the discovery of the talismans in the subterranean realm below lake Dongting (lake Tai 太湖 in modern Jiangsu).[44] Ge Hong wrote that *Writs of the Three Sovereigns* were hidden within all mountains, and could only be attained by entering into these hidden precincts.[45] A citation of the *Scripture of the Three Sovereigns* preserved in the *Yunji qiqian* claims that the text was revealed to Bao Jing as he meditated in a cavern within Mt. Songgao.[46]

Indeed, it may be that these early narratives were at the basis of the intriguing notion of cavern-heavens (*dongtian* 洞天) that developed in the Shangqing scriptures. Within these cavern-heavens, mundane space and time were abrogated, and they were perceived as distinct cosmic realms, possessing their own sun and moon, that were simultaneously below and beyond the mountains of our world. These cavern-heavens were also described as forming a subterranean network. As

---

43 YJQQ DZ 1032: 2.2b.
44 DZ 388: 7a6. For the literary antecedents and later contexts of this narrative, see Stephen R. Bokenkamp, "The Peach Flower Font and the Grotto Passage," *JAOS* 106 (1986): 171–9.
45 Wang, *Baopuzi neipian*, 19.336; see also the discussion in Schipper, "The true form," 99 ff.
46 YJQQ DZ 1032: 4.10b. It is difficult to ascertain the provenance of this passage.

I have shown elsewhere, the specific links between various caves in this network may be interpreted as refractions of actual socio-historical links between local cults and Daoist lineages. By the late Six Dynasties, the network of cavern-heavens formed one aspect of a Daoist sacred geography that also incorporated several other cosmographies.[47]

These connotations of "caves" may explain why in explicating the term "three caverns" the *Yunji qiqian*, citing the *Daomen dalun*, glosses cavern (*dong*) with its near homonym, *tong* (通), "to penetrate": "Cavern means to penetrate; penetrating to the mystery and reaching the marvelous."[48] Cavern is thus perceived as a hidden passage penetrating to the ultimate mystery of the cosmos. This gloss is certainly helpful in understanding the connotations of "cavern," but it is not evident in the use of the term in the Lingbao scriptures.

The significance of the *Writ of the Three Sovereigns* in the development of the notion of the Three Caverns may extend further than the association with caves. While the "caverns" of the Lingbao and Shangqing scriptures are associated with specific revelations in the fourth and early fifth centuries, the Sanhuang corpus consists of talismanic texts that had been in circulation among the southern elite for generations, and which were associated with a variety of lineages. The actual texts that constituted the Sanhuang corpus are no longer extant, except in fragmentary form.[49] It is clear, however, that the core text of this corpus was the *Writ of the Three Sovereigns*, which was revered by Ge Hong as the most efficacious text of all.

As discussed in Chapter 2, Ge Hong had received two versions of the *Writ of the Three Sovereigns*. The version transmitted by Bao Jing was eventually obtained by Lu Xiujing, who transmitted it to Sun Youyue, who, in turn transmitted it to Tao Hongjing.[50] This version was thus accepted as the canonic one. The earliest references to this textual corpus in the Lingbao scriptures are to the *Writ of the Three Sovereigns* alone.[51] According to the analysis of the various textual corpora in "Scriptures of the Three Caverns," the sixth chapter of the *Yunji qiqian*, this version of the *Writ of the Three Sovereigns*, which became the basis of the Sanhuang canon, included only four *juan*. It was Tao Hongjing who "analyzed the different branches of the transmitted texts and divided it into eleven *juan*."[52]

Ge Hong stresses the apotropaic efficacy of the text, and tells little of the content. However, fragmentary citations of the text suggest the text was a cosmological and historical narrative, detailing sequential eras of the Celestial, Earth, and Human Sovereigns (天, 地, 人皇). Ōfuchi Ninji has long ago shown that the

47 Raz, "Daoist Sacred Geography."
48 YJQQ DZ 1032: 6.1a5.
49 Schipper and Verellen, vol. 1, 260–69; Ōfuchi Ninji, *Dōkyō*, 219–96; Lü, *Tangqian*, 56–8.
50 DZ 1032: 6.5b–6a.
51 Entitled *Celestial Writ of the Three Sovereigns* (*Sanhuang tianwen* 三皇天文) in *Five Ascendant Talismans* DZ 671: 2.11a; and in *Taishang dongxuan lingbao benxing suyuan jing* 太上洞玄靈寶本行宿緣經 DZ 1114.10a1.
52 DZ 1032: 6.12a4.

notion of the Three Treasures developed in the Lingbao scriptures is based upon the Three Sovereigns.[53] The notion of the Three Caverns is thus traceable to some of the earliest texts associated with Ge Hong.

The Three Caverns in the Lingbao scriptures

The Lingbao scriptures elaborate the temporal sequence of the Three Sovereigns into a complex cosmogony that describes the emergence of the cosmos through a series of nine transformations. The most detailed formulations of this cosmogony in the Lingbao scriptures appear in the aforementioned *Scripture of Divine Stanzas Born in the Self-Generated Nine Heavens*.[54] Each of the Caverns here is perceived as a spatio-temporal locus of transformation, within which unfold three internal transformations that culminate with the production of a text. The opening passage of this text, entitled "Golden Books of the Macrocosm of the Three Treasures" 三寶大有金書, describes the appearance of the texts of the Three Caverns as part of the cosmogonic process, and prior to the appearance of the mundane world. The narrative describes the emergence in successive eons of Three Treasures, the Celestial Treasure (Tianbao 天寶), Numinous Treasure (Lingbao 靈寶), and Divine Treasure (Shenbao 神寶). The Three Treasures are deities, who are personified manifestations of the pneuma of three successive eons. Each of these temporal deities undergoes three transformations into various entities within their respective eons. These nine transformations eventually generate the texts associated with each of the Caverns:

> The Lord of Celestial Treasure is the revered deity of the Great Cavern.[55] The Elder of Celestial Treasure is the ancestral pneuma of the Lord of Celestial Treasure. The Elder is the pneuma of the Most Eminent Jade Emptiness of the Without-Prior Chaotic Cavern. Ninety-nine thousand nine-hundred and ninety-nine trillion pneumata (transformations) later, upon reaching the first year of the *Longhan* epoch, it transformed to generate the Lord of Celestial Treasure, and he brought forth a book. During this period he was entitled [ruler of] Most Eminent Macrocosmic 大有 Jade Purity Palace.
>
> The Lord of Numinous Treasure is the revered deity of the Cavern of Mystery. The Elder of Numinous Treasure is the ancestral pneuma of the Lord of Numinous Treasure. The Elder is the pneuma of the Mystic Eminent Purple Emptiness of the Supreme Without-Prior Red Chaos. Ninety-nine thousand nine-hundred and ninety-nine trillion pneumata (transformations) later, upon reaching the *Longhan* epoch, he unfurled the chart and transformed to generate the Lord of Numinous Treasure. Crossing through one

---

53 Ōfuchi Ninji, *Dōkyō*, 22–3.
54 *Dongxuan lingbao ziran jiutian shengshen zhangjing* DZ 318.
55 The *Perfected Scripture of the Great Cavern* (*Dadong zhengjing* DZ 6) is the most important of the Shangqing scriptures.

kalpa, and reaching the *Chiming epoch*, he brought forth a book of salvation. During this period he was entitled [ruler of] Supreme Clarity Mystic Capital Seven Treasures Purple Tenuity Palace.

The Lord of Divine Treasure is the revered deity of the Cavern of Divinity. The Elder of Divine Treasure is the pneuma of Most Supreme Pure Emptiness of the Mystic Pervasive Primordial of Silent Void. Ninety-nine thousand nine-hundred and ninety-nine trillion pneumata (transformations) later, upon reaching the first year of the Chiming epoch, it transformed to generate the Lord of Divine Treasure. Crossing through two kalpas, and reaching the first year of the *Shanghuang* epoch, he brought forth a book. During this period he was entitled [ruler of] Three Sovereigns Cavern of Divinity Great Purity Great Culmen Palace.[56]

The incomprehensibly vast stretches of time imagined in these passages are clearly a response to Buddhist ideas of time, yet the basic cosmological assumption of the narrative remains the well known cosmogony of the *Daode jing*, "the Dao generated one, the one generated two, two generated three, and three generated the myriad things".[57] As we noted in Chapter 4, this cosmogony formed the basis of the cosmogonic narratives of Celestial Master Daoism. The cosmogony of the *Divine Stanzas* continues by reiterating the underlying unity of the manifested pneumas:

> As for these three titles, although they differ in time and names, at root they are one. Divided, they constitute the three pneumas, the mystic, primordial, and inaugural, in order to administer [the respective eon]. The Three Treasures are the revered deities of the three pneumas. Under their respective titles, they each gave birth to three pneumas and successive titles, thus together producing nine pneumas.[58]

These lines resonate with well known passages from the *Daode jing* that emphasize the ultimate unity of all things within the Dao. Using similar structure and terms from the first chapter of the *Daode jing*, the first line emphasizes that, although named differently and apparently manifesting at distinct moments in time, the Three Treasures are ultimately one within the Dao and always were.[59] The second line is based on the cosmogonic narrative found in the Celestial Master text *Commands and Admonitions for the Families of the Great Dao*, which itself was an elaboration of the gnomic lines in *Daode jing* 42. Again, the emphasis here is on the ultimate unity of the various manifestations. The *Lingbao* narrative continues

---

56 DZ 318.1a.
57 Wang Chengwen, *Dunhuang*, 171.
58 DZ 318.1b7–9.
59 The line resonates with the line from the first chapter of the *Daode jing* "these two are the same, when they emerge they are named differently. When they are the same, this is known as mystery." 此兩者同出而異名, 同謂之玄 (*Daode jing* 1).

with further emergence within the primordial unity as the three pneumas multiply to produce nine, which are then further elaborated into the manifested cosmos:

> The nine pneumas emerged prior to the great void, and were hidden within the void cavern (*kongdong*). They were without light, without shape, without form, and without name… The three colors were indistinct in primordial chaos, sometimes existent and sometimes absent. Reaching the apogee through numerous revolutions and amplifications, the three pneumas shone forth. Some of the pneuma became clear and ascended, increasingly *yang* it formed heaven. Some pneuma congealed and coalesced, increasingly solid it formed earth. The nine pneumas were arrayed in proper order, and the sun, moon, constellations, yin-yang and five phases, humans, and all things received life together. As for the myriad transformations of heaven and earth, none could live were it not for the birthing by the three pneumas and guidance by the nine pneumas. The three pneumas are the ancestors of heaven and earth, the nine pneumas are the root of the myriad things.[60]

Thus, the cosmogonic narrative that began with the Three Treasures, and their respective self-generated texts, proceeds to explicate the appearance of the cosmos. Rather than generating the cosmos through successive transformative elaborations of the Five Talismans as we saw in the *Lingbao* texts discussed in Chapter 3, the *Divine Stanzas* stresses the primordial and cosmogonic quality of the texts of the Three Caverns. The crucible of the process is the Void Cavern wherein the undifferentiated primal pneuma transforms into creative pneumas that actually produce the manifested cosmos. The text continues by celebrating its own priority:

> The *Divine Stanzas of the Nine Heavens* are the flying mysterious pneumas of the three caverns. [This scripture] was thrice-harmonized to form tones and congealed to form the numinous script; merging in primordial chaos [it includes] the secret tones and esoteric names of the hundred spirits. The birthing pneumas congealed into form as self-generated stanzas 自然之章.[61]

The text now shifts to describe its own creative and transformative qualities. Indeed, it was through recitation of this text in primordial times by the Three Treasures that the cosmos came into being. The highest gods attained their form by reciting the text. The author then finally addresses the actual audience of the text, the Students of the Dao 學士, who are to recite this text if they are to rise to the heavens.

> The Celestial Treasure intoned this text in order to initiate the radiance of heaven and earth. The Numinous Treasure intoned this text in order to initiate

60 DZ 318.1b9–2a7.
61 DZ 318.3a2–4.

the ghosts and spirits of the long night of the nine abysses.[62] The Divine Treasure intoned this text in order to control the myriad numinae. The Great One intoned this text in order to complete the bodily spirits. The thearchical lords intoned this text in order to congeal their form. The nine heavens intoned this text in order to generate humanity. Students of the Dao intone this text in order to ascend to the heavens.[63]

The text continues by describing the attainments due to the "students of the superior way" 學上道 who revere the spirit transcendents. At first glance, the list of attainments seems to conflate terminology from distinct traditions, such as "release by means of a corpse," from the early seekers of transcendence, to Buddhist notions of nirvana (*miedu* 滅度) and transmigration (*zhuanlun* 轉輪). However, these attainments are in fact seen as partial, just like the traditions with which they are associated. Nevertheless, these attainments would eventually lead to the final attainment, when "at the end one returns to the way of transcendence. One's form and one's spirits will not depart from each other, and together will enter the perfection of the Dao."[64]

The Lingbao scriptures include several enumerations of the Three Caverns, indicating either different authors with different agendas, or negotiations within the emerging tradition of the meaning of this concept. The Lingbao scripture *Instructions for Holding Lingbao zhai by the Perfected of the Grand Culmen*, which is listed in Lu Xiujing's catalogue as one of the "new scriptures" revealed to Ge Xuan,[65] provides one vision of the Three Caverns. The importance of this text is that it is among the earliest manuals for performing the Lingbao *zhai*. The text thus directly confronts the Way of the Celestial Master by recasting Celestial Master practices and terminology into the Lingbao ritual framework. The ritual procedure is structured in the form that was to become the standard of the Lingbao ritual system, and includes complete instructions for the rite of "externalization of officials" (*chuguan* 出官), which was at the core of the early Celestial Master petitioning ritual.[66] In this rite, modeled upon the imperial bureaucratic procedure, the "officials," the bodily spirits, were activated through meditative breathing exercises in order to ascend and present petitions at the celestial courts. The list of officials in this Lingbao text is based on Celestial Master manuals, and includes several officials entitled *zhengyi*.[67] Intriguingly, the list also includes one of the earliest references to the fully developed Celestial Master sacred geography of "twenty-four parishes, thirty-six silent chambers, seventy-two blessed-sites, that

---

62 The "long night of nine abysses" refers to the netherworld and hells of the Lingbao cosmology.

63 DZ 318.3a4–7.

64 DZ 318.3b1–2 終歸仙道, 形與神同不相遠離, 俱入道真.

65 *Taiji zhenren fu Lingbao zhaijie weiyi zhujing yaojue* 太極真人敷靈寶齋戒威儀諸經要訣 DZ 532; Ōfuchi, "On Ku," 54; ZHDZ, vol. 4, 510c.

66 Lu Pengzhi, *Tangqian*, 25.

67 DZ 532.2a3, 2a8, 2a10.

were arrayed by the Celestial Master."[68] The performer of the Lingbao *zhai* begins by presenting himself as "Libationer of such-and-such parish."[69] The initial stages of the ritual are, therefore, heavily indebted to Celestial Master Daoism. It is at the stage of "reciting scriptures" (*zhuanjing* 轉經) that we find that the particular vision of three scriptural corpora of this text does not celebrate Celestial Master Daoism, but in fact rejects it. The first text to be recited is the *Daode jing*, which is defined as a scripture of the Great Vehicle (*dasheng zhijing* 大乘之經).[70] The next text to be recited is the core Shangqing scripture, the *Perfect Scripture of the Great Cavern* (*Dadong zhenjing* 大洞真經). The most important texts, however, are the Lingbao scriptures, defined as the "ultimate scripture of the Daoists, the mystic ancestor of the Great Vehicle."[71]

The relationship between *Daode jing* and Lingbao is a central concern of this text. The passage cited above, which introduces the three scriptures to be recited, ends with the lines:

> The myriad marvels are gathered in response to the Five-thousand Graphs![72]
> Taking great refuge [in the Way] is superior to all practices in the world. The Lingbao original *zhai* is the ancestor of all the various *zhai* rites.[73]

> 五千文感會眾妙, 大歸等耳勝得世間行也. 諸齋法皆上宗於靈寶本齋矣

While celebrating the *Daode jing*, this passage subtly elides the entire history of Daoism and asserts the Lingbao *zhai* is the ancestor of all practices. Stephen Bokenkamp has argued that the *Instructions for Holding Lingbao zhai* may have been composed by a distinct group of Lingbao practitioners specifically for the purpose of converting Celestial Master adherents. The ritual procedure in this text is heavily indebted to Celestial Master ritual protocols, indicating that it was an attempt to reformulate the old Celestial Master ritual while allowing new converts to locate their familiar deities and practices within the emerging Lingbao synthesis.

A Celestial Master response: the Inner Explanations of the Three Heavens

It is not quite clear how widespread the initial transmission of the Lingbao texts was, but, within a few years, they were well known and well received. It was, perhaps, the various ritual programs that led to the popularity of the Lingbao scriptures. Further evidence for the success of the Lingbao scriptures may be

---

68 DZ 532.3a; Gil Raz, "Daoist sacred geography."
69 DZ 532.4b1, 齋主自稱某治祭酒某先生.
70 DZ 532.12a.
71 DZ 532.12b.
72 Alluding to the final phrase of *Daode jing* 1: "gateway of the myriad marvels." 眾妙之門.
73 DZ 532.13a.

adduced from the spate of Celestial Master texts that attempted to respond to the Lingbao challenge. Evidently, the adherents of Lingbao and of Celestial Master Daoism did not see themselves as members of a single tradition, but rather as competitors.

Unlike most other Daoist texts, the *Inner Explanations of the Three Heavens* can be easily dated, and we even know the name of its author, Mister Xu, disciple of the Three Heavens (三天弟子徐氏). Unfortunately, we know nothing else about him. The text is clearly addressed to Liu Yu 劉裕 (356–422), who was about to claim the imperial throne in Jiankang and establish the Song dynasty (420–79). The first chapter of the text is fully translated and annotated by Stephen Bokenkamp,[74] so after a brief examination of the historical narrative in this part of the text, I will focus on the second chapter.

The *Inner Explanations* begins with a cosmogonic narrative that responds to the Lingbao narratives by placing the origins of Daoism, here defined exclusively as an idealized vision of Celestial Master Daoism, in an even more primordial moment. While this temporal vision is an elaboration of the cosmogonic narrative of *Daode jing* 42, its main claim is the complete identity between the Dao and Laozi. Significantly, this cosmogonic narrative leads directly to the appearance of different religions in the world. By placing these different religions within a unified narrative, the text provides a cosmological framework for distinguishing between these religions. Most importantly, this allows the author to assert the unique suitability of Celestial Master Daoism for China, and exclude all other religions. While the first *juan* provides the cosmological and historical narrative proving the priority and superiority of Daoism, in the second *juan* the author provides detailed criticism of specific practices. The text begins:

> The source of the Dao originally arose with nothing prior to it … without cause. Born in the void through self-actualization (*ziran* 自然), it transformed to give birth to the Elder of the Way and the Power, who appeared prior to the appearance of primal pneuma. Since he is the one revered within the Dao, he serves as the Elder of the Way and Power.[75]

The rhetoric of this passage resonates with the description of the Three Treasures in the *Self-Generated Stanzas* cited above. In that text, the Elders of each eon were defined as the ancestral pneumas of the Three Treasures, which in turn generate the primordial texts of the Three Caverns. Unlike the elders of the Three Treasures, however, the Elder of the Way and the Power is unique, and without peer. The text continues by describing the emanation of the three pneumas, followed by the full host of deities and spirits, culminating in the "twelve-hundred officials," the bureaucratic pantheon of the early Celestial Master community. We should note

74 Bokenkamp, *Early*, 186–229.
75 DZ 1205: 1.2a; I follow Bokenkamp's translation with emendations.

that while borrowing the label Elder, this passage does not refer to the Lingbao terminology of Treasures, Palaces, and eons:

> Based on this, there is the Illimitable Great Way of Great Clarity, with the Mystic, Primal, and Highest Three Heavens; the Most High Lord Lao, Most High Elder… and twelve-hundred officials.

The pantheon of the Celestial Master ecclesia is therefore part of the primordial cosmogonic order, and is in fact prior to the emergence of the cosmos itself. The term Great Clarity was used to name high heaven in Han cosmological writings, and it remained so in the early Celestial Master texts as well as in early alchemical works.[76] This heaven was demoted in importance in the Shangqing scriptures, which claimed their source to be in the Heaven of Highest Clarity (*Shangqing* 上清). An even higher heaven, Jade Clarity (*Yuqing* 玉清), was revealed in the Lingbao revelations. By emphasizing that Great Clarity is in fact prior to the emergence of the cosmos and its various heavens, this text recasts the early Celestial Master cosmology as the ultimate source of all teachings. The text can then reclaim the superiority of the Celestial Master ritual system:

> When mortals these days send up petitions to Great Clarity, they are directed at what is known as the celestial perfected.

The Shangqing and Lingbao scriptures claimed that the perfected dwelt in remote heavens far beyond the Great Clarity. The text here reasserts the supremacy of the petitioning rites by claiming that the celestial perfected, the transcendents favored in the Shangqing and Lingbao scriptures, are merely another term for the celestial bureaucracy envisioned by the Celestial Master. Significantly, this discussion of basic Celestial Master practice is included in the description of the earliest cosmogonic stage, "before there were primal pneumas." In the next passage, the narrative turns to describe the emanation of the cosmos through a series of transformations:

> After this, within Utter Darkness was produced Void Cavern; within Void Cavern was produced Grand Nullity. Grand Nullity transformed into the three pneumas, the Mystic, Primordial and Inaugural. Intermingled in undifferentiated chaos, they transformed to produce the Dark and Wondrous Mystic Maiden. After the generation of the Jade Maiden, the undifferentiated pneumas congealed within her, transforming and producing Laozi.

The first transformation produces the Void Cavern. As we saw above, in the Lingbao cosmology this cavern is the source of the scriptures.[77] Here, this

---

76 On early alchemy, see Pregadio, *Great Clarity.*
77 See the discussion of *Five Tablets in Red Script* in Chapter 3 and of the *Self-Generated Stanzas* earlier in this chapter.

transformation occurs after the entire Celestial Master pantheon of the Great
Clarity is already in place, thereby demonstrating the priority of the Celestial
Master cosmology. The sequence of cosmogonic emanation continues as the three
primordial pneumas coalesce within the undifferentiated chaos to form the Mystic
and Wondrous Mystic Maiden. Then, through yet another transformation of the
same pneumas, Laozi was produced within her womb. This cosmogonic transformation presages the "historical" birth of Laozi in the womb of Mother Li, who,
the text emphasizes, was not a distinct entity, but yet another transformation of
Laozi. This may well be a response to texts such as the *Scripture on Transformations
of Laozi*, in which references to Laozi's mother could be interpreted as referring
to a distinct, and hence prior, entity.[78] The narrative continues to emphasize Laozi's
unique cosmogonic role, as the physical transformation of the Dao whose own
body is the source of the pneumas that produced the manifested cosmos:

> Laozi transformed, and the pneumas became heaven, earth, humanity, and all
> things. This was the result of Laozi cyclically transforming himself, refining
> his form and pneumas. Lord Lao spread out the mystic, primordial, and inau-
> gural pneumas.[79]

These three pneumas eventually became the heavens, water, and earth. Laozi
then personally mixed these pneumas further, producing nine kingdoms, which he
populated with nine humans, six males and three females.[80] After the appearance
of the primordial couple, Fu Xi and Nu Wa, people took names.

At this stage, Laozi "issued forth three Ways to teach the people of heaven
(*tianmin* 天民)." These three Ways were correlated with the cosmological qualities of the people at their locales. Thus, "in the Central Kingdom where the yang
pneumas are pure and bright," Laozi initiated the Great Way of Inaction (*Wuwei
dadao* 無為大道). Outside this realm, in the 81 barbarian countries (*huguo* 胡國),
where yin pneumas flourish, he initiated the Way of the Buddha with its strict
injunctions and prohibitions in order to suppress the yin pneuma. In Chu and Yue
the pneumas of yin and yang are thin, so here Laozi initiated the Great Way of
Pure Contract (*Qingyue dadao* 清約大道). This was an ideal time, when "the rule
of the Six Heavens flourished and the three Ways were put into practice."[81]

Before discussing the three Ways mentioned here, we need to clarify the notion
of the Six Heavens, which was a new concept that appears in the reformist Celestial
Master texts of the fifth-century. In his *Abridged Codes*, for example, Lu Xiujing

---

78 See Introduction; and discussion in Livia Kohn, "The Mother of the Tao," *Taoist Resources* 1
    (1989): 37–109.
79 DZ 1205: 1.2a5–b8, Bokenkamp, *Early*, 207–8.
80 This odd placement of humans does not appear in other Celestial Master texts. It may be a reflec-
    tion of an idealized cosmography found in the *Taiping jing*: see Wang Ming, ed. *Taiping jing
    hejiao* (Beijing: Zhonghua shuju, 1960, rpt. 1988): 36–8; Barbara Hendrischke, *The Scripture on
    Great Peace* (Berkeley: University of California Press, 2006): 75, 95–9.
81 DZ 1205: 1.3a2–6, Bokenkamp, *Early*, 209.

describes the sorry state of humanity which motivated Laozi's revelation to the Celestial Master as a time when "the stale pneuma of the Six Heavens abrogated official titles… and as leaders of armies they roamed throughout the realm."[82]

According to Lu Xiujing, the practices revealed to the Celestial Master were to rectify this abominable situation into which humanity had fallen. Clearly, for Lu Xiujing, the Six Heavens are a source of demonic false practices, but the referent of this term is not immediately apparent. Scholars have held that this term refers to local religious practices, to the imperial ritual system, or perhaps to both ritual systems, which were characterized by blood sacrifices.[83] As we saw in Chapter 3, blood sacrifice was rejected by Daoists and this rejection extended to both imperial and local sacrificial cults. The extant early Celestial Master texts, however, do not use the term Six Heavens. The earliest uses of this term in Daoist texts seems to be in Shangqing texts, where it refers to the ghostly realm of the netherworld, Fengdu 豐都.[84] Is this the referent in the fifth-century Celestial Master texts?[85] It seems unlikely.

---

82 DZ 1127: 1a; Nickerson, "Abridged Codes," 352. See Chapter 2 for more details.

83 Kobayashi Masayoshi argues the Six Heavens are the six northern heavens Fengdu, the netherworld introduced in Shangqing scriptures; see Kobayashi, *Rikuchō*, 482–510. Zhao Yi 趙益 agrees with Kobayashi that the Six heavens are the demonic realms of the Fengdu netherworld, but suggests that demons there are in fact the gods of the local cults of common religion; see "Nanchao daojing 'Santian neijie jing' zaitan" 南朝道經 '三天內解經' 再探 *Nanjing xiaozhuang xueyuan xuebao* 3 (2006): 43–48. Bokenkamp cogently argues that the term probably refers to the sacrificial system envisaged in Zheng Xuan's 鄭玄 (127–200) commentaries on the Confucian classics; see *Early*, 200 n.21. Lü Pengzhi agrees that the term is based on Zheng Xuan's theory of the Six Heavens, and therefore applies to Confucian ritual as well as to the sacrificial cults of common religion; Lü, *Tangqian*, 228. I agree with Bokenkamp that the term harks back to debates among imperial ritualists regarding the correct interpretation of ritual classics. The debate among imperial ritualists centered upon the relationship of the five emperors and Great Unity. Zheng Xuan, following the Han weft-texts, argued that each of these entities was a heaven, hence there were six heavens. These heavens were personified as manifestations of the phases, and had arcane names. Perhaps, most importantly, the notion of the six heavens also entailed the idea that the ruling emperor was himself a manifestation of the ascendant phase, and hence extra-human. The rival opinion, usually associated with Wang Su 王肅 (195–256), was that the five emperors mentioned in the Confucian classics were simply ancient human emperors and not the arcane personifications introduced in the weft texts. Debates between proponents of both opinions continued throughout medieval China, and were only decided in the Tang, when Zheng Xuan's opinion was determined to be false. As I have shown elsewhere, the *jiao* ritual of the *Array of the Five Talismans* was composed in the context of this debate, and takes a position that at once expresses disapproval of the cosmology of the Six Heavens, while simultaneously advocating the notion of the ruling dynast as embodying the ascendant phase; see Raz, "Imperial Efficacy."

84 A detailed description of this demonic realm is preserved in chapter 15 of the *Declarations of the Perfected*. The text also provides a method for protecting oneself against demonic attacks while sleeping: "If people in the world know the names of the gateways to the six heavens of Fengdu then the hundred ghosts will dare not harm them." The text goes on to provide instructions for an incantation to be recited as one goes to bed (also in DZ 1016: 10.10a3).

85 Another intriguing reference in the *Declarations of the Perfected* refers to a text entitled *Correct Teachings of the Three Heavens, Writ for Expelling the Six Heavens* (*Chu liutian zhiwen santian zhengfa* 除六天之文三天正法 (DZ 1016: 5.2a6), which is not extant. This text seems to have been

While the term "stale pneumas of the six heavens" in the *Abridged Codes* refers to ghosts and demons, the point is that they have usurped unlawful positions in the temples and shrines of the people. The problem that Lord Lao was trying to resolve by revealing himself to the first Celestial Master was the improper cultic worship of the common religion.

In the *Inner Explanations*, the term Six Heavens is more complex and not entirely negative. Rather, it is used to describe a time at the beginning of human history when the three distinct and cosmologically proper religions were properly followed. This was when the "rule of the Six Heavens flourished." Later in the text, after continuing the historical narrative through the reigns of mythical ancient rulers who all had a manifestation of Laozi as counselor, the appearance of the "historical" Laozi, and the birth of Buddha,[86] the narrative describes the collapse of the idealized religious state, when "perversity and evil arose," and people "poured libations and made offerings to mediums and ghosts, not distinguishing between the true and false."[87] This state of decline is no longer in a mythical time, but is meant to describe the religious practices during the Han dynasty. The text ascribes the appearance of the *Taiping Jing*, and other teachings, as attempts initiated by Laozi to "aid the Six Heavens by correcting its deviant pneumas." These teachings, however, "could not rectify the pneumas of the Six Heavens."[88] The situation worsened, and during the Han "various deviant forces flourished and the pneumas of the Six Heavens flared up. The three Ways intermingled, and disease pneumas crisscrossed the land." The text then describes the deviant practices that arose as a result of the collapse of the Six Heavens:

Physicians and mediums flourished and blazed, and all abandoned the perfect [Way] and followed the false. They sang and danced to the sounds of strings and drums. They slaughtered and killed the six domestic animals, made libations, and sacrificed to the deviant ghosts.[89]

This led not only to the shortened lives and violent deaths of the people, but to the collapse of the Han dynasty itself. Among the symptoms of this collapse was the intermingling of peoples through miscegenation as well as the acceptance of Buddhist practice in the Central Kingdom.

an eschatological treatise describing the celestial cycles and predicting the imminent collapse of the current cosmic order. The text also provided apotropaic devices for use during the coming cataclysm. Parts of the text are preserved in two later texts: *Taishang santian zhengfa jing* 太上三天正法經 DZ 1203 (probably composed in early Tang) and *Shangqing dadong jiuwei badao dajing miaolu* 上清大洞九微八道大經妙籙 DZ 1395, and in numerous citations; for details see Robinet, *Révélation*, vol. 2, 87–91.

86 In this narrative, Laozi causes the guardian of the path, Yin Xi, to transform and enter Māyā's mouth (DZ 1205: 1.4b, Bokenkamp, *Early*, 212).
87 DZ 1205: 1.4b5, Bokenkamp, *Early*, 212.
88 Ibid.
89 DZ 1205: 1.4.b8–10, Bokenkamp, *Early*, 213.

It was at that time that Lord Lao, now named Newly Emerged Most High, revealed himself to Zhang Daoling and bestowed upon him the title "Master of the Three Heavens of Correct Unity and Pacified Pneumas of the Grand Mystic Capital," and entrusted him with the Way of Correct Unity of Covenantal Authority. The text explicitly states that, by this revelation, Lord Lao "abrogated the Six Heavens and their three Ways."[90] Despite this initial effort, the Way of the Celestial Master was soon also in peril, as it too was intermingled with "old matters of the Six Heavens."[91] Alongside improper practices by libationers who claim to follow the Celestial Master, the text also lists several "deviant" traditions, some of which are evidently sects that identified themselves as Daoist.[92]

The narrative finally reaches the immediate cause for its composition, the recognition that Liu Yu, the Song Thearch, is a descendant of the Liu clan, "a family whose fate is constantly linked with the Dao."[93] It is, therefore, the hope of the author, Xu, that the emperor would accept his fated role and rule as a Daoist monarch. The most important aspect of this would be to ensure the correct separation of the three Ways, and particularly reject Buddhism. The first chapter ends with a detailed comparison of the way of Buddha, which it defines as the way of yin and death, and the Way of Laozi, which is the path of *yang* and life.[94]

The term "Six Heavens" is used in the *Inner Explanations* as a label for the totality of the religious landscape in China. In ancient times, when the Six Heavens flourished, the three primordial paths, a generic form of Buddhism and two teachings resonant with Daoism, were practiced in their respectively appropriate regions. It is the collapse of this order that brings forth the corrupt practices of local religious practices, and the sacrificial imperial ritual system, as well as the sectarian Daoist groups. These are the stagnant fumes of the Six Heavens, which are to be replaced by the idealized Celestial Master ecclesia.

The historical narrative seems to imply that the three Ways are to be superseded by the Way of Correct Unity of Covenantal Authority. Yet, upon closer examination, we find that the only religion to be excluded is Buddhism. The Ways of Non-Action and of Pure Contract are two forms of ancient Daoism that are subtly conflated into the teachings of Laozi, and then into the Way of the Celestial Master. The scriptural revelations of the fourth century are also folded into the Celestial Master narrative, as the Lingbao revelations are reduced to one of many auspicious events auguring the rise of Liu Yu,[95] and the Mao brothers are described as Directors of Destinies within the bureaucratic hierarchy headed by the three

---

90 DZ 1205: 1.6.a1, Bokenkamp, *Early*, 216.
91 DZ 1205: 1.7.a3, Bokenkamp, *Early*, 218.
92 These include the Way of Banners and Flowers, condemned as merely Buddhism, and the adherents of Way of Clear Water who revered water as the Dao. The latter cult is also mentioned in other sources, and seems to have been quite important in the southeastern coastal region; see Bokenkamp, *Early*, 218.
93 DZ 1205: 1.9a.1, Bokenkamp, *Early*, 222.
94 DZ 1205: 1.9b6–8, Bokenkamp, *Early*, 222–23.
95 DZ 1205: 1.9a7, Bokenkamp, *Early*, 222.

Celestial Masters themselves.[96] The chapter ends celebrating the *Writ of the Five-thousand Characters*, the *Daode jing*, as a text that "leads one to maintain the Dao and have longevity beyond life and death. The ancestral root of the Dao resides in this scripture."[97]

The first chapter of the *Inner Explanations* thus provides a cosmogonic and historical narrative that proves the primacy and superiority of the Celestial Master teaching. While the chapter also provides an idealized vision of some of the correct practices to be followed by the adherents, it is in the second chapter that we get a more detailed discussion of actual practices.

The chapter begins with an exposition of meditative practice based on *Daode jing*, which:

> leads one to maintain his source and secure one's root... Therefore, one should contemplate perfection and meditate upon the Dao, and strengthen and solidify one's root. If one does not lose one's source, one may attain longevity and not die.[98]

We should note that contemplation of the Dao is not a metaphysical exercise, but a necessity to maintain life, for without the pneuma of the Dao 道氣 one would die. On the other hand, meditation would lead to transcendence. Importantly, this passage ends with a quote from an unnamed scripture:

> A tower of a hundred feet is served by its base.[99] This is precisely what this means.

The next passage begins with a series of sentences, which are elaborations of lines from the *Daode jing*, here adapted as a metaphysical exposition of the Dao's pneuma:

> The pneuma of the Dao is ultimately subtle, it cannot be seen and it cannot be heard.[100] If you wish to welcome it, it has no beginning; if you wish to follow it, it has no end. It envelops and encloses the six directions, it carries and supports heaven and earth. Its virtue is more honored than that of the superior

---

96 DZ 1205: 1.9a4, Bokenkamp, *Early*, 221.
97 DZ 1205: 1.10a8–9, Bokenkamp, *Early*, 224.
98 DZ 1205: 2.1a.
99 Cf. *Daode jing* 64: "A nine-storied tower arises from a pile of earth" 九層之臺起於累土.
100 Cf. *Daode jing* 14: "Gaze at it, it cannot be seen; naming it as 'subtle'; Listen to it, it cannot be heard ... Look up at it, one cannot see its head; Following it, one cannot see its back." 視之而弗見, 名之曰微; 聽之而弗聞, 名曰希 ... 迎之不見其首, 隨之不見其後. This phrasing follows the Mawangdui recension, which in this case seems closer than other recensions; Liu Xiaogan 劉笑敢, *Laozi gujin – wuzhong duikan yu xiping yinlun* 老子古今 – 五種對勘與析評引論 (Beijing: Zhongguo shehui kexue chubanshe, 2006): 182–3.

lords; its merit is more eminent than that of the two principles. It is the lord of the spirit-luminaries.

The text continues to elaborate on the ineffability of the Dao, while simultaneously insisting on applying this knowledge to one's body. One begins by the realization that Dao is non-existence 道者無也, and that all existent things emanate from non-existence. One is then to apply this realization: "If one is able to examine non-existence, then one [can] forget his body" 能察無則忘其身.[101] Importantly, this passage continues to cite and elaborate on lines from the *Daode jing*. This hermeneutic is particularly significant as it is among the earliest examples of a Daoist ritual manual that directly grounds its practice in the *Daode jing*. This hermeneutic is particularly significant when we read later in the text that:

> In studying the Dao nothing comes before the *zhai* 齋. Externally, one will then be without pollution, and internally, the five organs will be purified and emptied. The descending perfected will summon one's spirits to dwell together with the Dao. One who is able to practice the formal *zhai* will merge his perfection with the Dao 合道真. One must not offend the taboos and precepts. Hence, the Celestial Master transmitted this instruction.[102]

The most important point to note here is that the early Celestial Master did not practice *zhai* rituals. As discussed in Chapter 3, the *zhai* rituals were developed in the Lingbao scriptures. The Lingbao *zhai* served as the structural framework for Lu Xiujing's systemization of ritual, to be discussed in the next section. As we saw, however, in the *Questions of the Duke Transcendent*, the Lingbao scriptures claimed that Zhang Daoling did receive the teaching of the Lingbao *zhai*. In that case, I argued that the point was to reject the Celestial Master ritual scheme and suborn it to the Lingbao ritual. It is, therefore, striking that this passage claims that it was the Celestial Master who transmitted the *zhai* method. I suggest that *Inner Explanations* is responding to the Lingbao claims by, on the one hand, accepting the assertion that Zhang Daoling received the *zhai* ritual method, while, on the other hand, claiming that this method is indeed the teaching of the Celestial Master, and not of the Lingbao scriptures.

The importance of *zhai* in the *Inner Explanations* indicates that this text was indeed a response to Lingbao ritual. We may recall here that in the first chapter of the text the author explains the importance of offering five bushels of rice:

> Those who revere the Dao but do not offer five bushels of rice are not members of the Way of the Covenantal Authority of Correct Unity of the Three Heavens. The precise intent of five bushels of rice is an offering to the

101 DZ 1205: 2.1b.
102 DZ 1205: 2.2b1.

five Thearchs in order to let them know the people's desire to revere the Dao. The sages thoroughly merge with the pneumas from beginning to end. Therefore the sagely do not die. The allotments of commoners are joined to rice. If they have no rice and grain then they would starve to death. They thus take that which is most valuable and offer it to the dark and mysterious. It is not that [the Thearchs] desire or require this rice.[103]

The offering of rice, a practice that was at the core of the earliest community, is here explained in terms of reverence to the five Thearchs. The little evidence we have of early Celestial Master ideology does not provide the five Thearchs with important ritual significance. The explanation given here for the ancient practice is new, and should also be seen as responding to the role of the five Thearchs in the Lingbao system. The incorporation of the five Thearchs into the Daoist ritual system dates back to *jiao* rite of the *Array of Five Talismans*, which inspired the Lingbao *zhai* ritual system. In my discussion of these developments in Chapter 2, I noted that the rejection of the flesh offering in the original rite as it was explained in the commentary and later adapted into the Lingbao ritual system reflects a major trend among Daoists as they distinguished themselves and their practices from other contemporary traditions. While I would not argue that this is evidence of direct impact of Celestial Master ideology, it does indicate some interaction between lineages that rejected blood rites and the lineage which transmitted the *jiao* rite. On the other hand, the explanation we find in the *Inner Explanation* for the rice offerings, and particularly the care the author takes to explain the symbolism of the rice, suggests that the acceptance of the five Thearchs into the Celestial Master ritual scheme was recent.

The *Inner Explanations* continues by emphasizing the importance of purification, both outer and inner, as one prepares to perform *zhai*. The text then criticizes contemporary members of the Way of the Celestial Master who rely on their talismans and registers for protection instead of performing rituals:

> Whenever I see the vulgar libationers of the present generation, I find they carry an excessive number of talismans and registers, but perform very few audiences and rites. They describe themselves as [the following] "I am a master of the great Dao, an accomplished Perfected person and do not fear contamination and dirt." Grasping scriptures, they say that the Perfected of the Dao have no fears, entering fire they are not burnt, entering water they are not frozen, entering a contaminated [place] they are not infected, entering [a place of] weapons they are unhurt. They say that they themselves have attained the perfection of the Dao. Isn't this laughable?

After critiquing contemporary libationers who do not perform sufficient rituals, but only seek their own protection and transcendence, the text resumes the

---

103 DZ 1205: 1.7b8–8a2; Bokenkamp, *Early*, 219 with emendations.

discussion of different traditions and practices. While the first chapter of the *Inner Teachings* explicitly rejects Buddhism, here the text adopts Buddhist rhetoric in comparing and contrasting Buddhist and Daoist practices. Daoism is labeled Great Vehicle (*dasheng* 大乘), the common translation for Māhāyana, while Buddhism is labeled Small Vehicle (*xiaosheng* 小乘), that is Hinayana:

> In studying the Dao there are several levels. Students of the Great Vehicle should be joyous and tranquil as they meditate upon perfection and infuse the mysterious [into themselves] 怡心恬寂思真注玄.[104] Externally, they are as though empty, while internally, they are like a golden citadel. Using fragrance they communicate with pneuma,[105] while their mouths forget words. With compassion they consider all beings, first thinking of saving others, only then saving themselves. They always have their mind set on ascending to transcendence and do not think of material and money. They turn their hearts to ritual and propitiation and do not labor their bodily spirits.[106] They seek perfection within themselves, and then to communicate with the mysterious. They think of merging with the Dao, and do not boast. They may be said to inhale and exhale the six-directions of space or to traverse and observe the unknown.[107]

The Daoist practitioner is here portrayed as a Bodhisattva, bringing salvation to others before saving himself. Yet, the rhetoric harks back to some of the earliest Daoist practices of *qi* cultivation and "forgetting words." The main point is that

104 "Infuse the mysterious into themselves" translates the term *zhuxuan* 注玄. This term appears in several texts, as a reference to the inhalation of pneumas during meditation. For example, the *Jade Instructions* include instructions for the ingestion of the talismanic scripts, discussed in Chapter 3. The instruction for the ingestion of the sixteen graphs of central, yellow heaven are: "for guiding and directing the twelve pneumas of the yellow Thearch and ingesting the yellow sprouts, they must all be inscribed in vermilion on white paper. After entering full meditating state, swallow them at once. Then, above direct your primordial pneuma to the nine heavens, and below infuse the mysterious from your chest into your gate of marvels. The pneuma in your great granary (stomach) will of itself become replete, and your spleen will not be drained, but will spontaneously blaze forth." 導引黃帝十二炁, 服食黃牙, 皆赤書白紙上. 存思訖頓而服之, 則上引元炁於九天, 下注玄膺於妙門, 太倉氣糧而自充, 脾府不澳而自熏 (DZ 352: 2. 9b). A more difficult use is found in the *Five Ascendant Talismans*: "The *Writ of the Way and Power in Five–thousand Graphs* is the most profound of all the scriptures, the meaning of expounding the Dao, the complete instruction of the perfect and upright. Its graphs are blazing. If you recite it for a thousand days, your void heart will be infused with its mystery and you will ascend as a transcendent in broad daylight and become one of the four-floreate perfected, who are the ancestors of the eminent transcendents." 道德五千文, 經之至賾, 宣道之意, 正真之教盡也. 煥乎其文矣. 誦之千日虛心注玄白日昇仙上為太上四華真人此高仙之宗 (DZ 671: 2.13b–14a).

105 The mysterious phrase 香以通氣 may refer to meditatively journeying upon breath or incense for communication with the spirits.

106 *Huixin* 迴心, or more often 廻心, is a Buddhist term meaning "conversion" or "turn one's thought toward…," Digital Dictionary of Buddhism, "*Huixin*" (http://www.buddhism-dict.net/cgi-bin/xpr-ddb.pl?5e.xml+id('b5efb-5fc3').

107 DZ 1205: 2. 2b10.

transcendence and salvation require single minded purpose and relinquishing of mundane affairs. The focus of the practitioner of the Great Vehicle is contrasted with the scattered mind of the students of the Small Vehicle. Their lack of focus is indicated by the long list of desires, merging various mundane wishes with more transcendent goals and punctuated by the repetitive *you* 又, which I translate as "or":

> The students of the Small Vehicle are not at all like this. Considering much talk as good and a lot of affairs as proving their diligence, they knock their heads together, depleting and damaging their bodily gods. They compete with words, while their minds within are not focused. Grasping incense with three fingers, they endlessly boast about their attainment. Then they seek to transcend the world as divine transcendent and to ascend in flight to Upper Clarity. Or they wish to serve in office and rise in the ranks, and ride in five-horse chariots. Or they wish their family to flourish for generations with thousands of sons and myriad grandchildren. Or they wish to have money and accumulate goods, with slave men and women milling about. Or they wish to extend their years and avoid danger and to retain their vigor when old. Or they wish to manage the people and collect taxes to open myriad paths. Or they wish to open their heart to awakening and to have acuity of eyes and ears. Or they wish to drive far the hundred ghosts and to ensure illness does not enter their gate. Or they wish to be a compassionate father and filial son, a cherishing husband and have a chaste wife. Or they wish to have piercing vision and to penetratingly see to heaven's sources. Or they wish to exchange goods and welcome friends. Or they wish to contemplate perfection and meditate upon the Dao so that jade maidens descend to their chamber. What they seek is plenty and what they esteem is bothersome. This does not match with Laozi's original teaching of maintaining unity. Therefore, their mouth is exhausted with their pleading words, their body is worn-out by the pain of bending and twisting, their heart is weary from so much desire, and their spirits are tired from coming and going. The Scripture says: "excessive labor damages one's spirits, excessive talk damages one's pneuma, excessive walking damages one's muscles, excessive vision damages one's eyes, carrying heavy burdens damages one's muscles, eating too much causes illness, and engaging in meaningless business damages one's life-allotment." All these do not concur with the methods of self-cultivation.

There is nothing Buddhist about the practices and transcendent goals criticized here. Rather, they point to rival Daoist practitioners, such as those lesser practitioners who seek to ascend to the heaven of Upper Clarity, an oblique critique of the Shangqing scriptures. The main point, though, is the excessive engagement of other Daoists in the mundane practices and affairs of the world. Rather, the text advocates complete physical and sensory withdrawal, resonant with Laozi's teaching. The text recognizes that the practices pursued by the students of the Small Vehicle are efficacious in the mundane realm, and may even help in cultivating goodness, but they are insufficient for the ultimate goals of transcendence:

> Students of the Small Vehicle knock their teeth in the darkness and seek a numinous response. This way of transformation causes one to cultivate goodness, eradicate sins and correct one's errors, but it is not a method for managing the body, prolonging years, increased longevity, and ascending in flight. That is why they are called students of the Small Vehicle.[108]

The text now turns to a direct and explicit criticism of Buddhist meditation practice, which is contrasted with Daoist visualization techniques. Ironically, the Buddhist discourse of Great and Small Vehicle is here turned against the Buddhists themselves as their contemplative practice is reduced by the Daoist author to simple counting of breaths:

> The practitioners of Buddhism (*shamendao ren* 沙門道人) are students of the Small Vehicle. Hence when sitting in silence they count their own breaths. Upon reaching ten they start again. Year in and year out they do not even for a moment forget this. The Buddhist methods do not include visualization of the spirits of the body. Therefore, they depend on counting breaths in order to cut off external thoughts. Daoists (*daoshi* 道士) are students of the Great Vehicle. Hence they regularly contemplate the perfected spirits of the body: their form and shape, clothes and colors. They guide and lead the spirits to come and go, just as if facing a lord.[109]

While this passage is no more than a Daoist caricature of Buddhist meditation practices, such as that found in the *Sutra on Mindfulness of Counting Breaths* (*Ānāpānasmṛti*), translated by An Shigao,[110] its rhetoric stresses the distinction Daoists themselves made between their practices and those of Buddhists. Importantly, however, the Daoist practice celebrated here is of visualization (*cun* 存) of the "perfected spirits" 真神, the gods within the body. This terminology is indebted to the Shangqing scriptures, which had just been criticized in the previous passage.

We find here a complex rhetorical strategy, in which explicit criticism of Buddhism allows for silent erasure of rival Daoist lineages, while their practices are adopted into a new synthesis under the label of Celestial Master Daoism. The text concludes with a reiteration of the differences between practitioners of the Great Vehicle, who "do not stop for even a moment, so that external thoughts do not enter. The spirit perfected will descend to them if the heart is without many

---

108 DZ 1205: 2.3b5–4b2.
109 DZ 1205: 2.4b3–7. *Shamen* is a transcription of Śramana, and is among the earliest attested terms used in China to refer to Buddhists.
110 *Anpan shouyi jing* 安般守意經 T 602.

affairs." On the other hand, "students of the Small Vehicle have a hundred affairs that pull at them, or they are bound by worries, anxieties and external thoughts."[111] Finally, the text reminds the reader of the ultimate difference between the Great and Small Vehicle:

> The paths of the Great and Small Vehicles are different, and you must understand that they are not the same. The student of the Small Vehicle is good at argumentation and words; he may become a teacher of the age 世師. The student of the Great Vehicle conserves his pneuma, maintains the one, and treasures his bodily substance.

The final line may hint at the actual social situation of the author Xu. Those practitioners, be they Buddhist or of rival Daoist lineages, whom he considered of the Small Vehicle, were accorded high social status, patronage at court, or local support. This success, he argued, was due to their rhetorical skill. But it was indeed this very success in the mundane that would sap their strength and vigor. To those who would follow him, who would remain unencumbered by social and political demands, he promised salvation in their very bodies.

We should note, however, that the orthodoxy imagined in the *Inner Explanations* is not an explicit integration of different Daoist lineages and practices. Rather, it is an orthodoxy based on reformulated Celestial Master practices that include *zhai*, and discourse that includes the Bodhisattva ideal. Both of these notions were imported into this new vision of the Way of the Celestial Master from Lingbao, and are in fact a response to the evident success of Lingbao Daoism. However, as is made clear in the cosmogonic and historical narrative in the first chapter of the text, the only Way cosmologically appropriate for China is the Way of the Celestial Master. In fact, we may see the explicit criticism of Buddhism as oblique criticism of Daoist lineages that had adopted Buddhist ideas and practices, as exemplified in the Lingbao scriptures. Rather than explicitly attacking the Lingbao and Shangqing texts, Xu, the author, incorporated references demoting these texts to omens heralding the rise of the Liu-Song dynasty, in the case of Lingbao, or by asserting that the Mao brothers were, in fact, adherents of the Way of the Celestial Master.

Lu Xiujing's historical, ritual, and canonic project

Unlike the authors of many of the texts discussed so far, about whom we know very little if anything at all, Lu Xiujing's life is relatively well known. Besides references in the texts authored by Lu and others, much of our information is based on the biographical details preserved in Ma Shu's *Daoxue zhuan*.[112] Most

---

111 DZ 1205: 2.4b7–9.
112 The fragments concerning Lu Xiujing are collated and translated in Bumbacher, *Fragments*, 204–19. For a recent study, see Zhong Guofa 鍾國發, "Lu Xiujing pingzhuan" 陸修靜評傳, in *Tao Hongjing Pingzhuan* 陶弘景評傳 (Nanjing: Nanjing University Press, 2005): 527–613.

significantly, Lu's biography reveals close links with the Liu-Song court. These links may help explain both the context of his project of creating orthodoxy and the relative success of this project. Despite these details, it is difficult to date his texts. In particular, it is unclear when he wrote his *Abridged Codes for the Daoist Community*, which is an attempt to reform the Way of the Celestial Master, and when he switched his allegiance to Lingbao Daoism. Intriguingly, none of the preserved fragments of the *Daoxue zhuan* allude to his practices as a member of the Celestial Master community.

In his *Preface to the Lingbao Catalogue*, Lu introduces himself as Disciple of the Three Caverns. As this text dates to 437, I suggest that the *Abridged Codes* must have been written earlier. We should recall that Kou Qianzhi presented scriptures to the northern Tuoba Wei court in 423. In 425, emperor Wei erected the Altar of the Great Dao Temple 大道壇廟 at the capital for Kou Qianzhi. In the south, Liu Yu's rise to power may have motivated Master Xu to compose the *Inner Explanations*.[113] These two efforts at reforming the Way of the Celestial Master provide a suitable context in which Lu Xiujing could have composed the *Abridged Codes*, perhaps as response to Kou Qianzhi's success, however short lived, at establishing a new Celestial Master orthodoxy with himself as Celestial Master.

The fragmentary references to Lu Xiujing in the *Daoxue zhuan* provide us with a few biographical, albeit somewhat hagiographical, details. Lu was a scion of an elite clan in Dongqian in Wuxing county (in modern Zhejiang), in the southern coastal region. While still engaged in mundane affairs and married, he began practicing some austerities, including a regimen of celibacy: "although externally involved in worldly affairs, internally he maintained chastity and simplicity. At a young age he already cut off grains, and had a separate bed and slept alone".[114] He was still employed in an official capacity when he announced to a colleague: "It is difficult to get a second allotment of time. I will abandon wife and children, shed my official post, and concentrate my efforts on expounding the teaching, without wasting time on waking and sleeping".[115] He soon left his home and entered Mt. Yunmeng to live in reclusion. A narrative dating to this period of reclusion tells of a time Lu descended from the mountain and stayed with his family for a few days. One of his daughters suddenly became ill. As she was at death's door, a family member begged him to help save her. Lu replied:

> I have originally abandoned my wife and children and devoted myself to the mysterious ultimate. Today, when I pass my home its affairs are just as though I were in an inn; how can I once again have a mind concerned with

113 The historical narrative in the first *juan* begins with the primordial moment of emergence to the recent enthronement of Liu Yu, a moment which Master Xu describes as: "in one stroke, heaven totally eradicates the useless and regulates the correct, sweeping away the stale pneumas by means of the Dao. Is this not a pledge of good faith from the Most High?" DZ 1205: 1.9a; Bokenkamp, *Early*, 222.
114 Bumbacher, *Fragments*, 215.
115 Bumbacher, *Fragments*, 218.

desires? He then put on his coat and departed, without looking back. A day after he left, the daughter's illness was cured.

The main point of this narrative may be the daughter's miraculous cure in response to Lu's complete renunciation of his family. This emphasis of complete renunciation indicates a major shift in Daoist practice, and the beginning of Daoist monasticism.

Later sources report that he traveled throughout the realm to several sacred sites.[116] At some point, Lu took up residence by the Pubu cliff on the southeast face of Mt. Lu, where he built a monastery named Monastery of the Altar of Simplicity and Solitude (Jianji tanguan 簡寂壇館). Subsequently, the name of the monastery became his sobriquet.

It was in the 430s that Lu must have been initiated into Lingbao Daoism, for by 437 he had completed the *Catalogue of the Lingbao Scriptures*, which he addressed to Song emperor Wen (Liu Yilong 劉義隆 407–453, r. 424–53). Whether or not the emperor actually received this text is impossible to tell, but his fame certainly reached the court.[117]

Although he is best known as a systematizer of Lingbao ritual, his subsequent activities reveal that he continued to practice Celestial Master rites. The introductory passage to his *Writ of the Five Stimuli* reports that in the winter of 453, he performed with his acolytes a Retreat of Mud and Ashes of the Three Primordials (*sanyuan tutan zhai* 三元塗炭齋). This performance prompted him to compose the *Writ of the Five Stimuli*. In his own words, he had two purposes in writing the text. His first goal was to instruct his acolytes in a set of five meditations which he composed in order to "encourage and console" 勸慰 his acolytes in the freezing cold and hardship during the ritual.[118] The second purpose of the text, Lu tells us, was to provide a "complete and orderly list of the various *zhai* rites."[119]

This was the first such systemization of Daoist ritual. While the hierarchic scheme is centered upon nine Lingbao *zhai*, it includes two Shangqing rites at the head of the list. The Retreat of Mud and Ashes itself is listed last as an extraneous rite, following the nine Lingbao *zhai*. While Lu does not specify the source of this rite, it was probably based upon an earlier Celestial Master rite of repentance.[120] Later adherents of Celestial Master Daoism reintroduced the Retreat of Mud and Ashes as one of the basic rites in a reformulated Celestial Master ritual system, which was based upon the Lingbao models.[121]

---

116 Zhong, "Lu Xiujing," 531.
117 For a brief survey of Lu's relationship with the Liu-Song court, see Bokenkamp, "Buddhism, Lu Xiujing."
118 *Dongxuan lingbao wugan wen* 洞玄靈寶五感文 DZ 1278.1b8–10. For a study of the ritual and meditations in this text, see Stephen Bokenkamp, "Sackcloth and Ashes, Self and Family in the Tutan Zhai" in Florian C. Reiter and Poul Andersen, eds. *Scriptures, Schools, and Forms of Practices in Taoism* (Wiesbaden: Harrassowitz Verlag, 2005): 33–48.
119 DZ 1278.1b10.
120 Bokenkamp, *Early*, 401 n.58; Lü, *Tangqian*, 13, 222–3.
121 Lagerwey, *Wu-shang*, 156–8; idem, "Le rituel Taoïste selon lu xiujing," 13; Lü, *Tangqian*, 13, 222–5.

Lu's reputation grew so that in 467 Song emperor Ming (Liu Yu 劉彧 439–72, r. 465–72) summoned him to court, as the emperor "wished to spread the Daoist teaching" 思弘道教. After repeated refusals, Lu finally agreed to the summons citing as his models Laozi's support for the Zhou and Ge Hong's aid to the Wu court.[122] Lu participated in a debate at court between adherents of Dark Learning (*xuanyan zhishi* 玄言之士) and Buddhists (*shamen* 沙門). Lu bested all participants, and so impressed the audience of nobles that they reported his prowess to the emperor. Ten days later the emperor again convened a gathering. He personally asked about the Dao, and inquired about the utmost object of veneration 問道, 諮求宗極. Lu "explained the Gate of Mysteries 玄門,[123] and expounded upon samsara."[124] He was then asked about the "Daoist explanation of the three times" 道家說三世. The term "three times" is a Buddhist term referring to past, present, and future, used to explain the workings of karma across rebirth. Lu, however, explains this notion by citing both Laozi and Zhuangzi:

> The scripture says: "I do not know whose son it is, it is the image of the ancestor of Di."[125] When there is a 'before,' then there must be an 'after'; if there are before and after, then there must be a middle. Zhuangzi says: "as one is born, one dies."[126] These two lines explain the three times. But as their words are terse and their principles profound the world has not yet understood them."[127]

Lu's response implicitly asserts the priority of the ancient Daoist classics over the Buddhist explanations. By citing the *Daode jing* and *Zhuangzi* Lu may simply have opted to use texts familiar to all at court. But this choice may also be indicative of the hermeneutic we already saw in our discussion of *Inner Explanations*, which used citations from the *Daode jing* to explicate and authenticate specific practices. Lu Xiujing uses the same hermeneutic in his *Candle of the Law Scripture*.[128] This text consists of ten meditations composed by Lu Xiujing to be read prior to various stages of the *zhai* in order to explicate the rite and prepare the

---

122 *Fragments*, Bumbacher, 210–11. Laozi's position as Archivist to the Zhou court is mentioned in Sima Qian's biography of Laozi, SJ 104. Ge Hong served the Wu in a military capacity, but there is no record of his being summoned to aid the court after his retirement to Mt. Luofu in 306.

123 Referring to the last words of the opening verse of the *Daode jing*.

124 I follow Bumbacher's interpretation of the term *liutong* 流統, Bumbacher, *Fragments*, 213, n. 478.

125 *Daode jing* 4.

126 *Zhuangzi yinde*, 4.42; Angus C. Graham translates as "simultaneously with being alive one dies," see *Chuang-tzu, The Inner Chapters* (Hackett: Indianapolis, 2001): 52. See the discussion of this passage in Bokenkamp, "Buddhism, Lu Xiujing," 195–6.

127 Bumbacher, *Fragments*, 214.

128 *Taishang dongxuan lingbao fazhu jing* 太上洞玄靈寶法燭經 DZ 349. The first meditation is found in *Dongxuan lingbao zhai shuo guangzhu jiefa dengzhu yuanyi* 靈寶齋說光燭戒罰燈祝願儀 DZ 524, which includes explanations and instructions for performing *zhai* culled from Lu Xiujing's writings. Kristofer Schipper considers DZ 349 to be by Lu Xiujing (Schipper and Verellen, *Taoist Canon*, 253); the editors of *Zhonghua daozang* argue this text is a compilation by an unknown author of the Sui-Tang, similar in content to DZ 524 (*ZHDZ* 4.415).

participants. Significantly, each sermon ends with a quote from the *Daode jing* that is meant to sum up the meaning inherent in each aspect of the *zhai*.

The emperor was so impressed with Lu that he erected the Monastery for Venerating the Void (Chongxu guan 崇虛館), in the northern suburbs of the capital, where he installed Lu.[129] Based in this magnificent establishment, Lu expounded his teachings, and "the flourishing of Daoism (*daojiao*) began at that time."[130]

In 471, Lu again led his acolytes to perform the Exposure *zhai* of the Three Primordials (*sanyuan luzhai* 三元露齋, an alternative name to the *Tutan zhai*) on behalf of the ill emperor Wen. The ritual lasted for 20 days, until an auspicious yellow vapor appeared. The narrative in the *Daoxue zhuan* ends with the emperor returning to health.[131] The emperor, however, died within the same year.

Emperor Wen's relationship with Lu Xiujing is critical to our understanding of Lu's work, for the emperor not only established the Chongxu guan, but he also ordered Lu to compose a Daoist canon. Lu presented his *Catalogue of the Scriptures of the Three Caverns* to the emperor in 471.[132] Unfortunately, this *Catalogue* is no longer extant. We can only rely on Lu's extant writings to determine whether his canonization of the Lingbao scriptures, systemization of ritual, and construction of Daoist history cohere into a cogent project of creating orthodoxy.[133] Among the questions we need to address are:

1   Is the vision of the idealized Celestial Master community in the *Abridged Codes* superseded by Lu's works based on the Lingbao scriptures, such as the *Catalogue of the Three Caverns* and the ritual manuals?
2   Did Lu Xiujing envision an alternative community to the Celestial Master ecclesia, based on Lingbao ritual?

129 About thirty years later, in 491, emperor Xiaowen of the Northern Wei moved the Daoist altar (*daochang* 道場 or *daotan* 道壇) that was erected for Kou Qianzhi to the south of the capital Ye, and renamed it Monastery for Venerating the Void (Chongxu si 崇虛寺); *Weishu* 7B.168, 114.3055. The term Chongxu used to name the two Daoist institutions in the north and south harks back to the Celestial Master parish system. According to the *Taizhen ke*, an early Celestial Master codex (cited in the Tang encyclopedia *Yaoxiu keyi jielu chao* 要修科儀戒律鈔 DZ 463: 10.1a), the central structure in each of the Celestial parishes was named Hall for Venerating the Void (Chongxu tang 崇虛堂). This text is not extant except in fragmentary citations and is therefore very difficult to date. I thank John Lagerwey for this point.
130 Bumbacher, *Fragments*, 214; Zhong, "Lu Xiujing," 561.
131 Bumbacher, *Fragments*, 205.
132 Chen, *Daozang*, 106; Bokenkamp, "Buddhism."
133 Besides the works already mentioned above, his works on ritual include *Transmission Rites of Lingbao Scriptures Taishang dongxuan lingbao shoudu yi* 太上洞玄靈寶授度儀 DZ 528, *Documents and Writs of Lingbao Taishang dongxuan lingbao zhongjian wen* 太上洞玄靈寶眾簡文 DZ 410; "Ancient Protocol for Construction of *zhai* in the Nocturnal Invocation" 古法宿啟建齋儀 preserved as the main text in *juan* 16 of *Wushang huanglu dazhai licheng yi* 無上黃籙大齋立成儀 DZ 508, compiled by Jiang Shuyu 蔣叔輿 (1162–1223). For details on this compilation, see Schipper and Verellen, *Taoist Canon*, 1014–18.

3   Why did Lu Xiujing not include the Celestial Master texts in his canon, but restrict it to the texts of the Three Caverns, a notion introduced in the Lingbao scriptures?

It is clear that Lu's Daoist canon cannot be studied in isolation, but it must be placed in the context of his ritual systemization, and his formulation of the Lingbao canon itself. Stephen Bokenkamp argues that the absence of Celestial Master texts in the Three Caverns scheme may be explained by the claims made in the Lingbao scriptures regarding their own primordial nature. As we saw in Chapter 3, the Lingbao scriptures claimed they were elaborations of the primordial talismanic scripts. The Lingbao scriptures thus superseded all previous revelations. Zhang Daoling, the first Celestial Master, is himself co-opted into the Lingbao system as one of the deities present when Ge Xuan is first granted the Lingbao scriptures.[134]

The clearest presentation of Lu's full ritual system is in his *Writ of the Five Stimuli*. The twelve rites are presented in a ritual hierarchy, and divided into two groups. The list begins with two Shangqing rites from the Cavern of Perfection. This is followed by nine rites, which are defined as Lingbao *zhai*:

1   Retreat of Golden Register 金祿齋 to ensure harmony and peace in the state.
2   Retreat of Yellow Register 黃祿齋 to extinguish karmic offenses of ancestors to the ninth generation.
3   Retreat of Contract with the Perfected 明真齋 to save the souls of the Daoist's parents.
4   Retreat of Three Primordials 三元齋 to offer repentance for Daoist's own sins.
5   Retreat of Eight Nodes 八節齋 to offer repentance for the sins of all beings in the present generation.
6   Retreat of Spontaneity 自然齋 to dissolve disasters and avert misfortune.
7   Retreat of the Three Sovereigns 三皇齋 to expel all defilements by ritual purification and bathing.
8   Retreat of the Great One 太一齋 to honor unity of the universe.
9   Retreat of Instruction 指教齋 ritual for achieving mental clarity.

The list of the nine *zhai* 齋 includes a brief statement regarding their purpose, followed by a short note with instructions for performance. These instructions, however, are extremely brief and are probably no more than preparatory or mnemonic remarks. We do find detailed instructions for these rites in Lingbao scriptures, which were the source for Lu Xiujing's work, or in the sixth-century

---

134 Bokenkamp, "Buddhism, Lu Xiujing," 188–9.

compendium *Secret Essentials Without Peer* (*Wushang biyao* 無上秘要),[135] which is based to a large extent on Lu Xiujing's work.

Lu ends his list of rites in the *Writ of Five Stimuli* with the Retreat of Mud and Ashes, which is presented as a distinct rite and outside the other categories. As mentioned above, Lu may have composed this text in the context of performing the Retreat of Mud and Ashes in 453. This was a Celestial Master rite, but save for the details given here, the only instructions for this rite are given in the compendium *Wushang biyao*, which presents the performer of this rite as simultaneously ranked in the Celestial Master hierarchy and within the Lingbao ritual hierarchy.[136]

The list of rites in the *Writ of the Five Stimuli* resonates to some extent with the notion of the Three Caverns, but is not coherent with our understanding of the Three Caverns. While the list of rites is divided among Shangqing and Lingbao rites, albeit a preponderance of Lingbao rites, there is no distinct category of Sanhuang rites. The seventh of the Lingbao rites, however, is the Retreat of the Three Sovereigns of the Cavern of Divinity. Thus, the third of the Caverns is not presented as a distinct category, but is rather embedded within the Lingbao category.

Moreover, examination of the nine Lingbao *zhai* reveals the deep impact of Celestial Master rites on these rites. John Lagerwey's close study of this ritual scheme shows that the Retreat of Mud and Ashes was not the only Celestial Master rite that was included in Lu's ritual scheme. In fact, of the nine, three rites were developed in the early Celestial Master community: the Retreat of Spontaneity, the Retreat of the Great One, and the Retreat of Instruction. The other Lingbao *zhai* rites were also based, to a large extent, upon Celestial Master ritual models.[137]

Clearly, the ritual scheme of the *Writ of the Five Stimuli* does not reflect the textual collections of the Caverns as found in later compendia. Rather, the text seems to reflect a ritual scheme that suborns various Daoist practices under and within the Lingbao ritual. It may therefore seem surprising that the Shangqing rites are presented at the head of the list. We should recall that this was a rhetorical strategy in the Lingbao scriptures themselves. While being placed first, the Shangqing texts and rites are described as beyond, and indeed outside, the ken of practices for the current age.

Lu Xiujing defines the main difference between the Shangqing and Lingbao *zhai* in terms borrowed from the *Daode jing*. The former are introduced as "based in non-action 無為為宗,"[138] while the latter are defined as "based in action" 有為為宗. Although labeled *zhai*, thus suborning them within the Lingbao ritual

---

135 On this text, see comments in the Afterword.
136 The title of the main performer is given as "Parish-libationer of the Celestial Master and ritual master of the supreme three caverns of Most High Lingbao, master of the sacred peak…" 係天師某治祭酒太上靈寶無上三洞法師某嶽先生. See *Wushang biyao* 無上祕要 DZ 1138, *juan* 50; Lagerwey, *Wu-shang*, 156–58.
137 For details see John Lagerwey's unpublished manuscript, "Le Rituel Taoïste selon Lu Xiujing,"; also see Lü, *Tangqian*, 185–8.
138 DZ 1278.5a3–4, the text mistakenly has 無為為無宗; see Lagerwey, "Rituel," 1 n.3.

scheme, we should remember that Shangqing practices were not public rites and not systematized. Rather, they were diverse individual self-cultivation practices. Indeed, Lu's description of the Shangqing rites harks back to the Shangqing revelations texts and their antecedent methods of meditative cultivation:

> Breathe as a fetus, then you will observe the divine trigger in your heart: pacifying your belly, fasting, stilling the spirits, quieting the pneuma, relinquishing form, intention, and ego, in absence merge with the Dao.

> 胎息後視心時所神機, 寂胃, 虛申, 眠神, 靜炁, 遺形志體, 無與道合.

Lu glosses the final phrase: "the Dao embodies emptiness and void, the ego is full; hence there is distinction. Now that you are able to forget, you can attain mysterious merging 玄合."[139]

While defining the Shangqing rites as based on "non-action" would give them priority over the Lingbao rites that are defined as rooted in action, Lu clearly advocates the superior efficacy of the Lingbao rites for communal and individual salvation. Perhaps, Lu is suggesting that that the individual practices are beyond the ken of the community he sought to establish. Or perhaps with the Bodhisattva ideal of universal salvation introduced in the Lingbao scriptures, which as we saw was also accepted by the author of *Inner Explanations*, the individual practice seemed selfish and narrow. The Lingbao rites were in fact predicated on communal salvation, ranging from the state as a whole to the practitioners' own ancestors to the ninth generation.

For example, as we saw above, the *Questions by the Duke Transcendent* insists that the core of Daoist practice is salvation for others: "First, he saves others, and later saves himself."[140]

While this passage does not explicitly reject Shangqing practice, the first part of the *Questions by the Duke Transcendent* insists on the primacy of the Lingbao rite, and describes its practitioners as "masters of the Great Vehicle."[141]

The text continues by stating that there is a similar rite, known as the *zhai* method of the Three Heavens. This rite was revealed to the Celestial Master, here also entitled Ritual Master of the Three Heavens, who then composed the *Scripture of Instruction in the Teaching*. By thus asserting the primacy of the Lingbao *zhai* because of its focus on salvation for others, and claiming that the Celestial Master had received a version of this practice as well, there was little room left for placing the individualist Shangqing meditation methods, which thus seem lacking indeed.

Perhaps more importantly, the *Questions by the Duke Transcendent* claims that Zhang Daoling's *Scripture of Instruction in the Teaching* is somehow equivalent to the *Five Ascendant Talismans* that is described as the celestial version of the

---

139 DZ 1278.5a. Compare with *Daode jing* 56 "mysterious sameness" 玄同.
140 DZ 1114.5a–6a.
141 S 1351, lines 31–3, ZHDZ, vol. 4, 119c.

teaching. As we saw in Chapter 3, the *Five Ascendant Talismans* was among the earliest of the Lingbao texts, and reveals an early attempt at the synthesis achieved in the more developed scriptures. The text begins with a reformulation of the five Lingbao talismans as primordial and cosmogonic, while the second chapter recasts several older ritual practices into a rite by which an individual practitioner could transform his ritual space and time into the moment of establishment of the Han dynasty.[142] A particularly interesting aspect of this text is the introduction of a ritual scheme entitled Twenty-four Charts of Lingbao.

Most, if not all of these charts are based on practices mentioned in *Baopuzi*, but Ge Hong does not refer to the charts in any order, and they are scattered among his list of charts and talismans.[143] It seems that the concept of the Twenty-four Charts was an innovation by the author of the text, perhaps Ge Chaofu, who wished to collate and systematize the practices he found most important in his family's tradition into a unified, coherent, and hierarchical ritual order. This ritual scheme became the focus of another of the Lingbao scriptures, the aforementioned *Scripture of Twenty-four Charts*, which, as we saw, presents a slightly different version of the Three Caverns. In this text, the Twenty-four Charts are placed within the developed cosmology of the Lingbao scriptures. Like the talismanic writs, which were the primordial forms of the scriptures, the Twenty-four Charts too are said to have emanated in the Void Cavern, and to have been revealed by the Primordial Celestial Worthy at the beginning of human time, when the Fiery Brilliance (*chiming* 赤明) eon initiated its radiance.[144]

The centrality of the Five Talismans, recasting of old ritual forms in the idiom of visualization and Buddhism, and the collation and systemization of the Twenty-four Charts in the *Scripture of the Five Ascendant Talismans* are characteristic of the Lingbao synthesis. The further elaboration of the Twenty-four Charts into the cosmological pattern of the Three Caverns helps reveal stages in the development of the Lingbao scriptures. Most importantly, however, for our purpose here is that in the *Scripture of the Five Ascendant Talismans*, the word *zhai* does not refer to a developed ritual program, but is used in an older, more generic sense of "fasting, abstinence, ritual." For example, the instructions for transmission of the Twenty-four Charts include the following: "On an East-well day bathe in orchid infusion, purify and cleanse your body, abstain and follow the taboos when entering the chamber."[145]

142 For details, see Raz, "Time Manipulation."
143 See Raz, "Time Manipulation"; Bokenkamp, "Sources," 459–60. While Ge Hong lists a "Scripture of Twenty-four Life [bestowing charts?]" 二十四生經 in his bibliographic chapter, there is no evidence linking it and the various charts and talismans associated with the Twenty-four Charts (Wang, *Baopuzi*, 333).
144 DZ 1407: 1a1, 1b9. *Chiming* eon is the third cosmic era, in which the primal and inaugural pneumas appeared and heaven and earth divided; see Bokenkamp, *Early*, 381. See DZ 457.2a, DZ 23.11b, DZ 87: 2.7a.
145 DZ 671: 2.11a4. The word *zhai* appears several times in the text: 1.12a1: "You should obtain the Lingbao scriptures; abstain and purify and swallow talismans" 當得靈寶經, 齋潔服符; 1.11a5: "enter the ritual chamber" 入齋堂; 2.1a10: "purify and exorcise your hall to make it a ritual

The *Scripture of the Five Ascendant Talismans* thus does not include references to Zhang Daoling, or any obvious Celestial Master links, and it does not include a ritual scheme resembling the developed *zhai* rites. The importance of the text is in revealing an early version of the Lingbao synthesis, that is, the adaptation and reformulation of older ritual techniques into the new Lingbao ritual idiom. These rituals, however, are not the more developed Lingbao *zhai* rites. Indeed, the rituals actually presented in this text were not included among the *zhai* methods listed by Lu Xiujing. Nevertheless, this text is mentioned in the *Questions of Duke Transcendent* as the primordial *zhai* method taught to Zhang Daoling. Moreover, the *Ascendant Talismans* is said to be the primordial form of the *Scripture of Instruction*, attributed to Zhang Daoling. What are we to make of this claim?

As shown by Lü Pengzhi, the *Scripture of Instruction of the Teaching*, which provided detailed instructions for the Retreat, was composed within the Celestial Master community on the basis of the Lingbao scriptures and in response to the *Lingbao zhai*. Lü further argues that the now lost *Zhijiao jing* was composed after the emergence of the initial Lingbao revelations, the so-called "Ancient" texts, but prior to the appearance of the "New" Lingbao scriptures.[146] I agree with Lü's analysis, that the Retreat detailed in the *Scripture of Instruction* was an attempt to emulate the Lingbao *zhai*, while maintaining a distinct communal identity. I would add that the reference in the *Questions of Duke Transcendent* is thus a response by a Lingbao author to the *Scripture of Instruction of the Teaching*, placing it within the Lingbao cosmology. The reference to Celestial Master Zhang Ling is not a celebratory note, as much as an acceptance and subversion of a claim first made in the *Scripture of Instruction of the Teaching*. In compiling his list of Lingbao rites, Lu Xiujing accepted the claims made in the Lingbao scriptures concerning their temporal primacy and ultimate efficacy. His inclusion of rites, which may have originated within the Celestial Master tradition, was predicated upon the earlier adaptation and reformulation of these rites within the Lingbao scriptures. Thus, Lu Xiujing's systematization of the Lingbao rituals and compilation of a canon were part of a vision for a new dispensation that would replace what he may have perceived as an obsolete Celestial Master community. His earlier attempt to reform the Celestial Master community, expressed in his *Codes to the Daoist Community*, may not have been successful for several reasons. First and foremost, he had no way of enforcing his particular vision on diverse Celestial Master

chamber" 清除堂中為齋室; 2.4b1: "enter the ritual chamber" 入齋堂; 2.4b3: "ritual method of the six-jia" 六甲齋法; 2.13a4: "on an auspicious day bathe, abstain and be tranquil" 吉日沐浴齋靜. For the significance of "east well" see Raz, "Time Manipulation."

146 Lü Pengzhi, "A Study of the Zhijiao Fast of Celestial Master Daoism," in Florian C. Reiter, ed. *Foundations of Daoist Ritual* (Wiesbaden: Harrassowitz, 2009): 165–88. If we accept Lü's identification of a line referring to "Teachings left over by the Celestial Master" in *Inner Teachings of the Three Heavens* (DZ 1205: 2.2b4) as a reference to *Retreat of Instruction*, then we may date the *Zhijiao jing* to about 420 CE.

groups existing in the early fifth century. Second, he may have been sincerely committed to the cosmological and ideological vision of the Lingbao scriptures. The vision of a unified cosmos generated by efficacious texts and guaranteeing universal salvation, all explained within the Chinese traditional cosmology, would certainly have been attractive to a scion of an elite family in the southern coastal polity of the fifth century.

Conclusion

In this chapter, I examined attempts at creating Daoist orthodoxy. The best known, and arguably most influential of these efforts at integration, was the systemization of ritual and canonization of the Lingbao scriptures by Lu Xiujing. We must remember, however, that he was not the first, and certainly not the last, to promote a particular vision of Daoist orthodoxy. Lu seems to have first tried to reform the Celestial Master community, but his later efforts at ritual systemization and canon formation were based upon the Lingbao scriptures. The Lingbao scriptures should be seen as an elaborate attempt to create an integrated Daoist community that would replace the Celestial Master community. The Lingbao rituals and scriptures borrow heavily from both Buddhist and Celestial Master sources, but this should be seen as a strategy for incorporating particular notions and practices, while rejecting the institutional aspects of these traditions. As Stephen Bokenkamp has shown in several publications, the Lingbao adaptation of Buddhist terminology and practice was an attempt to dislodge, and even supplant, Buddhism from its privileged place in Chinese society.

While Lu's particular vision of Daoism was soon superseded by other efforts, several core aspects of his creative program had lasting impact. The Lingbao *zhai* ritual form, systematized by Lu, became the model for all Daoist rituals thereafter. The categories of Three Caverns and Twelve Divisions remained as basic textual organizational schemes in later canons, even as ever more texts and lineages came to be included.

The continuing interaction between the various Daoist lineages as they competed through texts and practices is far too complex to delineate fully. However, the brief examination of the development of the Celestial Master Retreat of Instruction as a response to the Lingbao challenge, and its subsequent incorporation within the Lingbao system itself provides a glimpse of this process. Previous scholars have noticed similar processes of "ceaseless coming and going" or "reverberation" between Daoism and local traditions.[147] However, here we can see

---

147 "Coming and going" is borrowed from Rolf Stein's classic analysis of the interaction between "popular customs" and the emerging Daoist religion in medieval China, see Stein, "Religious Taoism." The notion of "reverberation" was introduced by Paul Katz to describe the complex interaction in which "ideas, values, and beliefs change as they pass from person to person," see *Demon Hordes and Burning Boats, The Cult of Marshal Wen in Late Imperial Chekiang* (Albany: SUNY, 1995): 114–15.

that similar complex processes formed the emerging Daoist lineages themselves. The continual adaptation and manipulation of texts and practices reveals the ongoing competition between different Daoist lineages. As they negotiated, they tried to distinguish their identities while vying for support among the populace, the elite, and the court.

Afterword, in lieu of conclusion

The processes described in the previous chapters did not conclude during the fifth century. Indeed, debates regarding practices and efforts at establishing orthodoxy continued throughout the following centuries as numerous lineages of practice and local traditions were accepted into the Daoist fold, through complex reformulations of scriptures and practices.[1]

While there is no clear conclusion to the process by which Daoism emerged as a religion in medieval China, the integration of the various traditions and lineages that appeared by the fifth century, and which we traced in the previous chapters, did mark a new stage in the history of Daoism. Inherent in this complex and multifaceted process were two complementary trends. On the one hand, authors distinguished their own specific texts and practices by asserting their temporal priority and superior efficacy. On the other hand, these claims of superiority made Daoist canons grow more expansive and inclusive. Thus, we find ever more complex manuals of transmission that attempt to integrate and rank texts and practices in hierarchical ritual schemes.

The particulars of these complex processes are far beyond the scope of this book. In this final chapter, I briefly discuss responses to Lu Xiujing's efforts at textual canonization and ritual systemization that illustrate the continuing debates among Daoists following Lu Xiujing. Our discussion of the debates on orthodoxy in Chapter 5 showed that the Lingbao scriptures essentially rejected the Celestial Master texts and practices, even as they incorporated major elements into the new Lingbao ritual and scriptural synthesis. We should note, however, that the incorporation of Celestial Master texts and practices in Lingbao ritual texts is not

---

1 Among the better known examples of such local cults incorporated into Daoism are: (1) the cult to Wu Meng 吳猛 and Xu Xun in the southern coast 許遜 studied by Lee Fengmao, *Xu Xun yu Sa Shouxian: Deng Zhimo daojiao xiaoshuo yanjiu* 許遜與薩守堅: 鄧志謨道教小說研究 (Taipei: Taiwan Xuesheng, 1997); Kristofer Schipper, "Taoist Ritual and Local Cults of the T'ang Dynasty," in Michel Strickmann, ed. *Tantric and Taoist Studies*, vol. III (Institut Belge des Hautes Etudes Chinoises: Bruxelles, 1983): 812–34. (2) The cult of Zitong in Sichuan studied by Terry Kleeman, *A God's Own Tale*. (3) Cults on Mt. Huagai in Fujian, studied by Robert Hymes, *Way and Byway: Taoism, Local Religion, and Models of Divinity in Sung and Modern China* (Berkeley: University of California Press, 2002).

evidence for inclusion of the Way of the Celestial Master Daoism in the emerging synthesis of the Three Caverns, but its exclusion. Similarly, the incorporation of Celestial Master Zhang into the Lingbao revelations was not a celebration of the Celestial Master teaching. On the contrary, this inclusion was in order to reveal the primacy of the Lingbao revelations. Lu Xiujing's canon and ritual system, composed after his own conversion to Lingbao Daoism, expressed the same attitude to Celestial Master ritual.

The most important aspect of the debates following Lu Xiujing was the reintegration of Celestial Master texts and rituals into the Daoist canons. Lu Xiujing's effort at creating orthodoxy was thus only partially successful. While later Daoists accepted the Three Caverns as the core of the Daoist canon, succeeding canons were based on a far more expansive organizing principle that included the texts of the Celestial Master and many other texts excluded from the Three Caverns.

The significance of the debate may be highlighted, for instance, by the ritual scheme presented in the important Daoist compendium *Secret Essentials Without Peer*, which was composed at the behest of Emperor Wu of the Northern Zhou (Yuwen Yong 宇文邕, 543–78) during the mid 570s. This compendium was supposed to provide a ritual framework for the empire.[2] In the one hundred chapters of the *Secret Essentials Without Peer*, there is only one citation from a Celestial Master text.[3] The ritual system introduced in the text was based on the Lingbao rites and included only one of the Celestial Master rituals, namely the Retreat of Mud and Ashes.[4] The textual and ritual scheme of the *Secret Essentials Without Peer* thus follows the principles developed by Lu Xiujing, which were based on the Lingbao scriptures.

The *Complete Essentials Without Peer* includes some references to Celestial Master practices. Two chapters concerning the sacred geography of celestial and terrestrial realms (*juan* 21–3) conclude with a section entitled "Pneuma-Parishes of Orthodox Unity" (*Zhengyi qizhi* 正一炁治). This section provides a complete list of Celestial Master parishes and their astronomical correlates.[5] Three chapters regarding precepts and injunction of various ritual lineages (*juan* 44–6), concludes with a section on "Five Precepts of Orthodox Unity" (*Zhengyi wujie* 正一五戒).[6]

---

2   *Wushang biyao* DZ 1138. For the political motivation for the compilation of this compendium, see Lagerwey, *Wu-shang*, 32 ff; Wang Chengwen, "The Revelation and Classification of Daoist Scriptures," in John Lagerwey and Lü Pengzhi, eds. *Early Chinese Religion: the Period of Division (220–589 AD)* (Leiden: Brill, 2010): 866–71.

3   A third of the original chapters are lost. The Daozang version preserves 67 chapters. Several fragmentary manuscripts were found at Dunhuang, among them P 2861, which includes a complete table of contents of the text; translated in Lagerwey, *Wu-shang*, 49–71.

4   For a discussion of the rituals included in *Wushang biyao*, see Lü, *Tangqian*, 264–71; idem, "Daoist Rituals" in Lagerwey and Lü, 1342–4.

5   DZ 1138: 23.4a–9a, citing *Chart of the Pneuma-Parishes of Orthodox Unity* (*Zhengyi qizhi tu* 正一炁治圖); Lagerwey, *Wu-shang*, 103.

6   DZ 1138: 46.16b–18a, citing *Zhengyi fawen*; Lagerwey, *Wu-shang*, 147.

Importantly, the *Secret Essentials Without Peer* does accord the *Daode jing* a special place in its sections on royal governance (*wangzheng* 王正) and on cultivation (*xiuzhen yangsheng* 修真養生).[7] Moreover, transmission of the *Daode jing* is a critical step in the graded initiation system envisaged in the *Secret Essentials Without Peer*. According to this scheme, an initiate would first accept the "ten precepts" (*shijie* 十戒), then receive the Five-thousand Graphs (*Daode jing*), and then the Sanhuang, Lingbao, and Shangqing scriptures (*juan 35*). The protocol for transmission of the *Daode jing* is the first of the textual initiations given in the text (*juan* 37), followed by the transmission protocols for the Sanhuang corpus (*juan* 38), Lingbao (*juan* 39), and Shangqing (*juan* 40). We should note, however, that the transmission protocol follows the Lingbao ritual framework and Lingbao ritual manuals. The protocol includes citations from one manual specifically dedicated to the transmission of the *Daode jing*, but these citations include references to Ritual Master of the Three Caverns. This manual was thus probably redacted by a Lingbao author, and is not representative of early Celestial Master ritual.[8]

Adherents of Celestial Master Daoism, however, responded to Lu Xiujing's challenge almost immediately after his efforts at canonization and ritual systemization. One of the clearest and most succinct responses is the *Discourse on Orthodox Unity*, a late fifth-century Celestial Master text.[9] This text, as I discuss in detail below, claims higher efficacy and historical priority for the Celestial Master ritual scheme, thus asserting its superiority over the Lingbao ritual. On the other hand, this text sees both ritual schemes as part of a single tradition. This text thus responds to the challenge of Lu Xiujing's efforts by accepting the Lingbao rituals as authentic, yet secondary.

The *Discourse on Orthodox Unity* is only one of several texts composed by adherents of the Celestial Master traditions that appeared during the fifth century as responses to Lu Xiujing's challenge. Other important contemporary texts are the *Catalogue of the Seven Parts of the Jade Filaments* (*Yuwei qibu jing shumu* 玉緯七部經書目),[10] and the *Scripture of the Orthodox Unity* (*Zhengyi jing* 正一經), which provide an expanded vision of Celestial Master Daoism.[11] These texts presented a textual canon consisting of seven parts (*qibu* 七部) that included alongside the Three Caverns four other textual corpora: Great Clarity (*taiqing* 太清),

7 DZ 1138: 6.11a–12b, 7.1a3b; Lagerwey, *Wu-shang*, 39, 83–4.
8 DZ 1138: 37.2b9–3b3, 4a3–7 are citations from *Chuanshou wuqianwen luyi* 傳授五千文錄儀. This text is not extant.
9 *Zhengyi lun* 正一論 DZ 1228. Schipper and Verellen date this text to the Tang (*Taoist Canon*, 486). Wang Chengwen argues the text was composed during the Southern Dynasties; Wang, *Dunhuang*, 358–360.
10 Wang Chengwen argues that *Yuwei qibu jing shumu* was composed by Meng Zhizhou 孟智周 in the late fifth century; see Wang Chengwen, "The Revelation," 851–2.
11 Unfortunately, both of these texts are not extant and survive only in partial citations in later compilations, such as the eighth century encyclopedia *Pivotal Meaning of Daoism, Daojiao yishu* 道教義樞 DZ 1129.

Great Peace (*taiping* 太平), Great Profundity (*taixuan* 太玄), and Orthodox Unity (*Zhengyi*),[12] which was considered the most fundamental.

The texts of these four textual corpora originated in distinct lineages, and for the most part were earlier than the texts of the Three Caverns. Indeed, as discussed in the previous chapters, many of the practices and texts included in the Shangqing and Lingbao texts may be traced to antecedents in these very texts. The corpus labeled *Taixuan jing* included the *Daode jing* and its commentaries. The *Taiping* corpus seems to have been limited to the *Taiping jing*, although the version of the text referred to at this stage is difficult to ascertain.[13] The corpus of the *Taiqing jing* consisted of alchemical texts, but it is difficult to determine which texts were actually included in this category.[14] As we saw in Chapter 2, the transmission rites of several of these texts requires blood oaths, thus marking them as belonging to lineages of technical specialists, which should not be simplistically labeled Daoist. As I argued in Chapter 2, the reformulation of these oaths into "pure" transmission rituals that did not require blood, as in the case of the *Scripture of Transmuted Cinnabar*, marks the incorporation of the alchemical texts into the Daoist ritual scheme. Moreover, the hagiography of Zhang Daoling in the *Shenxian zhuan* presents him as a master alchemist and transmitter of the *Yellow Thearch's Scripture of Divine Cinnabar of the Nine Cauldrons*.[15] The Celestial Master tradition in the Jiang'nan region evidently adopted alchemy into its repertoire of practices.

Although it is difficult to ascertain which texts were included within each of these categories, the inclusion of the various texts that originated in distinct lineages in a single canon provides a glimpse of the new integrative vision of the tradition espoused by adherents of the Way of the Celestial Master. The exclusion of these early texts from the Three Caverns marked the orthodox vision that appeared in the Lingbao scriptures, and which was elaborated by Lu Xiujing in his catalogue. The inclusion of these texts in the canon of seven parts shows that, by the end of the fifth century, several of the older lineages were subsumed by the Celestial Master tradition. It is quite possible that the actual lineages in which

---

12 DZ 1129: 2.7b.
13 See the brief discussion in Wang, "Revelation," 858. The history and redaction of the *Taiping jing* is a complex question, and far beyond the scope of this book. Recent studies of this important text include an extensive annotated translation by Hendrischke, *Scripture on Great Peace*; and several publications by Grégoire Espesset. Particularly useful for the complexities attendant to the label *Taiping jing* is a review article of Hendrischke's work by Espesset, "Editing and Translating the Taiping Jing and the Great Peace Textual Corpus," *Journal of Chinese Studies* 48 (2008): 469–86.
14 For a study of the Taiqing alchemical tradition, see Pregadio, *Great Clarity*. It is unclear which of these texts, were included in this category.
15 The *Shenxian zhuan* passage is preserved in *YJQQ*, DZ 1032.109.20a. The *Scripture of the Nine Cauldrons* probably refers to the first chapter of *Huangdi jiuding shendan jingjue* 黃帝九鼎神丹經訣 DZ 885; see, Fabrizio Pregadio, "The *Book of the Nine Elixirs* and its Tradition," in Yamada Keiji 山田慶兒 and Takeda Tan 田中淡, eds. *Chūgoku kodai kagakushiron* 中國古代科學史論 (Kyoto: Jinbun kagaku kenkyūjo, 1991): vol. 2, 543–639. For a translation and discussion of Zhang Daoling's hagiography, see Campany, *To Live*, 349–56. Campany argues that this hagiography may well have been composed by Ge Hong.

these texts had originally circulated were no longer in existence, and that variant texts were being transmitted rather freely among practitioners. Most significantly, the integration of these texts from originally disparate lineages into a single canon transformed these texts and their associated practices into distinct stages within a single hierarchy of attainment. Later Daoist canons adopted the four categories advanced by the Celestial Masters authors, but placed them as Auxiliary categories to the Three Caverns. The first canonic effort to adopt this structure was by Wang Yan 王延 (d. 604) and his collaborators in the Tongdao guan 通道觀 in the capital of the Northern Zhou in the late 570s.[16] The *Scripture on Transformations of Laozi*, which I discussed in the Introduction, was copied in the context of this canonization project.

The most important of the new four textual categories was the corpus entitled *Zhengyi*. This category included texts of Celestial Master Daoism, and it may have been formed as an independent canon in the early fifth century, to rival the Three Caverns. Indeed, as it is difficult to gauge the popularity of Lingbao ritual, or the challenge posed by the canon of the Three Caverns, the establishment of a Celestial Master canon may be seen as evidence that the Lingbao scriptures were recognized as an attempt to establish an alternative community. What constituted the *Zhengyi* canon in the fifth century is unclear. Later texts refer to a Celestial Master codex named *Methods and Writs of Orthodox Unity* (*Zhengyi fawen* 正一法文). While numerous texts had evidently been lost over the centuries,[17] the Ming Daozang preserves several texts entitled *Zhengyi fawen*. Among the most important of these is the *Methods and Writs of Orthodox Unity*; *Precepts, Codes and Scriptures Taught by the Celestial Master* (*Zhengyi fawen tianshi jiao jieke jing* 正一法文天師教戒科經), which includes five originally independent texts, among them some of the earliest datable texts of Celestial Master Daoism.[18]

Among the most succinct responses by Celestial Master adherents to the Lingbao claims of primacy is the *Discourse on Orthodox Unity* (*Zhengyi lun* 正一論). This text is structured as a dialogue between a querying guest and an unnamed and untitled advocate of the Celestial Master. The Way of the Celestial Master is here discussed in terms of two rites, the Rite of Instruction (*zhijiao zhai* 旨教齋) and the Mud and Ashes rite of repentance (*tutan xieyi* 塗炭謝儀). As we

---

16 This catalogue, entitled *Zhunang jingmu* 珠囊經目, was in seven *juan* and "we may speculate on the possibility [it] was divided into seven parts" (Schipper and Verellen, *Taoist Canon*, 14). The first clear evidence for such a catalogue is the *Order of Succession of the Daoist Scriptural Legacy* [*Daomen jingfa xiangcheng cixu* 道門經法相承次序 DZ 1128] compiled by Pan Shizheng 潘師正 (585–682) in about 680; Schipper and Verellen, 17–20; Wang, "Revelation," 866–72.

17 The *Catalogue of Scriptures Missing from the Daoist Canon* DZ 1430, compiled in the Ming, mentions over 30 texts entitled *Zhengyi jing* or *Zhengyi fawen jing*, along with a codex of 60 scrolls entitled *Zhengyi fawen*.

18 *Zhengyi fawen tianshi jiao jieke jing* DZ 789. The five texts are: (1) Untitled Introduction to the codex (1a–12a); (2) *Dadao jialing jie* 大道家令戒 (12a–19a), translated in Bokenkamp, *Early*, 149–85; (3) 19b–20a *Tianshi jiao* 天師教, a hepta-syllabic verse; (4) *Yangping zhi* 陽平治; a history of the Yangping parish, the residence of the Celestial Master (20b–21b); (5) *Tianshi wuyan diwang shi* 天師五言帝王詩 (22a–23a).

saw in Chapter 5, the history of these rites is complex, and the Rite of Instruction, in particular, probably developed in response to the Lingbao rite. Nevertheless, this text asserts that the Rite of Instruction and the Retreat of Mud and Ashes were revealed together in a single scroll to Celestial Master Zhang Ling.[19] The passage continues with a rhetorical question:

> How can one practice the repentance rite of the Celestial Master and not prac-tice the Retreat of the Celestial Master? If the Retreat can be abbreviated, and the Repentance can be replaced and used [only] to augment the gaps in Lingbao [ritual], then I am afraid that this not only missed the profundity of the Celestial Master, but is also not the intent of Master Ge.

The Master Ge referred to here is Ge Xuan, the purported revelator of the Lingbao scriptures and rituals. The author of the text seems to be aiming at a com-munity that practiced the repentance rite of Mud and Ashes, which was part of the early ritual repertoire of the Celestial Master community, but which did not neces-sarily practice the Rite of Instruction, which was a more recent development.

We should recall here the community alluded to in Lu Xiujing's *Writ of the Five Stimuli*. Lu Xiujing and his disciples performed the rite of Mud and Ashes on at least two occasions, in 453 and in 471. Indeed, Lu Xiujing may have composed the *Writ of the Five Stimuli* on the occasion of the earlier performance as an aid in meditation. Lu listed the Rite of Instruction as the last of the nine Retreats in the ritual scheme of the text, while he placed the rite of Mud and Ashes outside this ritual scheme.

The author of *Discourse of Orthodox Unity* seems to allude to communities that practiced both Celestial Master and Lingbao rites, and used the former to augment the Lingbao rites. This form of practice would suggest the superiority of the Lingbao rites. Interestingly, the author argues that such practice contradicts Ge Xuan's own intentions, which are thus said to be complementary to the Celestial Master agenda.

Perhaps the most interesting aspect of this text is the reduction of the entire history of Daoism into a simple question of primacy of practices associated with the Celestial Master Zhang and Master Ge Xuan. The Rite of Instruction transmitted by Celestial Master Zhang is simply earlier than the Lingbao *zhai* revealed by Master Ge. The primacy of the Celestial Master rite is reiterated several times in this short text. We find a relatively detailed elaboration of this assertion in a response to a query as to whether the rite of Mud and Ashes and the Lingbao rites could be practiced together. The response presents a brief vision of the origins of Daoism:

> On the fifteenth day of the eighth month of first year of the *han'an* period (142 CE), the Celestial Master revealed the Rite of Instruction on Mt. Yangping, in order to instruct the various officers and lead them to enter

---

19 DZ 1228.2b.

the ranks of the transcendents. Wang (Chang) and Zhao (Sheng) practiced this, and upon death they ascended to the supreme Dao. At that time, when the Repentance Rite of Mud and Ashes was already being practiced, the Lingbao *zhai* had not yet spread. Only the Five Talismans were known. How can they be practiced together? Examining the chronology for verification suffices to show this is absurd. This is no more than fabricating minor branches and providing justification for the Perfect Writs. Accepting a few words as sufficient to practice the teachings of Zhang and Ge together is unacceptable, and you should have no faith in it![20]

Of course, the revelation to the Celestial Master, or appearance of the Celestial Master community, preceded the appearance of the Lingbao ritual system. Yet, this passage claims that the Rite of Instruction was a critical part of the original revelation to Zhang Daoling. Interestingly, this revelation is dated slightly later than that mentioned in the Celestial Master texts *Commands and Admonitions* and *Yangping zhi*.[21] While the initial revelation is usually said to have occurred on Mt. Heming, the revelation here is located on Mt. Yangping, which was the seat of the Celestial Master and thus the highest ranked of the 24 parishes. Interestingly, this passage recognizes the historical importance and antiquity of the Lingbao talismans.

The discussion then turns to efficacy, as the interlocutor asks: "The Rite of Instruction was used by the Celestial Master to instruct the parish officials, and that's all. It is a method of the Small Vehicle. It is not appropriate for Lingbao Daoists 靈寶道士 to practice it".[22] The Celestial Master respondent explains:

> ... this method was used to instruct the parish officials and the people of the Dao 道民 to avert calamities and become seed people of the latter age... if the parish officials do not cultivate [this] to become seed people how would they ford the ten hardships and eight difficulties.[23] Without merit they can have no salvation. It is difficult to talk of virtue with those who turn their back on Orthodox Unity.

20 DZ 1228.3a.
21 Both texts date the revelation to the first day of the fifth month; *Dadao jia lingjie* DZ 789.14b; Bokenkamp, *Early*, 171; *Yangping zhi* DZ 789.20b1.
22 DZ 1228.3b.
23 The term "ten hardships and eight difficulties" 十苦八難 is found numerous times in Lingbao scriptures, such as *Chishu yupian* DZ 22: 3.1a, *Taishang dongxuan Lingbao benxing suyuan jing* DZ 1114.14a, *Taishang dongxuan lingbao zhihui benyuan dajie shangpin* DZ 344.9a. While these hardships and difficulties are not specified, the latter may be traceable to Buddhist usage which refers to eight rebirths in which it is difficult to see Buddha or hear his teaching: (1) a hell-being, (2) hungry ghost, (3) animal, (4) in the long-life heavens (where life is long and easy), (5) in Uttara-kuru (the northern continent where all is pleasant), (6) as deaf, blind or dumb, (7) a worldly philosopher, (8) in the intermediate time between the life of a Buddha and his successor. Digital Dictionary of Buddhism (http://www.buddhism-dict.net/cgi-bin/xpr-ddb.pl?51.xml+id('b516b–96e3')).

As we saw in Chapter 5, the label of "small vehicle" was deployed as a criticism of Celestial Master Daoism in several Lingbao scriptures. Here, the Celestial Master author responds to this criticism by first asserting that the teaching is meant for both the "parish officials" and for the general members of the community, the people of the Dao. Second, the passage adopts the rhetoric of salvation, borrowed from the Lingbao scriptures, using originally Buddhist terminology. Salvation, however, is here dependent on becoming seed people. As we saw in Chapter 4, this attainment was the goal of Daoists in the early Celestial Master community, as expressed, for example, in the *Initiation Rite of the Yellow Book*.

This attainment is found in a similar context to the *Discourse of Orthodox Unity* in the *Orthodox Unity Protocol for the Retreat of the Instruction*. Here the attainment is included in the ninth of the twelve vows taken by a Ritual Master of the Three Heavens and Perfected of Orthodox Unity when performing the Retreat of Instruction:

> Vow to eradicate all illness, the ten hardships and eight difficulties, avoid the calamities of the age, and become a seed-person in [an age of] great peace.[24]

What is most significant in these passages is the adaptation of Lingbao terminology, which itself is heavily indebted to Buddhist notions and practice, into the Celestial Master ritual scheme. This should not be seen as grafting of new, even foreign, ideas onto older forms of practice. Rather, as Bokenkamp has shown for the Lingbao scriptures, this adaptation was a complex creative process from which a new synthesis arose.

This brief examination of fifth- and sixth-century Celestial Master texts shows that the competition and rivalry between lineages or communities of practice, which we detected in the early formation of Daoism, continued into the sixth century and beyond as attempts to integrate the various Daoist lineages that emerged in previous centuries gained momentum through imperial urging and sponsorship. Importantly, these Celestial Master texts reveal that the Lingbao scriptures and ritual were a real challenge, and that practitioners of these rites were seen as forming a competing community. At the same time, these texts reveal that debates with adherents of Lingbao were internal debates. Authors of Celestial Master texts and rites, as well as adherents of Lingbao, recognized each other's texts and practices, and those texts which came to be included in the Four Auxiliaries, as belonging to one tradition. Although they continued to debate the relative status of the texts and practices in competing hierarchical schemes of attainment, they recognized that certain texts and practices belonged within the Daoist canon, while others did not. How then did Daoists of various lineages and communities of practice recognize similarity and difference among their practices, and how did they create a distinct tradition that was styled Daoist? I suggest that it was precisely the complex debates discussed in the preceding chapters,

24 *Zhengyi zhijiao zhaiyi* 正一指教齋儀 DZ 798.4b.

and other similar debates regarding other practices, deities, and texts, that led to the emergence of Daoism.

Indeed, we may now return to the polythetic definition I suggested at the outset of this study. Regardless of their differences, the debate between the Lingbao and Celestial adherents reveals agreement in the points I suggested. One, the Dao is an overarching and effective force, both prior to the emanation of the cosmos and active in the manifested world. Second, the Dao can be effectively approached by humans through ritual means, and those who are successful with this quest achieve transcendence. Third, these ritual means are secret and guarded within strict line-ages of transmission. Fourth, these lineages reject all practices that do not revere the direct manifestations of the Dao, especially the blood sacrifices of the com-mon religion. The Way of the Celestial Master instituted a ritual system based on bureaucratic means of communication with the extra-human realm. The Lingbao ritual scheme elaborated on this model, creating an all encompassing cosmology, in which the cosmos itself was seen as emanating through successive scriptural stages. Finally, medieval Daoists were motivated by an eschatological vision, which transformed the early traditions of the seeker for immortality into a reli-gious quest for transcendence and salvation.

Bibliography

Bibliography abbreviations

AM: *Asia Major*

BEFEO: *Bulletin de L'Ecole Française d'Extrême-Orient*

BIHP: *Bulletin of the Institute of History and Philology of the Academia Sinica*, 中央研究 院歷史 語言所集刊

BPZ: *Baopuzi neipian*

CEA: *Cahiers d'Extrême-Asie*

DDB: *Digital Dictionary of Buddhism* http://www.buddhism-dict.net/ddb/

DJWH: *Daojia wenhua yanjiu* 道家文化研究

DJYS: *Daojiao yishu* 道教義樞 DZ 1129

EFEO: *École Française d'Extrême-Orient*

FSTY: *Fengsu tongyi* 風俗通義 by Ying Shao 應劭 (fl.189–94). Taipei: Chung-hwa, 1985

HJAS: *Harvard Journal of Asiatic Studies*

HNZ: *Huainanzi zhuzi suoyin* 淮南子逐字索引 Hong Kong: Chinese University of Hong Kong Institute of Chinese Studies, Shangwu, 1992: 11/99/13

HR: *History of Religions*

HS: *Hanshu* 漢書 Ban Gu (32–92)

HHS: *Houhanshu* 後漢書. Beijing: Zhonghua shuju, 1973

HYGZ: *Huayangguo zhi* 華陽國志 by Chang Qu 常璩 (fl.347), ed. Taipei: Taiwan Chunghua, 1978

HX: *Hanxue* 漢學

ICS: *Chinese University of Hong Kong Institute of Chinese Studies the ICS ancient Chinese texts concordance series*

IS   Yasui Kozan 安居香山 and Nakamura Shōhachi 中村璋八. *Ishō shusei i*緯書集成. Tokyo: Kangi bunka kenkyūkai, 1960–63. 6 vol.

JAOS: *Journal of the American Oriental Society*

JCR: *Journal of Chinese Religions*

KG: *Kaogu* 考古

LXZ: *Liexian zhuan*

SCC: *Science and Civilisation in China*

SDZN :   *Sandong zhunang* 三洞珠囊 DZ 1139

SGZ: *Sanguozhi* 三國志 by Chen Shou 陳壽 (233–97) and Pei Songzhi 裴松之 (372–451). Beijing: Zhonghua shuju, 1965

SJ: *Shiji* 史記, Sima Qian 司馬遷 (145–86 BCE)

SJZ: *Shuijing zhu shu* 水经注疏, comp. by Li Daoyuan, annotated by Yang Shoujing
         楊守敬 and Xiong Huizhen 熊會貞, Nanjing: Jiangsu guji chubanshe, 1989
SSJZS: *Shisan jing zhushu* 十三經注疏. Ruan Yuan, ed. (1764–1849). Beijing: Zhonghua
         shuju, 1980. 14 vols
SWJZ: *Shuowen jiezi zhu* 說文解字注, by Xu Shen 許慎 (Han), annotated by Duan
         Yucai 段玉裁 Taipei: Tiangong shuju, 1998
SXZ: *Shenxian zhuan*
TP: *T'oung Pao*
TPGJ: *Taiping guangji* 太平廣記. Mingren biji congshu series. Taipei: Xinxing shuju.
         1958
TPYL: *Taiping yulan* 太平御覽 comp. Li Fang 李方 Sibu congkan 四部叢刊, ed.
         Taipei: Shangwu
TR: *Taoist Resources*
TS: *Tōhō shūkyō* 東方宗教
WSJC :   *Weishu jicheng* 緯書集成, compiled by Yasui Kozan 安居香山 and Nakamura
         Shōhachi 中村璋八, Chinese rpt. Hebei renmin chubashe, 1994
WW: *Wenwu* 文物
YJQQ: *Yunji qiqian* 雲笈七籤, DZ 1032
YWLJ: *Yiwen leiju* 藝文類聚, compiled by Ouyang Xun 歐陽詢 (57–641). Shanghai:
         Shanghai guji, 1999
XEZ: *Xiang'er zhu* S. 6825
ZHDZ: *Zhonghua daozang* 中華道藏, chief-editor Zhang Jiyu 張繼禹. Beijing: Huaxia
         chubanshe, 2004

Traditional sources

Cai zhonglang ji 蔡中朗集 in *Hanwei liuchao yibaisan jia ji* 漢魏六朝一百三家集. 2:
    18b–19a; collated by Zhang Pu 張溥 (Ming) in *Congshu jicheng* 叢書集成. Beijing:
    Zhonghua shuju, 1985: chapters 389–90.
Chuxueji 初學記 (compiled in 728), modern edn. Beijing: Zhonghua shuju 1979.
Chuci buzhu 楚辭補注, Hong Xingzu 洪興祖 (1090–1155) comp. Taipei: Da'an, 1995.
Huainanzi zhuzi suoyin 淮南子逐字索引 Hong Kong: ICS, 1992.
Huayangguo zhi 華陽國志 by Chang Qu 常璩 (fl.347), ed. Taipei: Taiwan Chunghua,
    1978.
Ishimpō 醫心方, Tamba Yasuyori 丹波康賴 (911–995), comp. Taipei: Xinwenfeng, 1976.
Jinshu 晉書 (compiled under Fang Xuanling 房玄齡), Beijing: Zhonghua shuju, 1974.
Liji Zhengyi 禮記正義, with a commentary by Zheng Xuan 鄭玄, annotation by Kong
    Yingda 孔穎達 in SSJZS.
Liuchao shiji bianlei 六朝事跡編類 Zhang Dunyi 張敦頤 (Song) Congshu jicheng, ed.
    Taipei: Shangwu.
Li Xu 隸緒 comp. by Hong Kua 洪适 (1117–84). Taipei: Yiwen yinshuguan, 1966.
Lushi Chunqiu zhuzi suoyin 呂氏春秋逐字索引. Hong Kong: ICS, 1994.
Maoshi Zhengyi 毛詩正義, with a commentary by Zheng Xuan 鄭玄 and annotated by
    Kong Yingda 孔穎達 in SSJZS.
Morohashi Tetsuji 諸橋轍次 comp., *Dai kanwa daijiten* 大j漢和字典. Tokyo: Taishūkan
    shoten: 1957–60.
Mozi xiangu 墨子閒詁, compiled by Sun Yirang 孫詒讓 (1848–1908). Beijing: Zhonghua
    shuju, 2001.

Mozi zhuzi suoyin 墨子逐字索引. Hong Kong: ICS 2001.

Nanqi shu 南齊書 compiled by Xiao Zixian 蕭子顯, Beijing: Zhonghua shuju, 1972.

Nanshi 南史 Li Yanshou 李延壽. Beijing: Zhonghua shuju, 1965.

Sanguozhi jijie 三國志集解 Lu Bi 盧弼. Beijing: Zhonghua shuju, 1982.

Shennong bencaojing 神農本曹經 Sibu beiyao edn. Taipei: Chunghua, 1965.

Shuijing zhu 水經注, compiled by Li Daoyuan 酈道元 (d. 527). Taipei: Taiwan Zhonghua shuju, 1965.

Suishu 隋書 compiled by Wei Zheng 魏徵, 580–643. Beijing: Zhonghua shuju, 1973.

Taiyi shengshui 太一生水 in *Guodian Chumu zhujian* 郭店楚墓竹簡, Beijing: Wenwu chubanshe, 1998: 13–14; 125–6.

Wang Chong 王充, *Lunheng jiaoshi* 論衡校釋, comp. by Huang Hui 黃暉. Beijing: Zhonghua shuju, 1990.

Weishu 魏書 by Wei Shou 魏收 (506–72). Beijing: Zhonghua shuju, 1974.

Wenxuan 文選. Compiled by Xiao Tong (501–31). Taipei: Huazheng shuju, 1984.

Yang Xiong 揚雄, *Fayan zhuzi suoyin* 法言逐字索引 Hong Kong: ICS, 1995.

Yiwen leiju 藝文類聚, compiled by Ouyang Xun 歐陽詢 (57–641). Shanghai: Shanghai guji, 1999.

Zhouli Zhengyi 周禮正義 with a commentary by Zheng Xuan 鄭玄 and annotated by Jia Gongyan 賈公彥 in SSJZS.

Zhuangzi jishi 莊子集釋 Beijing: Zhonghua shuju, 1961, vol .1: 20.

Daoist and Buddhist sources

P: refers to Dunhuang manuscripts in the Pelliot collection at the Librarie Française.

S: refers to Dunhuang manuscripts in the Stein collection at the British Library.

T: refers to texts in *Taishō Shinshū Daizōkyō* 大正新脩大藏經 [Taishō Revised Tripiṭaka]. Chief-editor Takakusu Junjiro.

DZ 6 *Dadong zhengjing*

DZ 22 *Yuanshi wulao chishu wupian zhenwen tianshu jing* 元始五老赤書玉篇真 文天書經

DZ 23 *Taishang zhutian lingshu duming miaojing* 太上諸天靈書度命妙經

DZ 56 *Taishang yupei jindang taiji jinshu shangjing* 太上玉佩金璫太極金書上經

DZ 81 *Dongzhen taiwei huangshu tiandijun shijing jinyang sujing* 洞真太微黃書 天帝君石景金陽素經

DZ 87 *Yuanshi wuliang duren shangpin miaojing sizhu* 元始無量度人上品妙經四註

DZ 97 *Taishang lingbao zhutian neiyin ziran yuzi* 太上靈寶諸天内音自然玉字

DZ 165 *Lingbao ziran jiutian shengshen sanbao dayou jinshu* 靈寶自然九天生神 三寶大有金書

DZ 167 *Lingbao zhenling weiye tu* 靈寶真靈位業圖

DZ 177 *Huagai shan fuqiu wang guo san zhenjun shishi* 華蓋山孚丘王郭三真君 實

DZ 184 *Taizhen yudi siji mingke jing* 太真玉帝四極明科經

DZ 219 *Lingbao wuliang durenshangqing dafa* 靈寶無量度人上經大法

DZ 257 *Dongzhen taiwei huangshu jiutian balu zhenwen* 洞真太微黃書九天八籙真文

DZ 258 *Taixuan bajing lu* 太玄八景籙

DZ 294 *Liexian zhuan* 列仙傳

DZ 296 *Zhenxian tongjian* 真仙通鑒

DZ 303 *Ziyang zhenren neizhuan* 紫陽真人内傳

DZ 318 *Dongxuan lingbao ziran jiutian shengshen zhangjing* 洞玄靈寶自然九天生神章經

DZ 331 *Taishang huangting neijing yujing* 太上黃庭內景玉經.

DZ 332 *Taishang huangting waijing yujing* 太上黃庭外景玉經

DZ 335 *Taishang dongyuan shenzhou jing* 太上洞淵神咒經

DZ 344 *Taishang dongxuan lingbao zhihui benyuan dajie shangpin* 太上洞玄靈寶智慧本願大戒上品經

DZ 346 *Taishang dongxuan lingbao zhenyi quanjie falun miaojing* 太上洞玄靈寶真一勸戒法輪妙經

DZ 349 *Taishang dongxuan lingbao fazhu jing* 太上洞玄靈寶法燭經

DZ 352 *Taishang dongxuan lingbao chishu yujue miaojing* 太上洞玄靈寶赤書玉訣妙經

DZ 388 *Taishang lingbao wufuxu* 太上靈寶五符序

DZ 410 *Taishang dongxuan lingbao zhongjian wen* 太上洞玄靈寶眾簡文

DZ 420 *Shenxian fuer danshi xingyao fa* 神仙服餌丹石行藥法

DZ 421 *Dengzhen yinjue* 登真隱訣

DZ 434 *Xuanlan renniao shan jingtu* 玄覽人鳥山經圖

DZ 441 *Dongxuan lingbao wuyue guben zhenxingtu* 洞玄靈寶五嶽古本真形圖

DZ 442 *Shangqing housheng daojun lieji* 上清後聖道君列紀

DZ 457 *Taishang dongxuan lingbao zhihui zuigen shangpin dajie jing* 太上洞玄靈寶智慧罪根上品大戒經

DZ 463 *Yaoxiu keyi jielu chao* 要修科儀戒律鈔

DZ 508 *Wushang huanglu dazhai licheng yi* 無上黃籙大齋立成儀

DZ 524 *Dongxuan lingbao zhai shuo guangzhu jiefa dengzhu yuanyi* 靈寶齋說光燭戒罰燈祝願儀

DZ 528 *Taishang dongxuan lingbao shoudu yibiao* 太上洞玄靈寶授度儀表

DZ 532 *Taiji zhenren fu Lingbao zhaijie weiyi zhujing yaojue* 太極真人敷靈寶齋戒威儀諸經要訣

DZ 534 *Taishang tongling bashi shengwen zhenxingtu* 太上通靈八史聖 文真形圖

DZ 599 *Dongtian fudiyuedu mingshan ji* 洞天福地嶽瀆名山記

DZ 615 *Chisongzi zhangli* 赤松子章歷

DZ 639 *Huangtian shangqing jinque dijun lingshu ziwen shangjing* 皇天上清金闕帝君靈書紫文上經

DZ 671 *Taishang wuji dadao ziran zhenyi wuchengfu shangjing* 太上無極大道自然 真一五稱符上經

DZ 693 *Daode zhenjing zhigui* 道德真經指歸

DZ 785 *Laojun yinsong jiejing* 老君音誦誡經

DZ 789 *Zhengyi fawen tianshi jiaojie kejing* 正一法文天師教戒科經

DZ 790 *Nüqing guilü* 女青鬼律

DZ 798 *Zhengyi zhijiao zhaiyi* 正一指教齋儀

DZ 846 *Taiqing jing duangu fa* 太清經斷穀法

DZ 851 *Sanyuan yanshou canzan shu* 三元延壽參簪書

DZ 856 *Sanhuang neiwen yibi* 三皇內文遺秘

DZ 885 *Huangdi jiuding shendan jingjue* 黃帝九鼎神丹經訣

DZ 889 *Taiji zhenren jiuzhuan huandan jing yaojue* 太極真人九轉還丹經要訣

DZ 1016 *Zhen'gao* 真誥

DZ 1032 *Yunji qiqian* 雲笈七籤

DZ 1114 *Taishang dongxuan lingbao benxing suyuan jing* 太上洞玄靈寶本行宿緣經

DZ 1124 *Dongxuan lingbao xuanmen dayi* 洞玄靈寶玄門大義

DZ 1127 *Lu xiansheng daomen kelue* 陸先生道門科略

DZ 1128 *Daomen jingfa xiangcheng cixu* 道門經法相承次序

DZ 1129 *Daojiao yishu* 道教義樞

DZ 1138 *Wushang biyao* 無上祕要

DZ 1139 *Sandong zhunang* 三洞珠囊

DZ 1168 *Taishang laozi zhongjing* 太上老子中經

DZ 1185 *Baopuzi neipian* 抱朴子內篇

DZ 1203 *Taishang santian zhengfa jing* 太上三天正法經

DZ 1205 *Santian neijie jing* 三天內解經

DZ 1228 *Zhengyi lun* 正一論

DZ 1237 *Sandong xiudao yi* 三洞修道儀

DZ 1278 *Dongxuan lingbao wugan wen* 洞玄靈寶五感文

DZ 1281 *Wuyue zhenxing xulun* 五嶽真形序論

DZ 1294 *Shangqing huangshu guodu yi* 上清黃書過度儀

DZ 1343 *Dongzhen huangshu* 洞真黃書

DZ 1351 *Dongzhen* taishang feixing *yujing jiuzhen shengxuan shangji* 洞真太上飛行羽經九真昇玄上記

DZ 1382 *Shangqing jiudan shanghua taijing zhongji jing* 上清九丹上化胎精中記經

DZ 1395 *Shangqing dadong jiuwei badao dajing miaolu* 上清大洞九微八道大經妙籙

DZ 1407 *Dongxuan Lingbao ershisi sheng tujing* 洞玄靈寶二十四生圖經

DZ 1430 *Daozang quejing mulu* 道藏闕經目錄

DZ 1439 *Dongxuan lingbao yujingshan buxu jing* 洞玄靈寶玉京山步虛經

DZ 1465 *Xiaoyao xu jing* 消遙墟經 by Hong Zicheng 洪自誠

P 2256, P 2861 *Tongmen lun* 通門論 by Song Wenming 宋文明 also known as Lingbao jing yishu 靈寶經義疏

P 2356, P 2403 and P 2452: fragments of *Taishang taiji taku shangzhenren yan toishang lingbao weiyi dongxuan zhenyi ziran jingjue* 太上靈寶威儀洞玄真一自然經訣

P 2440 *Lingbao zhenyi wucheng jing* 靈寶真一五稱經

P 2789 is a fragment of *Shenzhou jing*

S 2295 *Laozi bianhua jing* 老子變化經

S 2750 *Taogong chuanshou yi* 陶公傳授儀

S 6825 *Laozi xiang'er zhu* 老子想爾注

S 1351 *Taiji zuo xiangong qingwen shang* 太極左仙公請問經上

T 55.602 Foshuo Anpan shouyi jing 安般守意經 *Xie Ao* 謝敷 *Anpan shouyi jing xu* 安般守意經序 (*Chu sanzang jiji* 出三藏記集)

Western-language sources

Abe, Stanley. "Heterological Visions: Northern Wei Daoist Sculpture from Shaanxi Province," *CEA* 9 (1996–7): 69–83.

Allan, Sarah. "The Great One, Water, and the Laozi: New Light from Guodian," *TP* 89 (2003): 237–85.

Andersen, Poul. "Talking to the Gods: Visionary Divination in early Taoism (The Sanhuang Tradition)," *TR* 5.1 (1994): 1–25.

—— "The Practice of BUGANG," *CEA* 5 (1989): 15–53.

—— *The Method of Holding the Three Ones*. London: Curzon Press, 1980.

Anderson, Benedict. *Imagined Communities: Reflections on the Origin and Spread of Nationalism*. London: Verso, 1983.

Arrault, Alain, and Jean-Claude Martzloff. "Calendriers," in Marc Kalinowski, ed. *Divination et Société Dans le Chine Médiévale*. Paris: Bibliothèque national de France, 2003.

Bai Bin, "Religious Beliefs as Reflected in the Funerary Record," in John Lagerwey and Lü Pengzhi, eds. *Early Chinese Religion: the Period of Division (220–589 AD)*. Leiden: Brill, 2010: 989–1073.

Barrett, Timothy H. *Taoism Under the T'ang: Religion and Empire During the Golden Age of Chinese History*. London: Wellsweep, 1996; rpt. Warren: Floating World, 2006.

Bell, Catherine. "Ritualization of Texts and Textualization of Ritual in the Codification of Daoist Liturgy," *HR* 27.4 (1988): 366–92.

—— *Ritual Perspectives and Dimensions*. New York and Oxford: Oxford University Press, 1997.

Bodde, Derk. *Festivals in Classical China*. Princeton: Princeton University Press, 1975.

Bokenkamp, Stephen R. See also Bo Yi 柏夷.

——"The 'Pacing the Void Stanzas' of the Lingbao Scriptures," unpublished M.A. Thesis, University of California Berkeley, 1981.

——"The Entheogenic Herb Calamus in Taoist Literature," *Phi Theta Papers* 15 (1982): 6–22.

—— "Sources of the Ling-pao Scriptures," in Michel Strickmann, ed. *Tantric and Taoist Studies* II, 1983: 434–86.

—— "The Peach Flower Font and the Grotto Passage," *JAOS* 106 (1986): 65–77.

—— "Time after Time," *AM* 7.1 (1994): 59–88.

—— "Declarations of the Perfected," in Donald S. Lopez, ed. *Religions of China in Practice*. Princeton: Princeton University Press, 1996: 171–9.

—— "The Yao Boduo Stele as Evidence for "Dao-Buddhism" of the Early Lingbao Scriptures," *CEA* 9 (1996–1997): 55–67.

—— *Early Daoist Scriptures*. Berkeley: University of California Press, 1997.

—— "Buddhism, Lu Xiujing and the first Daoist Canon," in Scott Pearce, Audrey Spiro, and Patricia Ebrey, eds. *Culture and Power in the Reconstitution of the Chinese Realm, 200–600*. Cambridge, MA and London: Harvard University Press, 2001: 181–99.

—— "The Prehistory of Laozi: His Prior Career as a Woman in the Lingbao Scriptures," *CEA* 14 (2004a): 403–21.

—— "The Silkworm and the Bodhi Tree: The Lingbao Attempt to Replace Buddhism in China and Our Attempt to Place Lingbao Taoism," in John Lagerwey, ed. *Religion and Chinese Society*. Hong Kong: Chinese University Press, 2004b, vol. 2: 317–39.

—— "Sackcloth and Ashes, Self and Family in the Tutan Zhai," in Florian C. Reiter and Poul Andersen, eds. *Scriptures, Schools, and Forms of Practices in Taoism*. Wiesbaden: Harrassowitz Verlag, 2005: 33–48.

—— *Ancestors and Anxiety: Daoism and the Birth of Rebirth in China*. Berkeley: University of California Press, 2007.

Bottero, Françoise. "Revisiting the *wén* 文and the *zì* 字: the Great Chinese Character Hoax," *Bulletin of the Museum of Far Eastern Antiquities* 74 (2002): 14–33.

Brown, Peter. *The Cult of the Saints: Its Rise and Function in Latin Christianity*. Chicago: University of Chicago Press, 1981.

—— *The Rise of Western Christendom: Triumph and Diversity, A.D. 200–1000*. Oxford: Blackwell, 2003.

Bujard, Marianne. "Le 'Traité des Sacrifices' du Hanshu et la mise en place de la religion d'État des Han," *EFEO* 84 (1997): 111–27.

—— *Le sacrifice au Ciel dans la Chine Ancienne: Théorie et Pratique sous les Han Occidentaux*. Paris: EFEO, 2000a.

—— "Le Culte de Wangzi Qiao ou la Longue Carrière d'un Immortel," *Études Chinoises* 19 (2000b): 115–58.

—— "State and Local Cults in Han Religion," in John Lagerwey and Mark Kalinowski, *Early Chinese Religion Part One: Shang through Han.* Leiden: Brill, 2009: 777–811.

Bumbacher, Stephan Peter. *Fragments of the Daoxue Zhuan: Critical Edition, Translation and Analysis of a Medieval Collection of Daoist Biographies.* Frankfurt am Main: Peter Lang, 2000.

Burke, Peter. *History and Social Theory.* Cornell University Press: Ithaca, 1992.

Cahill, Suzanne E. *Transcendence and Divine Passion: the Queen Mother of the West in Medieval China.* Stanford: Stanford University Press, 1993.

Campany, Robert F. *Strange Writing: Anomaly Accounts in Early Medieval China.* Albany: State University of New York Press, 1996.

—— *To Live as Long as Heaven and Earth: A Translation and Study of Ge Hong's Traditions of Divine Transcendents.* Berkeley: University of California Press, 2002.

—— "On the Very Idea of Religions (in the Modern West and in Early Medieval China)," *HR* 42 (2003): 287–319.

—— *Making Transcendents*: *Ascetics and Social Memory in Early Medieval China.* Honolulu: University of Hawaii Press, 2009.

Cedzich, Ursula-Angelika. "Das Ritual der Himmelmeister im Spiegel früher Quellen, Übersetzung und Untersuchung des liturgischen Materials im dritten *chüan* des *Teng-chen yin-chüeh*." Ph.D. Dissertation, Julius-Maximilians-Universität, Würzburg. 1987.

—— "Early Daoist Scriptures, Review Article," *JCR* 28 (2000): 161–76.

—— "The Organon of the Twelve Hundred Officials and Its Gods," *Daoism: Religion, History and Society* 1 (2009): 1–95.

Chavannes, Édouard. *Le T'ai chan: Essai de Monographie d'un Culte Chinois.* Paris: E. Leroux, 1910.

Chen Chi-yun. "Orthodoxy as a Mode of Statecraft: The Ancient Concept of *Cheng*," in Kwang-Ching Liu, ed. *Orthodoxy in Late Imperial China.* Berkeley: University of California Press, 1990: 27–52.

Chen Qiaoyi 陳橋驛, *Shuijing zhu jiaoshi* 水經注校釋. Hangzhou: Hangzhou daxue chubanshe, 1999.

Chenivesse, Sandrine. "Fengdu: Cité de l'Abondance, Cité de la Male Mort," *CEA* 10 (1998): 287–339.

de Crespigny, Rafe. *Generals of the South, The Foundation and Early History of the Three Kingdoms State of Wu.* Internet edition, 2004 http://arktos.anu.edu.au/chill/index.php/eic/; originally published as No. 16 of the Asian Studies Monographs: New Series of the Faculty of Asian Studies at The Australian National University, 1990 accessed August 10, 2005.

Csikszentmihàlyi, Mark. "Chia I's 'Techniques of the Tao' and the Han Confucian Appropriation of Technical Discourse," *AM* 10.1–2 (1997): 49–69.

—— "Traditional Taxonomies and Revealed Texts in the Han," in Livia Kohn and Harold David Roth, eds. *Daoist Identity: History, Lineage, and Ritual.* Honolulu: Hawaii University Press, 2001: 81–101.

—— *Readings in Han Chinese Thought.* Indianapolis: Hackett, 2006.

—— with Michael Nylan. "Constructing Lineages and Inventing Traditions through Exemplary Figures in Early China," *TP* 89 (2003): 59–99.

Dean, Kenneth. *Taoist Ritual and Popular Cults of Southeast China.* Princeton: Princeton University Press, 1993.

Despaux, Catherine. *Immortelles de la Chine Ancienne: Taoisme et Alchimie Feminine.* Puiseaux: Pardès, 1990.

DeWoskin, Kenneth J. *Doctors, Diviners and Magicians of Ancient China: Biographies of Fang-shih*. New York: Columbia University Press, 1983.

Dien, Albert E. "Turfan Funeral Documents," *JCR* 30 (2002): 23–48.

—— *Six Dynasties Civilization*. New Haven, Yale University Press, 2007.

Digital Dictionary of Buddhism, "*Huixin*" http://www.buddhism-dict.net/cgi-bin/xpr-ddb.pl?5e.xml+id('b5efb-5fc3'): accessed March 22, 2010.

Drexler, Monika. "Schriftamulette fu auf zwei Grabvasen der Östlichen Han-Zeit," *Monumenta Serica* 49 (2001): 227–48.

Duara, Prasenjit. "Superscribing Symbols: the Myth of Guandi, Chinese God of War," *JAS* 47.4 (1988): 778–95.

Dudink, Adrianus. "The Poem *Laojun bianhua wuji jing*, Introduction, Summary and Translation," in Jan A.M. De Meyer and Peter M. Engelfriet, eds. *Linked Faiths: Essays on Chinese Religions and Traditional Culture in Honor of Kristofer Schipper* Leiden: Brill, 2000: 74.

—— in Schipper and Verellen, eds. *The Taoist Canon: a Historical Companion to the Daozang*. Chicago: University of Chicago Press, 2004.

Durrant, Stephen "The Taoist Apotheosis of Mo Ti," *JAOS* 97 (1977): 540–6.

—— in Michael Loewe, ed. *Early Chinese Texts: a Bibliographical Guide*. Berkeley: Society for the Study of Early China: Institute of East Asian Studies, University of California, Berkeley, 1993.

Ebrey, Patricia B. and James L. Watson, eds. *Kinship Organization in Late Imperial China 1000–1940*. Berkeley: University of California Press, 1986.

Ehrman, Bart D. *Lost Christianities: the Battles for Scripture and the Faiths we Never Knew*. New York: Oxford University Press, 2003.

Eskildsen, Stephen. *Asceticism in Early Taoist Religion*. Albany: SUNY Press, 1998.

Espesset, Grégoire."Editing and Translating the Taiping Jing and the Great Peace Textual Corpus," *JCS* 48 (2008): 469–86.

—— "Later Han Religious Mass Movements and the Early Daoist Church," in John Lagerwey and Marc Kalinowski, eds. *Early Chinese Religion, Part One: Shang through Han (1250 BC–AD 220)* vol. 2, Leiden: Brill, 2010: 1061–102.

von Falkenhausen, Lothar. "The E Jun Qi Metal Tallies," in Martin Kern, ed. *Text and Ritual in Early China*. Seattle: University of Washington Press, 2005: 79–123.

Frankfurter, David. "The Magic of the Writing and the Writing of Magic: the Power of the Word in Egyptian and Greek Traditions," *Helios* 21.2 (1994): 189–221.

—— "Narrating Power: the Theory and Practice of the Magical *Historiola* in Ritual Spells," in Marvin Meyer and Paul Mirecki, eds. *Ancient Magic and Ritual Power*. Leiden: Brill, 1995: 457–76.

Furth, Charlotte. "Rereading van Gulik: Sexuality and Reproduction in Traditional Chinese Medicine," in Christina K. Gilmartin, Gail Hershatter, Lisa Rofel, and Tyrene White, eds. *Engendering China: Women, Culture and the State*. Cambridge: Harvard University Press, 1994.

Giele, Enno "Early Chinese Manuscripts: Including Addenda and Corrigenda to New Sources of Early Chinese History: An Introduction to the Reading of Inscriptions and Manuscripts," *Early China 23–24*, 1998–9: 247–337.

Goodman, Howard."Celestial Master Taoism and the Founding of the Ts'ao-Wei Dynasty, The Li Fu Document," *AM* 7 (1994): 5–33.

—— *Ts'ao P'i Transcendent: the Political Culture of Dynasty-founding in China at the End of the Han*. Seattle: Scripta Serica, 1998.

Graham, Angus C. *Disputers of the Tao*. La Sallel, Il. Open Court, 1989.

—— *Chuang-tzu, The Inner Chapters*. Hackett: Indianapolis, 2001.

van Gulik, Robert H. *Sexual Life in Ancient China*: *a Preliminary Survey of Chinese Sex and Society from ca. 1500 B.C., till 1644 A.D.* Leiden: E. J. Brill, 1961. Republished with a new introduction and bibliography by Paul R. Goldin, Leiden and Boston: Brill, 2003.

Harper, Donald. "The Sexual Arts of Ancient China as Described in a Manuscript of the Second Century B.C." *HJAS* 47 (1987): 539–93.

—— "Resurrection in Warring States Popular Religion," *Taoist Resources* 5.2 (1994): 13–28.

——"Warring States, Ch'in, and Han Periods," *JAS* 54 (1995): 152–60.

—— *Early Chinese Medical Literature*. London and New York: Kegan Paul International, 1998.

—— "Warring States Natural Philosophy and Occult Thought," in Michael Loewe and Edward Shaughnessy, eds. *The Cambridge History of Ancient China*. Cambridge, UK; New York: Cambridge University Press, 1999: 813–84.

—— "Contracts with the Spirit World in Han Common Religion: The Xuning Prayer and Sacrifice Documents of A.D. 79," *CEA* 14 (2004): 227–267.

Hawkes, David. *Ch'u Tz'u, The Songs of the South*. Boston: Beacon Press, 1962.

—— *The Songs of the South: an Ancient Chinese Anthology of Poems*. Harmondsworth, Middlesex, England; New York, NY: Penguin, 1985.

Henderson, John B. *Construction of Orthodoxy and Heresy: Neo-Confucian, Islamic, Jewish, and Early Christian Patterns*. Albany: SUNY Press, 1998.

Hendrischke, Barbara. *The Scripture on Great Peace*. Berkeley: University of California Press, 2006.

Ho Peng Yoke. "Alchemy on Stones and Minerals in Chinese Pharmacopoeias," *Chung Chi Journal* 7 (1968).

Holcombe, Charles. *In the Shadow of the Han: Literati Thought and Society at the Beginning of the Southern Dynasties*. Honolulu: Hawaii University Press, 1994.

Holzman, Donald. "The Wang Ziqiao Stele," in *Immortals, Festivals and Poetry in Medieval China*. Aldershot and Brookfield: Ashgate Publishing, 1998. Originally published in *Rocznik Orientalistyczny* 47.2 (1991): 77–83.

Hsieh Shuwei. "Image and Devotion: A Study of the Yao Boduo Stele." M.A. Thesis, Indiana University, 2002.

Hucker, Charles. *A Dictionary of Official Titles in Imperial China*. Stanford: Stanford University Press, 1985.

Hureau, Sylvie. "Buddhist Rituals," in John Lagerwey and Lü Pengzhi, eds. *Early Chinese Religion: the Period of Division (220–589 AD)*. Leiden: Brill, 2010a: 1213–27.

—— "Translations, Apocrypha, and the Emergence of the Buddhist Canon," in John Lagerwey and Lü Pengzhi, eds. *Early Chinese Religion: the Period of Division (220–589 AD)*. Leiden: Brill, 2010b: 758–60.

Hurvitz, Leon. "Wei Shou, Treatise on Buddhism and Taoism: An English Translation of the Original Chinese Text of Wei shu CXIV and the Japanese Annotation of Tsukamoto, Zenryū," in *Yün-kang: The Buddhist Cave Temples of the Fifth Century A.D. in North China*, vol. 16. Kyoto: Kyoto University, Institute of Humanities, 1956.

Hymes, Robert. *Way and Byway: Taoism, Local Religion, and Models of Divinity in Sung and Modern China*. Berkeley: University of California Press, 2002.

Janowitz, Naomi. *Icons of Power: Ritual Practices in Late Antiquity*. University Park: Pennsylvania State University Press, 2002.

Johnston, Ian. *The Mozi: A Complete Translation*. New York: Columbia University Press, 2010.

Kalinowski, Marc. "Les Instruments Astro-calendériques des Han et la Méthode *liu ren*," *BEFEO* 72 (1983): 309–420.

—— "La Transmission du Dispositif des Neuf Palais sous les Six-dynasties," in Michel Strickmann, ed. *Tantric and Taoist Studies,* vol. 3. Bruxelles: Institut Belges des Hautes Etudes Chinoises, 1985: 773–811.

—— "Les Traités de Shuihudi et l'Hémérologie Chinoise à la fin des Royaumes-Combattants." *TP* 72 (1986): 175–228.

—— "La Littérature Divinatoire dans le *Daozang*." *CEA* 5 (1989): 85–114.

—— *Cosmologie et Divination dans la Chine Ancienne. Le Compendium des Cinq Agents (Wuxing dayi, Vie siècle).* Paris: EFEO, 1991.

—— "Technical Traditions in Ancient China and Shushu Culture in Chinese Religion," in John Lagerwey, ed. *Religion and Chinese Society.* Hong Kong: Chinese University Press, 2004: 223–48.

—— "Divination et Astrologie dans l'empire Han: Sources Historiographiques et Découvertes Archéologiques Récentes," *Cahiers du Centre Gustave Glotz* 16 (2005): 275–96.

Kaltenmark, Max. *Le Lie-sien Tchouan.* Paris: Collège de France, 1953 (rpt. 1987).

—— "*Ling-pao* 靈寶: Note sur un Terme du Taoïsme Religieux," in *Mélanges Publiés par l'Institut des Hautes Études Chinoises*, Paris, 1960, vol. II: 559–88.

—— "Quelques Remarques sur le 'T'ai-chang ling-pao wou-fou siu'," *Zimbun: Memoires of the Research Institute for Humanities,* Kyoto University 18 (1981): 1–10.

Kaptchuk, Ted. *The Web that has no Weaver: Understanding Chinese Medicine.* New York: McGraw-Hill Professional, 2000.

Katz, Paul. *Demon Hordes and Burning Boats*, *the Cult of Marshal Wen in Late Imperial Chekiang.* Albany: SUNY, 1995.

Kirkland, Russell. *Taoism: the Enduring Tradition.* New York: Routledge, 2004.

Kleeman, Terry. *A God's Own Tale*: *the Book of Transformations of Wenchang, the Divine Lord of Zitong.* Albany: State University of New York Press, 1994a.

—— "Licentious Cults and Bloody Victuals: Sacrifice, Reciprocity, and Violence in Traditional China." *AM* Ser. 3, 7 (1994b): 185–211.

—— *Great Perfection*, *Religion and Ethnicity in a Chinese Millennial Kingdom.* Honolulu: University of Hawaii Press, 1998.

—— "Daoism in the Third Century," in Florian C. Reiter, ed. *Purposes, Means and Convictions in Daoism*, Wiesbaden: Harrasowitz, 2007: 11–28.

—— "Community and Daily Life in the Early Daoist Church," in John Lagerwey and Lü Pengzhi, eds. *Early Chinese Religion: the Period of Division* (*220–589 AD*), Leiden: Brill, 2010, vol. 1: 395–436.

Knechtges, David. *Wen xuan, or, Selections of Refined Literature,* vol. 1. Princeton: Princeton University Press, 1996.

Knoblock, John and Jeffrey Riegel. *The Annals of Lü Buwei.* Stanford: Stanford University Press, 2000.

Kohn, Livia. "The Mother of the Tao," *TR* 1 (1989): 37–109.

—— *Laughing at the Tao, Debates among Buddhists and Taoists in Medieval China.* Princeton: Princeton University Press, 1995.

—— *God of the Dao: Lord Lao in History and Myth.* Ann Arbor: Center for Chinese Studies, The University of Michigan, 1998.

—— *Daoism Handbook.* Leiden, Boston Koln: Brill, 2000a.

—— "The Northern Celestial Masters," in Kohn, *Daoism Handbook.* Leiden, Boston Koln: Brill, 2000b: 283–306.

—— and Russell Kirkland. "Daoism in the Tang (618–907)," in Kohn, *Daoism Handbook*. Leiden, Boston Koln: Brill, 2000c: 339–83.

—— *Daoism and Chinese Culture*. Cambridge: Three Pines Press, 2001.

Kroll, Paul. "In the Halls of the Azure Lad," *JAOS* 105 (1985): 75–94.

Lagerwey, John. *Wu-shang pi-yao somme taoiste du VIe siécle*. Paris: EFEO, 1981.

—— *Taoist Ritual in Chinese Society and History*. New York: Macmillan, 1987.

—— "Rituel Taoïste et Légimité Politique," *BEFEO* 84 (1997): 99–109.

—— "Deux Écrits Taoïstes Anciens," *CEA* 14 (2004): 139–171.

—— "Zhengyi Registers." *Institute of Chinese Studies Visiting Professor Lecture Series* (I), *Journal of Chinese Studies*, Special Issue (Chinese University of Hong Kong, 2005): 35–88.

—— "The Old Lord's Scripture for the Chanting of the Commandments," in Florian C. Reiter, ed. *Purposes, Means, and Convictions in Daoism*. Wiesbaden: Harrassowitz, 2007: 29–56.

—— and Marc Kalinowski, eds. *Early Chinese Religion, Part One: Shang through Han (1250 BC–220 AD)*. Leiden: Brill, 2010a.

—— and Lü Pengzhi, eds. *Early Chinese Religion: the Period of Division (220–589 AD)*. Leiden: Brill, 2010b.

—— "Le Rituel Taoïste selon Lu Xiujing." Unpublished manuscript.

Lai Chi-tim, "The *Demon Statutes of Nüqing* and the Problem of the Bureaucratization of the Netherworld in Early Heavenly Master Daoism." *TP* 88 (2002): 252–81.

Leban, Carl. "Managing Heaven's Mandate: Coded Communication in the Accession of Ts'ai P'ei, A.D. 220," in David T. Roy and Tsuen-hsuin Tsien, eds. *Ancient China: Studies in Early Civilization*. Hong Kong: Chinese University Press, 1978: 315–39.

Ledderose, Lothar. "Some Taoist Elements in the Calligraphy of the Six Dynasties," *T'oung Pao* 70 (1984): 246–78.

Legge, James *The Ch'un Ts'ew, with the Tso chuen in The Chinese Classics*; rpt. Taipei, Republic of China: Southern Materials Center, 1985.

Lewis, Mark E. "Ritual Origins of the Warring States," *BEFEO* 84 (1997): 73–98.

—— *Writing and Authority in Early China*. Albany: SUNY Press, 1999.

—— "The *feng* and *shan* Sacrifices of Emperor Wu of the Han," in Joseph P. McDermott, ed. *State and Court Ritual in China*. Cambridge: Cambridge University Press, 1999: 50–80.

Li Gang. "State Religious Policy," in Lagerwey and Lü Pengzhi, eds. *Early Chinese Religion: the Period of Division (220–589 AD)*. Leiden: Brill, 2010: 193–274.

Li Ling 李零. (Translated by Donald Harper), "An Archaeological Study of Taiyi (Grand One) Worship," *Early Medieval China* 2 (1995): 1–39.

Li Xueqin 李學勤. *Eastern Zhou and Qin Civilizations*. (Translated by K. C. Chang). New Haven: Yale University Press 1985: 399–417.

Lin, Fu-shi. "Chinese Shamans and Shamanism in the Chinag-nan Area During the Six Dynasties." Ph.D. Thesis, Princeton University, 1994.

Lipner, Julius J. "Ancient Banyan: an Inquiry into the Meaning of 'Hinduness'," in J. E. Llewellyn, ed. *Defining Hinduism*. Routledge: New York, 2005: 30–48.

Lippiello, Tiziana. "Interpreting Written Riddles: a Typical Chinese Way of Divination," in De Meyer, Jan A. M. and Peter M. Engelfriet, eds. *Linked Faiths: Essays on Chinese Religions and Traditional Culture in Honor of Kristofer Schipper*. Leiden and Boston: Brill, 2000: 41–52.

Little, Stephen with Shawn Eichman. *Taoism and the Arts of China*. Chicago: The Art Institute of Chicago, 2000.

Liu An, King of Huainan. *The Huainanzi: A Guide to the Theory and Practice of Government in Early Han China*. Translated and edited by John S. Major, Sarah A. Queen, Andrew Seth Meyer, and Harold Roth. New York: Columbia University Press, 2010.

Loewe, Michael. *Crisis and Conflict in Han China*. London: George Allen & Unwin, 1974.

—— *Ways to Paradise: the Chinese Quest for Immortality*. London: Allen and Unwin, 1979.

—— ed. *Early Chinese Texts: A Bibliographical Guide*. Berkeley: Society for the Study of Early China: Institute of East Asian Studies, University of California, Berkeley, 1993a.

—— *Early Chinese Sources*. Berkeley: Society for the Study of Early China, 1993b.

—— "The chüeh-ti Games: a Re-enactment of the Battle between Ch'ih-yu and Hsüan-yüan?" in Loewe, *Divination, Mythology and Monarchy in Han China*. Cambridge: Cambridge University Press, 1994: 236–48.

Lopez, Donald S., ed. *Religions of China in Practice*. Princeton: Princeton University Press, 1996.

Lü Pengzhi. "Daoist Rituals," in John Lagerwey and Lü Pengzhi, *Early Chinese Religion: the Period of Division (220–589 AD)*. Leiden: Brill, 2010: 1245–349.

—— "A Study of the Zhijiao Fast of Celestial Master Daoism," in Florian C. Reiter, ed. *Foundations of Daoist Ritual*. Wiesbaden: Harrassowitz, 2009: 165–188.

Lupke, Christopher, ed. *The Magnitude of Ming: Command, Allotment, and Fate in Chinese Culture*. Honolulu: University of Hawaii Press, 2005.

Major, John S. *Heaven and Earth in Early Han Thought*. Albany: SUNY, 1993.

Mather, Richard. "K'ou Ch'ien-chih and Taoist Theocracy at the Northern Wei Court, 425–451," in Holmes Welch and Anna Seidel, eds. *Facets of Taoism*. New Haven and London: Yale University Press, 1979: 103–22.

De Meyer, Jan A. M. and Peter M. Engelfriet, eds. *Linked Faiths: Essays on Chinese Religions and Traditional Culture in Honor of Kristofer Schipper*. Leiden and Boston: Brill, 2000.

Mollier. Christine, *Une Apocalypse Taoïste du Ve siècle: le Livre des Incantations Divines des Grottes Abyssales*. Paris: Collége du France, Institut des Hautes Études Chinoises, 1990.

Munakata, Kiyohiko. *Sacred Mountains in Chinese Art*. Champaign: Krannert Art Museum, University of Illinois at Urbana-Champaign; Urbana: University of Illinois Press, 1990.

Needham, Joseph. *Science and Civilization in China*. Cambridge: Cambridge University Press, 1954–98.

Needham, Rodney. "Polythetic Classification, Convergence and Consequence," *Man* 10 (1975): 349–69.

Ngo Van Xuyet. *Divination, Magie et Politique dans la Chine Ancienne*. Paris: Presses Universitaires de France, 1976.

Nickerson, Peter. "*Taoism, Death and Bureaucracy in Early Medieval China*." Berkeley University Ph.D. Thesis, 1996.

—— "Abridged Codes of Master Lu," in Donald Lopez, ed. *Chinese Religions in Practice*. Princeton: Princeton University Press, 1996: 347–59.

—— "The Southern Celestial Masters," in Livia Kohn, ed. *Daoism Handbook*. Leiden, Boston Koln: Brill, 2000: 256–82.

Nienhauser Jr, William H., ed. *The Indiana Companion to Traditional Chinese Literature*. Bloomington: Indiana University Press, 1986.

—— *The Grand Scribe's Records*. Bloomington: Indiana University Press, 1994.

Noegel, Scott, Joel Walker, and Brannon Wheeler, eds. *Prayer, Magic, and the Stars in the Ancient and Late Antique World*. University Park: Pennsylvania State University Press, 2003.

Ochi Shigaeki 越智重明. "Thoughts on the Understanding of the Han and Six Dynasties," *Memoirs of the Research Department of the Toyo Bunko*, 35 (1977): 1–75.

Ōfuchi Ninji. "On Ku ling-pao jing," *Acta Asiatica* 27 (1974): 33–56.

—— "The Formation of the Taoist Canon," in Holmes Welch and Anna Seidel, eds. *Facets of Taoism*. New Haven and London: Yale University Press, 1979: 253–67.

Pankenier, David W. "The Cosmo-political Background of Heaven's Mandate," *Early China* 20 (1995): 121–76.

Pearce, Scott, Audrey Spiro, and Patricia Ebrey, eds. *Culture and Power in the Reconstitution of the Chinese Realm, 200–600*. Cambridge, MA and London: Harvard University Press, 2001.

Pines, Yuri. "The Search for Stability: Late-Chun ch'iu Thinkers,"*AM* 10.1–2 (1997): 18–31.

—— "History as Guide to the Netherworld: Rethinking the *Chunqiu shiyu*," *JCR* 31 (2003): 101–26.

Poo Mu-chou. "Ghost Literature: Exorcistic Ritual Texts or Daily Entertainment?" *AM* 13.1 (2000): 43–64.

Porkert, Manfred. *Biographie d'un taoïste légendaire*: *Tcheou tseu-yang*. Paris: Collège de France, Institut des Hautes Études Chinoises, 1979.

Pregadio, Fabrizio. "The *Book of the Nine Elixirs* and its Tradition," in Yamada Keiji 山田慶兒 and Takeda Tan 田中淡, eds. *Chūgoku Kodai Kagakushiron* 中國古代科學史論. Kyoto: Jinbun kagaku kenkyūjo, 1991, vol. 2, 543–639.

—— *Great Clarity*: *Daoism and Alchemy in Early Medieval China*. Stanford: Stanford University Press, 2006.

Puett, Michael. *To Become a God: Cosmology, Sacrifice and Self-Divinization in Early China*. Cambridge, Mass and London: Harvard University Press, 2002.

Queen, Sarah A. *From Chronicle to Canon: the Hermeneutics of the Spring and Autumn, According to Tung Chung-shu*. Cambridge: Cambridge University Press, 1996.

Raz, Gil "Ritual and Cosmology: Transformations of the Ritual for the Eight Archivists." M.A. Thesis, Indiana University, 1996.

—— "Creation of Tradition: The Five Numinous Treasure Talismans and the Formation of Early Daoism," Ph.D. Thesis, Bloomington: Indiana University 2004.

—— "Time Manipulation in Early Daoist Ritual." *AM* (2005): 27–65.

—— "Imperial Efficacy: Debates on Imperial Ritual in Early Medieval China and the Emergence of Daoist Ritual Schemata," in Florian Reiter, ed. *Purposes, Means and Convictions in Daoism, a Berlin Symposium*. Wiesbaden: Harrasowitz 2007: 83–109.

—— "Daoist Sacred Geography," in John Lagerwey and Lü Pengzhi, eds. *Early Chinese Religion*: *Part Two, The Period of Division*. Leiden and Boston: E.J. Brill, 2010: 1399–442.

Read, Bernard, and C. Pak. *Chinese Materia Medica*, *A Compendium of Minerals and Stones*. Taipei: SMC Materials, 1977.

Reiter, Florian C., ed. *Purposes, Means and Convictions in Daoism*. Wiesbaden: Harrasowitz, 2007.

—— ed. *Foundations of Daoist Ritual*. Wiesbaden: Harrassowitz, 2009.

Robinet, Isabelle. *La Révélation du Shangqing dans l'Histoire du Taôisme*. Paris: EFEO, 1984.

—— *Taoist Meditation: The Mao-shan Tradition of Great Purity*, translated by Julian F. Pas and Norman Girardot. Albany: SUNY Press, 1993.

—— *Taoism: Growth of a Religion*. Translated by Phyllis Brooks. Stanford: Stanford University Press, 1997.

Robson, James. *Power of Place: The Religious Landscape of the Southern Sacred Peak (Nanyue* 南嶽*) in Medieval China*. Cambridge: Harvard University Asia Center, 2009.

Schafer, Edward. "The Restoration of the Shrine of Wei Hua-ts'un at Lin-ch'uan in the Eighth Century," *Journal of Oriental Studies* 15 (1977): 124–37.

—— "Wu Yün's 'Cantos on Pacing the Void'," *HJAS* 41 (1981): 377–415.

Schipper, Kristofer. See also Shi Zhouren施舟人

—— L'empereur Wou des Han dans la légende taoiste. Paris: EFEO 1965.

—— *Taoist Body*, *HR* 17 (1978): 355–86.

—— "Le Calendrier de Jade – Note sur le Laozi zhongjing," *Nachrichten der Gesellschaft für Natur und Völkerkunde Ostasiens* Hamburg 125 (1979): 75–80.

—— "Taoist Ritual and Local Cults of the T'ang Dynasty," in Michel Strickmann, *Tantric and Taoist Studies*, vol. III. Institut Belge des Hautes Etudes Chinoises: Bruxelles, 1983: 812–34.

—— "Taoist Ordination Ranks in the Tunhuang Manuscripts," in Gert Naundorf, Karl-Heinz Pohl, Hans-Hermann Schmidt, eds. *Religion und Philosophie in Ostasien: Festschrift für Hans Steininger zum 65 Geburtstag*. Würzburg: Königshausen und Neumann, 1985.

—— "Study of Buxu: Taoist Liturgical Hymn and Dance," in Tsao Peng-yeh and Daniel P.L. Law, eds. *Studies of Taoist Rituals and Music of Today*. Hong Kong: Society for Ethnomusicological Research in Hong Kong, 1989: 110–20.

—— "Le culte de l'immortel Tang Gongfang," in A. Forest, Y. Ishizawa, and L. Vandermeersch, eds. *Cultes Populaires et Sociétés Asiatiques*. Paris: EFEO, 1991: 59–72.

—— *The Taoist Body*. (Translated by Karen Duval.) Berkeley: University of California Press, 1993.

—— "Une stèle Taoïste des Han orientaux récemment découverte," in Jacques Gernet and Marc Kalinowski, eds. *En Suivant la Voie Royale, Mélanges Offerts en Hommage à Léon Vandermeersch*. Paris: EFEO, 1997: 239–47.

—— and Franciscus Verellen, eds. *The Taoist Canon*: *a Historical Companion to the Daozang* Chicago: University of Chicago Press, 2004.

—— "The True Form: Reflections on the Liturgical Basis of Taoist art," *Sanjiao wenxian* 4 (2005): 91–113.

Seidel, Anna. *La Divinisation de Lao Tseu dans le Taoisme des Han*. Paris: EFEO, 1969.

—— "The Image of the Perfect Ruler in Early Taoist Messianism: Lao-tzu and Li Hung." *HR* 9, 2/3 (November 1969/February 1970): 216–47.

——"Imperial Treasures and Taoist Sacraments – Taoist Roots in The Apocrypha," in Michel Strickmann, ed. *Tantric and Taoist Studies*, Bruxelles: Institut Belges des Hautes Etudes Chinoises, (1983), vol. II: 291–371.

—— "Taoist Messianism," *Numen* 31 (1984): 161–74.

—— "Traces of Han Religion, in Funeral Texts Found in Tombs," in Akizuki Kanei 秋月 觀映 *Dōkyō to shukyō bunka* 道教と宗教文化. Tokyo: Hirakawa, 1987: 23–57.

—— "Early Taoist Ritual," *CEA* 4 (1988): 199–204.

—— "Chronicle of Taoist Studies in the West," *CEA* 5 (1989–90).

—— "Taoism: the Unofficial High Religion of China," *TR* 7.2 (1997): 39–72. Originally published as "Taoismus, die inoffizielle Hochreligion Chinas." Tokyo, OAG Aktuell 41 (1989).

Sivin, Nathan. *Chinese Alchemy: Preliminary Studies*. Cambridge: Harvard University Press, 1968.

—— "On the Word 'Taoist' as a Source of Perplexity," *HR* 17 (1978): 303–30.

—— "Huang ti nei ching" in Michael Loewe, ed. *Early Chinese Texts: a Bibliographical Guide*. Berkeley: Society for the Study of Early China: Institute of East Asian Studies, University of California, Berkeley, 1993: 196–215.

—— "Taoism and Science," in *Medicine, Philosophy and Religion in Ancient China* Aldershot, UK and Brookfield, VT: Variorum, 1995a, VII.

—— "Text and Experience in Classical Chinese Medicine," in Don Bates, ed. *Knowledge and the Scholarly Medical Traditions*. Cambridge: Cambridge University Press, 1995b: 177–204.

—— "Drawing Insights from Chinese Medicine," *Journal of Chinese Philosophy* 34 (2007): 43–55.

Skemer, Don C. *Binding Words*: *Textual Amulets in the Middle Ages*. University Park: Pennsylvania State University Press, 2006.

Smith, Kidder. "Sima Tan and the Invention of Daoism, 'Legalism,' *et cetera*," *JAS* 62.1 (2003): 129–56.

Smith, Richard J. *Fortune-tellers and Philosophers*: *Divination in Traditional Chinese Society*. Boulder: Westview Press, 1991.

Smith, Thomas E. "Ritual and the Shaping of Narrative: The Legend of the Han Emperor Wu." University of Michigan Ph.D. Thesis, 1992.

Sørensen, Jørgen Podemann "The Argument in Ancient Egyptian Magical Formulae," *Acta Orientalia* 45 1984.

Soymié, Michel. "Les dix jours de jeûne du taoïsme," in *Yoshioka Yoshitoyo hakase kanri kinen Dōkyō kenkyū ronshū* 吉岡義豐博士還紀念道教研究論集. Tokyo: Kokusho kankōkai, 1977: 1–21.

Stein, Rolf. "Religious Taoism and Popular Religion from the Second to Seventh Centuries," in Holmes Welch and Anna Seidel, eds. *Facets of Taoism: Essays in Chinese Religion*. New Haven: Yale University Press, 1979: 53–81.

Strickmann, Michel. "The Mao Shan Revelations – Taoism and the Aristocracy," *TP* 63 (1977): 1–64.

—— "On the Alchemy of T'ao Hung-ching," in Holmes Welch and Anna Seidel, eds. *Facets of Taoism*. New Haven and London: Yale University Press, 1979: 133–92.

—— *Le Taoïsme du Mao Chan, Chronique d'une Révélation*. Paris: Mémoires de l'institut des Hautes Études Chinoises, 1981.

—— *Tantric and Taoist Studies,* vol. 2. Bruxelles: Institut Belges des Hautes Etudes Chinoises, 1983.

—— *Tantric and Taoist Studies,* vol. 3. Bruxelles: Institut Belges des Hautes Etudes Chinoises, 1985.

—— *Chinese Magical Medicine*. Stanford: Stanford University Press, 2002.

Sun Xiaochun and Jacob Kistemaker. *The Chinese Sky during the Han: Constellating Stars and Society*. Leiden, New York: Brill, 1997.

Tambiah, Stanley. *The Buddhist Saints of the Forest and the Cult of Amulets*: *a Study in Charisma, Hagiography, Sectarianism, and Millennial Buddhism*. Cambridge: Cambridge University Press, 1984.

Teboul, Michel. "Sur quelques particularités de l'uranographie polaire chinoise," *TP* 71 (1985): 1–39.

Twitchett, Denis, and Michael Loewe, eds. *The Cambridge History of China, vol. 1: the Ch'in and Han Empires, 221 BC–AD 220*. Cambridge: Cambridge University Press, 1986.

Unschuld, Paul. *Medicine in China, a History of Pharmaceutics*. Berkeley and Los Angeles: University of California Press, 1986.

—— *Huang Di Nei Jing Su Wen: Nature, Knowledge, Imagery in an Ancient Chinese Medical Text*. Berkeley: University of California Press, 2003.

Verellen, Franciscus. "The Beyond Within: Grotto-Heavens (*dongtian* 洞天) in Taoist Ritual and Cosmology," *CEA* 8 (1995): 265–90.

—— "The Heavenly Master Liturgical Agenda According to Chisong zi's Petition Almanac," *CEA* 14 (2004): 291–343.

Wang Chengwen. "The Revelation and Classification of Daoist Scriptures," in John Lagerwey and Lü Pengzhi, eds. *Early Chinese Religion: the Period of Division (220–589 AD)*. Leiden: Brill, 2010: 775–888.

Ware, James. "The *Weishu* and *Suishu* on Taoism," *JAOS* 53 (1933): 240–50.

—— *Alchemy, Medicine and Religion in the China of AD 230 The Nei P'ien of Ko Hung*. Dover Publications: New York, 1966; rpt. 1981.

Welch, Holmes and Anna Seidel, eds. *Facets of Taoism*. New Haven and London: Yale University Press, 1979.

Wile, Douglas. *Art of the Bedchamber*. Albany: SUNY Press, 1992.

Yamada Keiji. "The Formation of the Huang-ti nei-ching," *Acta Asiatica* 36 (1979): 67–89.

Yamada Toshiaki. "Longevity Techniques and the Compilation of the *Lingbao wufuxu*," in Livia Kohn, ed. *Taoist Meditation and Longevity Techniques*. Ann Arbor: University of Michigan, Center for Chinese Studies, 1989: 99–124.

Yü Ying-shih. "Life and Immortality in the Mind of Han China." *HJAS* 25 (1964): 80–122.

Chinese- and Japanese-language sources

Bo Yi 柏夷 (Stephen Bokenkamp), "Tianshidao hunyin yishi 'heqi' zai shangqing lingbao xuepai de yanbian" 天師道婚姻儀式 "合氣" 在上清靈寶學派的演變 *Daojia wenhua yanjiu* 16 (1999): 241–8.

Cao Wanru and Zheng Xihuang, "Shilun daojiao de wuyue zhenxingtu," *Ziran kexueshi yanjiu* 1987.6: 52–7.

Chen Guofu 陳國符. *Daozang yuanliu kao* 道藏源流考. Beijing, Zhonghua shuju, rpt. 1989.

Chen Qiaoy 陳橋驛. *Shuijing zhu jiaoshi* 水經注校釋. Hangzhou: Hangzhou daxue chuban-she, 1999.

Chen Xianyuan 陳賢遠. "Han 'Xianren Tang Gongfang bei' kao" 汉 '仙人唐公 房碑考, *Wenbo* 文博 1996.2: 27–8, 48.

Chen Yuan 陳垣. *Daojia jinshi lue* 道家金石略. Beijing: Wenwu, 1988.

Dong Xiansi 東賢司, "Yizhu Fei Zhi bei" 譯注 '肥致碑 *Dafen daxue jiaoyu xuebu yanjiu jiyao* 大分大學教育學部研究紀要 17.1 1995.

Fan Yousheng 樊有升. "Donghan Fei Zhi bei" 東漢肥致碑. *Shufa congkan* 書法從看 1992.2; collected in *Huaxiang zhuan shike muzhi yanjiu* 畫像磚石刻墓誌研究. Zhongzhou guji, 1994: 168–71.

—— "Donghan daoshi 'Fei Zhi bei' chuxi" 東漢道士'肥致碑' 初析. *Heluo chunqiu* 河洛春秋 1997.1: 21–7.

Ge Hong *Mozi zhenzhong wuxingji* 墨子枕中五行記 *BPZ* 19.333.

Gao Wen 高文. *Hanbei jishi* 漢碑集釋. Kaifeng: Henan daxue, 1997.

Hong Shi 洪石. "Dongzhou zhi jindai mu suochu wushu jiandu jiji xiangguan wenti yan-jiu" 東周至晉代墓所出物疏簡牘及其相關問題研究. *KG* 2001.9: 59–69.

Hsing I-tien 邢義田. "Donghan de fangshi yu qiuxian fengqi – Fei Zhi bei duji" 東漢的方士與求仙風氣 – 肥致碑讀記. *Dalu Zazhi* 大陸雜誌 94.2 (1997): 49–61.

Hu Fuchen 胡孚琛. *Weijin shenxian daojiao* 魏晉神仙道教 Beijing: Renmin, 1989.

Hu Fuchen and Lü Xichen 呂f錫琛, *Daoxue tonglun* 道學 通論 Beijing: Shehui kexue wenxian, 2004.

Huang Lie 黃烈. "Luelun tulufan chutude 'daojiao fulu'" 略論吐魯番出土的道教符籙 WW 1981.1: 51–6.

Hunansheng bowuguan 湖南省博物館, "Changsha liangjin nanchao sui mu fajue baogao" 長沙兩晉南朝隋墓發掘報告, Kaogu xuebao 1959.3: 75–103.

Ishii Masako 石井昌子. "Reihō gofukyō no ikkōsatsu" 靈寶五符經の一考察 *Sōka daigaku ippan kyōikubu ronshū* 創大學一般教育部論集 5 (1981): 1–20.

—— "Reihō kyō rui" 靈宝経類 in *Kōza tonkō* 4: *Tonkō to chūgoku dōkyō* 講座敦煌. 4: 敦煌と中国道教. Tokyo: Daitō, 1983: 164–7.

—— "Taijō reihō gofujo no ikkōsatsu" 太上靈寶五符序の一考察, in *Makio Ryōkai hakase shojū kinen ronshū Chūgoku no shūkyo shiso to kagaku* 牧尾朗海博士頌 壽記念論文集: 中國の宗教思想と科學. Tokyo: Kokusho kankōkai, 1984: 13–31.

Jao Tsung-I (Rao Zongyi) 饒宗頤. *Laozi xiang'er zhu jiaozheng* 老子想爾注校證. Shanghai: Shanghai guji, 1991 (a revised edition of *Laozi xiang'er zhu jiaozheng* 老子想爾注校證, Hong Kong: Tongnam, 1956).

—— "'Chuan Laozi shi' Rongcheng yishuo gouchen" '傳老子師' 容成遺說鉤沉, *Beijing daxue xuebao* 1998.3, rpt. in *Jao Tsung-I ershi shiji xueshu wenji* 饒宗頤二十世紀學術文集 Taipei: Xinwenfeng, 2004, vol. 5: 105–18.

Jiangsu sheng wenwu guanli weiyuan hui. "Jiangsu gaoyou shaojiagou handai yizhi de qingli" 江蘇高郵邵家溝漢代遺址的清理. *KG* 1960.10: 20–1.

Jiang Yuxiang 江玉祥 "Shilun zaoqi daojiao zai bashu fasheng de wenhua beijing" 試論早期道教在巴蜀發生的文化背景, *DJWH* 7: 323–37.

Kamitsuka Yoshiko 神塚淑子. "Hōshu seitokun omegutte – Rikuchō Jōsei Dōkyō no ikkōsatsu" 方諸青童君をめぐつて— 六朝上清派道教 の一考察. *TS* 76 (1990): 1–23.

—— "Reihō kyō to shoki kōnan bukkyo – inga ōhō sishō chōsin ni" 靈寶經と初期江南佛教 — 因果應報思想 中心に. *TS* 91 (1998): 1–21.

Kato Chie 加藤千惠. "Roshi chukyō to naitan sishō no genryū" 老子中經と内丹思想 の源流. *TS* 76 (May 1996a): 21–38; Chinese translation '老子中經' 與内丹思想的起源 in *Zongjiaoxue yanjiu* 1997.4: 40–7.

—— 加藤千惠, "Roshi chukyō to naitan shisō no kigen" '老子中經'と内丹思想的起源, *TS* 87 (May 1996b): 22–38, Chinese translation '老子中經' 與内丹思想的起源 in *Zongjiaoxue yanjiu* 1997.4: 40–7.

Kobayashi Masayoshi 小林正美. *Reihō sekisho gohen no sishō to seiritsu* 靈寶赤書五篇真文の思想と成 立. *TS* 60 (1982): 23–47.

——"Taijō reihō gofujo no sosei katei no bunseki" 太上靈寶五符序の成書過程の分析. (1) *TS* 71 (April 1988): 20–43. (2) *TS* 72 (October 1988): 20–44.

—— *Jōseikyō to reihō kyō no shūmatsuron* 上清經と靈寶經の終末論 *TS* 75 (1990a): 20–41.

—— *Rikuchō Dōkyōshi kenkyū* 六朝道教史研究. Tokyo: Sōbunsha, 1990b.

—— *Chūgoku no dōkyō* 中國の道教 Tokyo: Sōbunsha, 1998: 7.

Lee Fengmao 李豐楙. *Liuchao sui-tang xiandao lei xiaoshuo yanjiu* 六朝隋唐仙道類小說研究 Hsueh-sheng: Taipei, 1986.

—— "Liuchao de Li Hong tuchen chuanshuo" 六潮的李弘圖讖傳說, in *Liuchao Sui Tang xiandaolei xiaoshuo yanjiu* Taipei: Taiwan xuesheng shuju, 1986: 283–304.

_____ "'Dongyuan Shenzhou jing' de shenmoguan jiqi kezhishuo" '洞淵神咒經' 的神魔觀及其克制說. *Dongfang zongjiao yanjiu* 2 (1991a): 133–55.

—— "Tangdai 'Dongyuan Shen zhou jing' xiejuan yu Li Hong" 唐代 '洞淵神咒經' 寫卷與李弘. *Di'erjie Dunhuangxue guoji yantaohui lunwenji* 第二屆敦煌學國際研討會論文集. Taipei, Hanxue yanjiu zhongxin, 1991b: 481–500.

_____ "'Daozang' suoshou zaoqi daoshu de wenyi guan – yi 'Nüqing guilü' ji 'Dongyuan Shenzhou jing' xi weizhu" '道藏' 所收早期道書的瘟疫觀 – 以 '女青鬼律' 及 '洞淵神咒經' 系為主. *Zhongguo wenzhi yanjiu jikan* (1993): 417–54.

_____ "Chuancheng yu duiying: liuchao daojing zhong 'moshi' shuo de tichu yu yanbian" 傳承與對應: 六朝道經中 '末世' 說的提出與衍變, *Bulletin of the Institute of Literature and Philosophy* 9 (1996): 91–130.

_____*Xu Xun yu Sa Shouxian: Deng Zhimo daojiao xiaoshuo yanjiu* 許遜與薩守堅: 鄧志謨道教小說研究. Taipei: Taiwan Xuesheng, 1997.

—*Busi de tanqiu Baopuzi* 不死的探求抱朴子. Taipei: China Times, 1998.

Li Hsun-hsiang 李訓詳. "Muzhiming haishi cisi ti ke? — du Fei Zhi bei zhaji" 墓誌銘還是祠祀提科 — 讀肥致碑札記. *Dalu Zazhi* 95.6 (1997): 286–8.

Li Jianmin 李建民. "Zhongguo gudai 'jinfang' kaolun" 中國古代 "禁方" 考論. *BIHP* 68 (1997): 117–57.

—— *Sisheng zhi yu* 死生之域. Taipei, Academia Sinica, 2000.

Li Jinyun. "Tan Taicang chutu de wuyue zhenxing jing." *Wenwu* 1988.2: 177–8.

Li Liliang 李麗涼. *"Wushang biyao" zhi bianzuan ji daojing fenlei kao* '無上秘要' 之編纂及道經分類考. Taipei: Chengchih University MA, 1998.

Li Ling 李零. "Donghan weijin nanbeichao fangzhong jingdian liupai kao" 東漢魏晉南北朝房中經典流派考. *Zhongguo wenhua* 15/16 (1997): 141–58.

—— *Zhongguo fangshu kao* 中國方術考. Beijing: Dongfang, rev. edn 2000a.

—— *Zhongguo fangshu xukao* 中國方術續考. Beijing: Dongfang, 2000b.

Li Yuzheng 李域錚, Zhao Minsheng 趙敏生, and Lei Bing 雷冰. *Xi'an beilin shufa yishu* 西安碑林書法藝術. Xi'an: Shaanxi Renmin, 1983.

Li Xueqin "Taiyi shengshui de shushu jieshi" 太一生水的數術解釋, *DJWH* 17 1999: 9–12.

Lian Shaoming 連邵名. "Kaogu faxian yu zaoqi fu" 考古發現與早期符. *KG* 1995.12: 1125–30.

Lin Fu-shi 林富士. *Handai de Wuzhe* 漢代的巫者 Taipei: Daoxiang, 1988.

—— "Luelun zaoqi daojiao yu fangzhong shu de guanxi" 略論早期道教與房中術的關係, *BIHP* 72.2 (2001): 233–300.

Liu Dianjue 劉殿爵. *Mozi zhuzi suoyin* 墨子逐字索引 [A concordance to the Mozi]. Hong Kong: Shangwu yinshuguan, 2001.

Liu Lexian 劉樂賢. "Shaojiagou Handai mudu shang de fuzhou ji xiangguan wenti" 邵家溝漢代木牘上的符咒及相關問題. Taipei: Zhongguo wenhua daxue shixuexi, 1999.

Liu Shipei 劉 師 培. "Du daozang ji" 讀道藏記, rpt. in *Daozang yaoji xuankan* 道藏要籍選刊 Shanghai: Guji chubanshe 1989, vol. 10: 705–21.

Liu Tseng-Kuei 劉增貴. "Qinjian 'rishu' zhongde chuxing lisu yu xinyang" 秦簡 '日書' 中的出行禮俗與信仰. *BIHP* 72.3 (2001): 503–41.

Liu Xiaogan 劉笑敢. *Laozi gujin – wuzhong duikan yu xiping yinlun* 老子古今 – 五種對勘與析評引論. Beijing: Zhongguo kexue chubanshe, 2006.

Liu Yi 劉屹. "Dunhuang ben Laozi bianhuajing yanjiu zhiyi, Hanmo chengshu shuo zhiyi" 敦煌本老子變化經研究之一 – 漢末成書說質疑 *Wu Qixiang xiansheng bezhi huadan Dunhuang xue jikan* 吳其昱先生八秩華誕敦煌學季刊. Taiwan, 1998.

—— *Jingtian yu chongdao – zhonggu daojiao xingcheng de sixiangshi beijing zhi yi* 敬天與崇道中古道教形成的思想史背景之一 Beijing: Zhonghua shuju, 2005.

—— "Lun gu lingbao jing 'shengxuan buxu zhang' de yanbian" 論古靈寶經 '昇 玄步虛章' 的演變 in Florian Reiter, ed. *Foundations of Daoist Ritual*. Wiesbaden: Harrassowitz, 2009: 189–205.

Liu Zhaorui 劉昭瑞. "'Huangshen yuezhang' jiantan huangjin kouhao ji xianguan wenti" 論"黃神越章" 兼談黃巾口號的意義及相關問題. *Lishi yanjiu* 1996.1: 125–132.

—— *Kaogu faxian yu zaoqi daojiao yanjiu* 考古發現與早起道教研究. Wenwu: Beijing, 2007.

Liu Zhongyu 劉仲宇. "Daofu suyuan" 道符溯源. *Shijie zongjiao yanjiu* 1994.1: 1–10.

Long Xianzhao 龍顯昭 and Huang Haide 黃海德, eds. *Bashu daojiao beiwen jicheng* 巴蜀道教碑文集成. Chengdu: Sichuan Daxue, 1997.

Lü Pengzhi 呂鵬志. "Tianshi dao shoulu keyi – Dunhuang xieben S.203 kaolun" 天師道授籙科儀敦煌寫本考論. *BIHP* 77.1 (2006): 79–166.

—— *Tangqian daojiao yishi shigang* 唐前道教儀式史綱. Beijing: Zhonghua shuju, 2008.

Lü Zongli 呂宗力. "Donghan beike yu chenwei shenxue" 東漢碑刻與讖緯神學, in *Yanjiusheng lunwen xuanji* 研究生論文選集. Nanjing, 1984.

—— "Tōkan hikaku to shin'i shingaku" 東漢碑刻と讖緯神學, in Nakamura, 1993: 210–55.

Lu Yixing 陸錫興. "'Huangjun faxing' zhuzi kemingzhuan de tansuo" "黃君法行"朱字刻銘磚的探索. *KG* 2002.4: 85–8.

Ma Chengyu 馬承玉. "Cong Dunhuang xieben kan 'Dongyuan shen zhou jing' zai beifang de chuanbo" 從敦煌寫本看 '洞淵神咒經' 在北方的傳播. *DJWH* 13 (1998): 200–25.

Maeda Shigeki 前田繁樹. *Roshi chukyō oboegaki* '老子中經'覺書. in Sakade Yoshinobu 阪出祥伸, ed. *Chūgoku kodai yōsei shisō sogoteki kenkyū* 中國古代 養 生思想 綜合的研究. Tokyo: Hirakawa, 1988.

Meng Wentong, "Wanzhou xiandao fen sanpai kao" 晚周仙道分三派, in *Tushu jikan* 圖書季刊 8 (1946); rpt. in *Meng Wentong wenji* 蒙文通文集. Chengdu: Bashu shushe, 1987: v. 1, 335–42.

Miyakawa Hisayuki 宮川尚志. "Shindai dokyō no ikkosatsu – 'Taishō tōen shinju kyō' omegurite" 晉代道經の一考察 '太上洞淵神咒經' をめぐりて, in *Chūgoku shūkyō shi kenkyū* 中國宗教史研究. Kyoto: Dōhōsha, 1983: 149–74.

Nagata Hidemasa 永田英正. Kandai sekkoku shûsei 漢代石刻集成. Kyoto, Dôhôsha, 1994.

Oh Yi-han 吳二煥. 1982. *Rokutenstsu no haiekei* 六天說の背景 *(Japanese) Chūgoku shiso shi kenkyū* 5: 1–36.

Ōfuchi Ninji 大淵忍爾. Dōkyō shi no kenkyū 道教史の研究. Okayama: Okayama daigaku kyōzaikai shoseki, 1964.

—— *Tonkō dōkyō mokurokuhen* 敦煌道經目錄篇. Tokyo: Fukubu shoten, 1978a.

—— *Tonkō dōkyō zurokuhen* 敦煌道經圖錄篇. Tokyo: Fukubu shoten, 1978b.

—— *Shoki no Dōkyō* 初期の道教. Tokyo: Sōbunsha, 1991.

—— *Dōkyō to sono kyoten* 道教とその經典. Tokyo: Sōbunsha, 1997.

Ozaki Masaharu 尾崎正法. "Tōen shinju kyō" 洞淵神咒經, in *Kōza Tonkō, Tonkō to Chūgoku Dōkyō* ‧ 講座敦煌, ‧ 敦煌中國道教. Tokyo: Tohō, 1983, vol. 4, pp. 177–82.

Rao Zongyi (Jao Tsung-i) 饒宗頤, *Laozi xiang'er zhu jiaozheng* 老子想爾注校證 Shanghai: Shanghai guji, 1991 (a revised edition of *Laozi xiang'er zhu jiaojian* 老子想爾注校踐, Hong Kong: Tongnam, 1956).

Schipper, Kristofer. "Gogaku shingyo tzu no shinkō" 五嶽真形圖の信仰 *Dōkyō kenkyū* 道教研究 vol. 2 (1967): 114–162.

—— "Reihō kagi no tenkai" 靈寶科儀の展開, in *Nihon Chūgoku no shūkyo bunka no kenkyū* 日本‧ 中國の 宗教文化の研究. Tokyo: Hirakawa, 1991: 219–31.

Shi Zhouren 施舟人 (Schipper). "'*Laozi zhongjing*' *chutan*" '老子中經' 初探, in *DJWH* 16 (1994): 204–16.

—— "Lijing baishi xianghuo bushuai de Xianren Tang Gongfang" 歷經百世香火不衰的仙人唐公房, in Lin Fushi 林富士 and Franciscus Verellen 傅飛嵐 *Yiji chongbai yu shengzhe chongbai* 遺跡崇拜與聖者崇拜. Taipei, Yun-chen wenhua, 1998: 85–99.

Shi Shuqing 史樹青, "Jin Zhou Fangming qi Panshi yiwuquan kaoshi" 晉周芳命妻潘氏衣物券考釋, *Kaogu tongxun* 考古通訊, 1956.2: 95–99.

Tang Changru 唐長孺. "Fan Changsheng yu Bashi ju Shu de guanxi" 范長生與巴氏據蜀的關係. *Lishi yanjiu* 4 (1954): 115–21.

—— *Wei Jin Nanbei chao shilun shiyi* 魏晉南北朝史論拾遺. Beijing: Zhonghua shu ju, 1983: 218–232.

—— "Shiji he daojing zhong suojiande Li Hong" 史籍和道經中所見的李弘, in *Weijin nanbei chao shilun shiyi* 魏晉南北朝史論拾遺 (rpt. Beijing: Zhonghua shuju), 1983: 208–17.

—— "Weijin qixian beifang tianshidao de chuanbo" 魏晉期間北方天師道的傳播, in Tang Changru 唐長孺, *Wei Jin Nanbei chao shilun shiyi* 魏晉南北朝史論拾遺. Beijing: Zhonghua shu ju, 1983: 218–32.

Tsukamoto Zenryu 塚本善隆. *Gisho Shakurōshi* 魏書釋老志. Kyoto: Heibonsha, rpt. 1989.

Xiao Dengfu 蕭登福. *Chenwei yu Daojiao* 讖緯與道教. Taipei: Wenjin 文津, 2000.

Wang Chengwen 王承文. *Dunhuang gu lingbao jing yu jintang daojiao* 敦煌古靈寶經與晉唐道教. Beijing: Zhonghua shuju, 2002.

Wang Deyou 王德有 in *Laozi zhigui* 老子指歸. Beijing: Zhonghua shuju, 1994.

Wang Hui 王暉. "Chutu wenzi ziliao yu wudi xinzheng" 出土文字資料與五帝新證. *Kaogu xuebao* 2007.1: 1–28.

Wang Ming 王明, ed. *Baopuzi neipian jiaoshi* 抱朴子內篇校釋. Beijing: Zhonghua shuju, 1985.

—— *Taiping jing hejiao*. Beijing: Zhonghua shuju, 1960, rpt. 1988.

Wang Qing 王青. *Hanchao de bentu zongjiao yu shenhua* 漢朝的本土宗教與神話. Taipei: Hongye, 1998.

Wang Shumin 王叔民, *Liexian zhuan jiaojian* 列仙傳校箋. Taipei: Institute of Literature and Philosophy, Academia Sinica, 1995.

Wang Yi, Commentary to the *Chuci* 楚辭 poem "Yuanyou" 遠遊 in Hong Xingzu 洪興祖 (1090–155) comp., *Chuci buzhu* 楚辭補注. Taipei: Da'an: 251.

Wang Yucheng 王育成. "Donghan daofu shili" 東漢道符實例. *Kaogu xuebao* 1991.1: 45–56.

—— "Xu Fu diquan zhong tainshidao shiliao kaoshi" 徐副地券中天師道史料考釋. *Kaogu* 1993.6: 571–5.

—— "Donghan 'Fei Zhi bei' tansuo" 東漢肥致碑探索. *Zhongguo lishi bowuguan guankan* 1996a.2: 34–41.

—— "Wenwu suojian zhongguo gudai daofu shulun" 文物所見中國古代道符述論. *DJWH* 9 (1996b): 267–301.

—— "Donghan daojiao diyi keshi 'Fei Zhi bei' yanjiu" 東漢道教第一刻石'肥致碑' 研究. *Daojiaoxue tansuo* 道教學探索 10 (1997): 14–28.

—— "Luelun kaogu faxiande zaoqi daofu" 略論考古發現的早期道符. *KG* 1998.1: 75–81.

—— "Donghan tiandi shizhe lei daoren yu daojiao qiyuan" 東漢天帝使者類道人與道教起原. *DJWH* 16 (1999a): 181–203.

—— "Han tiandi shenshizhi lei daoren yu daojiao qiyuan" 漢天帝神使者類道人與道教
起源, paper presented at the International Conference on Daoist Studies (1996), published in *Daojia wenhua yanjiu* 道家文化研究 16 (1999b): 181–203.

—— *Daojiao fayin lingpai tan'ao* 道教法印令牌探奧. Beijing: Zongjiao wenhua chubanshe, 2000.

Yamada Toshiaki 山田利明. "'Taishō tōen shinju kyō' no zushin teki seikaku" '太上洞淵
神咒經' 的圖讖性質 – 關於其成立情況. *Taisho daigaku kenkyū kiyō, bun, bukkyō
gakubu* 大正大學研究紀要文佛教學部 66 (1981): 145–63.

—— "Reihō gofu no seiritsu to sono fuzuiteki seikaku" 靈寶五符の成立と その符瑞的
性格, in Yasui Kōzan 安居香山, ed. *Zen'i shisō no sōgōteki kenkyū*. 讖緯思想の綜合
的研究. Tokyo: Kokusho kankōkai, 1983: 165–96.

—— "Gofujo keisei kō – Gaku kochō megutte" 五符序形成考 - 樂子長をぐって in
Akizuki Kan'ei 秋月觀映 *Dōkyō to shukyō bunka* 道教と宗教文化. Tokyo: Hirakawa,
1987a.

—— "Futatsu no shinfu – Gogaku shingyōzu to Reihō gofu" 二つの神符 –五嶽真形圖と
靈寶五符 in *Tōyōgaku ronsō* 東洋學論叢 40 (1987b) (*Tōyō daigaku bungaku* 東洋大
學學部): 147–65.

—— *Rikuchō Dōkyō girei no kenkyū* 六朝道教禮儀の研究. Tokyo: Tōhō-shoten, 1999.

"Yanshi xian nancaizhuang xiang han Fei Zhi mu fajue jianbao" 偃師縣南蔡庄鄉漢肥致
墓發掘簡報. *WW* 1992.9: 37–42.

Yang Lien-sheng 陽聯陞. "*Laojun yinsong jiejing* jiaoshi." 老君音誦誡經校釋 *BIHP*
28.1 (1956): 33–92.

Yasui Kōzan 安居香山, ed. *Zen'i shisō no sōgōteki kenkyū*. 讖緯思想の綜合的研究.
Tokyo: Kokusho kankōkai, 1983.

Yoshikawa Tadao 吉川忠夫 and Mugitani Kunio 麥谷邦夫, eds. *Shinkō kenkyū* 真誥研
究. Kyoto: Kyoto daigaku jimbun kagaku kenkyūjo, 2000.

Yoshioka Yoshitoyo 吉岡義豐. *Dōkyō kyōten shiron* 道教經典史論. Tokyo: Dōkyō
kankōkai, 1955.

Yu Wanli 虞萬里. "Donghan 'Fei Zhi bei' kaoshi" 東漢肥致碑考釋. *Zhongyuan wenwu*
中原文物 1997.4: 95–101.

Yuan Weichun 袁维春. *Qinhan bei shu* 秦汉碑述. Beijing: Beijing gongyi meishu, 1990.

Zhang Chaoran 張超然, "Rudao yu xingdao: Zhao Sheng yixi tianshi jiaotuan de huangchi
jiaofa" 入道與行道: 趙昇一系天師教團的黃赤教法, *Taiwan zongjiao yanjiu* 3.1
(2003): 49–88.

Zhang Xunliao 張勛燎. "Donghan musang chutu de jiezhu qicailiao he tianshidao de
qiyuan" 東漢墓葬出土的 解注器材料和天師道的起源 *DJWH* 9 (1996): 253–66.

—— "Henan Yanshi xian nan caizhuang xiang donghan chutu daoren Fei Zhi bei ji youguan
daojiao yiwu yanjiu" 河南偃師縣南蔡庄鄉東漢出土道人'肥致碑'及有關道教遺物
研究. *Sichuan daxue kaogu zhuanye chuangjian sanshiwu zhounian jinian wenji* 四川
大學考古專業創建三十五周年紀念文集. Chengdu: Sichuan daxue, 1998: 301–11.

—— and Bai Bin. *Zhongguo daojiao kaogu* 中國道教考古. Beijing: Xianzhuang shuju,
2006.

Zhang Yan 張燕. *Beichao fodao zaoxiang bei jingxuan* 北朝佛道造像碑精选. Tianjin:
Tianjin guji, 1996.

Zhang Yincheng 張寅成. "Zheng Xuan liutian shuo de yanjiu" 鄭玄六天說的研究,
Shiyuan 15: 189–201.

Zhao Yi 趙益. "Nanchao daojing 'Santian neijie jing' zaitan" 南朝道經 '三天內解經' 再
探, *Nanjing xiaozhuang xueyuan xuebao* 3 (2006).

Zhong Guofa 鍾國發. "Lu Xiujing pingzhuan" 陸修靜評傳., in *Tao Hongjing Pingzhuan* 陶弘景評傳. Nanjing: Nanjing University Press, 2005: 527–613.

Zhu Yueli 朱越利. *Daozang fenlei jieti* 道藏分類解題. Beijing: Huaxia, 1996.

—— "Huangshu kao," 黃書考 *Zhongguo zhexue* 19 (1998): 167–88.

Zhuo Zhenxi 禚振西. "Shaanxi huxian de linagzuo hanmu" 陝西戶線的兩座漢墓. *Kaogu yu wenwu* 1980.1.

—— "Caoshi zhushuguan kaoshi" 曹氏朱書罐考釋. *Kaogu yu wenwu* 1982.2: 88–91.

Zuo Jianquan 左景权. "'Dongyuan Shen zhou jing' yuanliu shikao" 洞淵神咒經源流試考 *Wenshi* 23 (1984).

Index